TASFEER OF SURAH BAQARAH

BY

SERENA HUSAIN YATES

Copyright © *Serena Husain Yates*, 2025

All Rights Reserved

This book is subject to the condition that no part of this book is to be reproduced, transmitted in any form or means; electronic or mechanical, stored in a retrieval system, photocopied, recorded, scanned, or otherwise. Any of these actions require the proper written permission of the author.

DEDICATION

TO MY PARENTS MOHAMMED HUBDAR HUSAIN &
ZAITOON HUSAIN

MY CHILDREN TARIQ, SALMA, SARAH, SAMEENA

MY GRANDCHILDREN

LAYLA, MUSA, AARON, SETH, YACUB

KEYAAN, LEYAH, EVA, SIYANNA, NOAH

JASMINE, TARIQ ISMAIL, AMELIA,

OMARI, ZAYN, KEIRA, ADAM, AYDEN

TABLE OF CONTENTS

DEDICATION 3

MY LEGACY 8

VERSE 190 1

VERSE 191 11

VERSE 193 15

VERSE 194 17

VERSE 195 19

VERSE 196 23

VERSE 197 28

VERSE 198 32

VERSE 199 37

VERSE 200 39

VERSE 201 43

VERSE 202 45

VERSE 202 47

VERSE 204 49

VERSE 205 52

VERSE 206 55

VERSES 207 59

VERSE 208 62

VERSE 209 73

VERSE 210 78

VERSES 211 82

VERSE 212 91

VERSE 213 92

VERSE 214 110

VERSE 215 114

VERSE 216 119

VERSE 217	125
VERSE 218	132
VERSE 219	135
VERSE 220	143
VERSE 221	151
VERSE 222	160
VERSE 223	163
VERSE 224	166
VERSE 225	170
VERSE 226	173
VERSE 227	177
VERSE 228	179
VERSE 228	184
VERSE 229	192
VERSES 230	200
VERSE 231	202
VERSE 232	207
Verse 233	209
VERSE 234	213
VERSE 235	217
VERSE 236	221
VERSE 237	224
VERSES 238	228
VERSE 239	229
VERSES 240, 241 & 242	235
VERSE 243	239
VERSE 244	242
VERSE 245	243
VERSE 246	249
VERSE 247	253

VERSE 248	256
VERSE 249	259
VERSES 250	263
ALLAH SAYS IN VERSE 251:	266
VERSE 252	275
VERSE 253	280
VERSE 254	287
VERSE 255	291
VERSE 256	312
VERSE 257	318
VERSE 258	322
VERSE 258	327
VERSE 260	335
VERSE 261	341
VERSE 262	344
VERSE 263	348
VERSE 264	351
VERSE 266	353
VERSES 267	356
VERSE 268	358
VERSE 269	360
VERSES 270	364
VERSE 270	366
VERSE 271	367
VERSE 272	371
VERSE 273	376
VERSE 274	379
VERSE 275	382
VERSES 276	392
VERSE 277	394

VERSES 278	395
VERSE 279	398
VERSES 280	400
VERSE 281	404
VERSE 282	406
VERSE 283	418
VERSE 284	424
VERSE 285	432
VERSE 286	437

MY LEGACY

My children, My grandchildren, I leave this book as a legacy to you.

In this journey of life Allah has chosen me to be your guardian, your protector. Allah has entrusted me, gifted me with the best of treasures, my beautiful family. Live your life in the submission and affirmation to the one God. All that exists belongs to Him as He is the Originator of all. He, subhanahu, alone is worthy of worship and all other deities are to be shunned. Everything happens by the Qader (will) of subhanahu. What was never meant for you will never reach you and what is meant for you, you will nev er have missed. Live your life with kindness, gratitude. Live everyday as the last day of your life. Seek refuge in Allah from the accursed Shaitan who lies waiting to trap you. Fulfil your duties to one another. You might be four different families but live your life as one. There is nothing greater than kinship. Remember that happiness comes with a pure heart free from jealousy, hatred, arrogance. Establish your prayers regularly and with humility. Nothing in your life is more important than your Salaat. Prayer is your connection to Allah. Feel the hunger and thirst of others. Thank Allah in all conditions. He may know a thing that's good for and that what is bad.

Learn the lessons from the Prophets. Put your trust in Allah and avoid those who aim to cause mischief. Speak well of others and avoid slander and backbiting. Live your life with contentment and avoid excess. Have pleasure in giving than receiving. Be charitable to your neighbours and love for yourself what you love for your brother. Live your life with tolerance and be accepting of others, even if their beliefs differ from you. Ask forgiveness from those you harm and repent to Allah. I pray that Allah protect and guide each and everyone one of you and we meet again and live as one family in Jannatul Firdous. AMEEN

Mummy, Nani Serena

VERSE 190

Wa qaatiloo fee sabeelillaahil lazeena yuqaatiloonakum wa laa ta'tadooo; innal laaha laa yuhibbul mu'tadeen

Fight in Allah's cause against those who fight you, but do not overstep the limits: Allah does not love those who overstep the limits

Allah Almighty sent one heavenly message after another in order to keep life upright and just for humanity. From Adam to Noah, Abraham, Moses, Jacob, Solomon, Jesus and Muhammad —peace be upon them all-, the heavenly messages came to fight corruption, spread justice, and protect the rights of people, animals, and nature. Sadly, the call for justice and protection of everyone's rights always faces fierce opposition from those who benefit from the exploitation of others. The message of Islam, however, was granted a responsibility that no other message before it had. Prior to Islam, prophets and messengers would bring the heavenly curriculum and invite people to join and implement Allah's teachings; however, when it came to dealing with those who actively fought against Allah, His prophets, and teachings, the heavens interfered to protect the believers and discipline the corrupt. Prophet Noah invited his people to faith for decades, but it was Allah who punished those who opposed Noah and prevented people from hearing his message. Likewise, Prophet Moses spread the word of Allah amongst the people, but Allah was the one who drowned Pharaoh and his army after they spent years torturing the Children of Israel. When it came to Islam, however, the responsibility of upholding Allah's teachings and the responsibility of standing up to those who actively fight against justice was now the duty of the believers. In other words, while previously the heavens were responsible for disciplining the violators, now it is the duty of the believers.

Let's look at a historical example from the Quran. The Children of Israel did not have a duty to fight. At one point, they had asked Allah to be allowed to fight their enemies. The reason behind their request was not to uphold Allah's teachings; rather they had other motives in mind as the following verse illustrates:

Do you not consider what happened with the elders of the Children of Israel after Moses: once they appealed to a Prophet chosen for them, saying: "Set up for us a king and we will fight in Allah's cause." He said: "Isn't it possible that you would hold back from fighting if fighting were prescribed for you?" They said: "Why should we not fight in Allah's cause when we have been driven out from our homes and separated from our children?" But when fighting was prescribed for them, they did turn away, except a few of them. Allah has full knowledge of wrongdoers. (02:246)

So, the Israelites didn't ask to fight to defend their faith; they wanted to fight because they were exiled from their homes and forced to leave their children.

As for the nation of Prophet Muhammad (peace be upon him), Allah Almighty gave us the responsibility of restoring balance and justice. Keep in mind that this is neither a permit for aggression nor a license to force belief on anyone. To the contrary, it is a moral responsibility to preserve human dignity by assuring that people have the freedom of choice in belief and have full access to the truth that Allah sent. There is no compulsion in religion. Allah had legislated fighting for the nation of Prophet Muhammad (pbuh) not to coerce people into belief, but to protect their freedom in selecting what they see is right. It is a duty to stop tyrants and dictators –regardless of their claimed religion- and free people from being forced into that which they do not want.

Sadly, there have been many charges against Islam regarding the issues of fighting and war. Let's consider the two most common accusations: first, it has been said that Islam was spread by the sword, implying that when the Muslims won battles, they forced their enemies into Islam. Second: Islam has been criticized for imposing taxes –called Jezia-on the nonbelievers under its rule. We answer that these charges are frail and, in fact, contradictory. By imposing a Jezia tax on the non-believers, Islam officially recognizes their faith and their right to practice it. If the Muslims had forced people to embrace Islam, then there would have been no need to legislate the Jezia tax. Hence, Islam did not impose faith on anyone; to the contrary, Islam freed the people from the powers which dominated them and allowed the free practice of their faith. Jezia guarantees the right of non-Muslims to practice their faith freely, and guarantees them the protection of the state.

Here you may ask: if that was the case, then why did the Muslims go to wars to begin with? We answer that the Islamic wars were fought for two reasons: The first was to defend the community from outside aggression. And the second was to stand against those who repressed and imposed a dictatorial rule on others. Islam fought to give people the freedom to decide the most appropriate religion for themselves. Why? Because the believers were confident that when people were free to choose, and when they saw the exemplary life of the Muslim society, they would naturally find the truth in Islam. Allah says:

There is no compulsion in the Religion. The right way stands there clearly distinguished from the false. Hence he who rejects the tyrant powers of evil and believes in Allah has indeed taken hold of the firm, unbreakable handle; and Allah is All-Hearing, All-Knowing. (02:256)

Often, when people read this verse they overlook the actual reason behind the statement: "There is no compulsion in the Religion." Allah gave us the reason in the later part of the verse. He says: "The right way stands there clearly distinguished from the false." In other words, when the truth is crystal clear, there is no reason to force people to choose. People naturally want what is good for themselves. Allah wants faith to emanate from the heart, not through fear or compulsion. Allah says to the Messenger (peace be upon him):

Are you going to worry yourself to death because they will not believe? If We had wished, We could have sent them down a sign from heaven, at which their necks would stay bowed in utter humility. (26:03-04)

Allah –the All-Merciful- does not want bowed heads. Had He wanted bowed heads, then no one would have been able to escape what He has decreed. Allah wants enlightened minds and loving hearts. He who forces religion upon others is not a believer. He who oppresses people into Islam is not a believer. A true believer invites people to faith through reason and, more importantly, by being an example of what is good and upright. Only then would people accept faith wholeheartedly and apply its teachings willingly.

If you take a look at the world today, you find that there are many systems and governments –Muslim and otherwise- that impose their doctrines upon people by means of force and oppression. This fosters hatred, resentment and ultimately violence. Contrast that to governments –Muslim and otherwise- who allow people to choose freely; the entire society lives in peace and harmony.

Now, let's look at the issue of fighting from a historical point of view. Allah did not authorize fighting throughout the Meccan period of Islam which lasted for thirteen years –from the inception of the prophethood of Muhammad, until he, peace be upon him, migrated to Medina-. It was important to delay the legislation of fighting because Allah wanted the believers to focus first and foremost on their creed and the proper understanding and implementation of faith. More importantly, Allah wanted the early Muslims to become a good example for others even when they were abused and under tremendous pressure. Allah says:

Even after the truth has become clear to them, many of the People of the Book wish they could turn you back to disbelief after you have believed, out of their selfish envy. Forgive and forbear until Allah gives his command: He has power over all things. (02:109)

And in another verse:

Do not give in to the disbelievers and the hypocrites: ignore the harm they cause you and put your trust in Allah. Allah suffices as a Guardian. (33:48)

Fight in Allah's cause against those who fight you, but do not overstep the limits: Allah does not love those who overstep the limits. (Verse 190)

We discussed that Allah did not legislate fighting for the first 13 years of Islam. And even when it was legislated, it was allowed to defend against aggression or to free the oppressed and exploited from tyranny. Allah warned the Muslims against overstepping these limits.

Here you may ask, what was the reason for the gradual approach of disallowing fighting then legislating it? We answer that Allah Almighty knew that the call of Islam would enter many houses of the Arabs and Meccans. Early Muslims –just as early Christians and Jews- were subjected to unrelenting abuse and persecution. A household might have believers in Allah, and disbelievers under one roof. If Allah had prescribed fighting right from the beginning, there would have been a battle in each house.

Furthermore, Allah knew that the Arab tribes had many people who were hot-headed, foolish and reckless. They would go to war for trivial reasons. In fact, before Islam, a war had raged for forty years between two tribes over livestock dispute. A poet says:

There are people who, if evil flashed its teeth at them,

Rush to fight, whether in groups or alone;

They do not question their brother, as he places them

within the troops: 'Why are we going to battle?'

The Arab tribes and Bedouins of the time used to fight for any reason. Reckless zeal would drive them into battle with little thought. On the other hand, they always stood up for the weak and oppressed and rushed to defend any person who was treated unjustly regardless of the danger. Allah, the All-Merciful, wanted to extinguish the recklessness and zeal from their hearts while preserving their love for justice and integrity.

Take the example of when the early Muslims —mostly from the family of Hashim-were marginalized and boycotted by the elites of Mecca. This vulnerable group was forced to withdraw from society and ended up on the brink of starvation. Five of the most prominent families in Mecca —all enemies of the Hashim family- gathered and proclaimed: How can we eat, drink and enjoy life while our fellow Meccans are trapped in the valley without food, drink or trade? These prominent families were unbelievers who hated Islam, yet they stood up against the boycott of the family of Hashim and broke the siege. They all agreed to this decision because of their honour and commitment to what is right. These were the qualities that Allah wanted to preserve while dispensing with the qualities of fanaticism and tribalism. Changing ingrained social customs is not easy. Thus, Allah —the All-Wise- treated the Meccan society with leniency.

To those who ask: why didn't the Muslims fight their enemies from the first day and go after the leaders of disbelief in Mecca who were persecuting and torturing them? We answer that while there was fierce resistance to the new faith of Islam in Mecca, many of the leaders who used to fight the Muslims were the same ones who spread the banner of Islam years later after they embraced the faith. Khalid ibn al-Walid, for example, was a daring commander in the ranks of Quraish who fought the Muslims early in his life. Then Allah guided him to Islam, and he became one of the greatest Muslim military leaders. What would have happened if this great commander did not get a chance to hear the message of Islam, or see the Muslims practicing their faith? What if he had been killed at the hands of Muslims? Such an act would have deprived the Muslims of his talent, a talent that contributed to most of the Islamic conquests in the Syria and Iraq.

Allah's wisdom retained the likes of Khalid who were opponents of Islam because they had a great future role serving Islam and protecting the Muslims. Moreover, those who opposed Islam and persecuted the early Muslims served Islam with passion once they embraced the faith. They wanted Allah to forgive their earlier transgressions, so they worked tirelessly to serve the community. Take the example of Ikrima ibn Abi Jahl who was one of the fiercest enemies of the Muslims in Mecca. Later on, he embraced Islam. When he was fatally wounded in the battle of Yarmouk, he looked at his commander Khalid and asked: Are my deeds something the Messenger of Allah will be pleased with? As if he knew that Prophet Muhammad was angry with him before he became a Muslim.

There are many more examples of disbelievers who achieved high ranks once they embraced Islam such Amr ibn al-Aas who presided over Egypt after he won the hearts of its people with his wisdom and intelligence. He removed the hatred of Muslims from their hearts without a fight. Amr delivered the prophet's message to the Christians of Egypt –also known as Aqbat-. Prophet Muhammad peace be upon him said to Amr: "Take good care of the Aqbat of Egypt as they are our kin in blood and our kin in faith."

From all this, we understand the wisdom of delaying the legislation of fighting and war in Islam. Allah had preserved the Meccan society, allowed the early embracers of Islam to focus on their faith and disciplined them to bear the hardships of life in a hostile environment. That ensured that anyone who joined Islam –knowing the challenges ahead- had a firm belief in his or her heart. Those were the believers that carried Allah's message to all corners of the earth. They were true to themselves, true to their faith, and they were worthy of the responsibility of defending their faith and standing up for the weak and oppressed. That is why the order to fight came later and gradually. Allah says:

LET US NOW GO TO THE VERSE UNDERSTUDY

Fight in Allah's cause against those who fight you, but do not overstep the limits: Allah does not love those who overstep the limits. (Chapter 2: Verse 190)

Let's look at the historical events that lead to the revelation of this verse: Prophet Muhammad (peace be upon him) and his companions longed to visit the Sacred House in Mecca, and they planned to perform the pilgrimage trip of Umrah. They set off for Umrah in the month of thil-Qi'dah in the sixth year after the prophet's migration. When they reached a place called Hudaybiyah, the elites of Quraish stood in their way and said: Muhammad and his companions are not allowed to enter Mecca. The negotiations between the two parties continued, and the Messenger of Allah agreed to postpone his Umrah pilgrimage until the following year. It was agreed that Quraish would vacate Mecca for three days next year so the Muslims can perform Hajj.

The Prophet's companions –not aware of the agreement- had been ready with their Ihram clothes, and their hair cut short as required. They were excited and happy to visit Allah's sacred house. When they heard the news of postponing Umrah until next year, they were taken by surprise. They were only twenty kilometers away from Mecca! The companions were saddened, and some were angry. Omar bin al-Khattab (may Allah be pleased with him) said to the Prophet in anger: "are you not the Messenger of Allah? Are you not upon the truth?" Abu Bakr replied to him: "Omar, calm down, he is the Messenger of Allah."

It was the wisdom of Um Salama –the wife of the prophet- that defused the situation. Prophet Muhammad returned to her with sadness and concern. He –peace be upon him- said: "The Muslims have perished O Um Salama, I ordered them, but they did not comply." Um Sallama gave advice that showed her wisdom, compassion, and thoughtfulness. When she saw the look of concern on her husband's face, she said: excuse them O Messenger of Allah for they are in shock and grieve. They longed to enter the House of Allah, and as they drew closer, they were deprived of it. Muhammad, why don't you carry on the order of Allah by yourself. Do as you were commanded and do not speak to anyone. If they see you implementing Allah's orders, they will follow you." The Prophet (peace be upon him) took his wife's advice did as Allah commanded. Sure enough, when the companions saw the prophet, they all followed him.

Allah did not want those who had high hopes to visit His sacred house to leave with sorrow in their hearts. Thus, and before they returned to Madina, Allah revealed the actual reason behind the deal prophet Muhammad struck with Quraish. Allah says:

They were the ones who disbelieved, who barred you from the Sacred Mosque, and who prevented the offering from reaching its place of sacrifice. If there had not been among them, unknown to you, believing men and women whom you would have trampled underfoot, inadvertently incurring guilt on their account- Allah brings whoever He will into His mercy- if the believers had been clearly separated, We would have inicted a painful punishment on the disbelievers. (48:25)

Allah informed the Prophet and his companions that they had believing brothers and sisters in Mecca who hid their faith. Had you entered Mecca despite Quraish's warnings, they would have fought you, and you had to fight back. You would not have been able to distinguish between the two. Had the believers been known to you, we would have authorized you to fight. After the revelation of this verse, the Muslims understood the wisdom behind the deal. The Muslims, however, still feared that if they returned next year, Quraish might renege on their word. Thus, before their return, Allah Almighty authorized them to fight if the need arises. He, Almighty, says:

Fight in the way of Allah those who fight you but do not transgress. Indeed. Allah does not like transgressors. (2:190)

Perhaps, the most important phrase in this verse is "fight in the way of Allah." Allah wants to put an end to the tyranny and pride of human beings. Thus, it is necessary that the intention of fighting must be for Allah alone and not for gaining superiority or punishing an enemy or forcing your will upon them. There is no fighting for status, money, or to ensure access to markets and resources. Fighting is only allowed for protecting the weak and raising the word of Allah.

Allah further warns: "do not transgress. Indeed. Allah does not like transgressors" again emphasizing that Muslims must not fight those who did not fight them. Suppose, for example, that a group or a country came to fight the Muslims. But the residents of this country -such as the women, the children and the elderly- did not take part in the fight. It is not permissible to fight these residents, even if they support the policies of their government. The reaction of the Muslims must be according to the action taken against them and not a step further. Why? Because fighting civilian populations is an act of aggression and Allah Almighty does not like the aggressors. The fight must be only to repel aggression, not to start one

VERSE 191

Waqtuloohum haisu saqif tumoohum wa akhrijoohum min haisu akhrajookum; walfitnatu ashaddu minal qatl; wa laa tuqaatiloohum 'indal Masjidil Haraami hattaa yaqaatilookum feehi fa in qaatalookum faqtuloohum; kazaalika jazaaa'ul kaafireen

And kill them wherever you overtake them and expel them from wherever they have expelled you, and persecution is worse than killing. And do not fight them at the Sacred House until they fight you there. But if they fight you, then kill them. Such is the recompense of the disbelievers. But if they stop, then Allah is most forgiving and merciful.

In the previous sessions, we discussed the legislation of fighting in Islam and explained how Allah had entrusted the believers with the responsibilities of defending their faith against aggression and standing up to tyrants and oppressors. Before the advent of Prophet Muhammad –peace be upon him-, it was the responsibility of prophets and messengers to deliver Allah's teachings; while the heavens took on the responsibility of disciplining those who fought against Allah and spread corruption. We presented the example of Prophet Moses delivering the Torah and spreading the word of Allah; while the heavens intervened to punish Pharaoh and his followers. We also explained that verses such as: Do not give in to the disbelievers and the hypocrites: ignore the harm they cause you and put your trust in Allah. Allah suffices as a Guardian. (33:48), and Forgive and forbear until Allah gives his command: He has power over all things (02:109) are meant to help discipline one's self against fanaticism, extremism and the desire for revenge. Allah wants the believers to be wise, patient and careful in carrying out His teachings.

Allah wants the believers to resort to fighting only as a last option, and only after careful deliberation and reflection. Fighting should be a tool to defend values, not to seek gain, revenge or spread fear. For all these reasons, Allah legislated fighting gradually.

He says in verse 190: 'Fight in Allah's cause against those who fight you' setting defense as the sole reason to carry arms. Allah also made an exception for those who are attacked in sacred places or during sacred months to be able to defend themselves against those who take advantage of these sanctities.

He says in verse 194: 'A sacred month for a sacred month: violation of sanctity calls for fair retribution. So if anyone commits aggression against you, attack him as he attacked you.'

Allah gave a clear reason for this exception. He says: "persecution is worse than killing" meaning that those who are working tirelessly to spoil people's faith and create divisions among the believers have to be stopped. Preventing people from hearing Allah's message and joining the faith is one crime, but spreading corruption within the faith and creating divisions among the believers is a much more severe crime. This is yet another proof that fighting in Islam is legislated as a means for defence and to protect the Muslims against aggressors.

Here, we should ask a critical question:

Are the believers asked to fight to defend the Muslims only?

Or are they asked to fight in defence of every oppressed people regardless of faith? We answer that Allah has sent His message to humanity as a whole, so whoever is attacking the believers should be fought and stopped; and whoever is oppressing people –regardless of their faith- and forcing them into belief against their will should be fought and stopped, even if the oppressor claims to be Muslim. We defend the weak and the oppressed so that they are free in choosing their path in life. Allah says:

There is no compulsion in religion: true guidance has become distinct from error, so whoever rejects false Allahs and believes in Allah has grasped the firmest hand-hold, one that will never break. Allah is all hearing and all knowing. (2:256)

The real aim is fairness and justice, and the enemy are the tyrants and the unjust regardless of their faith. Allah says addressing the Muslims:

If two groups of the believers fight, you should try to reconcile them; if one of them is oppressing the other, fight the oppressors until they submit to Allah's command, then make a just and even-handed reconciliation between the two of them: Allah loves those who are equitable. (49:9)

This brings us back to the verse. Allah says: 'And do not fight them at the Sacred House until they fight you there' because it befits you as believers to respect the sanctity of Allah's sacred Mosque. But if your enemies dared to fight in the Sacred Mosque, then Allah has permitted for you to fight back. He says: 'And do not fight them at the Sacred House until they fight you there. But if they fight you, then kill them. Such is the recompense of the disbelievers. But if they stop, then Allah is most forgiving and merciful.'

Take note that Allah had asked the Muslims to stand against anyone who dares to violate Islam's sacred House, but to cease when the aggression stops. Allah – the All-Merciful- wants the heart of the believer to be free from the desire for personal revenge and the desire to turn from a defender of faith to an aggressor.

Take the example of Omar bin al-Khattab –one of the prophet's close companions- when a friend of his pointed out a man in the crowd and said: 'Omar, this is the man who killed your brother Zaid.' Omar replied: 'What can I do to him now that he has embraced Islam? Islam has sanctified his blood.' Omar put faith ahead of his personal desire for revenge.

Faith in Allah is dearer to the believer than his own blood. Whenever the Prophet (peace be upon him) would see Wahshi -the murderer of the Prophet's uncle Hamza- the most he would do was to turn his face away from him, but he did not kill him or avenge his Uncle. So, Islam is not a religion of hatred, revenge, or settling of scores; to the contrary, the more faith you have in your heart, the less these feeling find a way into it. Allah says:

But if they stop, then Allah is most forgiving and merciful. (2:192)

Meaning: As soon as the enemies of Islam stop their aggression and their efforts to break down the Muslims community, the Muslims ought to stop too.

VERSE 193

Wa qaatiloohum hatta laa takoona fitnatunw wa yakoonad deenu lillaahi fa-inin tahaw falaa 'udwaana illaa 'alaz zaalimeen

Fight them until there is no more persecution, and worship is devoted to Allah. If they cease hostilities, there shall be no reprisal except against the wrongdoers.

In the previous sessions, we explained how the responsibility of defending the believers against persecution and aggression, and the responsibility of defending those who are oppressed and subjugated – regardless of their faith- has been transferred from the heavens onto the believers. However, as soon as the aggressors and those causing corruption stop, the believers will neither have the right to continue the fight nor to hold grudges or seek revenge.

Let's take a moment to define 'persecution' which is translated from the Arabic origin 'Fitna.' We know that 'Fitna' is a test or trial. Allah says:

Do people think they will be left alone after merely saying 'We believe' without being put to the test? (29:02)

Allah puts our faith to the test because faith is a belief that has to be supported by actions. Is your faith strong enough to withstand trials and hardship? Or do you compromise at the first sign of trouble? There are those who get persecuted for their belief and have to defend it with their life. Take the example of the prophet's companions: They went through hardship after hardship, and some were martyred while defending against the enemies of the faith. This is how Allah guaranteed that only those with true faith and pure conviction would join Islam. They were worthy of carrying Allah message because they stood firm for what they believed. Allah says: 'Fight them until there is no more persecution, and worship is devoted to Allah' giving the believers a clear mission -not for worldly or material gain- but to give all humanity the chance to be free of persecution and tyranny; an opportunity to follow their creator not their equal; and an opportunity to be truly free from all forms of subjugation and imposed beliefs. Many belief systems and doctrines have been adorned for people to get them away from the path of their Creator. It is the duty of the believers to guide the human mind to the right direction and prevent it from submitting to anyone else but Allah Almighty. Our beloved prophet –peace be upon him- understood this mission.

Allah says:

We sent you only to bring good news and to give warning. Say, 'I am not asking for any reward for it, but anyone who wishes should take a path to his Lord.' (25:56,57)

If you look at the work of the prophets and messengers from an economic view, you find that they reduced corruption and spread fairness and generosity in societies. If you look at their work from a legislative view, you find that they set laws that helped individuals and societies alike. All this –and much more- deserves great material rewards in return. But Allah's messengers did not ask for any reward in this world because all pales in comparison to Allah's reward and recognition. In fact, no one can reward for faith except Allah Himself. He is the One who gives without limits.

The verse ends with: 'If they cease hostilities, there shall be no reprisal except against the wrongdoers' instructing the believers to refrain from fighting when their enemies stop. Moreover, Allah warns the believers against transgressing and against seeking revenge; rather, they should only stand up and respond to injustice. This is because when someone violates the rights of others, he or she is under the impression that it is easy to get away with it. Allah wants such a person to know that there are those who will stand firm and defend the weak.

Allah gives us the guidelines in verse 194.

VERSE 194

Ash Shahrul Haraamu bish Shahril Haraami wal hurumaatu qisaas; famani'tadaa 'alaikum fa'tadoo 'alaihi bimisli ma'tadaa 'alaikum; wattaqul laaha wa'lamooo annal laaha ma'al muttaqeen

A sacred month for a sacred month: violation of sanctity calls for fair retribution. So if anyone commits aggression against you, assail him in the manner he assailed you, but be mindful of Allah, and know that He is with those who are mindful of Him.

Tyrants and dictators are under the impression that no one can stand in their way. Allah is instructing the believers to stand for what is right and fair. So if a group violates a sacred month with aggression, Allah commands the believers to retaliate even during a sacred month. Likewise, if the assault targets and violates a sacred place, Allah commands the believers to retaliate in kind. This is because retribution means to treat the oppressor in the same way he or she oppressed the victim.

Here, many questions may come to mind: how is it possible that if someone does wrong and violates a sanctity that we are supposed to respond in kind? Are we permitted to do wrong? Are we expected to take revenge from the one who does something unlawful by doing the same as he or she did?

We answer: Of course not. Retribution is only done with matters that are authorized, and the punishment is only permissible in regards to deeds which are clear and have been proven without a doubt.

Suppose, for example, that it is your financial responsibility to take care of a relative and spend on him, but you neglect your duties. Your relative is now authorized to take from your wealth what is enough to meet his or her basic needs. Similarly, when Hind, the wife of Abu Sufyan, came to Prophet Muhammad –peace be upon him- complaining about her husband's stinginess and negligence. The prophet told her to take from his wealth that which is sufficient to feed and clothe herself and her children. Allah says: 'violation of sanctity calls for fair retribution. So if anyone commits aggression against you, assail him in the manner he assailed you.' Take note that Allah commands fairness against aggressors, whether they are believers or non-believers.

The verse ends with:

'but be mindful of Allah, and know that He is with those who are mindful of Him.' This is a warning not to assume that Allah gave any of us blank authority over others. Allah is the creator of us all, and each will be responsible before him for his or her actions.

VERSE 195

Wa anfiqoo fee sabeelil laahi wa laa tulqoo bi aydeekum ilat tahlukati wa ahsinoo; innal laaha yuhibbul muhsineen

Spend in Allah's cause: do not contribute to your destruction with your own hands, but do good, for Allah loves those who do good.

Defending one's faith requires action and commitment. Without commitment, the believers risk ruin of their faith. Allah warns: 'do not contribute to your destruction with your own hands.' To destroy something means to change it out of its functional state or to lose it completely. In fact, destruction is the opposite of life. Life is not mere breathing and movement; rather life is to perform your intended purpose. Animals are alive when they perform their intended function in nature. Likewise, plants have life and laws that govern their existence. By this measure, even inanimate objects have a life. It is not like yours or mine, but it is suitable to their function.

Allah says:

Do not call out to any other Allah beside Allah, for there is no Allah but Him. Everything will perish except His Face. His is the Judgement, and to Him you shall all be brought back. (28:88)

We are not the only ones who will perish; rather everything in existence will cease to be, including inanimate objects. Everything is created for a task which it has to perform, and that -in essence- is the definition of life.

Allah says: 'do not contribute to your destruction with your own hands' How can you avoid destroying yourself?

Allah says at the beginning of the verse "Spend in Allah's cause" because spending money is the means to build a strong economy, a strong social safety net, and a powerful military. Those who do not invest into building a strong economy are throwing their future into ruin. The minute that you stop investing in yourself is the minute when your competitors start gaining ground to overtake you. Moreover, when the enemy sees your complacency, he or she will become daring over you. There are countless historical examples where the mere act of preparing a powerful military prevented war. Allah wants to protect the believers and assure that they have a vibrant nation that is the envy of the world.

There is also another side to the phrase: 'do not contribute to your destruction with your own hands.' It is a warning to those who rush into war just because they can. Allah commands us to consider all matters and calculate carefully based on facts, not fanaticism. He warns us against inflammatory speeches, fake bravery, and zeal. Courage requires that you refrain from fighting where it is not appropriate so that you can gain victory over the enemy at a time when your preparations are complete.

So the verse strikes a balance between building an economy that serves all, building a military that deters the enemies, while at the same time exercising wisdom against aggression and zeal. Allah wants the believers to weigh every issue carefully. He wants the believers to be fully prepared for any possibility so they can defend the faith when it is appropriate. In this single sentence: 'Spend in Allah's cause: do not contribute to your destruction with your own hands' Allah gave us both: the command to build a vibrant nation, and the command to adequately and wisely defend it if the need arises.

Allah Almighty follows by saying:

"but do good, for Allah loves those who do good.' The word 'good' is translated from the Arabic origin 'ihsan' which means to go beyond obligation and expectations. Prophet Muhammad –peace be upon him- explained: "Ihsan is to worship Allah as if you see Him; for if you cannot see Him, then rest assured that He sees you." Sadly, some Muslims today are no longer governed by their conscience and their sense of good.

There are some who slacks on their jobs because no one is watching. Allah wants you to be your own judge; He wants your faith to direct you to do a perfect job even when no one is looking. Allah wants you to do a good job for the sake of the entire society, not for the sake of money or simply to get things done.

To do good is to perform with excellence and do for others what you would love others to do for you. If people lived by this principal alone, life would advance in all its aspects; industries would thrive, everyone's finances would improve, and the welfare of all members of society would be guaranteed. But if fraud is prevalent, then you would cheat others, and they would cheat you. All is lost.

Allah says: 'Spend in Allah's cause: do not contribute to your destruction with your own hands. but do good, for Allah loves those who do good.' The command here is general, covering all aspects of life. Hence, if excellence is required when spending money, then it is also necessary when earning it. Excellence is required in investment, and it is needed in charity. If you don't happen to have money to spare, then Allah wants you to give your effort to help others or share your knowledge to teach those around you and so on. Allah values your effort, earnings, and education. If you are strong, help protect the weak. If you are a lawyer, then stand up for the rights of others. If you live near a river or a lake, then help keep it clean and free of pollution. Practicing Ihsan is how societies earn respect and recognition.

Here, we must ask a crucial question: Why are the Muslim nations disrespected, bullied, and looked down upon all over the world today? We answer that the world judges the Majority of Muslim countries through the deeds of Muslims. Are our actions in line with Allah's teachings? When the early Muslims practiced their faith through actions and Ihsan, they set an example that all nations wanted to emulate. Islam spread to the furthest reaches of the east and west, not through wars and conquest, rather it spread because countries welcomed the Muslims and adopted their ways. Now it is up to each one of us to do the same. If we do good at the level of Ihsan, people of all faiths and backgrounds would see Islam as the system to adopt and emulate.

There are few among the western and eastern intellectuals who do not judge the religion of Islam by the actions of the Muslims. They understand that not all Muslims comply with Islamic teachings. These individuals should be given great credit and recognition for being able to see Islam in its pure and genuine form, not through how some Muslims miss-practice it today.

Moreover, the followers of other religions are aware that there are some acts that their religion condemns and labelled as crimes, yet people commit these acts anyways. These individuals do not represent the entire religion. Similarly, Islam has criminal laws and suitable punishments for criminal acts. The individuals who commit these acts are not representative of the Muslim community. For example, when you see a Muslim stealing do you say that all Muslims are thieves? No, you have to consider the Islamic legislations. Has Islam condemned theft? Has it set punishment for the one who steals? Of course it has. So, do not base your opinion about Islam by looking at the deeds of a few Muslims. You must look at the Islamic laws. Allah gave us the ability to do good and evil. He rewards for doing good deeds and punishes for evil ones. Intellectuals are the ones who judge the religion by looking at its principles. Our duty as Muslims is to correctly practice our faith by helping others and performing all tasks at an excellent level, a level of Ihsan.

VERSE 196

Wa atimmul Hajja wal Umarata lillaah; fain uhsirtum famas taisara minal hadyi walaa tahliqoo ru'oosakum hatta yablughal hadyu mahillah; faman kaana minkum mareedan aw biheee azam mir ra'sihee fafidyatum min Siyaamin aw sadaqatin aw nusuk; fa izaaa amintum faman tamatta'a bil 'Umrati ilal Hajji famastaisara minal hadyi; famal lam yajid fa Siyaamu salaasati ayyaamin fil Hajji wa sab'atin izaa raja'tum; tilka 'asharatun kaamilah; zaalika limal lam yakun ahluhoo haadiril Masjidil Haraam; wattaqul laaha wa'lamoo annal laaha shadeedul'iqaab

And complete the pilgrimage and the Umrah for the sake of Allah. If you are prevented from doing so, then whatever offering for sacrifice you can afford, and do not shave your heads until the offering has reached the place of sacrifice. If any of you is ill, or has an ailment of the scalp, he should compensate by fasting, or feeding the poor, or offering sacrifice. When you are in safety, anyone wishing to take a break between the Umrah and the Hajj one must make whatever offering he can afford. If he lacks the means, he should fast for three days during the Hajj, and seven days on his return, making ten days in all. This applies to those whose household is not near the Sacred Mosque. Always be mindful of Allah, and be aware that He is stern in His retribution.

The order of verses and topics in the Holy Quran is fascinating. A few verses earlier, Allah began by talking about fasting Ramadan, and after that He discussed the Hajj pilgrimage and its appointed times. The month of Ramadan comes before the months of Hajj, so the flow of the verses is consistent with the flow of time. These verses were also interjected by the discussion about the legislation of fighting –more specifically during the sacred months- which is also consistent with the flow of time.

The verse starts with:

"And complete the pilgrimage and the Umrah for the sake of Allah" indicating that the obligation of Hajj has already been established, and what Allah is asking you to do is to perform it to perfection. The Hajj pilgrimage and the Umrah share many rituals and acts of worship, but they differ in the fact the Hajj pilgrimage has a specific appointed time and requires the presence in Arafa. Take note that when Allah talks about obligation, He Almighty only mentions the Hajj pilgrimage –not the Umrah-. Allah says in the 97th verse of chapter 3:

The Hajj Pilgrimage to the House is a duty owed to Allah by people who are able to undertake it.

This is yet another proof that the Quran has to be studied as a whole and not taken out of context. More specifically, you should gather all the verses and Prophet narrations that discuss a certain topic and study them together. It is the best way to assure that you have a complete understanding of the subject. Here is an example from the 3rd verse of chapter 9. Allah says:

And a proclamation from Allah and His Messenger to all people on this day of the Major Pilgrimage: that Allah disavows those who associate partners with Him, and His Messenger likewise.

In this verse, the phrase "Major Pilgrimage" refers to the Hajj, and indicates to you that there are other types of pilgrimage which you can only learn about from other verses and narrations. Likewise, when you read the prophet's narration that says: "Hajj is Arafa" you understand that the main event during Hajj is the event of standing at Mount Arafa, which is not a requirement of the Umrah pilgrimage. As you see, a higher level of understanding can only be obtained by looking at all the Quranic verses and prophet's narrations regarding the topic on hand.

Here is a commonly asked question: Since Hajj and Umrah are two distinct acts of worship, can they be performed together, or should they be done separately? Scholars have differed regarding this issue. Some said that doing an exclusive trip for Hajj is better, while others encouraged doing both on the same trip and in the same Ihram. This means to perform Umrah first, stay in the state and attire or Ihram until the Hajj duties are completed. A third opinion is to break your state of Ihram between Hajj and Umrah. In other words, you arrive and perform Umrah, get out of Ihram and begin a new one for Hajj. Allah says: 'When you are in safety, anyone wishing to take a break between the Umrah and the Hajj one must make whatever offering he can afford.'

The verse continues: "And complete the pilgrimage and the Umrah for the sake of Allah." Allah is aware that some people may only perform the superficial rituals of the pilgrimage; there will be others who will go to Hajj to take advantage of the high season for trade. This verse is a reminder to all of us that the pilgrimage should be performed and perfected for the sake of Allah. In fact, even the thought and planning you put into making this trip should be done with Allah exclusively in mind. Purity of intention will serve you well in other matters too. If your intention to perform the pilgrimage of Hajj and Umrah is for Allah's sake, then you would make sure that the money you use to make this trip is earned by lawful means. The Hajj trip should be pure in all its aspects, whether spiritual, financial or social. Prophet Muhammad –peace be upon him- said: "Those of you who properly perform the Hajj pilgrimage without committing indecent acts or mischief will be cleared of their sins as if they were born today."

Sadly, some people misunderstand this narration as an excuse to do whatever they like before Hajj because all sins will be forgiven. We answer that the purity of your intention and the purity of your finances start well before the actual pilgrimage trip. Moreover, it is crucial to clarify which of your sins will be forgiven. Allah will forgive all your sins and shortcomings in your duties towards Him. In other words, if you have wronged yourself in your relationship with Allah –such as not performing your prayers, or fasting carelessly- then Allah will forgive these shortcomings. However, if you have wronged your fellow man, then these sins have to be addressed justly. Allah will forgive your sins towards Him, but He will not forgive your sins towards other people. So make sure that your dealings with people are just and fair, and seek forgiveness from those you have wronged. If you owe somebody money, you cannot go to Hajj until you pay what you owe, or at the very least obtain that person's permission to go to Hajj. Such are the steps on the road to purity before you go on the actual trip to Mecca.

Allah also knows that –despite your best efforts-, there will be circumstances outside your control. You may fall ill before your trip and be advised by doctors against traveling. Border authorities may prevent you from leaving your country or entering the Holy Land. This is similar to what happened to the Prophet and his companions in Huddaibya when they were prevented from entering Mecca. Allah –the all merciful- wants to give you peace of mind, and to honor your efforts and intentions. He says: 'If you are prevented from doing so, then whatever offering for sacrifice you can afford, and do not shave your heads until the offering has reached the place of sacrifice.' You have the option of earning great rewards by sacrificing an animal –if you have the means to do so- in cases where you trip was unsuccessful.

Allah gives yet another permit to those who are ill or have scalp issues to compensate by fasting, giving charity or sacrificing an animal. Here again, you can see the beauty of Islam. Allah gave three choices for the ill on a progressive scale. First, there is the option of fasting which only benefits the person who fasts. Second, at a higher level, there is the option of giving charity, which helps the believer and a few poor people; yet for those who strive to do better, the third option of animal sacrifice is given, which is enough to feed tens of poor people. You can choose what you want to do based on your level of faith, finances, and desire for reward.

Here, we should take a moment to study the true meaning of the phrase "If he lacks the means." Sadly, we see some people who –as soon as they make it to Mecca or Medina for Hajj- rush to the market to buy gifts and souvenirs. And when the time comes for the animal sacrifice, they are out of money and claim that they do not have the means to do so. We answer that 'not having the means' should be applied faithfully. In other words, it should be a valid excuse to those who are in true poverty or had a real financial emergency. Buying gifts and spending money on luxuries should only be done after all the necessities of worship have been satisfied. The phrase: 'If he lacks the means, he should fast for three days during the Hajj, and seven days on his return, making ten days in all' has been explained by the scholars to apply to those who know beforehand that they would not be able to afford an animal. It does not apply to those who put themselves in a situation where they run out of money. The prescribed fast for the poor are three days of fasting that can start as early as the 2nd day of Eid, and seven days on the way back home or as soon as the traveler returns. Allah says: 'making ten days in all' so we understand that it is not a choice between fasting three and seven days, but an obligation to fast a whole ten. Moreover, those who fast these days because they honestly could not sacrifice an animal will earn the full reward from Allah as if they had sacrificed.

The verse ends with: 'Always be mindful of Allah, and be aware that He is stern in His retribution.' Why would Allah warn us of severe punishment just after He offered such ease and accommodation? We answer that Allah does not want you to take advantage of or abuse His permits. They are reserved for those in poverty, those who are ill, or those who run into real emergencies, not for the lazy or the opportunist.

VERSE 197

Al-Hajju ashhurum ma'-loomaat; faman farada feehinnal hajja falaa rafasa wa laa fusooqa wa laa jidaala fil Hajj; wa maa taf'aloo min khairiny ya'lamhul laah; wa tazawwadoo fa inna khairaz zaadit taqwaa; wattaqooni yaaa ulil albaab

The Hajj pilgrimage takes place during the well-known months. So whoever undertakes the duty of Hajj in them, there should be no indecency, mischief, or quarrelling during the pilgrimage- whatever good you do, Allah is well aware of it. Provide well for yourselves: the best provision is to be mindful of Allah- always be mindful of Me, you who have understanding-

You may have noticed that when it came to fasting, Allah specified the month of Ramadan by name. He says in verse 185 of Surah Baqarah:

"It was in the month of Ramadan that the Quran was revealed as guidance for mankind, clear messages giving guidance and distinguishing between right and wrong. So anyone of you who is present that month should fast."

But, in this verse, the months of the Hajj pilgrimage —which are Shauwal, Thil Q'ida, and the first ten days of Thil Hijja- were not specified. This is because the obligation of fasting was new and had to be clarified; while the Hajj pilgrimage season was well known in Arabia and the entire region even before Islam. Allah gave us the reason for not naming the months and said: "The pilgrimage takes place during the well-known months."

The verse continues: "So whoever undertakes the duty of Hajj in them." This phrase is interesting because Allah set the duty of Hajj for us. Yet, it is you and I who commit ourselves to undertake this duty. In other words, through your planning for this trip, you commit yourself to the duty and you are bound by it.

Allah continues: "there should be no indecency, mischief, or quarrelling during the pilgrimage." Indecency is any lewd act of sexual nature. The eye can commit indecency by gazing at the opposite genger; the tongue can commit indecency by speaking about sexual issues or harassing the opposite sex. So any action or speech that has to do with sexual matters or may lead to intercourse is prohibited during the Hajj pilgrimage. While these things are usually allowed for married couples outside Hajj, they are forbidden for all –married and unmarried- during Hajj.

'Mischief,' on the other hand, is prohibited at all times. So, this is a double warning from our Lord that even if you occasionally commit mischief outside the Hajj, you should be extra vigilant during the pilgrimage out of respect for Allah and the sacred places. Allah wants you to break your bad habits because one of the goals of the Hajj trip is to purify yourself from all sin.

'Quarrelling' which is a lesser offense, is allowed in our day-to-day life. But, it is disallowed during Hajj. Our beloved prophet –peace be upon him- said: "Those of you who properly perform the Hajj pilgrimage without committing indecent acts or mischief will be cleared of their sins as if they were born today." Note that in this narration, quarreling was not mentioned as a pre-condition to forgiveness. This is mercy from our Lord and our beloved prophet because Allah is aware of the circumstances that may face travelers during the long, hard, and very crowded trip. 'Quarrelling' are back and forth arguments to prove a point or express displeasure. Allah gives us some leeway in this matter because when people are placed in an over-crowded, unfamiliar environment, they often get agitated and short tempered. Arguments and quarrels are disallowed during Hajj, but allowed otherwise. Allah says:

Call people to the way of your Lord with wisdom and good advice. Argue with them in the most courteous way, for your Lord knows best who has strayed from His way and who is rightly guided. (16:125)

So even if you are away from the comforts of home, even if you are sharing accommodations and bathrooms with strangers, and even if a few people around you are rude and ignorant, you should refrain from arguing during Hajj. Allah knows these hardships and He –the All-Merciful- wants you to come back from the Hajj pilgrimage having left the best of impressions on those around you. He says: 'Whatever good you do, Allah is well aware of it.' Allah –after prohibiting you from indecency, mischief, and quarreling- is rewarding you for doing the opposite. Lowering your gaze, helping others, and speaking with kindness will earn you immense rewards from your Lord. Even if those actions are small and those around you are not aware your efforts, rest assured that 'Allah is well aware of it.'

The verse continues with: 'Provide well for yourselves.' In the olden days, the Hajj trip was long and hard, often taken on foot, or on the backs of animals. It required plenty of planning and preparation to manage food and water supplies. Moreover, people often carried everything with them: from threads and needles to mend clothes to coffins in case of death on the road. It is very different nowadays, where people often buy luxuries and return from Mecca with gifts. Allah wants you to plan your trip well, and provide all the necessities for yourself and your family so your focus would be on worship alone. Allah does not want you to be preoccupied with your next meal; rather you should be preoccupied with your Lord in prayer. Those who go to Hajj with nothing, claiming that Allah will take care of them, often end up begging or committing theft to meet their basic needs; thus Allah reminds you of your responsibility. He says: 'Provide well for yourselves.'

More importantly, Allah –The All-Wise- is not only asking you to prepare provisions for your daily life needs, He also wants you to prepare provisions for your eternal life needs. He says: 'the best provision is to be mindful of Allah' reminding you to properly take care of all your needs both material and spiritual. Let's take an example from the Quran. Allah says in the 26th verse of chapter 7:

Children of Adam, We have given you garments to cover your nakedness and as adornment for you

Take note that Allah provided us with the basics to cover our private parts and provided us with the luxuries to look good and stylish. Allah continues:

the garment of Allah-consciousness is the best of all garments- this is one of Allah's signs, so that people may take heed.

If you enjoy beautiful clothes that look good, conceal your private parts, and protect you from the heat and cold, then imagine your joy with the cover that will provide you with protection from the heat of hellfire on the Day of Judgment.

This brings us back to the verse. Allah says: 'Provide well for yourselves: the best provision is to be mindful of Allah- always be mindful of Me, you who have understanding.' Allah is inviting you to think about your needs in this world and the next, to prepare the provisions that allow you to focus on worship during the Hajj pilgrimage, and prepare the best spiritual provisions that earn you paradise in the hereafter.

VERSE 198

Laisa 'alaikum junaahun an tabtaghoo fad lam mir rabbikum; fa izaaa afadtum min 'Arafaatin fazkurul laaha 'indal-Mash'aril Haraami waz kuroohu kamaa hadaakum wa in kuntum min qablihee laminad daaalleen

It is no crime in you if ye seek of the bounty of your Lord (during pilgrimage). Then when ye pour down from (Mount) Arafat, celebrate the praises of Allah at the Sacred Monument, and celebrate His praises as He has directed you, even though, before this, ye went astray.

Scholars have differed in regards to the origin of the name 'Arafa'. In the Arabic language, 'Arafa' means to acknowledge, to recognize, or to learn. Sometimes an adjective or a description becomes a name for a place or person; on other occasions, a name is used in hopes of changing a place or a person. For example, a father who hopes for his newborn daughter to grow up to be a lady may name her 'Grace.' A couple wanting their newborn son to grow up to be honest and trustworthy may call him 'Frank' and so on. These names are not actual descriptions of the children, but aspirations.

The word 'Arafa' is now a name for the place where pilgrims stand to seek Allah's mercy. It is important to note that 'Arafa' –also known as Arafat- does not only refer to Mount Arafa; it also includes the valley and the area surrounding it. Prophet Muhammad –peace be upon him- said: "The Hajj pilgrimage is Arafa." Some people have the misconception that if they do not climb the mountain called 'Mount of Mercy' which is in Arafa then their Hajj is incomplete. We answer that standing in Arafa includes the mountain and a large area of the valley around it. The mountain is only a part of the entire area of Arafa.

There is a difference of opinion as to why it has this name. Some scholars say: it is named 'Arafa' because Adam descended to earth in one place, while Eve descended in another. They both kept searching for each other until they met at this location. People have questioned the reason behind separating Adam and Eve from each other after they were created as a couple. You can imagine the state of Adam who was sent alone into a vast universe unknown to him, he looks around but finds no one like him. Would he not long for a companion to bond with? Imagine his happiness when he met up with Eve. Allah Almighty caused them to part so they would appreciate and acknowledge the desire, affection, and intimacy that men and women can now share.

Another opinion regarding the name 'Arafa' is related to the Angles coming to Adam and Eve in that location and asking them to reflect on their sin and repent to the Lord. Allah says:

They said: "O our Lord, we have wronged ourselves. If You do not forgive us and have mercy upon us, we shall certainly be lost." (07:23)

So it is claimed that at that location, Adam and Eve (peace be upon them) recognized their mistake and learned to repent.

Yet another opinion regarding the name 'Arafa' comes from the incident when Allah wanted to put Abraham's faith to the test. Abraham saw himself in a dream sacrificing his son Ishmael. That dream presented a very difficult test for Abraham from three aspects: first, the vision of sacrifice was a dream, not a revelation. Second: He saw himself sacrificing Ishmael –his only son at the time-. And lastly, it was Abraham himself who was slaughtering his own son. It was surely a difficult matter for Abraham –peace be upon him-, and many thoughts must have rushed through his mind. Was it a vision or something else? Abraham knew that the dreams of prophets were true visions, and the place where he acknowledged the dream as Allah's command is now called 'Arafa.' Moreover, such a difficult test presented an excellent opportunity for satan to distance Abraham from the Lord. So when satan came to

Abraham in a man's form and tried to talk him out of Allah's command, Abraham stoned him away with seven pebbles. Satan returned for a second attempt. Abraham did the same. Then satan tried a third time, and Abraham stoned him again and chased him away. Abraham ran from the place fearing another confrontation. The place where Abraham retreated to is now called 'Muzdalifa.' The word 'Muzdalif' in the Arabic language is used to describe a person who rushes away.

Some scholars are of the opinion that 'Arafa' is the place where the Archangel Gabriel taught Abraham –peace be upon him- the rituals of worship. Gabriel would then ask: Did you learn this? To which Abraham would reply: I learned –'Araftu' in Arabic-.

Perhaps, most importantly, Arafa is the place where Muslims come to meet their Lord during in prayer and supplication while performing one of the pillars of Islam. It is a place and a time to seek Allah's vast mercy and get closer to the Lord in supplication. The day of Arafa is the day when pilgrims are granted pardon from hellfire. Prophet Muhammad –peace be upon him- said: There is no day in which more people are pardoned from Hellfire than the Day of Arafat. Allah is close to the pilgrims on that day. He tells before the angels and says: 'Look at my servants; they made it here from all places, scruffy and tired, seeking my mercy. I want you to bear witness that I have forgiven them.' The Angels would say: 'Our Lord, among them is so and so who has overburdened himself with sin.' Allah answers: 'I have forgiven them.'

There is no blame on you for seeking bounty from your Lord. But when you depart from Arafa, remember Allah at the sacred landmark. And remember Him, as He has guided you, for indeed, you were before that among those astray. Verse 198)

The phrase "There is no blame on you for seeking bounty from your Lord" means it is neither a sin nor frowned upon to trade and earn money during the hajj pilgrimage. Traditionally, people gave the name 'Hajji' to a person who performed the Hajj pilgrimage and 'Dajji' to the person who went to Mecca exclusively to trade. We answer that you can do both. It is not objectionable to do some business while performing Hajj. The millions of people who perform the pilgrimage annually need plenty of services after all. Those who do Hajj and trade together facilitate the trip for others and fulfill a real need.

Take note of the precise words of the phrase: "for seeking bounty from your Lord." Allah did not use the word 'provision' –translated from the Arabic 'Rizq'-; rather He used the word bounty –translated from the Arabic 'Faddl'-. Why, you may ask? We answer that Allah has already made it clear in the previous verse that it is your duty, before you leave for pilgrimage, to take enough provisions with you to meet your basic needs. Allah does not want you to set out on your trip empty handed hoping to earn money to survive. Whatever you make from trade should be an extra bounty above and beyond your needs. Hence, you should take with you all you need of provisions, and, if you choose to, you can make a reasonable profit from trade as a bounty. If every pilgrim brings his or her basic needs, there wouldn't be any price gouging to exploit the needs of others.

Moreover, both the seeker of basic needs and the seeker of extra bounty must bear in mind that everything is from Allah. He says: "There is no blame on you for seeking bounty from your Lord." Don't say: 'I earned lots of money because I am more intelligent and more disciplined than others.' Or say: "I earned my money because I do great work and had an excellent education." Everything you and I earn is the result of Allah's favour upon us. We seek and credit our Lord -the Creator and the Sustainer- for everything we have. It is our duty to work hard, educate ourselves, and do the best that we can to earn money, but Allah is ultimately the One who grants and withholds.

The verse continues: 'But when you depart from Arafa, remember Allah at the sacred landmark.' The word 'depart' is translated from the Arabic origin 'Afadtum.' The root of this word is 'Fa Da' which means to overflow. For example, if you fill a glass with milk to the rim, then add just a little more it will start to spill over. Allah had decreed –even before this verse was revealed- that Arafa will be so crowded with pilgrims it will cause people to overflow from it.

If you have ever witnessed this scene –may Allah enable all Muslims to perform Hajj – you know exactly what is meant here. When the pilgrims leave Arafa and head to Muzdalifa, you wonder: where did all these people come from? You see valleys and roads filled with people moving like a river. You see buses moving as if they were a single train, and you won't be able to distinguish between individuals as they all seem to become one.

The verse continues: 'you depart from Arafa, remember Allah at the sacred landmark. And remember Him, as He has guided you.' The sacred landmark –translated from 'Mishar Al-haram' in Arabic- is in the area of Muzdalifah.

Allah is the one who made this marvellous journey possible for you; He brought you to His Sacred House and all the sacred places around it; On top of all these great blessings, He –the All-Merciful- grants you the bounty of forgiveness for your efforts and sincerity. Shouldn't you then, as a bare minimum, remember your Lord with appreciation and gratitude? He says: 'remember Allah at the sacred landmark. And remember Him, as He has guided you.' Allah's guidance and teachings are the shortest path that will lead to success. It is a blessing from Allah to His creation, and blessings deserve proper appreciation and remembrance.

Allah concludes the verse with: 'for indeed, you were before that among those astray.' Before Islam, many Meccans and people from around the region performed pilgrimage in ignorance. There were idols in the Ka'ba, and rituals lost all meaning. Now, with Allah's guidance, we perform Hajj as Allah intended.

VERSE 199

Summa afeedoo min haisu afaadan naasu wastagh firullaah; innal laaha Ghafoor ur-Raheem

Then stream out from where the people stream out, and plead to Allah for forgiveness; indeed Allah is All-forgiving, all-merciful.

The word 'then' implies that there should be a pause between the two events. In other words, there should be time spent in Arafa and Muzdalifa before heading out. This verse supports those who argue that it is necessary to stay overnight in Muzdalifa.

This verse was revealed because the people of Quraysh used to see themselves as the special people of the Sacred House. They assumed that they do not have to do what the rest of the pilgrims are commanded to do. For example, they saw no need to go and join the pilgrims in Arafa. Allah, however, wants equality between Muslims. Prophet Muhammad (peace be upon him) said in the Farewell Pilgrimage: "you are all the children of Adam, and Adam was created from dust; let people stop taking pride in their forefathers for Allah holds no weight to such trivial matters." Allah says: 'Then stream out from where the people stream out' indicating to Quraysh and the residents of Mecca that they should follow the same guidelines all Muslims follow.

Some scholars believe that the phrase 'Then stream out from where the people stream out' means to follow the footsteps of Prophet Abraham in pilgrimage just as Allah taught him. Here you may ask: How could the scholars claim that Prophet Abraham is referred to in this verse, while the plural 'people' is used? We answer that the plural 'People' had been used in the Quran to speak about a single person when he or she embodies the best traits of many people. Allah has described Abraham as a 'nation' as the following verse illustrates:

Abraham was a community in himself, exemplary, obedient to Allah, a man of pure natural belief. He was not one of the idolaters. (16:120)

The verse ends with: 'and plead to Allah for forgiveness; indeed Allah is All-forgiving, All-merciful.' Allah is informing you that regardless of your best effort, you will not be able to fulfill Allah's rights to perfection. Thus, you should always be in remembrance of Allah and asking him for forgiveness. Allah, after all, is the 'All-forgiving, All-merciful.'

VERSE 200

Fa-iza qadaitum manaa sikakum fazkurul laaha kazikrikum aabaaa'akum aw ashadda zikraa; faminannaasi mai yaqoolu Rabbanaaa aatinaa fiddunyaa wa maa lahoo fil Aakhirati min khalaaq

When you have completed your rites, remember Allah as much as you remember your own fathers, or even more. There are some who pray, 'Our Lord, give us good in this world,' and they will have no share in the Hereafter

The phrase 'have completed' is translated from the Arabic origin 'Qadaytum'. The root 'Qada' has various meanings; all share the core meaning of completing a task with proficiency and wisdom. Here are two examples of the use of the word 'Qada' in the Quran. In the following verse, 'Qada' it is translated into 'to decide,' or 'to rule':

So decide whatever you will: you can only decide matters of this present life- (20:72)

In another verse, it means: to issue a ruling. Allah says:

When Allah and His Messenger have decided on a matter that concerns them, it is not fitting for any believing man or woman to claim freedom of choice in that matter: whoever disobeys Allah and His Messenger is far astray. (33:36)

Getting back to the verse,

'And when you have completed your rites, remember Allah," the word 'rites' includes all places of worship. 'Arafat' is the place of standing before Allah in remembrance and supplication; Muzdalifa is where the pilgrims spend the night in remembrance afterward. Mena is also a place where the pilgrims spend the night. Every place has a particular rite attributed to it.

You have probably noted that the remembrance of Allah is repeatedly mentioned throughout the verses of the Hajj pilgrimage. As though Allah is reminding you that the hajj trip was made possible for you through His blessings and favours. In other words, you must not be deluded by your own abilities, and wealth. Rather, remember Allah who blessed you with Islam, legislated worship for you, gave you the physical and financial strength to perform the pilgrimage, and supported you thought-out the entire process.

Allah wanted to put an end to what the Arabs had become accustomed before Islam. During the pre-Islamic Hajj season, all the tribes would get together in Mena and each would bring forward their best poets and speakers to boast about their feats and the feats of their ancestors. They would announce all the things they were proud of, and use the gathering to pay blood money on behalf of members of their clan, then brag about their wealth and generosity. The gathering would also turn into a display of wealth. Prophet Muhammad recalled that there were food pots large enough to provide him with shade from the sun when he was young. Thus, Allah wanted to stop this arrogance and wasteful lavishness. He says: "remember Allah as much as you remember your own fathers, or even more."

Allah wanted the pilgrims to attribute all matters to Him. You remember your parents and your ancestors because they did so much for you and provided you with everything. But, who is the Creator of your parents and ancestors? Who is the provider of all good –whether wealth, strength or knowledge-? All good in this world is due to Allah. So if you remember your fathers for the favours they did for you, then you owe Allah –The real provider- more praise and more remembrance. Every person deserves to be remembered according to the good work her or she has done. Without Allah, there would be no good in this world. Hence you must reserve the highest praise and tribute to Allah Almighty.

Islam discourages you from taking pride in your lineage; rather pride of a believer should stem from within; more specifically from the good deeds he or she does to serve others. In the Arabic tradition, a person who takes pride in his or her forefathers is taking pride in bones and graves. Allah wants you to be proud in the good deeds you have done, not in what your predecessors have done. Your ancestor's deeds are for themselves, and you will only have your own deeds on the Day of Judgment.

A poet said:

Do not ascribe yourselves to bones,

Taking pride in their past, while your life is in ruins

Nobility inherited from the past does no good

Save for those who are eager to maintain this nobility

If a tree bears no fruit, no matter how high it grows

The people see it as nothing but firewood

Another poet said:

Our youth are not the ones who say: 'My father was so and so',

But rather the ones who say: 'Here I am!'

Pride comes from humility in serving others. Pride comes from feeding the poor, helping the weak and treating the sick. Most importantly, pride is to provide something enduring and influential to the disenfranchised in the world. It comes from spreading Allah's teachings to humanity. Allah says: 'remember Allah as much as you remember your own fathers, or even more' because Allah alone is the one capable of providing you with genuine support to become a leader in your community. He alone can guide you to help establish justice, peace, and mercy to those around you. These values are something a person can be proud of.

This brings us back to the verse: Allah says: 'There are some who pray, 'Our Lord, give us good in this world,' and they will have no share in the Hereafter.' When the pilgrim completes the rites, he or she should turn to Allah in supplication. People ask Allah for countless things. Each person asks depending on his or her desires and aspirations. Allah is guiding you not to preoccupy yourself with worldly material needs. In other words, do not supplicate: 'O Lord, give me cars, give me wealth, and give me a farm and livestock. O Lord, give me as you gave my father.' Allah wants you to think about the things that are eternal in their benefit and pleasure. Here, the true advantage of faith is on display. If you were only to ask Allah for the pleasures of this world, then what is the difference between you and the people of ignorance?

After you have spent days completing the rites of worship, you get the chance to stand before Allah and supplicate. Make sure to ask for things in accordance with the status and ability of the Giver. Let's clarify this point further. Say, for example, that you wanted to ask a person for money. If this person is a multi-millionaire, would you ask him or her for a £10? Or would you ask for tens of thousands? The richer the person, the more you can ask of him or her. Allah is the provider of all good, He is the creator of all good, to him belongs the heavens and the earth. When you ask of your Lord, make sure you ask according to His ability. Ask for the ultimate everlasting rewards; ask for forgiveness and paradise in the hereafter.

VERSE 201

Wa minhum mai yaqoolu rabbanaaa aatina fid dunyaa hasanatanw wa fil aakhirati hasanatanw wa qinaa azaaban Naar

And there are others who say, 'Our Lord, give us good in this world, and good in the Next World, and safeguard us from the punishment of the Fire.'

Allah wants to elevate you to higher levels. By performing the Hajj pilgrimage rituals, you have purified yourself for supplication to Allah. It is your chance to ask for the most beneficial things. Do not fall to a level where you show a lack of spirit and faith by exclusively asking for worldly and temporary matters. Allah wants to elevate the spirits of your faith, and in this verse, He teaches you the best supplication. The All-Merciful says:

And there are others who say, 'Our Lord, give us good in this world, and good in the Next World, and safeguard us from the punishment of the Fire.' (Chapter 2: Verse 201)

Take note of the beauty of Allah's teachings. In the verse under study, Allah is guiding you towards the finest supplication. Yet, He –the All-Merciful- did not omit "give us good in this world" from the prayer. The supplication combines both, blessings in this world and blessings and protection in the hereafter. We find that all scholars agree on what is meant by good in the Hereafter; it includes all things that lead to forgiveness, mercy, and Paradise. There is, however, some differences in opinion in regards to the good in this world. Some scholars have narrowed the meaning down to a righteous spouse and a good family. Others have said that 'good in the world' means proper knowledge because deeds are built upon it. I say: Why don't we take the good in this world in more general terms. Thus, it would mean: O Lord, give us all that which is good for the worldly life in Your sight.

The verse ends with: "safeguard us from the punishment of the Fire." Allah's favours on the Day of Judgment are on two levels. First, Allah saves His servants from Hellfire; and second He admits them into Paradise. This picture comes into full display when you read the descriptions of the Day of Judgment. On that day, after each person has been taken to account. A bridge will be erected across hellfire for everyone to cross. Every person will travel on this terrible bridge at a speed determined by his or her good deeds. Some will cross it with the speed of light, while others will cross it slowly and so on. The disbelievers, on the other hand, having no good deeds to carry them across, will fall into the fire. Here you may ask: why are the believers asked to cross such a bridge? We find the answer in the following verse talking about hellfire:

but every single one of you will approach it, a decree from your Lord which must be fulfilled. We shall deliver those who took heed for themselves, and leave the evil-doers kneeling there. (19:71-72)

While entrance into paradise is a great blessing, the believers cross this bridge to witness the terrible torment their faith has protected them from. They will sense the great blessing and immense mercy of their Lord. The believer would say: 'Praise be to Allah, for faith has saved me from the torment of fire.' Then a short while later, he or she will again say: 'Praise be to Allah, for He has blessed me with Paradise.' Allah says:

Every soul will taste death and you will be paid in full only on the Day of Resurrection. Whoever is kept away from the Fire and admitted to the Garden will have triumphed. The present world is only an illusory pleasure (03:185)

VERSE 202

Ulaaa'ika lahum naseebum mimmaa kasaboo; wal laahu saree'ul hisaab

Those will have a share of what they have earned, and Allah is swift in account.

The phrase 'have earned' is translated from the Arabic origin 'Kasabu.' The verb 'Kasaba' is usually used to describe lawful, beneficial earnings, while the verb 'Iktasaba' is used to describe unlawful or harmful earnings. Why the different verbs, you may ask? We answer that unlawful gains do not come natural and usually require extra effort; thus we use the longer verb 'Iktasaba' to convey this meaning. Take the example of a person stealing for the very first time. He or she would plan for days and may hesitate whether to steal or not. After the theft is committed he or she would worry for days about every sound and every movement. You can say that this person 'Iktasaba' the stolen goods and money. As for good deeds, they occur more naturally and do not involve excessive concern.

"Of what they have earned" in this verse is referring to what they have earned by completing the rituals of Hajj such as ihram, remembrance, circumambulation, visiting Mena, standing in Arafa, stoning the Jamaraat and so on. Each of these rites is a step for the servant towards earning the honour of the Hajj pilgrimage.

The phrase "Allah is swift in account" should remind you that speed is to use less time to do a certain task. More importantly, recall that the time needed to do a task is inversely related to the power, ability, and resources of the doer. Let's clarify this point with some examples. It may take you five hours to walk from your house to the airport, but if you take a car which has much more power, the trip would take 30 minutes; if you use a helicopter, the same exact trip may take less than 10 minutes. In essence, the more power and resources under your control, the less time you need to perform the same task. Likewise, it may take you a whole day to manually add a thousand four digit numbers, but if you have a calculator that time is cut by more than half. If you use a computer, the same task would take a few seconds because of the power at your disposal. Allah Almighty is the All-Powerful, All-Knowledgeable, All-Encompassing, the Bountiful, thus, by the same principal, Allah requires no time at all to complete a task. He only commands it 'be' and it becomes. Allah is swift in judging people to the degree of immediacy. Moreover, Allah is neither distracted nor preoccupied with one task over another. You and I may not be able to perform well when we multitask, and our abilities are even less when we are distracted. Allah Almighty's abilities are above all abilities. Allah is infinite in power and speed.

Imam Ali bin Abi Talib was asked: How will Allah take all of his creation to account at the same time on the Day of Judgment? Ali answered: just as He provides for all of them at the same time in this world.

VERSE 202

Wazkurul laaha feee ayyaamin ma'doodaatin; faman ta'ajjala fee yawmaini falaaa ismaa 'alaihi wa man ta akhara falaaa isma 'alayhi; limanit-taqaa; wattaqul laaha wa'lamooo annakum ilaihi tuhsharoon

Remember Allah on the appointed days. If anyone is in a hurry to leave after two days, there is no blame on him, nor is there any blame on anyone who stays on, so long as they are mindful of Allah. Be mindful of Allah, and remember that you will be gathered to Him.

Here again, the remembrance of Allah is common in all Hajj pilgrimage rituals. The 'appointed days' are the known as Days of Tashreeq –The Eastern days-. They are the eleventh, twelfth and thirteenth of the month of Thu'l-Hijjah. On the ninth day, the pilgrims stay in Arafa, and the night of the tenth is spent in Muzdalifa. Then the pilgrims depart and head to the Jamarat where the symbolic stoning of the devil takes place. After this point, some people head back to the Ka'ba to perform the circumambulation of Ifadha and that completes their Hajj. Others choose to stay behind, slaughter their animal sacrifice, and then head to the Ka'ba for the circumambulation of Ifadha.

The 'appointed days' which are the Days of Tashreeq or The Eastern days were named so because in the olden times, whenever the animals were slaughtered, the pilgrims would hang the meat facing eastward to dry up and be preserved under the sun rays.

The verse continues: "If anyone is in a hurry to leave after two days, there is no blame on him, nor is there any blame on anyone who stays on, so long as they are mindful of Allah.' The phrase 'If anyone is in a hurry to leave after two days' suggests that the "appointed days" are greater than two. But Allah Almighty has applied the same ruling for a two day and three day stays. Whether pilgrims stay two or three days, they will earn their reward in full. How can this be, you may ask? We answer that the issue here is not the time you spend, rather it is having the right intention of worship and purity of faith. For example, you may remain there for three days without being mindful of Allah or without being focused on worship. In this case, is the longer stay beneficial? Of course not! Allah made the condition of your stay clear: He says: 'nor is there any blame on anyone who stays on, so long as they are mindful of Allah.' So be cautious against measuring deeds in minutes, hours or days. It is the intention and piety that counts.

The verse ends with: "Be mindful of Allah, and remember that you will be gathered to Him.' Allah is referring to the gathering on the on the Day of Resurrection. He used the word 'gathered' because the enormous crowds during Hajj should remind you of the gathering of all creation on the Day of Judgment.

VERSE 204

Wa minan naasi mai yu'jibuka qawluhoo fil hayaatid dunyaa wa yushhidul laaha 'alaa maa fee qalbihee wa huwa aladdulkhisaam

And from among the people are those whose words about worldly life please you, and he cites Allah as witness to what is in his heart. Yet he is the fiercest of opponents. And when he turns his back, he strives about the earth to foment disorder and corruption; destroying crops and future generations. Allah does not like corruption.

Allah presents us with a very important issue: every human interaction has two sides: an apparent side and a hidden one. It is possible for some of us to master appearances and deceive others by hiding our true motives. How would you protect yourself from such people? The answer is simple: Always be in the company of Allah who has knowledge of everything: hidden and apparent.

Even better yet, if each and every individual in the society is Allah conscious, and if each and every individual believes in the Lord who knows all our secrets, then we would all commit ourselves to honesty and respect. There would be no deception or corruption. It is often said: "if you manage to evade the justice of this world, rest assured that you will never evade the justice of the world to come." We thank Allah and praise Him for His knowledge of the unseen, because He is the One who will protect each one of us from others and He will be the judge on the Day of Resurrection.

Moreover, it is a true bounty from Allah that He concealed our inner thoughts from one another because we are impulsive beings. Suppose, for example that you and I were long time friends. At one point of time, I might have been annoyed by something you did. Had you learned what I truly thought about you at that very moment, you might detest me. You may never forget or forgive a bad opinion I had about you once. My opinion about you, and yours about me, are mere thought that often change over time. Had we known each other's inner thoughts, life would have become very difficult.

Allah warns us about a certain type of people. He says: 'And from among the people are those whose words about worldly life please you, and he cites Allah as witness to what is in his heart.' They pretend to be good but conceal evil within. Is it wrong to be impressed or to like what someone else is saying, you may ask? No, but do not be deceived by speech related to worldly things; true good is in the speech related to hereafter, and that is the conversation that should attract and please you.

There are many examples of those who come up to others with kind words of praise, while harbouring ill feelings and bad intentions. Some people may praise their co-workers in a meeting, and then mock them behind their backs minutes later. Allah is alerting you to an important matter: If someone flatters you through his or her words, remind yourself that the best of speech is that which reminds you of good deeds and the everlasting life in the hereafter.

The Caliph of the Muslims wrote to Imam Jaffar As-Sadiq saying: 'Why don't you visit us as other people visit us O' grandson of the prophet?' Imam As-Sadiq wrote back: 'I have nothing in this world which I fear losing and you have nothing of the Hereafter which I seek.' As if Imam Jaffar wanted to tell the ruler: leave me alone; all that you are looking for are more people who sit around you in praise and eulogy, while ignoring the fact that most of them harbour ill feelings towards you.'

The verse: 'And from among the people are those whose words about worldly life pleases you, and he cites Allah as witness to what is in his heart' was revealed in regards to Al-Akhnas Ibn Shareeq Al-thaqafi who turned back and abandoned the Army of Quraish on the day of the battle of Badr. He excused himself from fighting the Muslims saying that the caravans of Quraish had escaped the Muslims safely, so there was no need to fight. He was a good looking well spoken man; when he would run into the prophet later, he would pretend to be a Muslim, soften his speech and claim love for Allah and the Messenger. However, he was a hypocrite who burnt the crops of the Muslims and killed their livestock when he had the chance. Although this verse was revealed in regards to al-Akhnas, it is general and applies to all the hypocrites.

"And from among the people are those whose words about worldly life pleases you, and he cites Allah as witness to what is in his heart. Yet he is the fiercest of opponents. And when he turns his back, he strives about the earth to foment disorder and corruption; destroying crops and future generations. Allah does not like corruption".

When it comes to your daily affairs, try not to claim that Allah is a witness to what you say; rather if you need proof, bring witnesses to testify to the authenticity of your statement. When you say: "Allah is my witness," you are declaring that Allah is on your side and claiming that He, Almighty, will vouch for your statements. This is not true. You have no knowledge of Allah; and if you intend to bring credibility to your statements do not involve Allah in the matter. Similarly, when you hear someone say to you: 'Allah is my witness,' say to him or her: this is an assertion from you that Allah is on your side, but you may be wrong. I prefer that you bring two people as witnesses and not involve Allah in this matter'

The verse continues: 'Yet he is the fiercest of opponents.' Allah is referring to those who are entrenched in disobedience and sin; those who go too far in argument and dispute supporting unjust matters. The Prophet (peace be upon him) said: "indeed the most detested men to Allah is the fierce disputant." Why are the hypocrites the fiercest of opponents? Because the person who openly confronts you with a matter makes his stand known, and allows you to take precautions. But the one who appears to be friendly while working behind the scenes to hurt you may catch you off guard. Thus, the opponent who makes things obvious and clear is better.

VERSE 205

Wa izaa tawallaa sa'aa fil ardi liyufsida feeha wa yuhlikal harsa wannasl; wallaahu laa yuhibbul fasaad

"And when he turns his back, he strives about the earth to foment disorder and corruption; destroying crops and future generations."

Here, you can see the core of hypocrisy: a person says things that please you to your face, but as soon as he or she turns away, this person shows the reality which was hidden and acts to cause corruption and harm. The earth was created and maintained without human intervention as a good, peaceful and thriving place. Corruption is almost exclusively the result of human action. Take a look around you; wherever you see pollution and destruction of nature, you see human interference. Why have we complained of food shortages but not of air shortages? Because food production and distribution is controlled by humans, while there is no human involvement in air production and distribution. We have intervened in fresh water management and as a result we have polluted and wasted it. In fact, corruption is often proportional to the extent of human intervention.

Thus, there is a dire need for faith to guide people. It is the framework that governs our actions and respects the rights of people and nature alike. There are no guiding scriptures for animals or plants because Allah created them to faithfully and instinctively perform their task. Livestock obey their owner even when lead to slaughter. A tamed bull would neither stop you from putting your load on it, nor refuse to plough. And on the rare occasions when the animal refuses to act, it is often due to illness or for being physically overburdened.

As for us humans, who enjoy freedom of choice, there is a need for a religion and a guiding book to direct us to do certain things and refrain from others. If we commit ourselves to the Quran and its teachings, life would be balanced and the corruption of man and nature would diminish. This is what we understand from the verse: "And when he turns his back, he strives about the earth to foment disorder and corruption; destroying crops and future generations." It shows that corruption requires effort, cunning, and a life away from Allah's teachings. Leave nature alone as Allah created it, and you will find it working beautifully to perfection. Allah says regarding the hypocrites:

When it is said to them, 'Do not cause corruption in the land,' they say, 'We are only putting things right,' No indeed! They are the corrupters, but they are not aware of it. (02:11-12)

Allah is the creator of the earth, and He is best aware of the needs of nature. Any work done outside the frame of Allah's teachings will cause corruption and destruction of nature. We have the freedom of choice in our actions, thus, Allah has given us heavenly guidance to protect us and protect our environment. Look at the stupidity and short-sightedness of those who cause corruption on earth. Do these individuals or companies think that they alone are allowed to benefit from the land, while spoiling it for others? The plunder of natural resources affects each and everyone of us, even those who think they are benefiting in the short term.

The word 'crops' in the phrase 'destroying crops and future generations' is translated from the Arabic origin 'Harth.' 'Harth' can hold two meanings, it could mean plants and crops, and could mean women. Let's take them one by one:

Allah blessed us with fertile earth that we can cultivate. We loosen the soil and plant seeds, and then utilize the resources Allah granted us to grow the crop. Keep in mind that Allah is the one who created the seed, the land, the water and the sun. All are essential components for the growing plants. Allah reminds you:

Consider the seeds you sow in the ground, Is it you who make it germinate or are We the Germinator? If We wished We could have made it broken stubble. You would then be left devoid of crops, distraught (56:63-66)

The second meaning of 'Harth': women, can be found in the following verse:

Your wives are the bearers of your seed; so, approach your tillage however you wish and send good ahead for yourselves. Act in due reverence for Allah, and know that you are to meet with Him; and give glad tidings to the believers (02:223)

The verse ends with: "Allah does not like corruption." Allah is telling you that if you do intend to work in nature, then the very least that you could do is to leave matters as Allah has created them.

This verse gives an example to one of the ways in which Islam was received and fought. There were a group of hypocrites who infiltrated the Muslim society, pretending to be believers and saying things that were pleasing to the Muslims; in reality, they were there to spy and cause damage. We should look at hypocrisy as an indicator of strength for the Muslims. How can that be, you may ask? We answer that you lie and try to deceive someone only if you are afraid to confront him or her. Hypocrisy did not arise in Mecca because the Muslims were few and weak. When Islam grew stronger in Medina, the hypocrites appeared. Allah says:

Some of the desert Arabs around you are hypocrites and some of the people of Medina are adamant in their hypocrisy. You do not know them but We know them. We will punish them twice over and then they will be returned to a terrible punishment. (9:101)

While in Mecca, the Muslims were few and weak, so their enemies confronted them directly with torture, boycott and physical attacks. But in Medina, Islam became strong, so the enemies changed tactics and the hypocrites were born. Hence, the presence of hypocrisy in Medina was a healthy phenomenon that indicated a strengthening and wide spreading faith; even those who had no faith started to claim it. They would say good and beautiful things and hide what is in their hearts. When they were in charge of land or life, however, they would work to destroy it.

VERSE 206

Wa izaa qeela lahuttaqil laaha akhazathul izzatu bil-ism; fahasbuhoo jahannam; wa labi'sal mihaad

When he is told, 'Beware of Allah,' pride in sin takes hold of him. Hell is sufficient for him: a dreadful resting place.

In the previous verses, we discussed hypocrisy in the Muslim society of Medina. We mentioned the story of Al-Akhnas who pretended to have faith, said what pleased the Muslims, yet worked to damage crops and livestock. Hypocrisy was a sign of a strengthening Muslim society because the enemies of Islam no longer wished to confront it directly with force; rather they now preferred to hide and damage it from within.

The Muslims, however, were vigilant to those who might have malicious intents within the society. More importantly, Prophet Muhammad -peace be upon him- and his companions had the Lord on their side informing them of those who wished them ill. The verse under study is one proof to this fact. Allah says:

When he is told, 'Beware of Allah,' pride in sin takes hold of him. Hell is sufficient for him: a dreadful resting place. (Chapter 2: Verse 206)

You would not say to a person "Hey man, why don't you fear Allah" unless you know that he is acting in a way not appropriate for a believer. We understand from this verse that a believer should be alert and should measure actions around him or her according to Allah's teachings. You should not surrender you mind, act without thinking, and blindly accept what you are told. You should not rely on divine inspiration to show you the truth; rather, you should have your own identity and put your mind to work in all matters around you.

When someone is told: "Fear Allah" it indicates that the person's actions at the time contradict what is right regardless of what he or she is saying. The old adage: "actions speak louder than words" comes to mind. A person may be praying in the first row; he or she may talk passionately about religious issues, but it is his or her actions towards others that count. Your advice to someone to "fear Allah" means that you are asking him or her to act righteously. It is not enough to say the right things or speak what others like. Allah wants your deeds to reflect what is in your heart.

The believer must be intelligent and socially astute in order to weigh the true actions of others, rather than take matters at face value. Pleasing words have to be backed up by proper actions. More importantly, if you suspect that someone is not being true to his or her words, you should bring that fact up to that person in order to limit the time of his or her hypocrisy. The moment you say: "fear Allah," the person would understand that his or her hypocrisy has been exposed, and perhaps this would be as a future deterrent.

This brings us back to the verse: Allah says: "When he is told, 'Beware of Allah,' pride in sin takes hold of him." The association of pride and sin in this verse suggests that pride may also be associated with something other than sin. Allah Almighty declared pride for himself, for the Prophet and for the believers. He says:

They say: "As soon as we return back to Medina, the proud should evict the weak from the city. They do not realize that all pride belongs to Allah, his messenger and the believers. (63:08)

The pride Allah declared is pride in the truth and not in sin. What is the difference between the two, you may ask? Let's study the Quran to understand the difference. We start with the story of the magicians that represented Pharaoh against Prophet Moses —peace be upon him-. Allah narrates in the Nobel Book:

They threw their ropes and staffs, saying, 'By Pharaoh's pride, we shall be victorious.' (26:44)

This was pride in sin and a total fabrication. In another chapter, Allah says:

Yet the disbelievers are steeped in pride and hostility. (38:02)

This, also, is a false pride. But pride in the following verse is different. Allah says:

Exalted is your Lord, the Lord of pride, above what they describe. (37:180)

It is real pride because pride is the power that prevails and no one can overcome it. As for pride in sin, it is false arrogance mired in sin. Allah Almighty says to all those who want this sort of pride in sin: if you truly have a pride, then no one should be able to overcome you. But O Magicians of Pharaoh, O you who have the pride of Pharaoh, you were the ones who fell in prostration before Moses as the following verse illustrates:

They said, 'We believe in the Lord of all the worlds, the Lord of Moses and Aaron.' (26:47-48)

Pride in Pharaoh did not benefit you, because it was pride in sin. Pride in the truth overcame pride in sin. Allah further describes the nature of pride in the truth in the following verse:

Allah will soon replace you with people He loves and who love Him, people who are humble towards the believers, proud on the disbelievers (from 5:54)

Allah informs us that for pride not to be in sin, it must be against the disbelievers. He says:

Muhammad is the Messenger of Allah. Those who follow him are strong towards the disbelievers and compassionate towards each other. You see them kneeling and prostrating, seeking Allah's bounty and His good pleasure: on their faces they bear the marks of their prostrations. This is how they are pictured in the Torah and the Gospel: like a seed that puts forth its shoot, becomes strong, grows thick, and rises on its stem to the delight of its sowers. So Allah infuriates the disbelievers through them; Allah promises forgiveness and a great reward to those who believe and do righteous deeds. (48:29)

One of the clearest signs of pride in truth is humility in the hour of victory. We have the example of our beloved prophet Muhammad. Early in the call to Islam, he migrated from Mecca because he could not protect the weak from amongst the believers. Years later, he –peace be upon him- returned to Mecca victorious. He entered the city with his head so bowed down in humbleness to Allah that it almost touched the saddlebow of his mount. This is pride in truth. Contrast that to pride in sin which in the case of victory people exercises transgression, humiliation, and devastation towards their enemies.

For such false pride, Allah prescribes: "Hell is sufficient for him: a dreadful resting place." Any pride that leads to hellfire is not pride at all; rather it is humiliation. There is no good in any deed that leads to fire, and there is no evil in any deed that leads to Paradise. Thus, if you want to be dignified, then consider the ultimate outcome of your actions.

The phrase 'resting place' is translated from the Arabic origin 'Mihad.' It refers to a paved and flattened surface that is comfortable for sitting, walking and living. In fact, a child's cradle is called 'Mahd.' Here, the question that comes to mind: Is the word 'Mihad' appropriate for a place like Hellfire? We answer: yes it is, because he who sits in a crib has no strength to leave or even move out of it. Thus, the person who's resting place is hellfire, has truly ended up in the most dreadful of resting places.

VERSES 207

Wa minan naasi mai yashree nafsahub tighaaa'a mardaatil laah; wallaahu ra'oofum bil'ibaad

And among the people is the one who sells himself in pursuit of Allah's good pleasure. Allah is All-Compassionate towards His servants

The verb "sells" is translated from the Arabic origin 'Shara.' When Allah uses this verb in the Quran it could mean either selling or buying. In chapter 12, narrating the story of Prophet Joseph, Allah uses the verb 'shara' in the following way:

and they sold him for a small price, a few pieces of silver: so little did they value him. (12:20)

It is the context of the verse that determines if the verb 'shara' means to buy or to sell. This is one of the aspects of the true beauty of the Arabic language. It is a language that invites people to communicate with an alert mind, and to let the context dictate proper understanding of the meaning.

This brings us back to the verse under study. From the phrase: "And among the people is the one who sells himself in pursuit of Allah's good pleasure.' We understand that it is a transaction in which one loses him or herself in exchange for something else. So, it is a process of selling: sacrificing one's self in exchange for Allah's pleasures. Allah grants paradise to the person who sells himself in exchange. He says in verse 111 of chapter 9:

Indeed Allah has bought from the faithful their selves and their possessions for paradise to be theirs

But what if we were to look at the verse under study from the opposite angle? What if we were to examine the verse with the verb

'Shara' indicating buying one's self? In this case, you would buy yourself back –in essence saving yourself from ruin- by offering what you have in exchange. Let's look at two examples from the prophet's companions:

The verse was revealed in regards to a companion named Suhaib bin Sinan al-Rumi. He embraced Islam in Mecca and wanted to migrate to Medina to join the prophet –peace be upon him-. A spokesman for Quarish told him: By the Allahs, we shall not let you leave with your life and money. You came to Mecca weak and poor; we welcomed and helped you; now look at all the wealth and strength you have. Suhaib answered: "What would you say if I leave you all my wealth? Would you let me go?" The spokesman said: "Yes," and so it was. Thus, Suahib bought his faith and freedom in exchange for all his wealth. Before Suhaib reached Medina, the Angel Gabriel narrated his story to Prophet Muhammad. He (peace be upon him) said to Suhaib as he arrived: "Your trade has been fruitful." So the meaning of the verse, and more specifically the meaning of the verb 'Shara' is to purchase one's self with wealth and sacrifice. This is one of the miracles of Quranic performance, where one word serves two opposing meanings in a single verse without violating the context.

Let's look at another example of a companion where the story supports the opposite meaning: in essence to sell one's self. During the battle of Badr, the elites of Quraish had gathered to fight the Muslims. The Muslims managed to kill some of Quraish's leaders and to capture some. Amongst the ones killed was Abu Uqbah al-Harith. He was killed by a companion named Khubaib from the Aws clan of Medina. After their defeat, some of the disbelievers conspired and said to the Prophet: "we have embraced Islam, so send us men who would teach us the religion." The Messenger of Allah (peace be upon him) agreed and sent ten of his companions to teach them the Qur'an. The disbelievers betrayed and killed them except Khubayb who managed to escape along with another companion named Zayd. Quraish went in their pursuit and captured Khubayb. One of his captors recognized him as the killer of Abu Uqbah. He sold him to the son of Abu Uqbah so that he could take revenge for his father. The son did not want to kill him; rather he chose to crucify him. When Quraish gathered for the crucifixion, Khubaib requested a few moments to perform a prayer. They agreed. After completing his prayer he said: "I would have asked for more time for prayer, but I don't want you to think that I am afraid and trying to delay my death" Then, he said the following poem:

I have no concern as I face death

As long as it is on the path of Allah that I face it

These were Khubaib's last words. While he was left hanging, the Prophet learned about the incident. He (peace be upon him) asked his companions: "Whoever amongst you can bring back the body of Khubaib from the cross will earn for himself a spot in paradise." Zubair and Miqdad replied: "we can bring him back, O Prophet of Allah." They departed to Mecca on this very dangerous journey knowing that they may not make it back. When they reached the place of the crucifixion, they waited till the guards fell asleep and took the body back. Quraish realized what had happened, and followed their trail. Zubair caught a glance of the knights approaching, so he placed Khubaib's body on the ground. The body immediately sank into the sand. Thereafter, Khubaib was given the title "the one whom the earth had swallowed." Zubair turned to the disbelievers, exposed his face and said: "I am Zubair, my mother is Safiyya, and this Miqdad my companion. If you have the courage to stop us then do so. If not, then leave us alone." When the Quraishies saw that they did not have the body anymore, they turned around and headed back. Hence, Khubaib earned Paradise. So did Zubair and Miqdad, selling themselves, putting everything –including their lives- on the line.

The verse ends with "and Allah is All-Compassionate towards His servants.' Allah –the All Merciful- is not asking every Muslim to go through these exceptional sacrifices in order to prove his or her faith and earn paradise. Allah gave each one of us a mission in life, and it is up to each person to carry out the message of Islam.

VERSE 208

Yaaa ayyuhal lazeena aamanud khuloo fis silmi kaaaffatanw wa laa tattabi'oo khutuwaatish Shaitaan; innahoo lakum 'aduwwum mubeen

You who believe, enter wholeheartedly into submission to Allah and do not follow in Satan's footsteps, for he is your sworn enemy.

The verse begins by addressing those who have believed in Allah. As if the Almighty is saying: 'O you who have believed in Me, listen to what I have to say.' Allah does not assign any obligation to those who do not believe in him; He only addresses those who love him. When you love someone, you look forward to things that bring you closer to him or her. Thus, religious obligations are a pleasure for the one who loves Allah.

Allah says: "You who believe, enter wholeheartedly into submission to Allah." The preposition 'into' indicates that something is completely engulfed within something else. For example, you go into a building, or you get into serious trouble, both examples show immersion with little chance of escape. Here is another example from the Quran:

Pharaoh said, 'How dare you believe in him before I have given you permission? This must be your master, the man who taught you witchcraft. I shall certainly cut off your alternate hands and feet, then crucify you into the trunks of palm trees. You will know for certain which of us has the fiercer and more lasting punishment.' (20:71)

Crucifixion is always done on something. However, in this verse pharaoh is threatening the magicians to tie them so harshly to the tree trunks that their bodies would sink into the tree. Let's clarify this picture. Get a match stick and place it on your finger, then tie very tightly with a thread, you will notice that the stick would appear to sink into your finger.

This brings us back to the verse. Allah says: ""You who believe, enter wholeheartedly into submission to Allah." The phrase "submission to Allah' is translated from the Arabic origin 'Silm;' The word 'Silm' carries different meanings, all of which are proper for this verse. 'Silm' means the religion of Islam, and it also means peace. Peace is the opposite of war and Islam came to put an end to the conflict between you and the universe around you. How is that, you may ask? We answer that Allah is your Creator and the Creator of the universe in which you live. The heavens, the earth, and everything in between follows Allah's will. You, on the other hand, are free to follow Allah's path or go against it. If you choose to follow your Lord's teachings, you become aligned in tranquillity with the entire universe. This is truly the pinnacle of wisdom and sound judgment because when you submit to Allah, you entrust your affairs to the All Wise who knows you best, the Possessor of all strength who does not treat unjustly, and the Provider of provision and blessing. Moreover, when you adhere to Allah's teachings, everything around you rejoices. How? We answer that the plants, animals and even inanimate objects that Allah created for your service follow Allah's will and exalt Him. So, when you follow Allah's will and exalt Him too, you become in harmony with everything around you. Even your own body, hands, legs and tongue that Allah has subjected to your will celebrate. Let's clarify this point further. Your tongue, for example, will follow whatever order you give it. It can happily proclaim that "there is no Allah but Allah, and Muhammad is His messenger." It can also proclaim faith in other Allahs if you choose, but it only utters these words while it curses you. Keep in mind that your control over your tongue —and over all your body parts- will end on the Day of Resurrection. These body parts will bear witness against you on that day: your legs, hands, eyes, ears will confess to Allah about what you did with them. Control on that day will only belong to the Supreme Creator. He says:

The day when they will emerge, nothing about them will be hidden from Allah. 'To whom does the sovereignty belong today?' 'To Allah, the One, the All-paramount!' (40:16)

And in another verse:

on the day when witness shall be given against them by their tongues, their hands, and their feet concerning what they used to do. (24:24)

Thus, Islam is an invitation for you to be in harmony with the universe around you, in harmony with your own self and body, all of which Exalt Allah and follow His will. This is the true path to peace.

Allah also calls you to enter into Islam completely, meaning not to take some of the religion and leave the rest. Take Islam as a whole and apply it entirely because Islam is one complete structure with known principles and clear laws. You cannot adhere to some rules and leave out the rest putting the whole system out of balance.

Sadly, we often see this in everyday life. For example, a husband and wife may have severe disagreements. The man may eventually divorce the woman. At that time, we find those who accuse Islam because it gave the man more control in the matter of divorce. We say to them: why do you blame Islam now? Did the couple enter into the marriage according to Islamic teachings? Did the man and woman live their life according to Allah's recommendations? Had they done that, you would have known that Islam fully preserves the dignity of women and men.

Many people enter into marriage without consideration for Islamic teachings, but when they fall into crisis they blame Islam. Did the man choose a life partner properly? The prophet, peace be upon him, said: "A woman is wedded for four things: for her wealth, for her beauty, for her noble descent, and for her pious adherence to religion; so aim to get the pious woman if you want real prosperity." Did the man prefer a pious woman over all else? Or was that the last thing on his mind? Similarly, when the man came to propose, did the woman and her family value his faith and good character? Or did they look at material things first? If you disregard Islamic teachings when you get married, then do not rush to blame Islam when you divorce.

Allah is inviting you to 'enter wholeheartedly into submission to Allah' and to live life by the high standards of faith. When you do so, you bring the entire universe to your side. You will have inner peace and love. Otherwise, the natural forces within yourself will be at war with one another and with the universe around you.

Your whims and desires drive you to chase after life, money, and the opposite gender causing friction, stress, and unhappiness. Allah says:

Had truth been subject to their whims the heavens and the earth and all those within them would have gone to ruin. In fact, We had sent them their reminder, but they turned away from good advice. (23:71)

You who believe, enter wholeheartedly into submission to Allah and do not follow in Satan's footsteps, for he is your sworn enemy. (Chapter 2: Verse 208)

Why submit to Allah? That seems to be a key question. Perhaps a more fitting question: Is there any person who is superior to you in every single way that he or she deserves to be followed? Do you have more to offer so people would follow you? We answer that in the laws of subordination, the subordinate has to be convinced that whoever he or she is following has far superior abilities, both physical and mental. But human beings can never have absolute superiority. Each one of us is talented in his or her way, and we all need one another to survive and thrive. Thus, the only logical answer is for all human beings to follow a power that is truly above them all. When every one of us believes and submits to Allah, we enter into peace and end all contradictions between powers. I am not subjected to you, and you are not subjected to me; you and I both surrender to a higher power. More importantly, the force you and I willingly follow does not need us. In other words, when Allah legislates, it is for our benefit and not His, so there is no exploitation or abuse.

Human legislators take into account their own interests when they set laws. The communist legislators set laws that serve them and antagonize other governing systems such as capitalism. Likewise, the capitalist legislator set laws to serve the elites and allow exploitation of resources. The only legislator that does not benefit from the laws He sets is Allah Almighty.

He says: 'enter wholeheartedly into submission to Allah.' In essence, Allah is issuing two invitations. First He is inviting all humanity to enter into Islam. Second, He is inviting the believers to embrace faith in its entirety without picking and choosing what they like and dislike. There is one common reason behind these two invitations: if we do not enter into Islam completely, then those who commit themselves to faith suffer from the actions of those who do not. A righteous person who does not lie or steal from others makes life easy for all those around him or her; while a corrupt person who lies and steals makes life miserable for those around him or her. Thus, in order for the entire society to be upright and live in happiness, every person must be committed to Allah's teachings. People who do not understand this fact often misinterpret some verses from the Quran. Let's take this verse as an example. Allah says:

O you who believe! Your responsibility is your selves. Those who go astray can do you no harm if you yourselves are guided. To Allah is the return of all of you, and He will make you understand all that you were doing. (05:105)

Contrary to what some people think, part of your own guidance and part of your faith is to invite others to join Islam. It is in your best interest for all those around you to become Allah conscious. If you commit yourself to Allah's teachings, then the fruits of your faith and ethics would be enjoyed by those around you. People would trust working with you because you do not lie or cheat. People would listen to you because you are honest and so on. The opposite is also true; a person who does not commit him or herself to higher Islamic values may become a source of corruption and misery in society. So it is in your interest to bear the burden of inviting others to enter into Islam. Don't say: "this will be a waste of my time. I am only responsible for myself" No, keep in mind that inviting others to faith will guarantee you opportunities in life, and will protect you and your family from the evils of disbelief.

Every time you recite the first chapter of the Quran 'Al-Fatiha' in your prayers, you say: "You alone we worship, and you alone we ask for help, Guide us to the straight path. The path of those whom You have blessed, not the way of those who earned Your anger, nor of those who went astray. (1:5-7) In essence, you are asking Allah to help guide you and all humanity to the straight path of Islam so life can be enjoyed by all. This is the true meaning behind the verse: 'enter wholeheartedly into submission to Allah.'

As for the verse: 'O you who believe! Your responsibility is your selves. Those who go astray can do you no harm if you yourselves are guided,' it means, that you will not bear the burden of the sins of others after you give good advice and sincerely direct them to the straight path.

You who believe, enter wholeheartedly into submission to Allah and do not follow in Satan's footsteps, for he is your sworn enemy.

Allah is advising the believers to practice their faith in its entirety. In other words, apply Allah's teachings as a whole; do not pick and choose what you like and what is convenient. Prophet Muhammad, peace be upon him, explained that Islam has foundations known as the five pillars. You cannot apply three pillars and leave two out because the architecture of faith is based on all five.

Take for example the following scenario :

The words of an engineer:

"we can build a sturdy structure on two, three or four foundation pillars."

One might say to him:

"But when you build the structure on four pillars, and the load is distributed properly, is it possible for you to remove a pillar or two and keep the structure intact?" He said: "No, it will collapse." I replied: "This means that a structure is set from the very beginning on the basis of your plan. Its load and integrity are distributed equally on the number of foundation pillars you decided in your plan -whether three, four or five pillars-. After the structure is built, you cannot make changes to the foundation pillars. Likewise, Allah –the All-Wise- laid the foundations of Islam on five pillars, and based on that foundation Islam is structured. Thus, when you build your personal faith, beware of leaving a pillar out. Take Islam as a whole."

Most of the maladies of the Islamic world today are the result of selectively applying Islamic rules, and picking and choosing what is convenient. Islam is meant to be adopted completely. Allah says: 'You who believe, enter wholeheartedly into submission to Allah.'

Sadly, nowadays, most rulers of Muslim countries and many of those in charge of the affairs of Muslims apply Islam selectively when it is expedient for their political purposes. For example, many rulers cite this verse as proof that they should be obeyed. Allah says:

You who believe! obey Allah and obey the Messenger and those in command among you. If you have a dispute about something, refer it back to Allah and the Messenger, if you truly have faith in Allah and the Last Day. That is better and more favourable in outcome. (4:59)

We say to these rules: When it comes to obedience, why do you focus on the part of the verse that says: 'and those in command among you' and leave the first –and most important- part of the verse out? Allah did not prescribe blind obedience to those in authority; rather He –the All wise- said: "You who believe! obey Allah and obey the Messenger and those in command among you" to show that obedience of the person in authority stems from his or her obedience to Allah and the Prophet. In other words, the leader has to correctly implement the teachings of Allah and our beloved prophet first, before he or she can command obedience from the people. This is the only way to guarantee a just and peaceful society.

Allah invites people to Islam to protect them from the corruption caused by their whims and desires. Most of the ills of nations stem from the changing whims and desires of those in charge. Governing systems such as capitalism, socialism, and communism try to spread their influence and exploit fractions within societies. Left, right, progressive and conservative political movements tout their ideology and spread hatred among people. This type of competition for rule leads to wars and destruction. Allah invites humanity to rise above these made up differences and follow the heavenly teachings that treat everyone justly and equally.

Allah gave us room to compete and advance via scientific exploration. We are free to ponder Allah's creations and rise by working our minds towards scientific progress. And when a person or a nation discovers a secret from the secrets of the universe, all humanity benefits and enjoys the fruits of discovery. Scientists explore the mysteries of our world through experimental science which all people can agree upon and benefit from. What humans differ in and fight over are things emanating from their own desires; each one of us wants to follow his or her own desires often at the expense of others. Allah wants to protect us from these desires, so he said: "You who believe, enter wholeheartedly into submission to Allah." In other words, follow the teachings of your Lord to avoid the contradiction of desires in society.

You can personally apply this concept. Be true to yourself so your tongue does not contradict with what is in your heart; do not be a believer by words, yet corrupt by heart and deed. Spare yourself the addictions of whims and desires. This also happens to be the best way for you to be in harmony with the universe, with the heavens, earth, animals, and plants. All those creatures are creations of Allah; they flawlessly perform their tasks and follow Allah's command. So do not single yourself out as the only creature going against Allah's teachings.

If you are a sinner, you are in disharmony with your surroundings of time and place. In other words, both the time and the place in which you disobey Allah will curse you. Allah –the All-Generous- gave you the ability to be blessed and loved by time and place when you do good deeds. The Prophet (peace be upon him) used to spread peace and blessings in time and place. He, for example, would fast most of the days of the month of Sha'ban. When the companions asked him about this, he told them that Sha'baan is neglected by people because it is between the months of Rajab -which is one of the four holy months- and Ramadan. Thus, he wanted to pay attention to a month which was overlooked by most people. It is as if the Messenger of Allah wanted to give importance and peace to a particular time by fasting in it. Places also can gain peace and pleasure from your deeds. Ali ibn Abi Talib -the prophet's cousin- (may Allah be pleased with him) said: "When a believer dies two places weep over him: one on earth and another in the heavens.

The place on earth where he used to pray weeps for him, and so does the place where his good deeds used to ascend to in Heaven."

You who believe, enter wholeheartedly into submission to Allah and do not follow in Satan's footsteps, for he is your sworn enemy. (Chapter 2: Verse 208)

In the phrase 'do not follow in Satan's footsteps, for he is your sworn enemy,' Allah is warning you against following the devil because his goal is to keep you away from Allah's path. In fact, satan's animosity for humankind is ancient; it started from the time of Adam. Allah, the All-Merciful- conveys this animosity to us by narrating what satan said as he stood before Adam:

He said, "I swear by Your Glory! I will tempt them all, Except Your servants among them, endowed with sincerity in faith and worshipping You." (38:82-83)

By clearly narrating the story of Adam, Eve and satan at the beginning of the Quran, Allah gave us immunity and protection from satan's actions. This is similar to when you want to protect your body from vile diseases such as the measles and polio. You would familiarize your body with that disease through vaccination early in life. Satan will not take you by surprise, for Allah has alerted you early on of his actions and intentions.

In the Quran, the words: 'satan' and 'the devils' refer to the disobedient jinn in general. The Jinn have believers just like humans have believers, and the Jinn have disbelievers known as the devils who spread corruption just as there are disbelieving people. However, we should not blame all corruption and sin on the devil; there are many sinful actions we do out of our own selfish desires.

So, the key question to ask is: How can you distinguish between the sins that Satan adorns to you from the sins that are adorned to you by your own self desires? In other words, some sins stem from your own self, and some sins come from the devils' whispers, how can you tell the difference between the two? We answer that there is an easy way to distinguish between the two. If you find yourself insisting on committing a specific kind of sin, then know it is from your own self. This is because each self has a certain desire and weakness that it wants to satisfy, so it insists on a particular type of sin. A person may love money, so his or her self would obsess over accumulating wealth by any means. He or she would rationalize sinful acts for the purpose of making money. Another person may love to be recognized and praised, so his or her self would always obsess with being recognized even if it has to cheat and lie. Each self has a goal of satisfying a specific urge, so it always pushes in that direction. Thus, if you always find yourself struggling with a specific weakness, coming back to it again and again, then know that it is from yourself.

Satan, on the other hand, does not insist on a particular type of sin. If he sees you standing strong and refraining from a certain sin, he will shift tactics and push you towards another one. This is because satan wants you to be a sinner regardless of what the sin is. For instance, if you are careful in your prayers, the devil would attempt to sway you regarding wealth, urging you not to pay the zakat almsgiving. If you are upright when it comes to money, the devil may turn you to the allure of bad company and slander and so on. Satan is unrelenting in his attempts to deceive humans because he does not want to be the only sinner. He disobeyed and was expelled from Allah's mercy.........why can't others be sinners like him? It does not matter what we do as long as we sin. Allah warns you: 'do not follow in Satan's footsteps, for he is your sworn enemy.'

When you know the source of your sin, you can develop specific tools to protect yourself from falling into it. Let's look into the best way to guard yourself against the whispers of the devils. Allah says:

O children of Adam, let not Satan tempt you as he removed your parents from Paradise, stripping them of their clothing to show them their private parts. Indeed, he sees you, he and his tribe, from where you do not see them. Indeed, We have made the devils allies to those who do not believe (7:27)

How can you fight something that you cannot see, you may ask? We answer that satan is a creation of Allah, and so are you. It is logical then that in a struggle between two of Allah's creations, the most powerful and persistent of the two will win. But if one of the two happens to be in Allah's company, then no one can ever overcome him or her. This is why Allah wants you to seek refuge in Him so you can be in his company against Satan. As soon as you entertain the thought of a sin, Allah teaches you to say and repeat: 'I seek refuge in Allah from Satan the accursed.' Now you are in Allah's company, and no one can overcome you. But if you deviate from Allah's path then the devil can defeat you, because the struggle in this case, would be between two parties detached from Allah.

VERSE 209

Fa in zalaltum minba'di maa jaaa'atkumul baiyinaatu fa'lamoo annallaaha 'Azeezun hakeem

If you slip after the clear proofs of the truth have come to you, then know that Allah is All-Mighty, All-Wise.

To slip means to sin. The word is derived from Arabic 'Zala' which means to move away from being upright. Everything has its balance, and moving away from that integrity is a slip. Similarly, sins and disobedience are moving away from Allah's straight path.

The verse continues: "after the clear proofs of the truth have come to you." Allah explains that we have no excuse to deviate from His path because He has made all matters clear to us. Allah gave each one of us a thoughtful mind to weigh truth and falsehood. Moreover, Allah did not leave us to our own devices; He, the All-Merciful, sent prophets and messengers just in case we slip from His path. He says:

Whoever accepts guidance does so for his own good; whoever strays does so at his own peril. No soul will bear another's burden, nor do We punish until We have sent a messenger. (17:15)

It is from Allah's mercy that He sent messengers to show us the right path. Allah also left some matters to us so we can exercise our minds to come up with rules and solutions. Islam came and approved some of the rulings and wisdom that prevailed at the time, and changed matters that were unwise. This shows that if you use your mind naturally and logically, it is often able to direct you towards the truth.

Take the example of Omar, one of the prophet's companions. When problems faced the Muslims, he weighed the matters then suggested solutions, and the Prophet (peace be upon him) often agreed. Soon after, verses of the Quran would be revealed confirming the ruling Omar proposed in these cases. Here, you may ask: Shouldn't these solutions come from the Prophet peace be upon him? We answer: if those views came from the Prophet, it would have been said that the prophet is infallible and he was receiving revelation. Allah wants to teach us that when the mind is pure and thoughtful, it will naturally lead to the right judgment, even if it is not receiving revelation from the heavens. Omar had such a mind, and many Islamic rulings came from him and were then approved by Allah and His messenger.

Some critics of Islam have asked: is there no one other than Omar? Why do you keep referring to him? We answer: Omar was raised in the school of the Prophet. Whatever he said was taken from the Prophet's teachings. Omar acknowledged this and said: 'what would Omar be without Islam?' We give the example of Omar because he is a human and not a messenger; whatever applies to him, applies to each one of us. He did not receive revelations, nor was he infallible. Allah wants us to have the ability to think clearly, understand and deduce so we can all be like Omar. By tapping into our pure nature and sincere faith, we can find the right path.

Take note that Allah, the All-Merciful, did not burden us with unnecessary obligations. Rather, His obligations are in line with sound mind and clear judgment. Allah's obligations protect us from the whims, desires, and material greed that often cloud our minds. It is important to note that the enemies of sound mind and good judgment are whims and desires. Allah said to Prophet David:

'David, We have made you a trustee on earth. Judge fairly between people. Do not follow your desires, lest they divert you from Allah's path: those who wander from His path will have a painful torment because they ignore the Day of Reckoning.' (38:26)

So the opposite of fair and truthful judgment is to follow one's whims and desires.

Here a story that is told in the Egyptian:

A woman had her son and daughter both marry on the same night. They were all poor, so she and the newlyweds -her daughter and the new husband, and her son and the new wife- all stayed in one small house. After laying in bed for a little while, the mother got up, went to her daughter and said to her: "provide warmth for your husband and satisfy him for the night is cold." Then she went to her son and said: "Stay away from your wife and leave space between you, for the weather is too hot." The place was the same, and the weather is one, but the mother let her jealousy get the best of her. She gathered summer and winter under one roof.

Allah says:

If the truth were to follow their whims and desires, the heavens and the earth and everyone in them would have been brought to ruin. No indeed! We have given them their Reminder, but they have turned away from it. (23:71)

When Allah legislates, He protects us from ourselves. Even in the best-run governments, the laws set by humans are often deficient and limited. That is why these laws are in constant need for changes and amendments. Whoever initially set the laws had either an incomplete knowledge of the present, a limited vision of the future, or was self-serving. People are fed up with conflicting governments and ever-changing laws. Interestingly, if you take a look at how laws change, they are often modified to comply with Allah's rulings and move closer to Islamic law. Governments that allow the free use of Alcohol often come back again and again to restrict its use to a certain age, certain locations, and certain amounts.

Someone once asked the question:

Why didn't Islam prevail over all other religions as claimed in the Quran? He was implying that billions of people are not Muslim and referring to the following verse: Allah says:

He is the One Who has sent His Messenger with the guidance and the Religion of truth that He may make it prevail over all religions, however detested this may be to those who associate partners with Allah. (9:33)

The answer:

"You have to pay attention to the entire verse, not just part of it. Allah says: 'however detested this may be to those who associate partners with Allah.' Islam is not meant to be the sole religion in the world. The phrase: "however detested this may be to those who associate partners with Allah" suggests that Islam will always be at a time when non-believers and polytheists exist. Had there not been any disbelievers, then the verse would be wrong. The true power of Allah's teachings is often observed when non-Muslim legislators resort to Islamic rulings when their system fails. They resort to Allah's teachings not as a religion but as a guide to set laws. Their application of Islamic disciplines further confirms the validity of Islam. Of course, if these rulings were adopted as religious teachings, the legislators would be accused of fanaticism. But despite their hatred for the religion of Islam, they were forced to mimic its teachings because it happens to be the best solution.

I'll give you an example here. The Catholic Church did not allow divorce and considered it against a woman's right. But the circumstances of life and marital problems forced them to rethink the rulings related to divorce. Did they become lenient towards divorce because Islam had permitted it? Of course not, they became lenient because they found it to be the best solution. Similar is the Alcohol issue I mentioned earlier. It was not Islam that forced changes and limitations in laws, rather it was the family, public health, and death related issues that compelled lawmakers to revisit the issue of Alcohol use over and over. Hence, the verse "He is the One Who has sent His Messenger with the guidance and the Religion of truth that He may make it prevail over all religions, however detested this may be to those who associate partners with Allah" means that non-Muslims will have to resort to the Islamic system to resolve their issues, even if they do not accept Islam as a religion."

This brings us back to the verse. Allah says: "If you slip after the clear proofs of the truth have come to you, then know that Allah is All-Mighty, All-Wise." Allah is informing you that if you decide to leave Allah's path, don't be under the illusion that you got away from Allah's judgment; do not think that you have escaped your obligation to your

Creator. Allah is the Almighty; His might prevails and is never prevailed over. He manages our affairs with mercy and wisdom, and to Him we are destined to return.

VERSE 210

Hal yanzuroona illaaa ai ya'tiya humul laahu fee zulalim minal ghamaami walmalaaa'ikatu wa qudiyal amr; wa ilal laahi turja'ul umoor

Are these people waiting for Allah to come to them in the shadows of the clouds, together with the angels? But the matter would already have been decided by then: all matters are brought back to Allah.

What are the disbelievers waiting for? Allah asks. Are they waiting to be distracted by life until they find themselves in a universe that has entirely changed on the Day of Judgment? The worldly life they see around them with its luxuries will turn into dry remnants scattered by wind as man stands before Allah to be taken to account.

The phrase "waiting for" is translated from the Arabic origin 'Yanzoroon.' It holds two meanings: to wait for, and to look at. Interestingly, if you are waiting for something, you start to imagine it in your mind's eye. In fact, people often ask "do you see?" when they are explaining something intangible. 'Yanzoroon' applies to both: tangible things through eye vision, and intangible things through understanding.

The verse starts with: "Are these people waiting for Allah to come to them?" Meaning, are they really waiting for the Day of Judgment to believe? Are they procrastinating until the hour comes and takes them by surprise? The Last Hour will not occur at a known time, but it does have minor and major signs warning about its approach. These signs are the pieces of evidence Allah lays before us so we can wake up and repent for our mistakes. The door of repentance will remain open until the sun rises from the west.

When you hear the words: "Are these people waiting for Allah to come to them?" you question: What is delaying their entry into Islam? What are they waiting for? Just as you say to a student who has been playing video games and watching TV all year: 'What are you waiting for?

The exam is just around the corner!' Likewise, Allah –the All-Merciful- urges us to embrace faith before it is too late.

The verse continues: Are these people waiting for Allah to come to them in the shadows of the clouds, together with the angels?" When you hear phrases regarding Allah's being such as "for Allah to come" or verses referring to Allah's face and hand, do not try to understand such verses with what is familiar to you. Rather, remember the following: Allah says in the 11th verse of chapter 42:

There is nothing whatever like Him.

Always keep in mind that there is nothing whatsoever like Allah. Allah exists and you exist, but your existence is not like His. Allah is alive, and you are alive; is your life like His? Of course not. Allah hears, and you hear, but are His hearing and yours alike? No. Allah sees, and you see but is your vision like His? Again, the answer is No. So, always remember that all the attributes that are common to humans and Allah come under the principle:

There is nothing whatever like Him.

Some scholars explain phrases such as 'Allah's Face' to mean Allah's essence, and "the hand of Allah" to mean the power of Allah. We answer that we do not need to go into such explanations. If we believe that there is nothing whatsoever like Allah, then we would have protected ourselves from making an error in understanding Him because we do not equate Allah with His creation, neither do we strip the text from its literal meaning.

We believe in Allah and keep our faith in Him within the framework that: 'There is nothing whatever like Him.' If you happen to imagine Allah as something familiar to you, then rest assured that He is contrary to what you imagine. Man can only imagine known images or combinations of known images. Allah does not resemble His creation. He says:

There is nothing whatever like Him.

The moment when Allah Almighty will reveal Himself on the Day of Judgment, those who have painted images in their minds will be surprised because He will not resemble anything they had imagined. It is of Allah's greatness that the mind cannot perceive Him in a material form. Allah explains that we have a hard enough time understanding what is within ourselves, let alone our Creator. He says:

In the earth are signs for those who have conviction And within yourselves. Can you not perceive? (51:20,21)

Allah is referring to the soul that exists within our body and gives us life. In fact, when the soul departs, the body turns into a decaying carcass. The soul that is within each one of us is something beyond our imagination and understanding. We cannot determine its place or form. So ask yourself: If I cannot imagine the soul created by Allah, then how can I even come close to imagining my Creator?

Thus, Allah is warning the non-believers not to wait until it is too late. He says: Are these people waiting for Allah to come to them in the shadows of the clouds, together with the angels? But the matter would already have been decided by then.' Are they waiting to see the great universe scattered, the sun wrapped in darkness and the stars dispersed? More importantly, are they waiting to be standing before their Lord to be judged for their actions? Allah is advising us to seize the opportunity before that happens before the door of repentance is closed forever. Why do the non-believers procrastinate entering into Islam? If they are waiting for Allah to change or for Allah to change His commandments, they should know that it will never happen.

Here, we emphasize once again that there is nothing whatsoever like Allah. His coming does not imply leaving one place to go to another, rather He exists in all places and that is His greatness. Allah has the attributes of absolute perfection; His orders do not require specific time or place. He says "Be, " and it becomes.

The verse continues "in the shadows of the clouds" to provide us with the grandeur and terror of that moment. When something overwhelming shadows you, you feel helpless. Allah says:

When the waves loom over those on board like giant shadows they call out to Allah, devout and sincere in their faith. But, when He has delivered them safely to land, some of them waver- only a treacherous, thankless person refuses to acknowledge Our signs. (31:32)

This is a description of the panic that hits those at sea when they are engulfed by a violent storm. Yet, far more terrifying to the non-believers is when the entire universe is scattered on the Day of Judgment. The believers would be prepared because Allah has repeatedly warned of these horrors.

The verse continues 'But the matter would already have been decided by then,' indicating that the opportunity for repentance is gone. So whoever did not return to Allah before that time would have missed his or her chance. This brings us back to the core question and message of this verse: What are you waiting for? Are you waiting for that day to come? You must seize the opportunity to return to your Lord, or all will be lost.

The verse ends with: 'all matters are brought back to Allah.' When you read the Quran, you will find that this phrase comes in two variations: The first is: 'matters are brought back to Allah' translated from the Arabic origin: Turjaoun; and the second is: 'matters come back to Allah' translated from the Arabic origin: Tarjeoun. Let's explain the difference. In the first, 'Turjaoun' matters are taken to Allah against their will. This applies to the disbelievers who are terrified of the evil they have done and the punishment awaiting them. In the second, 'Tarjeoun' the matters are longing to be with Allah because of the good they have done, and the award awaiting them.

VERSES 211

Sal Banee Israaa'eela kam aatainaahum min aayatim baiyinah; wa mai yubaddil ni'matal laahi mim ba'di maa jaa'athu fa innallaaha shadeedul'iqaab

Ask the Children of Israel how many clear proofs We gave to them. And whoever changes Allah's blessing after it has come to him: surely Allah is severe in retribution.

Allah wants the children of Israel to acknowledge the immense bounties He had given them.

Allah tells the Prophet (peace be upon him) to ask the children of Israel about the good He blessed them with. Allah knows their answer will be in accordance with what is in the Quran. Their words will also be used as evidence against the way they have been acting.

Allah says: "Ask the Children of Israel how many clear proofs We gave to them." When you hear the phrase "how many" in this context, it is not meant to inquire about the exact number, rather it is an indication that the favours and proofs Allah gave the Israelites are too numerous to count. Likewise, when you say to your friend: "Do you know how many times I helped John out of trouble!" You are suggesting that you had helped John too many times.

In the verse "Ask the Children of Israel how many clear proofs We gave to them" Allah is relating to us the example of people who received His bounties and denied His favours. Asking them is actually one way to get them to talk and admit their actions, because, despite their arrogance and rejection, Allah knows that they cannot deny His favours when asked. Did He not part the sea to save them from Pharaoh's army? Did He not make the staff of Musa, may peace and blessings of Allah Be

Upon Him come to life? Didn't He shade them with clouds when they wandered the desert? Didn't He grant them Manna, Quail, and springs of water in a place that was barren? All of these bounties, and countless more, yet they chose to be ungrateful to Allah. This is how they earned Allah's wrath as He seized them with years of famine and hunger.

Even though Allah specifies to His Messenger to "ask the children of Israel," the question is meant as a reminder for the Muslims and whole humanity. Allah provided each and every one of us with countless blessings, favours, and signs of His existence.

The verse continues: 'And whoever changes Allah's blessing after it has come to him: surely Allah is severe in retribution.' How can a person change Allah's blessings, you may ask? We answer that when you receive a bounty, you must receive it with appreciation and acknowledgment. To appreciate is to attribute the favour to its Creator on the one hand, and to be ashamed of disobeying Him on the other. If you receive Allah's blessings otherwise, it means that you have changed them. Allah says:

Do you ever consider those who exchanged Allah's blessing for ingratitude and unbelief, and caused their people to settle in the abode of ruin – (14:28)

From this verse, we understand that faith and gratitude are what is required when you receive the bounties of your Lord. In fact, Allah's blessings are meant to draw you closer to Him in gratitude and reverence.

The verse ends with: 'And whoever changes Allah's blessing after it has come to him: surely Allah is severe in retribution.' You may understand that the phrase "severe in retribution" is related to the Hereafter. However, some people think that the Hereafter is far off, and others who do not believe in it at all. If Allah's punishment is limited to the Hereafter, then such people would spread evil on earth because they see no consequence to their actions. An individual who believes in the Hereafter, where he or she will be taken to account, would behave accordingly. Likewise, an individual who has no faith in the Hereafter would behave accordingly and often cause suffering to all around him or her. Thus, if Allah does not hasten some punishment for those who do not believe in the Hereafter, the world would go to ruin. So those who do not accept Allah's teachings, and exchange His bounties for disbelief must see punishment in this world. In this manner, such people would fear the consequences of their actions in this world. If an oppressor knows that oppressors before him were brought to justice, he may think twice before acting. Allah does not postpone all punishments to the Hereafter; rather He gives a taste of it in this world. He says:

But whoever disregards My remembrance, he shall have life of hardship, and on the Day of Resurrection We shall raise him blind. (20:124)

Some of the righteous people used to supplicate: "Dear Allah, the unjust people see Your Hereafter as being far-off, and Your patience has deluded them; so take them to task as only the Almighty who controls all things can!"

Worldly life has been glamorized for the faithless, and they ridicule the faithful. But those who are Allah consious shall be above them on the Day of Resurrection; Allah provides immeasurably for whoever He pleases. (Chapter 2: Verse 212)

Allah Almighty wants to explain the place of man in the universe. Man was created as a master in the universe whereas all other creations are at his service. We know that inert matter such as the soil, rocks, air, and water serve the plants, and both the inert matter and the plants serve the animals, and all three of them serve us humans. Thus, humans are the masters among creation. And since humans are not the creators of all that is around them, it is natural to ask: Who is superior to us? Who is the creator? Who made all these things that serve us? How are we to run and manage this kingdom? These questions have been asked by all humans across cultures over centuries. We, as humans, are in desperate need for guidance towards the right path to properly take care of all that is around us.

Thus, when a Messenger comes and explains: 'Allah is Supreme, He is your one Lord, and He is the Creator of all you see' People should welcome this message because it solves the mystery that all humans experience by instinct. More importantly, people should be happy when Messengers and Prophets deliver Allah's curriculum and instruction. When you study Allah's teachings, you find that unlike all the objects, plants, and animals that serve us, Allah is self-sufficient. He does not need anything from us. We are only required to worship Allah as an acknowledgment and gratitude for all the creation He put at our service. So the believer is situated between two levels: Subjected servants below such as inert matter, plants and animals, and the One who bestowed all these bounties from above: Allah Almighty.

Sadly, people often take one and leave the other. They take what is lower and leave what is most superior. Allah invites you to rise and choose the most superior. If you would like an increase in gifts from those who serve you, then ask for that increase from One who is higher than you; the One who subjected things to your service.

This brings us back to the verse. When Allah says: "Worldly life has been glamorized for the faithless." Allah wants us to know that the standards of the disbelievers are debased because they find beauty in the lowest most inferior things. It is poor judgment for a person to run after what is inferior to him or her and prefer it over the most superior.

Whenever the verb 'Glamorized' is mentioned in the Quran, it comes in the passive tense —where the doer is not mentioned-. Here is another example from the Quran. Allah says:

Glamorized for the people are the desires of women, offspring, and of heaped up piles of gold and silver, of pedigree horses, cattle, and sown fields. These are the enjoyments of the worldly life, but with Allah is the best return. (03:14)

Note that in this verse Allah says: "Glamorized for the people," while in the verse under study He says: "glamorized for the faithless" What is the difference? We answer that when Allah talks about the disbelievers, He mentions worldly life as a whole because the disbelievers do not have anything beside this life. For them, it is the ultimate goal and the only place of enjoyment. People of faith, on the other hand, have this life and the hereafter. So in the verse where Allah addresses the faithless, He only mentions worldly life. On the other hand, in the verse where Allah addresses all people –the faithful and faithless-, He mentions the enjoyments of this world and the ultimate goal of the hereafter. He says: "Glamorized for the people are the desires of women, offspring, and of heaped up piles of gold and silver, of pedigree horses, cattle, and sown fields. These are the enjoyments of the worldly life, but with Allah is the best return.' Allah, the All-Merciful, is advising you to keep this worldly life in perspective. It has very little value compared to the pleasures and eternity of the hereafter. You should take life as a mission to get closer to the One who blessed you with it. Whenever you see something beautiful around you, acknowledge the creator and say: "Subhan Allah" "Exalted is Allah."

Another way to look at this issue is that Allah has glamorized life by instilling instincts and temptations within us. People are driven towards the opposite gender, towards gathering wealth and power. Here we should ask: Did Allah instill these instincts within us, and then leave us without guidance of how to manage them? Of course not, Allah gave us instincts and gave us the tools to channel them in a proper and healthy manner. He says:

Wealth and children are an adornment of the present worldly life, but the good, righteous deeds which endure are better in the sight of your Lord in bringing reward and better to aspire for. (18:46)

Worldly life has been glamorized for the faithless, and they ridicule the faithful. But those who are Allahwary shall be above them on the Day of Resurrection; Allah provides for whoever He pleases without account. (Chapter 2: Verse 212)

When Allah says: 'Worldly life has been glamorized for the faithless,' He exposes those who believe that there is no existence after this life. We say to them: Be careful, your values are out of balance and you are making a poor judgment. How can you chase after what is clearly inferior, and ignore what is far superior and longer lasting? What is even stranger is that you make fun of those who made better choices and focused on the hereafter. Allah says: 'and they ridicule the faithful.'

The believers commit themselves to the principals of faith. When you are committed, you restrict your movement in life. For example, you refuse to earn money from illegitimate sources, or through cheating others. Those who do not believe, on the other hand, are free to do whatever they please with no restrictions or fear of consequences. They go after life full force. Thus, you often see honest people of faith living a modest lifestyle within their lawful means; while dishonest people exploit others and build illegitimate wealth. They usually dress better, ride luxury cars, and live in bigger homes. And when the two meet, the people who cheat mock the ones who live on lawful income, why? Because they consider themselves better with higher standards of living; they have more money, better lifestyle and access to power. Allah answers: "But those who are Allahwary shall be above them on the Day of Resurrection" Why on the Day of Resurrection, you may ask? Shouldn't that be the case now as well? We answer that Allah is addressing what is visible to people. We look at appearances and possessions, while we don't see the psychological comfort and the tranquillity of the believers. When an honest person goes to sleep, he or she has a clear conscience free of spiritual and moral guilt. He or she has not hurt others, has not accepted a bribe, or slandered anyone. Do you think this person will get a good night sleep? You bet. Such a state of comfort cannot be bought with all the money of the world. These comforts are invisible to others, so Allah did not include them in the comparison. He, the All-Wise, focused on the matters that will be clear for all to see. Allah says:

The wicked used to laugh at the believers— they would wink at one another when the believers passed by them; And when they returned to their families, they would return mocking; And when they saw the believers, they said: "They have indeed gone astray." though they were not sent to be their keepers- (83:29-33)

Allah then moves from the scene of this world to the scene on the Day of Judgment:

So today the believers are laughing at the disbelievers, on luxurious couches gazing in wonder. Have the disbelievers been rewarded for they used to do? (83:34-36)

We answer: Yes our Lord, they have.

Here we should pause and take note that Allah used the word "Allahwary" in the verse under study. He did not use the word 'believers.' It would have made sense if the phrase had read: "But those who have believed shall be above them on the Day of Resurrection." Why did Allah choose to use "Allahwary" instead, you may ask? We answer that Allah is not looking for names or titles. Anyone who says "I believe in Allah and His messenger" is called a believer. But that is not enough to earn the high rewards of the hereafter. Allah wants action and deeds, not mere words.

There are billions of people around the world who say: "I am a believer," and "I am Muslim." We say to them: becoming a believer does not mean to label yourself as one; rather, it is the daily commitment to heavenly teachings. Thus, the All-Wise did not say: 'those who believe will be above them on the Day of Resurrection.' Instead, Allah put the focus on actions and said: 'But those who are Allahwary shall be above them on the Day of Resurrection.'

The verse ends with: 'Allah provides for whoever He pleases without account.' The verb 'provides' is translated from the Arabic origin 'Yarzuq' which also shares the root with the word 'rizq' or provision. What are provisions? Provisions are anything lawful that benefits you. Sadly, People often limit the word 'rizq' to money. But the word has a much broader meaning. For example, your physical health and ability is a provision. The knowledge and experience you have is also wealth. Likewise, wisdom and humility are rizq. Anything that can be used for the betterment of life is wealth.

Allah says:

And Allah has favoured some of you above others in provision. And yet, those who are more favoured do not consent to share their provision with those whom their right hands possess so that they might be equal with them in this respect. How then do they deny Allah's grace and bounty? (16:71)

Allah wants His creations to share their provisions with one another, whether it is money, knowledge, physical strength, or anything that may help advance the society as a whole. So, make sure that you don't limit the word 'Rizq' to money; we all have something beneficial to give and share with others.

Keeping this in mind, what is the meaning of 'Allah provides for whoever He pleases without account'? We answer that Allah gives without account because there is no authority higher than him that could question: why have you given so and so more than what he or she deserves? Allah gives without account because His depositories never run out; He is not governed by any law and He is the All-Generous, the All-Abundant. You and I do accounting because we have limited resources. But when all is limitless, there is no need for account. For example, if you have a thousand pounds in reserves and you give someone a hundred, you are left with £900 in savings. Soon, you would have to be careful as you give more and more. Allah, on the other hand, gives without the need to subtract from reserves because Allah is limitless. Allah multiplies the rewards of a good deed by seven-hundredfold and more. He says:

The metaphor of those who spend their wealth in the Way of Allah is that of a grain which produces seven ears; in every ear there are a hundred grains. Allah gives such multiplies and increases to whomever He wills. Allah is All-Encompassing, All-Knowing. (2:261)

So, when you read 'Allah provides for whoever He pleases without account' then know that Allah may not give you according to the amount of your work, rather He increases by multiples, and no one can hold Him to account. He says:

What you have runs out but what Allah has endures, and We shall certainly reward those who remain steadfast according to the best of their actions. (16:96)

Thus, the phrase " Allah provides for whoever He pleases without account" is a reminder to all of us not to question Allah when we see someone who has been granted more than us in this life. We are not aware of Allah's wisdom behind his provisions. More importantly, Allah's provisions are often a test for the one who receives them and for the one who does not. The Almighty says:

And for man – when his Lord tries him by bestowing favours on him – says: "My Lord has honoured me." but when He tries him through the restriction of his provision, he says, 'My Lord has humiliated me.' Not at all – but rather you do not honour the orphan. (89:15-16)

Take note that Allah answered both: the one who claims that provisions in this world are a sign of Allah's pleasure, and the one who claims that poverty in this world is a sign of Allah's displeasure, with the same answer: He says: 'Not at all.' Indeed, you are wrong if you consider Allah's provision a reward, and you are also wrong if you consider the deprivation of bounties as an insult. Allah's provisions are a blessing only if you use them for good and to help others. Allah's bounties should bring you closer to him in gratitude and appreciation, rather than distract you away from Him. Likewise, the lack of provisions is a blessing if it gets you closer to your Lord in prayer and humility, rather than make you angry at the world.

VERSE 212

Zuyyina lillazeena kafarul hayaatud dunyaa wa yaskharoona minal lazeena aamanoo; wallazeenat taqaw fawqahum yawmal Qiyaamah; wallaahu yarzuqu mai yashaaa'u bighairi hisaab;

Worldly life has been glamorized for the faithless, and they ridicule the faithful. But those who are Godwary shall be above them on the Day of Resurrection; God provides immeasurably for whoever He pleases.

Another wonderful benefit of the phrase: 'Allah provides for whoever He pleases without account" is to help you avoid falling into the trap of estimating provision strictly based on the amount of work you do. Often, you are mistaken in your calculation. For example, a farmer who sows seeds estimates his earnings and future income based on what he calculates the land to produce. However, he may get hit by bad weather or pests that destroy the produce. You and I must work hard using the means Allah put at our disposal, yet at the same time we should not rely on and make calculations based on these factors alone. We should do good honest hard work while putting our trust in Our Lord for results. Allah says in the 2nd and 3rd verses of chapter 65:

Allah will find a way out for those who are mindful of Him, and provide for him from where he does not expect. Whoever puts his trust in Allah – He will be enough for him. Allah always achieves His aim. Certainly Allah has set a proper measure for everything.

VERSE 213

Kaanan naasu ummatanw waahidatan fab'asal laahun Nabiyyeena mubashshireena wa munzireena wa anzala ma'ahumul kitaaba bilhaqqi liyahkuma bainan naasi feemakh talafoo feeh; wa makh talafa feehi 'illallazeena ootoohu mim ba'di maa jaaa'athumul baiyinaatu baghyam bainahum fahadal laahul lazeena aamanoo limakh talafoo feehi minal haqqi bi iznih; wallaahu yahdee mai yashaaa'u ilaa Siraatim Mustaqeem

Mankind was a single community, then Allah sent prophets to bring good news and warning, and with them He sent the Scripture with the Truth, to judge between people in their disagreements. It was only those to whom it was given who disagreed about it after clear signs had come to them, because of rivalry between them. So by His leave Allah guided the believers to the truth they had differed about: Allah guides whoever He will to a straight path.

Perhaps the first question that comes to mind when you read this verse is: if people were one nation and Allah sent them Messengers and Prophets as a single nation, then where have all these divisions and disputes come into play? To understand this issue, you have to look at the Quran as a whole, and consider all the verses that address this matter. Allah wants you to study the Quran in its entirety because parts of the Quran will often help you better understand other parts of it. Allah says in chapter 10:

All people were originally one single community, but later they differed. If it had not been for a word from your Lord, the preordained judgment would already have been passed between them regarding their differences. (10:19)

Before Allah sent the prophets, people were one nation following Adam. Allah guided Adam and gave him the heavenly teachings. Adam taught his children, and they taught the next generation. So people remained on one faith and there was no dispute between them. Moreover, the world was vast with plenty of resources serving very few people, so there was little need for competition and envy. Whoever wanted something –whether fruits or land- could simply take it.

Suppose that you have three children and you brought home 20 oranges. Every child can eat his or her fill with no need to worry about others. But if you only bring two oranges then you may have a problem between the competing kids. Likewise, people were one nation when resources were plentiful. Most of our problems and differences today are over insatiable greed and dwindling resources.

Adam (peace be upon him) taught his children the heavenly guidance; his children, in turn, were supposed to carry on these values, but some of them rebelled against Allah's teachings, and after that, greed and differences arose. The story of Abel and Cain explains this:

Tell them the truth about the story of Adam's two sons: each of them offered a sacrifice, and it was accepted from one and not the other. One said, 'I will kill you,' but the other said, 'Allah only accepts the sacrifice of those who are mindful of Him. (05:27)

We know that Adam and Eve are the origins of humanity. Eve gave birth to twins every time, and Adam wanted his children to marry. But how can they be married, while they are all siblings? Allah's law gave a solution to this problem. Adam's children born from one pregnancy were considered siblings, while children born from other pregnancies were not considered their siblings. Thus, children from one pregnancy were married to children from another.

It is narrated to us from Ibn Abbas and Ibn Mas'ud (may Allah be pleased with them) that 'Adam used to marry the male of one pregnancy to the female of another, and that Abel wanted to marry the sister of

Cain. He was older than Able, and Cain's sister was beautiful, but Cain wanted to take her for himself rather than let her marry his brother. Their father Adam ordered him to let her marry Abel but he refused, and the dispute grew. So Adam ordered both of them to make a sacrifice to Allah. Abel -who owned sheep- offered a healthy fat lamb, while Cain – a farmer- offered a bundle of his worst crop. A fire came down and consumed Abel's offering, and rejected Cain's. Cain became angry and said, 'I will kill you so that you won't marry my sister.' He replied, "Allah only accepts the sacrifice of those who are mindful of Him."

So the birth of the first conflict happened when two people competed over a desire and a limited resource. This was a clear example of what could happen when resources are scares and people put their greed and desire before all else.

'Mankind was a single community, ' but they differed the moment man let desires get the best of him. If Allah had wanted to make Adam's religion the only religion until the last day, He would have done so. But He –the All-merciful- knows His creation, and He knows that we are prone to forgetting and falling into error. Thus, He sent a procession of prophets and messengers. He says: "then Allah sent prophets to bring good news and warning, and with them He sent the Scripture with the Truth, to judge between people in their disagreements." The task of preaching and warning is to remind people that there is paradise and hellfire and that our actions in this world determine the outcome of the next. Each prophet gave the glad tidings of paradise to whoever believed and did good and warned those who disbelieved and spread corruption of hellfire. Moreover, Allah instilled within each one of us the instinct that guides us towards Him as the following verses illustrate:

When your Lord took out the offspring from the loins of the Children of Adam and made them bear witness about themselves, He said, 'Am I not your Lord?' and they replied, 'Yes, we bear witness.' So you cannot say on the Day of Resurrection, 'We were not aware of this,' Or lest you should say: "Our forefathers used to associate partners with Allah before us, and we were their offspring just following after them.

Will You, then, ruin us for what those did who rejected Your Lordship and invented that false way (07:172-173)

Here, Allah informs us that at the beginning of creation, he took entire mankind and made them bear witness to His Lordship and bear witness that there is no Allah but Him. This is where the instinct to seek the creator and the natural feeling that there is a higher power in this universe come from. Allah -the All-Merciful- did not leave us alone with just instinct. When Adam descended, Allah gave him the heavenly teachings to protect mankind from their greed and desires even before any problems started. It is the love of exclusive ownership, and the greed to have more and more even at the expense of others that creates divisions and ill feelings in the world.

There is no issue when resources are plentiful, and markets are stocked. You can buy whatever you want at any time you like. In such times, there are no crises. However, when supplies are low and cannot meet demand, people dogfight to gain access and secure their needs. So it is from the mercy of our Lord that He sent messengers to remind and warn us. He says: "Allah sent prophets to bring good news and warning, and with them He sent the Scripture with the Truth, to judge between people in their disagreements." Allah did not want to leave people to differ and fight. In fact, it is the people's disregard for the Lord's teachings that spread such differences. Allah says: "It was only those to whom it was given who disagreed about it after clear signs had come to them, because of rivalry between them."

The verse continues: "So by His leave Allah guided the believers to the truth they had differed about: Allah guides whoever He will to a straight path." Allah explains that He guides and guards those who believe and follow His Messengers. Sadly, with the passage of time, people become negligent, and their desires begin to overcome them. Allah follows by sending another Messenger to remind and to restore people to the right path. This was the process throughout the centuries until Allah sent Muhammad -the final Messenger- with Islam to entire humanity till the end of time. A unified religion guarantees that all mankind share the same creed and faith. Thus, we must cling to the teachings of Islam; otherwise, our future outcome will be similar to those of the former nations. Allah says:

Allah commands you to return things entrusted to you to their rightful owners, and, if you judge between people, to do so with fairness: How excellent is what Allah advises you to do; assuredly, Allah is All-Hearing, All-Seeing. You who believe, obey Allah and the Messenger, and those in authority among you. If you are in dispute over any matter, refer it to Allah and the Messenger, if you truly believe in Allah and the Last Day: that is better and fairer in the end. (4:58,59)

Mankind was a single community, then Allah sent prophets to bring good news and warning, and with them He sent the Scripture with the Truth, to judge between people in their disagreements. It was only those to whom it was given who disagreed about it after clear signs had come to them, because of rivalry between them. So by His leave Allah guided the believers to the truth they had differed about: Allah guides whoever He will to a straight path. (Chapter 2: Verse 213)

We know that Prophet Muhammad (peace be upon him) is the Seal of the Prophets. Moreover, Prophet Muhammad is the only messenger that Allah had entrusted to legislate on his own. In other words, Allah – the All-Wise- allowed Muhammad (peace be upon him) to legislate new religious laws on behalf of Allah as he saw fit. Allah says in verse 7 of chapter 59:

Whatever the Messenger gives you, you should accept, and whatever he forbids you, you should forgo.

Allah made it to clear to us that we should follow the command of our beloved Prophet, because what he instructs us to do is good for us, and he only forbids what is harmful. Obedience to the Prophet is part of our obedience to Allah. The Almighty says:

Whoever obeys the Messenger certainly obeys Allah; and as for those who turn their backs, We have not sent you to keep watch over them. (04:80)

And in another verse:

Say, 'Obey Allah and the Messenger.' But if they turn away, indeed Allah does not like the faithless. (03:32)

Allah has authorized His Messenger to legislate for mankind because he (peace be upon him) does not speak out of inclination or to self-serve. So always keep in mind that your obedience to Allah requires obedience to the Prophet.

Another blessing for the Muslim nation is that Allah gave us the right to use reasoning and thorough study to find proper religious solutions to new issues. This is known as 'ijtehad' in matters where there is no text in the Quran or Sunnah, or there is a text, but it could have more than one meaning. 'Ijtehad' is a safeguard for Muslims to settle any of their differences and address life's modern issues.

Another blessing you will notice is that the differences between the Muslim communities do not involve matters of creed; rather they are differences of understanding of the texts of the Quran or the narrations of the Messenger. In other words, every Muslim –even when strongly disagreeing with others- wants to draw his or her evidence from the book of Allah and the Sunnah of our beloved prophet. We have not left the source; rather each one of us wants to draw the right judgment from it.

So, if all of us –even when differing- go back to the Quran and the prophet's teachings, then where is the problem? We answer that problems arise when people who do not have proper knowledge, scholarship, or intelligence involve themselves in religious disputes and issue rulings. So, while disputes among Muslims did not reach the extent it reached previous religions –where creed and the authenticity of heavenly books are in question- we must be alert, and we must elevate our knowledge to correctly understand the Quran and avoid attributing false meanings to it. Allah's word should not be interpreted according to whims and desires, but according to what the Prophet said and taught. Allah's word should not be interpreted by people who did not properly study and research. Allah has entrusted the Quran and the message of Islam to the nation of Muhammad; He protected the Quran against alteration and distortion. We, as Muslims, are required to be knowledgeable, so we do not fall victim to those who abuse power and fabricate religious rulings to advance their agenda.

Just as the consumption of water brings life to our physical matter, so are the teachings of Islam. They are meant to bring life to our spirit. Water has no colour, taste or smell; it is the universal drink that we seek by instinct. Once colour, taste or smell is added to water, it is no longer called water; it turns into juice, tea or soda. Some people prefer a particular flavour of juice or a particular kind of tea; others may not like it. But everyone loves water, and the body flourishes with water. So is Islam, it is meant to be pure and nourishing for the soul. Thus, if you see religion been tainted by a group to give it a particular flavour, or colour, then know that it is outside the scope of true Islam. Anyone who tries to make alterations in Allah's religion takes it away from its original universal pure nature.

The scholars of Al-Azhar institute in Egypt have worked over the centuries to protect Allah's teachings and adhere to the foundations of knowledge. Thus, every scholar of Islam owes some of his or her knowledge to Al-Azhar. Al-Azhar strikes a balance between the love of the family of the Messenger of Allah (peace be upon him) and the love of his companions without being extreme in either direction. We find Islam to be gentle and easy to adhere to rather than harsh and overburdening. It is the Islam of purity and intuition that penetrates the soul. Allah says:

The indelible marking of Allah. And who marks better than Allah! And for Him we are worshipers. (02:138)

We must say to those who try to alter the religion in any form or ritual: you are taking Islam out of its origin which Allah intended, and you must stop.

Previous

Next

Mankind was a single community, then Allah sent prophets to bring good news and warning, and with them He sent the Scripture with the Truth, to judge between people in their disagreements. It was only those to whom it was given who disagreed about it after clear signs had come to them, because of rivalry between them. So by His leave, Allah guided the believers to the truth they had differed about: Allah guides whoever He will to a straight path. (Chapter 2: Verse 213)

We know that guidance refers to that which takes you directly towards your goal. There are two types of Guidance: first there is Allah's general guidance, and second, there is His divine guidance. General guidance is universal for entire mankind. More specifically, Allah calls everyone to the right path; He sends prophets and messengers and supports them with miracles and scripture to deliver his message to everyone. Allah clarifies the outcome of those who follow His path and those who abandon it. So whoever wants to follow the right path can do so, and whoever chooses to abandon it can do so.

As for those who choose to follow Allah's general guidance, the Lord supports them with his divine guidance; he endears faith and piety to their hearts and facilitates for them the actions that lead to paradise. Allah protects them from evil and helps them through hardship. This divine guidance is specific for the believers. Allah says:

As for those who follow true guidance, He leads them far ahead in their right ways and grants them piety and restraints from evil suited to their condition. (47:17)

Let's clarify the difference between general and divine guidance with an example. Say that you were lost and asked a policeman for directions towards your destination. The policeman gives you a map to help you find your way; it is the same general map he gives to everyone. If you show appreciation for him and say: "thank you for your help, you have made things so much easier for me." The policeman may decide to help you further by highlighting the best way for you to take. He will warn you about roads that have construction and traffic and about areas that are not safe at night.

Allah guides all humanity towards His path and then guides the believers even further by being with them every step of the way. Allah says:

As for the tribe of Thamood, We gave them guidance, but they preferred blindness, so they were struck by a blast of humiliating punishment for their misdeeds. Yet We saved those who believed and were mindful of Allah. (41:17-18)

You can further see the distinction between the two types of guidance in the following two verses. In the first verse, Allah addresses the Prophet and says:

You cannot guide everyone you love to the truth; it is Allah who guides whoever He will: He knows best those who will follow guidance. (28:56)

And in another verse, Allah also addresses the prophet and says:

and you certainly guide them to the right path (42:52)

At first glance these two verses are in contradiction: One verse denies the prophet guidance, and the other affirms that the prophet guides. How can this be? We answer that our beloved prophet Muhammad is the means of delivering Allah's book and general guidance to humanity. He lit the path towards heaven for everyone. Allah confirms: 'and you certainly guide them to the right path. On the other hand, the verse 'Surely you cannot guide whom you love, but Allah guides whom He pleases' means that while the prophet delivers the message, Allah is the one who makes guidance —His divine guidance— penetrate into the heart of a person. Allah says: Say, 'Indeed it is the guidance of Allah which is the true guidance.' (2:120)

Some people try to dissociate themselves from the responsibility of faith and deed and blame Allah for their disbelief. They use verses like this one for evidence:

What about those whose evil deeds are made alluring to them so that they think they are good? Allah leaves whoever He will to stray and guides whoever He will. Do not waste your soul away with regret for them: Allah knows exactly what they do. (35:08)

The disbelievers think that the phrase ' Allah leaves whoever He will to stray and guides whoever He will' will save them from hell-fire on the day of resurrection because Allah is responsible for misguiding them. They claim that since Allah had willed them to disbelief, what were they to do? We answer that a person who blames Allah for a choice that he or she made has not studied the Quran. Let's look at the following verses:

That is because they preferred the worldly life over the Hereafter and that Allah does not guide the disbelieving people. (16:107)

And in another verse:

Abraham said, "So indeed it is Allah Who brings the sun from the East - you bring it from the West!" - the disbeliever was therefore baffled; and Allah does not guide the unjust. (2:258)

And lastly,

Say, 'If your fathers, sons, brothers, wives, tribes, the wealth you have acquired, the trade which you fear will decline, and the dwellings you love are dearer to you than Allah and His Messenger and the struggle in His cause, then wait until Allah brings about His punishment.' Allah does not guide those who are corrupt. (9:24)

These verses clearly highlight the three groups of people who do not receive Allah's guidance: the disbelievers, the corrupt and the unjust. Allah sent His Prophets & Messengers, His scriptures, and His guidance to all mankind. Moreover, He created the universe and subjected it to our service, so each one of us may ponder the creation. Sadly, many people opposed Allah, refused to listen to His Messengers, followed their own desires, and took the beauty of creation for granted.

The truth is: Allah has blessed humanity with His general guidance, and provided all of us with countless bounties. He came forth with love and mercy. Those who responded to this love with denial, and chose disbelief did so with their own free will. In response, Allah left them for what they chose and did not force belief upon them.

Had Allah wanted to force belief or disbelief on us, He would have done so. In fact, Allah has demonstrated to you that He can have absolute power over you if He so wills. Take the examples of your internal organs; they operate entirely outside your will. Your heart, blood circulation, kidneys, and liver are subjected to Allah's will. Likewise, the calamities that may happen to you are out of your control. You cannot prevent disease, a car crash or a rock from falling on you.

Allah, however, did not want to force belief or disbelief on anyone. He gave you full control over one area of your life: your choices and actions. Are you going to use these great gifts to practice Allah's teachings? This freedom of choice is what you and I will be responsible for on the day of resurrection. If you choose disbelief for yourself, Allah does not force you to believe; rather, He informs you of the consequences. Allah wants you to freely turn to Him out of love. He does not benefit from your faith and deeds; the benefits and rewards will be for you alone. Faith in Allah and the actions that support that faith are your personal treasures on the day of resurrection; they are your salvation on that terrible day.

Do you suppose that you will enter the Garden without first having suffered like those before you? They were afflicted by misfortune and hardship, and they were so shaken that even the messenger and the believers with him cried, 'When will Allah's help arrive?' Truly, Allah's help is near. (Chapter 2:Verse 214)

Do you think that the road leading to Paradise will be easy and comfortable? It will not. In fact, it is necessary for you to prove yourself and shoulder the burden of faith in order to earn the fabulous gift of paradise. If faith meant saying few words, then life would have been a breeze; but the difficulty is not in saying the words, it is in implementing of those words in everyday life.

The disbelievers at the time of the Prophet understood this concept. They were people of character who respected their words. They did not want to lie to themselves, to those around them, or to be hypocrites. They understood that saying 'There is no deity but Allah, and Muhammad is His messenger' meant that all their daily actions had to change, and they would have to act according to the requirements of faith. They chose not to say these words of belief. It was a terrible decision, but at least they were honest with themselves and respected their words.

Allah says: "Do you suppose that you will enter the Garden without first having suffered like those before you? They were afflicted by misfortune and hardship" Recall that the previous verses were addressing the children of Israel who thought that they would enter Paradise without being tested. They distorted the religion to match their whims and wishes. They did not respect the words of faith. Allah is warning the nation of Muhammad to be prepared for tests and trials and to hold firm to their faith and true to their words. Let's take an example from the Quran. Allah says:

The Desert Arabs said: "We are believers." Tell them: "You have not believed yet; you may simply claim that you are Muslims. It is a long way for faith to penetrate inside your heart. If you obey Allah and His Prophet, He will not diminish anything from the reward promised for your good deeds as Allah is the Most Forgiving, the Most Merciful. (49:14)

When the Bedouins heard this, they said: 'we praise Allah, there is still hope that we will become believers.' Allah wanted the Bedouins to be true to themselves. Some scholars say that this verse was revealed specifically for the tribe of Asad. They came to Medina during a year of famine and proclaimed before the Prophet (peace be upon him): "There is no Allah but Allah, and Muhammad is the Messenger." Then they asked for the zakat charity and reminded the Prophet of their kindness as they did not fight the Muslims like others did. Thus, this verse was revealed to clarify to them that faith is much more than saying "I am Muslim." The verse does not mean that they were hypocrites; rather, it is a reminder that faith is the work of the heart that has to be reflected in every aspect of the believer's life.

This brings us back to the verse: "Do you suppose that you will enter the Garden without first having suffered like those before you?" Allah is informing you not to expect to enter heaven unless you have suffered trials like those who preceded you of nations. You and I must be tested and afflicted by adversity and tribulation, and whoever stays firm deserves Allah's reward. We must not think that we are special over other nations when it comes to life's tests and trials. To the contrary, because the nation of Muhammad has been granted the great blessings of Islam, their tests would be proportional to the bounties they enjoy. We have been blessed with the final message that was sent to entire humanity until the end of time, and we have to expect great tests to assure that each generation is worthy of this gift. The phrase: "…without first having suffered like those before you" signifies that afflictions similar to what struck the previous nations before will continue happening to each generation of believers.

Let's study the phrase "and were so shaken." It is translated from the Arabic origin "zulziloo" and it shows the beauty of the Arabic language where even the way a word sounds help express its meaning. "Zalzala زلزلة" means earthquake, and this word has two sections Zal, Zal "زل,زل". The word "Zal" means to fall from one's place. Thus, both sections of the word put together reflect a fallback and forth in opposite directions just as in an earthquake. It is a series of repeated jerks forwards and backward, left and right, that occur repeatedly.

The phrase "and were so shaken" expresses the great tribulations and succession of tragedies our beloved prophet and his companions endured. Harsh events tested their faith, their family ties, and their physical endurance. Such difficulties continued until the Prophet (peace be upon him), and those who believe with him said: 'When will Allah's help arrive?' Allah –The All-Merciful- answers: "Truly, Allah's help is near."

Here we should ask: Did the believers ask first, and then return to their senses and respond to themselves with "truly, the help of Allah is near?" or did their feelings go back and forth between "when will Allah's help arrive?" and "truly, the help of Allah is near"? Regardless of how difficult and stressful Allah's trials were, regardless how badly they were shaken, Prophet Muhammad (peace be upon him) and his followers continued to hold firm to faith. The question "when will Allah's help arrive?" gives us insight that help was delayed at first, and then Allah gave them the good tidings of: "truly, the help of Allah is near." There was no doubt or suspension of aid, rather, this delay was part of Allah's trial. People had all sorts of thoughts, some of them would say "when will Allah's help arrive?" while other voices from the community would answer "unquestionably, the help of Allah is near." The context of the verse suggests that those who said: "when will Allah's help arrive?" were the companions, and the reply "truly, the help of Allah is near" came from the Prophet (peace be upon him).

hey ask you as to what they should spend. Say, 'Whatever good you spend, let it be for parents, relatives, orphans, the needy, and the traveler.' And whatever good that you may do, Allah indeed knows it. (Chapter 2: Verse 215)

It is a sign of healthy faith that the believers were asking the Prophet questions. More specifically, they asked about matters that were not obligated knowing fully-well that the answer may lead to obligation and restriction. The Messenger (peace be upon him) said: "Don't ask me about things that I did not bring up, for those who came before you perished by the frequency and multiplicity of their questions and their disagreement with their prophets. If I command you of something, then do it the best that you can, and if I forbid something then leave it." The companions asked about the finer details of life; a phenomenon that confirms their love for Allah's teachings, and their desire to base all their actions on the foundation of Islam.

Amr ibn al-Jamouh asked the question in this verse, and he was an old man. He said: O Messenger of Allah, I have a lot of wealth, so what should I give in charity and to whom? He did not ask just for himself; he meant to ask the question that was on the mind of many. Thus, Allah gave a general answer to all believers.

Take note of the phrase: 'They ask you as to what they should spend' because it shows that spending was understood and accepted. The companions were not wondering whether they should spend or not spend, they just wanted to know what the best way to give is. Allah answers: "Say, 'Whatever good you spend, let it be for parents, relatives, orphans, the needy, and the traveler.'" At first glance, it may seem that the question was about what to spend, yet the answer came regarding to whom the spending goes. But if you take a closer look, you will notice that Allah –The All-Wise- had answered the original question: He said that spending must be from whatever 'good' you have; whether knowledge, wisdom, physical help or money that you earned from lawful means. Allah added the advice of who deserves to receive your good wealth. The ones to whom good and wealth are given should be from your close social circles. In other words, your parents, close relatives, and neighbours. Allah wants you to have secure, well-supported family, friends, and neighbours. In this way, the entire community will be taken care of. When you help those in need from your family, and when each one of us does the same, all will be taken care of. My circle of close relatives and neighbours will intersect with your circle of close relatives and neighbours. Allah further extends this care to the orphans and the poor to ensure that all members of the community are well cared for.

As mentioned earlier the questioner in this verse was Amr ibn al-Jamouh. He is a man with an amazing story. He was lame limping when he walked. Allah had excused the blind and the lame from fighting. Ibn al-Jamuh came to the Prophet (peace be upon him) when he was about to leave for battle and said: 'O Messenger of Allah, do not deprive me of being by your side in battle; my children do not allow me to go because of my lame leg.' The Prophet (peace be upon him) said to him: "Allah has excused you amongst those He has excused." He answered: "but, O Messenger of Allah, it is my wish to step onto the ground of paradise with this lame leg."

This was the person who asked about what Muslims should spend. Allah says: 'let it be for parents, relatives, orphans, the needy, and the traveller.' Here you may ask: Is every orphan in need? Perhaps the orphan inherited plenty of money; We answer that the issue here is not limited to fulfilling the financial needs of orphans; rather it is to stand beside the weak and show social solidarity. When a child becomes an orphan -even if he or she inherits plenty of money- he or she is still in dire need of compassion and parental support. Such care will bring about the feelings as if the father is still alive, and will drive away the feelings of envy towards other children who have their biological fathers besides them. If the orphan is neglected, he or she may rail against Allah and the entire society for the father's death. The orphan may question: "why am I the one whose father died? Why me??" But when the orphan feels that all people are taking care of him or her in a fatherly manner, he or she will feel secure. In a truly Islamic society, those who have their biological fathers only receive the love of one father, whereas the orphan receives the loving care of many people. As a result, love spreads in the Muslim society as people feel content with what Allah has decreed for them. No one objects to fate, blames Allah or the society for the misfortunes of life. Allah may have taken the child's father, but He –the All-Merciful- gave this child many fathers in return. Those who deny an orphan affection and kindness because his or her father left enough money are ignoring the tremendous moral and emotional reward of love. It is not a question of material needs, but an emotional, spiritual and personal need.

I would like to take a moment to remind you that Allah –the All-Wise- does not take a parent away from a child while there is a need for him or her on earth. I am sure that you can think back to a situation in your own life when you heard about the death of a father or mother of young children. You probably grieved and wondered about how the children would fare without one or both parents. After some years, when you meet those same children, you often find that they achieved a lot in their lives. They may own successful businesses or be highly educated and have families of their own. When a parent passes, Allah showers the children with an abundance of mercy.

This brings us back to the verse, after spending on orphans, Allah asks you to spend on the needy and the traveller. A traveller is a person who is far from family and wealth.

The verse ends with: "And whatever good that you may do, Allah indeed knows it." Allah is addressing your human nature that expects to be rewarded and recognized by other people after you help someone or do them a favour. Allah is reminding you to seek your rewards from Him and no one else. In other words, do not let others know that you spend on relatives, orphans, and the traveller, because those who you want to tell cannot reward you or benefit you in any meaningful way. Allah's knowledge of your deeds is sufficient for you. When you spend to help others and look for people's approval, you often get the opposite result. You may face indifference, denial, envy and even defamation. You end up losing the money that you spent and losing the reward of the Hereafter. On the Day of Judgment, Allah will say to those who spend to be praised by people: "You spent so people would say: 'so and so is generous,' and they said it; I will leave you to collect your reward from the ones you wanted to please." Allah says:

You who believe, do not void out your charitable deeds with flaunting and hurtful words, like someone who spends his wealth only to be seen by people, not believing in Allah and the Last Day. Such a person is like a rock with soil on it: heavy rain falls and leaves it completely bare. Such people get no rewards for their works: Allah does not guide the disbelievers. (2:264)

Thus, your sole purpose when spending to help others should be Allah's pleasure. You will find your rewards multiplied many times over when you need it the most on the Day of Resurrection. Moreover, Allah will endear you to the hearts of the people around you. Spending in secret is one of the best deeds you can do. Prophet Muhammad –peace be upon him- said: "There are seven types of people to whom Allah will provide shade on the day when there will be no shade except the shade of the Almighty. They are: a just ruler; a young person who grew up in the worship of Allah; a person whose heart is in love with mosques; two people who befriend each other in Allah's cause and separate in Allah's cause; a man who was seduced by a woman with status and beauty, yet he said 'No, I fear Allah'; a person who spends secretly in Allah's way so his left hand does not know what his right hand gave, and a person who remembers Allah in solitude and his eyes fill with tears."

Giving secretly is best when it comes to voluntary charity –also known as Sadaqa-; but when it comes to the obligatory alms –Zakat-, it is better to give publicly so others would follow your lead and fulfill their obligation. Similarly, it is better to perform obligatory prayer openly in mosques, while optional and voluntary prayers are better offered in private.

VERSE 214

Am hasibtum an tadkhulul jannata wa lammaa yaa-tikum masalul lazeena khalaw min qablikum massathumul baasaaa'u waddarraaaa'u wa zulziloo hattaa yaqoolar Rasoolu wallazeena aamanoo ma'ahoo mataa nasrul laah; alaaa inna nasral laahi qareeb

Do you suppose that you will enter the Garden without first having suffered like those before you? They were afflicted by misfortune and hardship, and they were so shaken that even the messenger and the believers with him cried, 'When will Allah's help arrive?' Truly, Allah's help is near.

Do you think that the road leading to Paradise will be easy and comfortable? It will not. In fact, it is necessary for you to prove yourself and shoulder the burden of faith in order to earn the fabulous gift of paradise. If faith meant saying few words, then life would have been a breeze; but the difficulty is not in saying the words, it is in implementing of those words in everyday life.

The disbelievers at the time of the Prophet understood this concept. They were people of character who respected their words. They did not want to lie to themselves, to those around them, or to be hypocrites. They understood that saying 'There is no deity but Allah, and Muhammad is His messenger' meant that all their daily actions had to change, and they would have to act according to the requirements of faith. They chose not to say these words of belief. It was a terrible decision, but at least they were honest with themselves and respected their words.

Allah says: "Do you suppose that you will enter the Garden without first having suffered like those before you? They were afflicted by misfortune and hardship" Recall that the previous verses were addressing the children of Israel who thought that they would enter Paradise without being tested. They distorted the religion to match their whims and wishes. They did not respect the words of faith. Allah is warning the nation of Prophet Muhammad(pbuh) to be prepared for tests and trials and to hold firm to their faith and true to their words. Let's take an example from the Quran. Allah says:

The Desert Arabs said: "We are believers." Tell them: "You have not believed yet; you may simply claim that you are Muslims. It is a long way for faith to penetrate inside your heart. If you obey Allah and His Prophet, He will not diminish anything from the reward promised for your good deeds as Allah is the Most Forgiving, the Most Merciful. (49:14)

When the Bedouins heard this, they said: 'we praise Allah, there is still hope that we will become believers.' Allah wanted the Bedouins to be true to themselves. Some scholars say that this verse was revealed specifically for the tribe of Asad. They came to Medina during a year of famine and proclaimed before the Prophet (peace be upon him): "There is no Allah but Allah, and Muhammad is the Messenger." Then they asked for the zakat charity and reminded the Prophet of their kindness as they did not fight the Muslims like others did. Thus, this verse was revealed to clarify to them that faith is much more than saying "I am Muslim." The verse does not mean that they were hypocrites; rather, it is a reminder that faith is the work of the heart that has to be reflected in every aspect of the believer's life.

This brings us back to the verse: "Do you suppose that you will enter the Garden without first having suffered like those before you?" Allah is informing you not to expect to enter heaven unless you have suffered trials like those who preceded you of nations. You and I must be tested and afflicted by adversity and tribulation, and whoever stays firm deserves Allah's reward. We must not think that we are special over other nations when it comes to life's tests and trials. To the contrary, because the nation of Muhammad has been granted the great blessings of Islam, their tests would be proportional to the bounties they enjoy. We have been blessed with the final message that was sent to entire humanity until the end of time, and we have to expect great tests to assure that each generation is worthy of this gift. The phrase: "...without first having suffered like those before you" signifies that afflictions similar to what struck the previous nations before will continue happening to each generation of believers.

Let's study the phrase "and were so shaken." It is translated from the Arabic origin "zulziloo" and it shows the beauty of the Arabic language where even the way a word sounds help express its meaning. "Zalzala زلزلة" means earthquake, and this word has two sections Zal, Zal "زل,زل". The word "Zal" means to fall from one's place. Thus, both sections of the word put together reflect a fallback and forth in opposite directions just as in an earthquake. It is a series of repeated jerks forwards and backward, left and right, that occur repeatedly.

The phrase "and were so shaken" expresses the great tribulations and succession of tragedies our beloved prophet and his companions endured. Harsh events tested their faith, their family ties, and their physical endurance. Such difficulties continued until the Prophet (peace be upon him), and those who believe with him said: 'When will Allah's help arrive?' Allah –The All-Merciful- answers: "Truly, Allah's help is near."

Here we should ask: Did the believers ask first, and then return to their senses and respond to themselves with "truly, the help of Allah is near?" or did their feelings go back and forth between "when will Allah's help arrive?" and "truly, the help of Allah is near"? Regardless of how difficult and stressful Allah's trials were, regardless how badly they were shaken, Prophet Muhammad (peace be upon him) and his followers continued to hold firm to faith. The question "when will Allah's help arrive?" gives us insight that help was delayed at first, and then Allah gave them the good tidings of: "truly, the help of Allah is near." There was no doubt or suspension of aid, rather, this delay was part of Allah's trial. People had all sorts of thoughts, some of them would say "when will Allah's help arrive?" while other voices from the community would answer "unquestionably, the help of Allah is near." The context of the verse suggests that those who said: "when will Allah's help arrive?" were the companions, and the reply "truly, the help of Allah is near" came from the Prophet (peace be upon him).

VERSE 215

Yas'aloonaka maazaa yunfiqoona qul maaa anfaqtum min khairin falil waalidaini wal aqrabeena walyataamaa wal masaakeeni wabnis sabeel; wa maa taf'aloo min khairin fa innal laaha bihee 'Aleem

They ask you as to what they should spend. Say, 'Whatever good you spend, let it be for parents, relatives, orphans, the needy, and the traveller.' And whatever good that you may do, Allah indeed knows it.

It is a sign of healthy faith that the believers were asking the Prophet questions. More specifically, they asked about matters that were not obligated knowing fully-well that the answer may lead to obligation and restriction. The Messenger (peace be upon him) said: "Don't ask me about things that I did not bring up, for those who came before you perished by the frequency and multiplicity of their questions and their disagreement with their prophets. If I command you of something, then do it the best that you can, and if I forbid something then leave it." The companions asked about the finer details of life; a phenomenon that confirms their love for Allah's teachings, and their desire to base all their actions on the foundation of Islam.

Amr ibn al-Jamouh asked the question in this verse, and he was an old man. He said: O Messenger of Allah, I have a lot of wealth, so what should I give in charity and to whom? He did not ask just for himself; he meant to ask the question that was on the mind of many. Thus, Allah gave a general answer to all believers.

Take note of the phrase: 'They ask you as to what they should spend' because it shows that spending was understood and accepted. The companions were not wondering whether they should spend or not spend, they just wanted to know what the best way to give is. Allah answers: "Say, 'Whatever good you spend, let it be for parents, relatives, orphans, the needy, and the traveller." At first glance, it may seem that the question was about what to spend, yet the answer came regarding to whom the spending goes. But if you take a closer look, you will notice that Allah –The All-Wise- had answered the original question: He said that spending must be from whatever 'good' you have; whether knowledge, wisdom, physical help or money that you earned from lawful means. Allah added the advice of who deserves to receive your good wealth. The ones to whom good and wealth are given should be from your close social circles. In other words, your parents, close relatives, and neighbours. Allah wants you to have secure, well-supported family, friends, and neighbours. In this way, the entire community will be taken care of. When you help those in need from your family, and when each one of us does the same, all will be taken care of. My circle of close relatives and neighbours will intersect with your circle of close relatives and neighbours. Allah further extends this care to the orphans and the poor to ensure that all members of the community are well cared for.

As mentioned earlier the questioner in this verse was Amr ibn al-Jamouh. He is a man with an amazing story. He was lame limping when he walked. Allah had excused the blind and the lame from fighting. Ibn al-Jamuh came to the Prophet (peace be upon him) when he was about to leave for battle and said: 'O Messenger of Allah, do not deprive me of being by your side in battle; my children do not allow me to go because of my lame leg.' The Prophet (peace be upon him) said to him: "Allah has excused you amongst those He has excused." He answered: "but, O Messenger of Allah, it is my wish to step onto the ground of paradise with this lame leg."

This was the person who asked about what Muslims should spend. Allah says: 'let it be for parents, relatives, orphans, the needy, and the traveller.' Here you may ask: Is every orphan in need? Perhaps the orphan inherited plenty of money; We answer that the issue here is not limited to fulfilling the financial needs of orphans; rather it is to stand beside the weak and show social solidarity. When a child becomes an orphan -even if he or she inherits plenty of money- he or she is still in dire need of compassion and parental support. Such care will bring about the feelings as if the father is still alive, and will drive away the feelings of envy towards other children who have their biological fathers besides them. If the orphan is neglected, he or she may rail against Allah and the entire society for the father's death. The orphan may question: "why am I the one whose father died? Why me??" But when the orphan feels that all people are taking care of him or her in a fatherly manner, he or she will feel secure. In a truly Islamic society, those who have their biological fathers only receive the love of one father, whereas the orphan receives the loving care of many people. As a result, love spreads in the Muslim society as people feel content with what Allah has decreed for them. No one objects to fate, blames Allah or the society for the misfortunes of life. Allah may have taken the child's father, but He –the All-Merciful- gave this child many fathers in return. Those who deny an orphan affection and kindness because his or her father left enough money are ignoring the tremendous moral and emotional reward of love. It is not a question of material needs, but an emotional, spiritual and personal need.

I would like to take a moment to remind you that Allah –the All-Wise- does not take a parent away from a child while there is a need for him or her on earth. I am sure that you can think back to a situation in your own life when you heard about the death of a father or mother of young children. You probably grieved and wondered about how the children would fare without one or both parents. After some years, when you meet those same children, you often find that they achieved a lot in their lives. They may own successful businesses or be highly educated and have families of their own. When a parent passes, Allah showers the children with an abundance of mercy.

This brings us back to the verse, after spending on orphans, Allah asks you to spend on the needy and the traveller. A traveller is a person who is far from family and wealth.

The verse ends with: "And whatever good that you may do, Allah indeed knows it." Allah is addressing your human nature that expects to be rewarded and recognized by other people after you help someone or do them a favour. Allah is reminding you to seek your rewards from Him and no one else. In other words, do not let others know that you spend on relatives, orphans, and the traveller, because those who you want to tell cannot reward you or benefit you in any meaningful way. Allah's knowledge of your deeds is sufficient for you. When you spend to help others and look for people's approval, you often get the opposite result. You may face indifference, denial, envy and even defamation. You end up losing the money that you spent and losing the reward of the Hereafter. On the Day of Judgment, Allah will say to those who spend to be praised by people: "You spent so people would say: 'so and so is generous,' and they said it; I will leave you to collect your reward from the ones you wanted to please." Allah says:

You who believe, do not void out your charitable deeds with flaunting and hurtful words, like someone who spends his wealth only to be seen by people, not believing in Allah and the Last Day. Such a person is like a rock with soil on it: heavy rain falls and leaves it completely bare. Such people get no rewards for their works: Allah does not guide the disbelievers. (2:264)

Thus, your sole purpose when spending to help others should be Allah's pleasure. You will find your rewards multiplied many times over when you need it the most on the Day of Resurrection. Moreover, Allah will endear you to the hearts of the people around you. Spending in secret is one of the best deeds you can do. Prophet Muhammad –peace be upon him- said: "There are seven types of people to whom Allah will provide shade on the day when there will be no shade except the shade of the Almighty. They are: a just ruler; a young person who grew up in the worship of Allah; a person whose heart is in love with mosques; two people who befriend each other in Allah's cause and separate in Allah's cause; a man who was seduced by a woman with status and beauty, yet he said 'No, I fear Allah'; a person who spends secretly in Allah's way so his left hand does not know what his right hand gave, and a person who remembers Allah in solitude and his eyes fill with tears."

Giving secretly is best when it comes to voluntary charity –also known as Sadaqa-; but when it comes to the obligatory alms –Zakat-, it is better to give publicly so others would follow your lead and fulfill their obligation. Similarly, it is better to perform obligatory prayer openly in mosques, while optional and voluntary prayers are better offered in private.

VERSE 216

Kutiba alaikumulqitaalu wa huwa kurhullakum wa 'asaaa an takrahoo shai'anw wa huwa khairullakum wa 'asaaa an tuhibbo shai'anw wa huwa sharrullakum; wallaahu ya'lamu wa antum laa ta'lamoon

Prescribed for you is fighting, though it is disliked by you. It may well be that you dislike something but it is good for you, and it may well be that you like something but it is bad for you. Allah knows, and you do not know.

Most people hate fighting. It is a natural and innate feeling. Here, Allah the creator of humanity acknowledges our dislike and addresses our feelings directly. In other words, Allah did not say: 'what is the big deal about fighting?' Rather He begins by saying: 'I know fighting is detested, and I want you to know that I take your feelings seriously.' If the issue of the fear of fighting had been ignored, people might have been turned off by Allah's message, and they may have felt that Allah makes light of something very grave.

Allah is warning the believers that they are coming upon hardships, troubles, and threats to their wealth and comfortable lifestyles. Historically, you often find that senior skilled politicians who excel in leadership do not like for their people to fight unless there was a dire need. If they saw a need for war, they would communicate to their people and soldiers that by enduring war, they are averting something worse than fighting. They mobilize the human spirit to face the situation with all its will and powers.

Allah says: "Prescribed for you is fighting, though it is disliked by you." Allah explains to us: I know that you detest fighting, but I want you to know that you should not judge significant matters according to your knowledge and feelings because your understanding is incomplete; rather look at issues through my knowledge. I am the one who legislates what you do not like; and I am the one who knows when the consequences are good. You may love something that leads you to ruin; you may hate something that is good for you, but I am your Creator, and I know the true essence of each matter.

Take the example of a father who loves his 3-year-old daughter and would do anything for her. When the daughter gets sick, the father would force her to take a bitter medicine that she hates. To the child, who does not have full knowledge, the act of forcing her to take the bitter medicine may seem cruel and only adds to the misery of her sickness. To the father, who has full knowledge, it is an act of love and mercy towards his daughter. More importantly, when the child has trust and love for her father, she would accept the bitter medicine that she hates because she knows that her dad loves her and would only do what is best for her.

There was a story of a local Chinese leader who owned a vast land and had many horses. There was one horse that was most beloved to him. One day his favourite horse went out of the pasture and did not return. The leader became sad. So the town's people came to console him for his loss; he smiled and said: 'Why are you here to comfort me? Who knows, maybe this is not a bad or evil thing.' A few days later, the man was surprised by the return of his horse leading a flock of wild horses to his land. When the people saw that, they rushed to congratulate him. The man smiled and said: 'How do you know that this is good for me?' Later, his son decided to go on a ride to tame one of the horses; he fell over and broke his leg. The people came again to console the man. He said: 'Why are you here to comfort me? Who knows if this is a good or a bad thing?' After some time, the government declared war and ordered all young men to join the army; but the young son was excused for his leg was broken. Friends came again to congratulate the father. He said: 'what are congratulating me for? Are you absolutely sure this is a good thing for me?'

Thus, we must not make judgments by looking at superficial matters, whether good or evil. In fact, we must consider all life issues through the light of the following verse: Allah teaches us:

No misfortune can happen, either in the earth or in yourselves, that was not set down in writing before We brought it into being- that is easy for Allah-. So you need not grieve for what you miss or gloat over what you gain. Allah does not love any vain or boastful person (57:22, 23

Prescribed for you is fighting, though it is disliked by you. It may well be that you dislike something but it is good for you, and it may well be that you like something but it is bad for you. Allah knows, and you do not know. (Chapter 2: Verse 216)

How many times did each one of us chase after something he or she really wanted only to regret it later? How many times did each one of us expect good to come out of an action only to be sorry to see evil? The opposite is also true.

Allah –the All Wise- had clarified this concept for us through the story of Prophet Moses (peace be upon him). He says:

Moses said to his servant, 'I will not rest until I reach the place where the two seas meet, even if it takes me years!' But when they reached the place where the two seas meet, they had forgotten all about their fish, which made its way into the sea and swam away. When they had gone a distance further on, he said to his servant, 'Bring us our lunch. Truly this journey of ours has made us tired.' He said, 'Remember when we were resting by the rock? I forgot about the fish- and none but Satan made me forget to mention it to you- and it made its way into the sea in an amazing way!' Moses said, 'Then that was the place we were looking for.' So the two turned back and retraced their footsteps. (18:60-64)

Prophet Moses was once walking towards the junction of the two seas accompanied by a young man helping him. Moses was searching for a wise man that he wished to meet. They carried with them a supply of salted fish to eat from on their journey. The trip was long, hard, and tiring. As they were walking, the young man noticed the salted fish miraculously make its way to the sea. When Moses and his companion rested from fatigue, Moses asked for the fish to eat. The young man apologized for forgetting to tell him what he saw of the fish. Moses said to him: 'this is exactly what we have been looking for. It is a sign from Allah that we have reached our destination, and the man we are supposed to meet –named Al Khidr- is at the place where the fish made its way to the sea.'

Moses, peace be upon him, traced his steps back and met the righteous servant. Allah taught Al-Khidr from the divine knowledge which He only gives to His righteous servants as a reward for their devotion and piety. Moses, peace be upon him, asked the Lord's servant to teach him from his knowledge. But Al Khidr whom Allah granted more knowledge than the human capacity can entertain replied:

The man said, 'You will not be able to bear with me patiently. How could you be patient in matters beyond your knowledge? (18:67-68)

Allah –the All-wise- had given prophet Moses a hint of what is to come. Moses knew that the loss of his fish food supply was a bad thing, but it was actually for his own benefit because it was a sign that led to the meeting place of the righteous servant. The same blueprint would continue throughout the verses as events unfold with Moses & Al Khidr –may Allah be pleased with them-. The verses narrate event after event that appears evil and unjust but in reality hold good and wisdom. Prophet Moses wanted to learn from the divine knowledge that Al Khidr was given. But Al Khidr warned him that he might see events that would test the limits of his patience. Moses insisted and promised to be a polite learner, to remain quiet, and not to object nor inquire about the reasons behind what he sees until it is explained to him. Allah narrates what happened next:

So they set forth until, when they embarked on the boat, he made a hole in it. Moses said: "Have you made a hole in it in order to drown its people? You have certainly done an awful thing!" He replied, 'Did I not tell you that you would never be able to bear with me patiently?' (18:71,72)

Prophet Moses couldn't hold himself back from asking when he saw the Al-Khidr destroy a ship which belonged to poor men; then he remembered his promise.

He said, 'Forgive me for forgetting. Do not make it too hard for me to follow you.' (18:73)

Allah continues:

And so they travelled on. Then, when they met a young boy and the man killed him, Moses said, 'How could you kill an innocent person? He has not killed anyone! What a horrible thing to do!' He replied, 'Did I not tell you that you would never be able to bear with me patiently?' He said, 'If I question you about anything after this, do not keep me in your company. You have obtained from me an excuse." So they went on until when they came upon the people of a township, they asked its people for food, but they refused them hospitality. They found there a wall which was on the verge of tumbling down, and the man restored it. Moses said: "If you had wished, you could have taken payment for it." (18:74-77)

After this, Al Khidr and prophet Moses –peace be upon them- separated. But before they left, the righteous man explained to Moses the reasons behind the events that he was unable to be patient over due to his lack of knowledge. Al Khidr said: 'I put a hole in the ship to save it from a king who seized every ship by force; I damaged it so the king would find the defective ship unappealing to take from the poor men. As for the young boy I killed. He was the son of righteous parents; this son would grow up to bring them tyranny, misery, and disbelief; Allah wanted to give them another son who is humble and righteous. By killing the boy before the age of puberty, he was guaranteed heaven, and so were his righteous parents. Finally, the wall that I rebuilt for the town had treasure buried underneath it that belonged to two orphans from the village. Their father was a pious man, so it was necessary to rebuild the wall and preserve it from the town's rude and greedy people until the orphans reached the age of strength to extract the treasure. Then Al-Khidr said:

I did not do these things of my own accord: these are the explanations for those things you could not bear with patience.' (From 18:82)

And there lies the key to the whole story: Al-Khidr did not attribute these acts to himself; rather he attributed them to the divine Creator who taught him. Allah is teaching you not to assume that good is always in what you like, nor is evil always in what you hate. Allah says: "It may well be that you dislike something but it is good for you, and it may well be that you like something but it is bad for you." Thus, keep this fact in mind when it comes to fighting wars when necessary. Moreover, remember that Allah only issues commands of 'do' and 'do not do' to those who loved and believed in Him. Allah does not obligate anything on the disbelievers.

Here you may ask: how come Allah urges the believers to do something they do not like and leaves the disbeliever alone? We answer that Allah asks of those who love Him to do what is good and beneficial in this world and the next. The believers have entrusted Allah with their affairs, so He –the All-Merciful- takes care of them. Allah does not interfere with your freedom of choice. Allah orders you to do things only after you chose to believe and declare your faith in Him. Perhaps most importantly, and as a reminder, Allah says at the end of the verse: 'Allah knows, and you do not know.'

VERSE 217

Yas'aloonaka 'anish Shahril Haraami qitaalin feehi qul qitaalun feehi kabeerunw wa saddun 'an sabeelil laahi wa kufrum bihee wal Masjidil Haraami wa ikhraaju ahlihee minhu akbaru 'indal laah; walfitnatu akbaru minal qatl; wa laa yazaaloona yuqaatiloonakum hatta yaruddookum 'an deenikum inis tataa'oo; wa mai yartadid minkum 'an deenihee fayamut wahuwa kaafirun fa ulaaa'ika habitat a'maaluhum fid dunyaa wal aakhirati wa ulaaa'ika ashaabun Naari hum feehaa khaalidoon

They ask you about the sacred month and fighting in it. Say, 'Fighting during the month is a great offense, but to bar others from Allah's path, to disbelieve in Him, prevent access to the Sacred Mosque, and expel its people, are still greater offenses in Allah's eyes: persecution is worse than killing.' They will not stop fighting you until they make you revoke your faith, if they can. If any of you revoke your faith and die as disbelievers, your deeds will come to nothing in this world and the Hereafter, and you will be inhabitants of the Fire, there to remain.

The verse starts with the phrase: 'They ask you about the sacred month and fighting in it.' The question being asked is not about the sacred months because these months were well known even before Islam; rather the question is about fighting during these months. What is the point of the question? We answer that the question was meant to be a provocative one, and there is a story behind it.

We know that there are twelve months in a lunar year, and Allah made four of them sacred: Rajab (which is the 7th month), and then three consecutive months: Thul Qi'dah (which is the 11th month), Thul Ḥijjah, and Muḥarram (which is the first month of the Hijri year.) They are called sacred months because fighting is forbidden in them. Allah knows that people, especially adversaries, have pride over each other; thus Allah made shields to protect people's lives and pride. From amongst these shields is the ban on fighting during the sacred months and in sacred places. War may harm the warrior, but his pride and anger often prevent him from stopping the fight; so wars often rage for years at terrible costs to all parties. Allah –the All-Merciful- says to the warriors: stop fighting during these months because I have forbidden it. Leaders and soldiers may wish deeply that someone would intervene to stop the war, but their pride and anger prevents them from stepping back. They do not want to look weak or cowardly. But when the divine law intervenes, each side has a valid reason to back off while protecting its pride against shame. Similarly, Allah made some places sacred so people can say that Allah is the One who forbade fighting in their vicinity; such places also provide a path for peace while protecting everyone's pride.

Our Lord wants to guard man against bloodshed. If waring countries abstain from fighting for three consecutive months, they will get a taste of peace, comfort, and tranquillity; people start to favour peace and would think twice before fighting again. On the other hand, if war raged throughout the year, the fire of anger would remain kindled in every soul.

The story behind this verse is one where Quraysh and the Jewish tribes of Medina tried to stir up divisions and foster doubt within the Muslims. Prophet Muhammad (peace be upon him) used to routinely send a small number of fighters to scout enemy positions and movements. Once, the Prophet dispatched a unit consisting of nine individuals headed by his cousin Abdullah al-Asadi. He, peace be upon him- handed Abdullah a letter and instructed him not to open it until two days into the journey. This was a measure of precaution to assure that no one knew where the scouts were headed. After proceeding for two nights, Abdullah opened the letter. It instructed the group to go to Nakhla -a place between Mecca and Taif- to survey the caravans of Quraysh. The letter also instructed for this mission to be voluntary, so each person in the team had the freedom to go or not.

During travel, Saad bin Abi Waqas' and Uqba bin Ghazwan's camels wondered off, so they went looking for them leaving only six fighters with Abdullah. The six men proceeded to Nakhla where they found Amr ibn Hadrami along with three other men with the caravan of Quraysh. A skirmish started and turned into a full fight in which the son of Al-Hadrami was killed, and two of Quraysh's fighters were captured.

The companions thought it was the last day of the month of Jumada, while in reality, it was the first day of Rajab which is a sacred month. When the companions found out, they realized that they had killed, captured and gathered spoils during a sacred month. In short, they had inadvertently acted contrary to Islamic teachings. This incident exposed the Muslims to the wrath of the Arabs who started to say that Muhammad claims to respect sanctities, yet his people fought in the holy month, shed our blood, took our money, and captured our men. So the Prophet (peace be upon him) abstained from taking the spoils and the prisoners until Allah sent His ruling in the following verse:

They ask you about the sacred month and fighting in it. Say, 'Fighting during the month is a great offense, but to bar others from Allah's path, to disbelieve in Him, prevent access to the Sacred Mosque, and expel its people, are still greater offenses in Allah's eyes: persecution is worse than killing.' They will not stop fighting you until they make you revoke your faith if they can. If any of you revoke your faith and die as disbelievers, your deeds will come to nothing in this world and the Hereafter, and you will be inhabitants of the Fire, there to remain. (2:217)

Allah explains: We acknowledge that fighting in the sacred month is a grave sin, but O Quraysh look at what you have done; compare your actions to ours. You claim that fighting in the sacred month is a great sin, while you disbelieve in Allah, prevent people from Allah's path, deny the Muslims access to the Sacred Mosque, and force the Muslim residents of Mecca out of their homes. These sins are far greater in the sight of Allah than fighting in a sacred month. People who behave like you should not be morally outraged over one day of fighting during a sacred month that happened by error. Do not use one aspect of faith as an excuse to attack others when your behaviour on a daily basis is a violation of faith as a whole. Yes, it is true that fighting in the Holy Month is a great sin; but working tirelessly to corrupt the believer's faith and violating the sanctity of the Sacred House by worshipping idols in it is far worse.

They ask you about the sacred month and fighting in it. Say, 'Fighting during the month is a great offense, but to bar others from Allah's path, to disbelieve in Him, prevent access to the Sacred Mosque, and expel its people, are still greater offenses in Allah's eyes: persecution is worse than killing.' They will not stop fighting you until they make you revoke your faith, if they can. If any of you revoke your faith and die as disbelievers, your deeds will come to nothing in this world and the Hereafter, and you will be inhabitants of the Fire, there to remain. (Chapter 2: Verse 217)

We explained how the disbelievers –who had violated every sanctity in the book- wanted to attack the Muslims over an error during a sacred month. Allah warns the Muslims that this type of behaviour will not stop, and He exposes the true intentions of the disbelievers. He says: "They will not stop fighting you until they make you revoke your faith, if they can." Don't think that the disbelievers will respect sacred months or sacred places; rather their purpose is either to kill you or drive you away from your faith. The phrase "If they can" is a challenge to the enemies of Islam that they will not be able to achieve their goal.

Allah continues "If any of you revoke your faith and die as disbelievers, your deeds will come to nothing in this world and the Hereafter, and you will be inhabitants of the Fire, there to remain." This part of the verse is similar to another verse in chapter 5. Allah says:

The deeds of anyone who rejects faith will come to nothing, and in the Hereafter he will be one of the losers. (from 5:05)

Note that the first verse mentions dying in the state of disbelief as a condition for losing one's good deeds, while the second verse does not mention death. Scholars agree that whoever leaves Islam, becomes a disbeliever, and dies in the state of disbelief will lose all of his or her good deeds on the Day of Judgement. The scholars, however, differed regarding the deeds of a person who starts off as a Muslim, leaves Islam to become a disbeliever for a period of time, then returns to Islam. This person does not die as a disbeliever, instead, he or she returns to Allah's path after a period of disbelief. Would this person's good deeds before they disbelieved become worthless or not? For example, if this person performed Hajj, then became a disbeliever, and later returned to Islam, would their Hajj be accepted, or would it have to be redone?

Imam al-Shafe'i holds the view that the good deeds of the person who rebels against Islam become worthless if he or she dies in the state of disbelief. But if this person returns back to Islam before death, then his or her previous good deeds will be restored. Imam Abu Haneefa has a different opinion. He says: the verse in chapter five is general and does not mention death. Accordingly, whoever turns to disbelief after Islam would lose all his or her good deeds regardless if he o she returns to Islam afterward.

Let's go back to the example of a person who performed the obligatory Hajj then decided to leave Islam. After some time, this person repents and comes back to faith. Would he or she have to perform the obligatory Hajj again or would the previous hajj suffice? This is the point of contention. According to Imam al-Shafe'i, this person's Hajj is not wasted by the period of disbelief if he or she returns to faith before death because Allah had specified: "If any of you revoke your faith and die as disbelievers, your deeds will come to nothing." But Imam Shafe'i argues that this person will not be rewarded for their Hajj. How could this be, you may ask? We answer that Al-Shafe'i has turned our attention to something that many people overlook. Hajj is a pillar of the pillars of Islam. If you are able to perform the obligatory Hajj pilgrimage and choose not to, you will be punished for this shortcoming. However, if you perform Hajj, you will be rewarded twice. The first reward is that you will be spared the punishment of those who do not perform Hajj.

And the second reward is that you will earn good deeds for performing the rituals of the Hajj pilgrimage. Al-Shafe'i said: if a person does a good deed –such as performing Hajj- then disbelieves, then returns to Islam, he or she will be spared the punishment of those who did not perform Hajj. Yet at the same time, he or she will lose the rewards of performing the rituals of Hajj. Imam Abu Haneefa is of the opinion that such person would not only lose the good deeds of performing the rituals of Hajj, but he or she would also be treated as a person who never performed Hajj.

The phrase "will come to nothing" is translated from the Arabic origin Habittat Like many words of the Quran, Habittat has its origin in the desert environment. It is used to describe a disease that befalls livestock and causes swelling of the abdomen and may sometimes lead to the death of the animal. The cattle catch the disease by consuming particular plants. Prophet Muhammad (peace be upon him) said: "Some of the plants spring produces can cause death by swelling, or almost cause it." The Prophet is warning us that evil maybe mixed with good as in the example of some poisonous spring plants that attract grazing cattle. People falsely assume that the cattle are healthy because it looks well fed with full stomach only to realize that it is a swelling caused by a disease. Similar are the deeds of the disbelievers. Their deeds may appear to be good but turn out to be worthless on the Day of Judgment.

Some people ask: is it conceivable that a person who comes up with an invention that saves thousands of lives would not benefit on the Day of Judgment? Could great inventors and researches that helped humanity end up in hellfire if they are disbelievers? We answer that you earn your reward from the one you worked for. If, for example, you work as an engineer for BMW and you design a great new safety feature, would you expect to get a salary from Mercedes Benz or Pepsi? Of course not, that is not who you worked for. Let's apply this concept to great inventors who happen to be disbelievers. Did they come up with all these inventions while keeping Allah in mind? Or was humanity, money, and fame their goal? These inventors have received their reward. They have university halls named after them; they have statues and books commemorating them, and some have earned great wealth. They should not expect a reward from Allah if they did not seek and do their work with Him in mind. Allah says:

But the actions of the disbelievers are like a mirage in the desert. A thirsty man mistakes it for water but when he reaches it, he finds it to be nothing at all, and he finds Allah there. He will pay him his account in full. Allah is swift at reckoning. (24:39)

Every believer must strive towards discovery, invention and the renaissance of the Muslim world. Muslim scientists must be beacons energized by the light of faith, and should not let others beat them to discoveries while they lounge around. Islam encompasses both moral values and worldly affairs. It is a religion of science and progress, and it guarantees for those who practice its teachings, the happiness in this world and the rewards of the Hereafter.

This brings us back to the verse. Allah says: 'They will not stop fighting you until they make you revoke your faith, if they can. If any of you revoke your faith and die as disbelievers, your deeds will come to nothing in this world and the Hereafter, and you will be inhabitants of the Fire, there to remain.' An upright person who strives for a fair and peaceful world is in harmony with Islamic principles. On the other hand, the same principals of faith become an obstacle and a problem to those who want to steal the sweat and efforts of others. They would do everything they can to turn people away from proper faith.

VERSE 218

Innal lazeena aamanoo wallazeena haajaroo wa jaahadoo fee sabeelil laahi ulaaa'ika yarjoona rahmatal laah; wallaahu Ghafoorur Raheem

Surely those who believe, those who emigrate and strive in Allah's cause – they are the ones who may hope for the mercy of Allah. Allah is All-Forgiving, All-Compassionate.

The verse lists three types of people: the first type are those who have believed, second are those who emigrated, and the third type are those who have struggled and fought in Allah's cause. In essence, they are people who were sincere in their faith, held Allah above all their affairs and worldly possessions, and strived to spread the word of Allah. They did all of that hoping for Allah's pleasure and mercy. Here you may ask: Why did they go to such lengths? Weren't they sure about Allah's love and forgiveness? We answer that a believer takes nothing for granted. You may have forgotten about some of your sins; you may not have repented from other sins properly. You should approach each task you do with Allah in mind. You should perform your daily job to the best of your ability and be an excellent example of a good Muslim. Don't allow your whims and desires get in the way and spoil your deeds. Prophet Muhammad peace be upon him used to supplicate: "Dear Allah, I seek refuge in you from knowledge that is wasted, from a deed that is not worthy to be raised to you, and from a supplication that is not worthy to be heard."

Our beloved prophet took the utmost care to assure that his deeds were done with pure intentions. He taught us that our thoughts and desires could sometimes spoil our work; he –peace be upon him- also taught us to be hopeful of the mercy of our Lord. A true believer would never say: 'I did my prayers and worship, so Allah owes me reward and mercy.' We answer that our worship is a display of gratitude for all Allah has blessed us with. Any reward we get from Allah for worship is a bounty and mercy from Him far above what we deserve. Allah gave us life, health, a beautiful world to live in; He guided us with clear signs, messengers, and heavenly books. He grants us food, water, family, and countless blessings. Our worship is mere gratitude and appreciation for all Allah has done for us. Even if you spend every minute of your life in worship and remembrance, it won't be enough to pay for a fraction of what Allah had blessed you with. So, whatever good comes to you after worship, whether it is an increase in blessings or mercy and paradise in the Hereafter, is a bounty from Allah that you did not really earn. That is why a believer is always hopeful -not certain- of Allah's mercy. Allah says:

They think they have done you a favour by entering Islam. Say, 'Do not consider your submission a favour to me; it is Allah who has done you a favour by guiding you to faith, if you are truly sincere.' (49:17)

Your relationship with Allah should be a relationship of love equally balanced between hope and fear. Let's clarify this with an example of a child who loves her father. She looks up to him and hopes that he helps her achieve her dreams, yet she fears him getting upset with her if she misbehaves. Both emotions are necessary for a healthy relationship between the daughter and her father, and if one emotion overtakes the other, the child's life goes out of balanced.

So is your relationship with Allah. If you fear Allah and do not trust His mercy, then your faith is unbalanced. Likewise, if you feel that the mercy of your Lord is guaranteed, then your faith is unbalanced. Both: reverence and aspiration should coexist within your heart. Take a moment to think about the religious obligations Allah asks of you. You will soon realize that you receive countless benefits from Allah, far beyond what you ought to have. Allah's blessings are something you can hope for, not something that you are entitled to. Allah says:

Call on your Lord humbly and privately- He does not like those who transgress His bounds. Do not cause disorder and corruption on the earth seeing that it has been so well ordered, and call upon Him with fear and hope. Indeed, Allah's mercy is to those devoted to doing good. (7:55-56)

This brings us back to the verse. Allah says: 'they are the ones who may hope for the mercy of Allah.' What is Mercy, you may ask? Mercy is to be spared suffering and pain. In other words, it is to be free from troubles to begin with. Allah says:

We send down the Quran as healing and mercy to those who believe; as for those who disbelieve, it only increases their loss. (17:82)

Take note that healing means to be cured of a disease that you are already afflicted with. Mercy, on the other hand, means that you are spared the affliction entirely. Allah knows that none of his servants are free from sin. If every nitty gritty is counted and have to be repaid, then we will all suffer. Thus, I advise you to recite the following prayer: "Dear Lord, treat us with your bounty, not your justice; treat us according to your kindness, not according to our deeds; and treat us with your leniency, not according to what we deserve."

Prophet Muhammad taught us that it is not our deeds that grant us Paradise, but it is Allah's grace, mercy, and forgiveness. He -peace be upon him- said: "None of you shall enter paradise because of your deeds.' They said, 'Not even you, O Messenger of Allah?' He said, 'Not even me shall enter paradise unless Allah showers me with His mercy."

VERSE 219

Yas'aloonaka 'anilkhamri walmaisiri qul feehimaaa ismun kabeerunw wa manaafi'u linnaasi wa ismuhumaa akbaru min naf'ihimaa; wa yas'aloonaka maaza yunfiqoona qulil-'afwa; kazaalika yubaiyinul laahu lakumul-aayaati la'allakum tatafakkaroon

They ask you about intoxicants and gambling: say, 'There is great sin in both, and some benefit for people: the sin is greater than the benefit.' They ask you what they should give: say, 'Give what you can spare.' In this way, Allah makes His messages clear to you, so that you may reflect

The word 'intoxicants' –sometimes translated to 'alcoholic drinks'- is derived from Arabic origin 'Khamr.' The word 'Khamr' has in its origin the meaning of 'to hide' or 'to conceal.' The word 'khimar' refers to a type of headscarf worn by Muslim women to cover their hair. So do drugs, intoxicants, and alcoholic drinks, they cover the mind in a haze and conceal intelligence.

Drinking and gambling were very popular in the pre-Islamic era, along with their associated personal and societal problems. When Islam came to fix the prevailing systems, it confronted the pagan society in two ways. First, in matters related to creed, such as polytheism the worship of idols, Islam addressed things head-on with no compromise or leniency. From day one, the banner of: "There is no deity but Allah and Muhammad is His Messenger" was raised to deal with the issue of polytheism at its roots. Second, Islam dealt with common social and personal habits gradually and with leniency. It began by raising awareness that such habits are unsuitable for a healthy society.

One of those habits was the use of alcoholic drinks and intoxicants. As explained, such substances cover the mind and cloud one's judgment, and at higher doses, may cause one to lose consciousness. Allah created us as the caretakers on earth and honoured us with intellect and thought. Allah loves and cares for His creation. Thus He does not want you to waste the gift of intelligence even for a short period of time. Being drunk or high on drugs is a rejection of Allah's gift. Those who drink alcohol or abuse substance justify their actions by saying that they want to forget their worldly problems. We ask: will ignoring the problems make them go away? Or will it make them worse? Allah invites you to live through your worries so you can face them with the best tool you have: your thoughtful mind. Islam does not want you to forget your problems; rather it encourages you to confront and solve them. Thus, it is necessary to keep your mind alert at all times.

How about problems and calamities beyond your control, you may ask? How about issues that cannot be solved? We answer that in such matters, Allah wants you to know that you can rely on Him; He takes care of His creation. In matters that are out of your control, you can relax your mind and leave things to the One always in control.

Let's look at how Islam wisely and gradually handled the issues of intoxicants. Allah says:

And from the fruit of the date-palm and the grape-vine, you derive both intoxicants and wholesome provision. There is certainly a Sign in that for people who use their intellect. (16:67)

Take note that when Allah mentioned 'intoxicants,' he passed by it without comment. But when 'provision' was mentioned, the Almighty described it as 'wholesome.' Through this verse, Allah paved the way for a future position on alcohol and intoxicants in Islam. The subtle omission of good and wholesome as descriptions indicated that once fruits and other healthy provisions are used to make intoxicants, they can no longer be described as good. There is a difference between using grapes as a source of nutrition and fermenting them to drink.

Another matter to note in the verse is the difference between legislation and advice. When you advise someone about a matter, you would often say: 'I will tell you the advantages and disadvantages, and then you are free to take my advice or leave it.' But when a ruling is issued, you order the person to do as you say and it is no longer an option. Both verses –the one in chapter 16 and the one under study- are advice and reminders of the harms of intoxicants; the final judgment was left to the believers at that time. Allah says: 'They ask you about intoxicants and gambling: say, 'There is great sin in both, and some benefit for people: the sin is greater than the benefit.'

Had Allah not pointed out the benefits of alcohol and gambling, some people would have objected and said: 'We reap so many economic benefits from alcohol and gambling; we earn a good living; people have fun and forget their troubles.' These are undeniable benefits, but Allah –the All Wise, All Knowledgeable- explains that the damage to families and societies outweighs any benefits. That is a fair assessment. Again, at this point, the verse only intended to advise and guide, not to rule or prohibit.

The phrase "the sin is greater than the benefit" was another step in the gradual process of addressing and ultimately prohibiting intoxicants. It is the best approach to tackle entrenched social and economic habits. Habits are hard to break, and changing such habits always elicits emotional agitation. Thus, it is better to address the issue gradually.

The process of prohibiting intoxicants began when one of the Muslim men came to the mosque to pray while he was drunk. He had slurred speech and misquoted the Quran. He said: "say, O disbelievers, I worship what you worship;" while the verse actually says: 'say, O disbelievers, I worship not what you worship.' Soon after, the following was revealed:

You who believe, do not come anywhere near the prayer if you are intoxicated, not until you know what you are saying; nor if you are in a state of major ritual impurity- though you may pass through the mosque- not until you have bathed; if you are ill, on a journey, have relieved yourselves, or had intercourse, and cannot find any water, then find some clean sand and wipe your faces and hands with it. Allah is always ready to pardon and forgive. (04:43)

This verse was a command to those who were accustomed to drinking to stay away from prayers and places of worship while drunk. By dissociating prayer from drinking, a person waking up in the morning cannot drink because he or she has to offer the Fajr morning prayer; He or she cannot get drunk because soon the time for the Zuhr midday, and Asr afternoon prayer will be due. So is the case for the Maghrib sunset and Isha night prayers. This only leaves the person with night-time after Isha prayer to drink and get drunk. Hopefully, after drinking a glass or two, he or she will fall asleep. In this manner, Allah made the time a believer abstains from alcohol longer than the time he or she drinks. Another step on the way to prohibition was completed.

During this time, some differences and problems arose among the companions regarding intoxicants which prompted them to ask Prophet Muhammad(pbuh) to clarify things. At that time, the following verses were revealed:

You who believe, intoxicants and gambling, idolatrous practices, and divining with arrows are repugnant acts- Satan's doing- shun them so that you may prosper. With intoxicants and gambling, Satan seeks only to incite enmity and hatred among you, and to stop you remembering Allah and prayer. Will you not give them up? (05:90-91)

The companions replied: we have ceased our Lord. Hence, with prohibition, Allah protected the minds of people, the integrity of society, and preserved the intellectual ability of men and women at all times.

They ask you about intoxicants and gambling: say, 'There is great sin in both, and some benefit for people: the sin is greater than the benefit.' They ask you what they should give: say, 'Give what you can spare.' In this way, Allah makes His messages clear to you, so that you may reflect (Chapter 2: Verse 219)

One of the main goals of religion is to safeguard the five indispensable necessities of life: personal safety, security of family ties, wealth preservation, the integrity of the mind, and the integrity of faith.

All religious legislations revolve around the preservation of these five matters. If you look even closer at these necessities, you find that each begins with the integrity of the mind. Your mind is what makes you think about faith, family, wealth and safety. Sound reasoning gives you the ability to manage all matters of your life. It is perfectly logical then, that Allah does not want you to intoxicate your mind with drinks or substances because you may waste all of your life's essentials.

Take note that Allah mentioned intoxicants and gambling together. Why, you may ask? Because Allah wants to protect you from negligence. Consider the life of a compulsive gambler. He or she will spend and waste his or her own money, and will not benefit from the money won by gambling. In the case of the winner, the money is acquired easily and spent without care. As for the loser, he or she suffers pain and agony for the loss. A gambler will go into poverty, risk the wellbeing of his or her children, and may even sell all of his or her valuables and belongings; all under the false hopes of future riches that never come.

Even when gambling is done in small games among friends, it causes great harm. The aim of the game is for one friend -the winner- to take money from all his or her friends. Each player is keen to send the other home with empty pockets; what kind of friendship is this? This type of game is adorned to all players by Satan. Moreover, when a person becomes accustomed to easy earnings from gambling, he or she will shun hard work. If no games are to be found, he or she may turn to borrowing from family members or even theft. Gambling -gradually but surely- turns a person towards immorality. A gambler often ends up with no friends, no money, and is often cursed by his or her own family. Allah says:

O you who believe! Intoxicants, games of chance, sacrifices to idols, and divination by arrows are a loathsome evil of Satan's doing; so turn wholly away from it so that you may prosper. With intoxicants and gambling, Satan seeks only to incite enmity and hatred among you, and to stop you remembering Allah and prayer. Will you not give them up? (05:90-91)

The verse moves on to the following question: "They ask you what they should give: say, 'Give what you can spare.'" The prophet was previously asked this question by Amr ibn al-Jumouh; Allah answered in an earlier verse:

They ask you as to what they should spend. Say, 'Whatever good you spend, let it be for parents, relatives, orphans, the needy, and the traveller.' And whatever good that you may do, Allah indeed knows it. (2:215)

In the verse under study, the answer is given in another form: Allah says: 'Give what you can spare' meaning to give to the poor whatever is in excess of your basic needs. It is translated from the Arabic origin "Al Afu." Interestingly, this word carries two meanings; both are valid for the verse under study. 'Al Afu' could mean excess; it also means to leave behind or pardon. Allah says:

You who believe, fair retribution is prescribed for you in cases of murder: the free man for the free man, the slave for the slave, the female for the female. But if the culprit is pardoned by his aggrieved brother, this shall be adhered to fairly (from 02:178)

Whoever pardons and leaves the feelings of hatred and revenge behind —in essence practices Al Afu- earns a great reward from Allah. So when Allah says: "They ask you what they should give: say, 'Give what you can spare,' the word 'spare' or 'Al Afu' implies both meanings: what exceeds your need, and what you can leave behind and forget about. In fact, spending from what you do not need promotes love and well-being in society. Take the example of a man who owns land and grows his own food. After keeping the amount required for him and his family and selling what he can, would he let the excess rot and go to waste? Or would it be wiser to give it to relatives and neighbours in need? Of course the latter is more logical. This was the religious recommendation before the Zakat almsgiving was introduced.

Here you may ask: what is the reason for changing 'Al Afu' to 'Zakat'? We answer that Allah —the All-Wise- does not want to overburden you with Almsgiving Zakat. He made the Zakat amount proportional to the effort required and to the natural recourses available. Let's clarify this point further. The Zakat on mineral and other resources excavated from earth is set at 20% of what is extracted. Each year, if you extract from the ground above a minimum amount –also known as Nisab- you give 20% of the excess to charity. As for the Zakat of agricultural products, it is 10% of whatever is irrigated naturally by rain, and 5% of whatever is irrigated by human effort and groundwater. Lastly, in the day to day trades and jobs, the Zakat almsgiving is 2.5% of earnings and savings above a certain minimum Nisab amount. Take note that the amount of prescribed Zakat is proportional to the amount of work you put in, and the natural resources Allah put at your disposal. When the work is harder, and there are fewer natural resources available, Allah asks you to pay less in Zakat.

Zakat almsgiving allows the stronger members of society to contribute more to the poor and disadvantaged. A person who spends his money on his family guarantees them security. And by spending on extended family, the circle of safety widens. Thus, by ordering the Zakat almsgiving, Allah protects people's wealth from the ravages of inequality and ill feelings in society. Another point to consider is that by specifying that Zakat is due on excess idle money, Allah encourages trade and investment. Here is how it works: If you have money saved in the bank, and you have to give 2.5% each year to charity, you will lose more than half your savings in 30 years. Wouldn't it be better to put that money to good use by starting a business or investment? Allah wants you to benefit yourself and to benefit the entire society around you. Take for example a man who has money saved, and decides to construct a small apartment building to rent out. He would dream and calculate how much he will receive each month in rental income. Although he may only be thinking of earning a profit, by starting the project and investing his money he will benefit many members of the society. Before this man makes a single penny, he will have to hire and pay an architect, an engineer, a project manager, many labourers, carpenters, blacksmiths, plumbers and others. Impoverished members of the society will all have benefited from the money of this man before he does. Allah gave him an idea, so he took out all of his savings and gave it to the workers as his idea turned into reality. This man may have had to force himself to pay the Zakat almsgiving on the saved money each year, but he will gladly spend it all on constructing a small apartment building. The more business this man does with his money, the less Zakat he has to pay. Either way, Allah benefits the poor. In this way, Allah encourages hard work and investment and discourages laziness and dependency. Prophet Muhammad (peace be upon him) said: "There is no better way to eat than from what your have personally earned through hard work. I want you to know that Prophet David —peace be upon him- used to gather and prepare his own food."

VERSE 220

Fid dunyaa wal aakhirah; wa yas'aloonaka 'anil yataamaa qul islaahullahum khayr, wa in tukhaalitoohum fa ikhwaanukum; wallaahu ya'lamul mufsida minalmuslih; wa law shaaa'al laahu la-a'natakum; innal laaha 'Azeezun Hakeem

In this world and the next. They ask you about orphans: say, 'It is good to set things right for them. If you combine their affairs with yours, remember they are your brothers and sisters: Allah knows those who spoil things and those who improve them. Had He so willed, He could been hard on you: He is Almighty and Wise.'

Allah begins this verse with the phrase "In this world and the next" to remind you that religious obligations and prohibitions have consequences now and later. Do not fall under the illusion that punishment or reward for what you do is only in the Hereafter; you will also experience some in this world. You can probably think of many examples of righteous people around you who have committed themselves to the truth. You often find that they were rewarded with contentment, happiness and safety in this world to the extent that people question: how did so and so raise his children and educate them, even though he was poor? So and so is very lucky because his or her children were lovely teenagers who did not rebel or cause headaches. What people often overlook is that Allah's blessings were with the righteous as he or she worked and raised the children. Allah takes care of His servants in this world and the next.

In the hereafter, the rewards would be multiplied many times over and would be clear for all to see. It is a gift and a blessing from our Creator. Prophet Muhammad (peace be upon him) said: "None of you will enter Paradise by his or her deeds alone' The companions asked, 'Not even you, Messenger of Allah?' He replied, 'Not even me, unless Allah showers me with mercy.'"

In the phrase "In this world and the next" Allah is reminding you that the Islamic teachings He sent will help you get the most out of life and help save you from the psychological and material troubles you would fall into if you follow your whims and desires.

In fact, in the previous verses, Allah compared two categories of people from the society: the first category is the hypocrites who put out an appearance that does not match what is in their hearts. Allah says:

And from among the people are those whose words about worldly life please you, and he cites Allah as witness to what is in his heart. Yet he is the fiercest of opponents. And when he turns his back, he strives about the earth to foment disorder and corruption; destroying crops and future generations. Allah does not like corruption. (2:204, 205)

Perhaps if such people realized their mistake, they would return to the truth. Sadly, this is not the case. If a hypocrite is approached by a sympathetic and compassionate person, he or she would often go deeper into sin. Allah says:

When he is told, 'Beware of Allah,' pride in sin takes hold of him. Hell is sufficient for him: a dreadful resting place. (2:206)

In contrast, Allah highlighted the second category of people who sell themselves for the sake of Allah. They dedicate all there is: whether material possessions or time and effort to Allah's cause. The Almighty said:

And among the people is the one who sells himself in pursuit of Allah's good pleasure. Allah is All-Compassionate towards His servants. (2:207)

Then Allah invited all to enter into peace and faith altogether. Embracing Islam means to bring all kinds of peace in your life and your hereafter. Islam brings you peace with yourself because your actions are in harmony with your beliefs; peace with nature because you and all the creation around are on the same path to Allah; and peace with the society as you invite those around you to submit to the creator and not to each other or their desires. Allah says:

You who believe, enter wholeheartedly into submission to Allah and do not follow in Satan's footsteps, for he is your sworn enemy. (2:208)

All of this provides proof that Allah did not leave the creation uncared for; rather He –the All-merciful- sent messengers, books and teachings to guarantee our safety and salvation in this world and the next. If you see disorder and fear in the world, then know that people have not adhered to some of Allah's teachings. Allah commands us to enter into peace entirely. There is no alternative because Allah is the All-Wise the Almighty that cannot be overcome; He is the All-Powerful, the All Competent who does everything with perfect wisdom. Those who think that they are insulting Allah by not adhering to His teachings are actually insulting themselves and demeaning their intelligence.

The most important warning Allah reminds us of over and over is the coming of the hour and the Day of Judgment. It will occur suddenly, and it will be a shattering catastrophe. Be careful of being struck by the hour unprepared. The words of the Quran are not mere historical events and legal theories. They are the words of Allah who ruled over the universe long before the call of Muhammad -peace be upon him-. Allah says:

People, be mindful of your Lord, for the tremor of the Last Hour will be a mighty thing: on the Day you see it, every nursing mother will think no more of her baby, every pregnant female will miscarry, you will think people are drunk when they are not, so severe will be Allah's torment. (22:1-2)

How many of Allah's signs did the children of Israel turn away from? How did they and their families fare when they ignored Allah's teachings? Allah wants you to look deeply into history, and to study matters rather than take everything at face value. You must not be fooled and distracted by the adornments of this life because life is short and unpredictable. How many years will you live in strength and good health? 20? 40? 80?

People before us differed and lost their way when they ignored Allah's teachings and followed their own whims and desires. Despite that, Allah did not abandon them; He sent Messengers and prophets, one after the other. Every time people immersed in immorality and corruption, Allah sent a Prophet. Muhammad, the final Messenger, was sent with the comprehensive message of Islam as the seal of all messengers. He, peace be upon him, is distinguished from all other Prophets because his teachings are to remain until the last day. His nation is also distinguished by its responsibility to carry this message and preserve it for all future generations.

Allah warns us of another pitfall: the pleasures of paradise are not attained easily. The road to heaven is surrounded by tough tasks and hard work; so you must keep your eye on the goal and keep your motivation up on a daily basis. Just like a top athlete has to go through hard training and pain daily to attain the championship. Prophet Muhammad (peace be upon him) said: "Paradise is surrounded by hardship while Hellfire is surrounded by desires." Allah, however, did not leave you to face this challenge without proper tools. He granted you a high status in the universe; He gave you a thoughtful mind, an able body, and He subjected matter, plants, and animals to your service. So all the tools needed for the job are at your disposal.

Allah also reminds you to work and provide for your needs and the needs of your family and not to forget about your relatives in poverty. Make sure to give them a share of your excess effort and wealth. In this way, the divine doctrine secures the entire society by providing the weak with a safety net earned from the efforts of their able Muslim brothers and sisters. Keep in mind that Zakat is not only an obligation that takes from you; it is –in fact- a safety net for you and for your family in case you run into trouble and need help.

The circumstances of life are ever changing; the powerful do not remain powerful forever; the rich do not stay rich forever. Allah Almighty rotates the good days and the bad days among people. Thus, everyone is asked to do their part. Allah only asks you to do extra when you are able; likewise, He will ask others to give you when you are in need. The more work and investment you do, the more you keep for yourself. You have the responsibility of spending on poor relatives and neighbors. This is the small sector of society that you are responsible for; whereas the responsibility of the orphans should be shared by all members of the community whether they are related or not. Orphans are our relatives because Allah has entrusted us to nurture and care for them. Indeed Allah's teachings are our salvation 'In this world and the next.'

In this world and the next. They ask you about orphans: say, 'It is good to set things right for them. If you combine their affairs with yours, remember they are your brothers and sisters: Allah knows those who spoil things and those who improve them. Had He so willed, He could been hard on you: He is Almighty and Wise.' (Chapter 2: Verse 220)

A wise man once said, "No good deed goes unpunished." In other words, there will always be enemies against the right path. Why, you may ask? Because many people make a living, earn a profit, and increase their power by exploiting others and robbing them of their rights. It is a direct result of people following their own desires while ignoring the teachings of their Lord. Corruption enriches the elites, and they will always fight with their money, power and media to keep the status quo. Thus, the believers have the responsibility to always remain vigilant of such people and their actions. You cannot be complacent, and more importantly, you should be prepared to sacrifice time, money and effort to free people from oppression and guarantee equality and justice for all. Allah says:

Surely those who believe, those who emigrate and strive in Allah's cause – they are the ones who may hope for the mercy of Allah. Allah is All-Forgiving, All-Compassionate. (2:218)

For these reasons, Allah has legislated fighting as a tool to prevent corruption if necessary as illustrated in the following verse:

Prescribed for you is fighting, though it is disliked by you. It may well be that you dislike something but it is good for you, and it may well be that you like something but it is bad for you. Allah knows, and you do not know. (2:216)

The ultimate goal is for all people to enter into peace and follow the teachings of their Lord wholeheartedly.

Then Allah draws our attention towards the value of the most essential organ of our body: the brain. The brain is the key to sound judgment and careful planning. You must protect your mind from any substance that may —even temporarily- disable it from functioning properly. Alcohol, drugs, and even actions such as gambling cloud the mind's judgment. Such matters are prohibited even in the smallest of quantities. People who claim that they drink or use drugs to forget about their problems should know that the one thing problems absolutely require to get solved or at least to move past is a sound and healthy mind. Gambling is also prohibited to ensure that everyone makes an honest effort to earn money without deceiving others. All the previous teachings and verses share the core of the phrase: "In this world and the next" because Allah's path guarantees our safety and happiness in both worlds.

This brings us back to the verse. Allah says: 'They ask you about orphans: say, 'It is good to set things right for them. If you combine their affairs with yours, remember they are your brothers and sisters: Allah knows those who spoil things and those who improve them. Had He so willed, He could been hard on you: He is Almighty and Wise.' Security and happiness should also extend to all members of the society. Allah explains that the issue of the orphan is not only material or financial one —an orphan, after all, may have inherited a sizable amount of wealth-; rather the entire community needs to compensate the orphan for the loss of his or her father. Such care will extinguish the feelings of bitterness against other children whose parents are still alive. This is only possible when the orphan receives enough attention and love.

In the olden times, the guardian of the orphan would often mix his or her wealth with that of the child to make daily matters easy. If the guardian had to keep everything separate, every decision would have to be tailored to the orphan. In other words, buying plates and spoons and buying bread would have to be split between the family's money and the orphan's money. Life is difficult as is, and it does not need that level of complexity. Thus, Allah had permitted the guardian to combine his or her wealth with the orphan's wealth. However, when the following verses were revealed, people started shying away from the responsibility of caring for an orphan. Allah says:

Stay well away from the property of orphans, except with the best intentions, until they come of age; give full measure and weight, according to justice'- We do not burden any soul with more than it can bear- ' when you speak, be just, even if it concerns a relative; keep any promises you make in Allah's name. This is what He commands you to do, so that you may take heed'- (06:152)

And in another verse:

People who consume the property of orphans unjustly consume nothing in their bellies except fire. They will roast in a Searing Blaze. (04:10)

People avoided bearing the heavy responsibility of the orphans fearing that they may not do it justice, but Allah wanted to make things easier for the orphans and guardians. Thus He revealed: "They ask you about orphans: say, 'It is good to set things right for them. If you combine their affairs with yours, remember they are your brothers and sisters." Allah wanted the feelings of love and brotherhood to be the primary factors in caring for an orphan. Combining the wealth of the orphan to that of the guardian is OK as long as it is done with caution and with the intention to avoid harm. Then Allah issued a warning: He says: 'Allah knows those who spoil things and those who improve them.' So you must understand that Allah knows who the corruptor is and who the reformer of the orphan's affairs is. It is not enough for the guardian to say that I have opened my house to the orphan and I am taking good care of him or her while money is being stolen behind the scenes. Allah is the All-Knowledgeable, the All-Seeing and Hearing.

The verse continues: "Had He so willed, He could been hard on you." In other words, if Allah had not allowed combining of the orphan's wealth with the guardian's then the matter would have become very difficult for the believers. Earlier we gave the simple example of having to separate the orphan's food and utensils from that of the family. The orphan's spoon and plate would have to be washed with his or her dish detergent, not that of the family, and so on. Even in today's advanced banking and accounting software, this would be very difficult to do. Allah, however, wants ease for us, not hardship. Thus He allowed mixing, so there is no difference in the way the orphan and the guardian live.

Here we should pause and study the beautiful accuracy of the Quranic expression. More specifically, the word Allah used for combining the affairs of the orphans to that of the guardian. The word 'combine' is translated from the Arabic origin 'Khalata'. 'Khalata' is used for mixing solids or items that can still be identified and separated later. For example, when you mix beans with lentils, or rice with hazelnuts, you can separate them later. It is different from mixing liquids —known in Arabic as 'Mazaja' where things cannot be separated once mixed. Allah Almighty guides us to combine our affairs with those of the orphans, but not to mix them because one day the orphan will reach the age of maturity, and the guardian will have to separate the orphan's wealth from his or her own.

Again here we should remember that 'Allah knows those who spoil things and those who improve them' because the guardian may claim in public that he takes care of the orphan's rights, and respects his or her interests, but the reality and intention is what counts. Accountability of actions is not based on what people see; it is based on what Allah knows.

VERSE 221

Wa laatankihul mushrikaati hattaa yu'minn; wa la amatum mu'minatun khairum mim mushrikatinw wa law a'jabatkum; wa laa tunkihul mushrikeena hattaa yu'minoo; wa la'abdummu'minun khairum mimmushrikinw wa law 'ajabakum; ulaaa'ika yad'oona ilan Naari wallaahu yad'ooo ilal Jannati walmaghfirati biiznihee wa yubaiyinu Aayaatihee linnaasi la'allahum yatazakkaroon

Do not marry the women who associate partners with Allah until they believe. A believing servant-girl is better than a free woman who associates partners with Allah, even though she pleases and attracts you. Nor give your women in marriage to men who associate partners with Allah until they believe. A believing slave is better than a free man who associates partners with Allah, even though he pleases and attracts you. Those call to the Fire, while Allah calls to Paradise and forgiveness by His leave. He makes clear His Revelations to people, that they may remember

Marriage is the basis of progress in life and the bedrock of a healthy society. Allah has honoured us and made us trustees on the land, and subjected all creations to our service. He wants to ensure the stability and happiness of humankind.

As we discussed earlier, what spoils life and creates conflict are the ever-changing whims and desires of people; thus, Allah wants you to build your family on a healthy social soil and a pure spring of faith. This fertile ground will produce healthy offspring who will grow in an environment of harmony and love. Therefore, it is imperative to choose the right person from which your offspring will come into being.

Allah starts with: "Do not marry the women who associate partners with Allah until they believe" because the woman is the cornerstone of building a family and a community. If the woman is a non-believer, what will happen? We answer that a mother will raise her children in a manner that reflects her values and beliefs. The father has a role too, but it often comes later. By then, some traits and habits have already been engrained into the children. So do not marry disbelieving women because this corrupts your family system. The mother's actions affect the baby from the moment he or she starts to develop awareness. A child spends the first couple of years in the mother's lap. As the baby grows up, so will the attachment to the mother. Attachment to the father strengthens later. So, if the mother is a polytheist and the father is a believer, the child will be introduced to faith well after being exposed to polytheism.

Out of all creatures, humans have the longest childhood. The length of childhood is often an indicator of the significance of the creature's mission in life. This is because childhood is the stage that prepares the creature for life. Let's, for example, look at the childhood of a house fly; it only lasts for a few hours because a fly has a short and straightforward mission in life. As for humans, Childhood continues for a decade because humans are entrusted with a great mission and a heavy responsibility. The prolonged childhood is needed to learn physical skills, language skills, social norms and moral values. Allah says:

When your children reach puberty, they should ask your permission to enter, like their elders do. This is how Allah makes His messages clear to you: Allah is all knowing, all wise. (24:59)

So a child remains a child until he or she reaches puberty. And if the child's mother is a polytheist, then the child will be surrounded by polytheistic values for over a decade. After such a long time, changing beliefs will be difficult. Even if the child becomes a Muslim due to the father's influence, it is often an overpowering influence, unlike the gentle ways of a mother. Such faith has internal conflicts and deep seeded doubts. Allah, the All-Merciful, wants the early years of childhood and youth to be grounded in faith, not conflict. He says: "Do not marry the women who associate partners with Allah until they believe." In other words, do not set low standards for yourself and your family. Adhere to the highest standards of Allah's teachings. He says: "A believing servant-girl is better than a free woman who associates partners with Allah, even though she pleases and attracts you." Allah is advising you that admiration for a woman which is not based on faith and morals is short-lived. The physical appearance of a woman is temporary; so is the attraction. As years pass, beauty begins to fade, and only values and character remain. Especially, when a woman bears children, her energy and time is fully occupied by raising her children and providing for them, and she will no longer prioritize taking care of herself and her husband.

Marriage has to be based on firm foundations, not merely on physical attraction. If you select a woman based on her physical appearance only to later realize that she lacks strong morals, you will live in regret. You would have to endure an unhealthy marriage for the sake of the children. Allah advises you to choose first and foremost based on faith and deed. He says: "Do not marry the women who associate partners with Allah until they believe." Allah continues: "A believing servant-girl is better than a free woman who associates partners with Allah, even though she pleases and attracts you." The attraction Allah is referring to is physical admiration. Allah advises you to put the everlasting values of faith and character over the fleeting values of physical beauty and social status.

Prophet Muhammad, peace be upon him, said: "A woman is wedded for four reasons: for her wealth, for her beauty, for her noble descent, and for her pious adherence to faith; so aim to get the pious woman if you want real prosperity."

Do not marry the women who associate partners with Allah until they believe. A believing servant-girl is better than a free woman who associates partners with Allah, even though she pleases and attracts you. Nor give your women in marriage to men who associate partners with Allah until they believe. A believing slave is better than a free man who associates partners with Allah, even though he pleases and attracts you.

Those call to the Fire, while Allah calls to Paradise and forgiveness by His leave. He makes clear His Revelations to people, that they may remember (Chapter 2: Verse 221)

Take note of the accuracy of the Quranic text. Allah started this verse by addressing the believing men directly and advising them not to marry disbelieving women. Then, Allah advises women not to marry polytheistic men. However, Allah used the expression: "Nor give your women in marriage" in essence addressing men again. Why, you may ask? Because in Islamic jurisprudence, the man –in this case, the father- is the guardian of his daughter and he has the responsibility to help her navigate marriage. The father's consent is a prerequisite for a proper marriage contact. Allah, the All-Wise, did not address the woman directly, because a young woman may make life-changing marriage decisions based on her passion and dreams, while her guardian can see the bigger picture.

This does not mean that the woman is not asked for her opinion. To the contrary, the woman has the main say in her marriage, and she has to be consulted in regards to the proposal. Her approval and consent are essential for a proper marriage contract. The guardian has the responsibilities of weighing all issues, offering advice, and giving or withholding consent. Then, the woman has the final say.

Islam calls for the woman's opinion, the father's logic, and the mother's experience so that a proper decision can be made in forming a new family. Every marriage conducted in this manner has a solid foundation and a real chance at success. In cases where the woman does not agree to a proposal, it is not permissible for the guardian to force her into the marriage.

Many marriages have failed because Allah's teachings were not followed when entering into the relationship. Sadly, when these marriages fail, the parties often turn to Islamic laws to find solutions. We ask: Why didn't you consider Allah's teachings when you entered into the marriage contract? If you knew better than your Lord at that time, use your knowledge to solve your problems now. It is unjust for you to involve Muslim scholars to help you get out of a situation of your own creation.

More importantly, if marriages based on un-Islamic principals flourished and succeeded, people would say that Allah's teachings had little value. Thus, problems had to occur for people to appreciate the values faith guides them to adopt. Prophet Muhammad –peace be upon him- said: "If a man comes to you in a marriage proposal, and you know he is of good faith and noble character, then facilitate the marriage. If you do not, you will end up with widespread immorality and corruption."

This brings us back to the verse. Allah says: "Nor give your women in marriage to men who associate partners with Allah until they believe." While the message of this verse is general, it was revealed to deal with a specific case. Prophet Muhammad (peace be upon him) sent one of his companions -named Marthad ibn Abi Murthad- to Mecca to help evacuate a group of new Muslims. While he was there, he saw 'Anaq' the woman he was in love with before Islam. He said to her: "Islam has come between us so we cannot be together." When she repeatedly asked him to marry her; He replied: "I will marry you, but I would like to consult the Prophet first." Soon after, he returned to Medina and asked the prophet. The verse under study was revealed. Allah says: "Do not marry the women who associate partners with Allah until they believe. A believing servant-girl is better than a free woman who associates partners with Allah, even though she pleases and attracts you."

As for the part of the verse that states: "A believing servant-girl is better than a free woman who associates partners with Allah;" it is said to have been revealed in regards to Khansaa. She was a slave-girl who belonged to Huthayfah ibn Al-Yaman. She was very unattractive and had a dark complexion. Huthayfah said to her: "O Khansaa, you have been mentioned in the highest gathering and Allah has included you in his Nobel book." After that, Huzayfah freed her and married her.

The verse continues: "Nor give your women in marriage to men who associate partners with Allah until they believe. A believing slave is better than a free man who associates partners with Allah, even though he pleases and attracts you." Note the balance and equality in the criteria for both sexes in choosing a life partner. The ultimate goal is the same: to build a family on a solid basis and to focus on values over everything else. In other words, if necessary, you are advised to overlook some superficial and temporary matters —such as physical beauty or wealth- to secure a solid foundation for a healthy family. Do not tread a path filled with roses while ignoring the long-term consequences of your temporary desire. Allah says: "Those call to the Fire, while Allah calls to Paradise and forgiveness by His leave. He makes clear His Revelations to people, that they may reflect and be mindful" The people who call to the fire are the people of disbelief. As for Allah, He calls to Paradise and forgiveness. Imam Ali (may Allah be pleased with him) said: "There is no good in any matter that leads to hellfire, and there is no evil in any matter after which is Paradise."

Do not marry the women who associate partners with Allah until they believe. A believing servant-girl is better than a free woman who associates partners with Allah, even though she pleases and attracts you. Nor give your women in marriage to men who associate partners with Allah until they believe. A believing slave is better than a free man who associates partners with Allah, even though he pleases and attracts you. Those call to the Fire, while Allah calls to Paradise and forgiveness by His leave. He makes clear His Revelations to people, that they may remember (Chapter 2: Verse 221)

Let's take a few moments to study the phrase "that they may remember." It is also translated into "perhaps they may remember." This phrase is repeated numerous times in the Quran. What does it exactly mean? Remembering makes you recall an issue you already know but forgot due to negligence. When someone mentions something that you have been careless about, you become alert and remember. The tragedy happens when you neglect an important issue for so long that you forget about it entirely.

There are two different types of remembering. The first type is to remember what you had known before but forgot about. Sometimes you may have to learn it all over again if you neglected it for too long. For example, if you learned algebra in school but have not used it for a long time, you need someone to remind you of the rules of algebra, or you may need someone to teach you algebra all over again. The second type of remembering is to start practicing what you already know. For example, you already know that exercise is good for you, but you do not go to the gym. When someone reminds you of the benefits of exercise, you get motivated and start going to the gym. You apply your knowledge.

In the verse under study, Allah reminds you of the values you should seek in your spouse. Allah wants to protect you from making the wrong choice and wants to ensure that your family is built on one common faith. If the beliefs of the two parents are in contradiction, so will be their actions. When that happens, life becomes a corrupted mess with daily fights and struggles. Simply put, marry a good-hearted believing man or woman, not a disbelieving one.

If you are a believing man, you should not marry a disbelieving woman because she is the one who will bear and raise your child while you are occupied with work. The child will look to his or her mother as the primary source of knowledge and the beliefs that she teaches her children will contradict yours.

Likewise, if you are a believing woman, you must not marry a polytheistic man because, after marriage, you will move into his world, his family, and his relatives. Your child will be repeatedly exposed to a polytheistic environment and to values that contradict your faith.

Allah -the All-Wise, the All-Merciful- wants to protect your child from being raised in an environment full of contradiction. He says:

A believing slave is better than a free man who associates partners with Allah, even though he pleases and attracts you. Those call to the Fire, while Allah calls to Paradise and forgiveness by His leave. He makes clear His Revelations to people, that they may remember (Chapter 2: Verse 221)

All this is specifically designed to preserve a healthy environment in which your baby is born.

Here, we should stop and examine an important issue: Allah has permitted the believers to marry women of scripture. He says:

Today all good things have been made lawful for you. The food of the People of the Book is lawful for you as your food is lawful for them. So are chaste, believing, women as well as chaste women of the people who were given the Scripture before you, as long as you have given them their bride-gifts and married them, not taking them as lovers or secret mistresses. The deeds of anyone who rejects faith will come to nothing, and in the Hereafter he will be one of the losers. (05:05)

The scholars have two positions in the regards to a Muslim man marrying a Christian or Jewish woman. The first position is against allowing this type of marriage. The scholars argue that over time, the people of the book have deviated away from their monotheistic beliefs and associated partners with Allah. Is there any greater sin than to claim a man as Allah or the son of Allah? The second position the scholars took in this matter is to permit a man to marry a woman of scripture, but they advised to make sure that she believes in Allah as the only deity. If the matter of disagreement is in regards to which prophet to follow, then there should not be a problem. If the matter of dispute is ascribing partners to Allah, then the differences are dire and the marriage should not happen.

When a believing man marries a woman of scripture, she will most probably move to his place and will be surrounded by the Islamic environment of his family. The father's family influence may counterbalance the influence of the mother on her children. But if the man fears that the children will be affected by the polytheistic values of the woman, then he should choose a Muslim woman as his life partner. When the child is raised in a harmonious environment free of conflict, he or she will grow up with sound beliefs and self-confidence.

Allah is reminding you of the enormous role of the mother in the child's life. A baby learns everything from his or her mother and passes through a period in which the mother is everything, and cannot be shared by anyone whether a sibling or even the father. Allah says:

We have instructed man to be good to his parents. His mother bore him with difficulty and with difficulty gave birth to him; and his bearing and weaning take thirty months. Then when he achieves his full strength and reaches forty, he says, 'My Lord, keep me thankful for the blessing You bestowed on me and on my parents, and keep me acting rightly, pleasing You. And make my descendants righteous. I have repented to You and I am truly one of the Muslims.' (46:15)

VERSE 222

Wa yas'aloonaka 'anil maheedi qul huwa azan fa'tazilun nisaaa'a fil maheedi wa laa taqraboo hunna hattaa yathurna fa-izaa tatah-harrna faatoohunna min haisu amarakumul laah; innallaaha yuhibbut Tawwaabeena wa yuhibbul mutatahhireen

And they ask you about menstruation. Say, 'It is a mild harm, so keep apart from women during menstruation and do not approach them until they have purified themselves. But once they have purified themselves, then go to them in the way that Allah has enjoined on you.' Allah loves those who turn back from wrongdoing and He loves those who purify themselves.

In this verse, Allah addresses the marital relations with women during the period of menstruation. When this ruling was revealed, people were of two schools of thought. Some people believed that a woman is so unclean during her period that her husband cannot have intimate relations with her, eat with her or even stay in the same house. In fact, even the children could not be with a menstruating woman under one roof. On the other extreme, people believed that a menstruating woman is like any other woman, and there is no reason to abstain from conjugal activity. So Islam came to sort this issue out and had a moderate middle view. Allah says:

And they ask you about menstruation. Say, 'It is a mild harm, so keep apart from women during menstruation and do not approach them until they have purified themselves.

Allah referred to menstruation as 'mild harm' translated from the Arabic 'Atha.' Since this description came from the Lord, our creator, we accept it regardless of what medicine has to claim. Once you hear that something is harmful, you prepare the mind to learn how to avoid harm. Allah made the menstrual cycle a part of a woman's life as it is necessary for childbearing. He instructs men to avoid intimate relationships with their wives during this period because it is harmful. Here you may ask: Is menstruation harmful to the woman or the man? We answer that it is harmful for both because the verse used the general term of harm and did not specify further. It suggests that intimate relations during this period may cause issues such as infections or diseases to both the male and female private parts.

Allah created the woman's womb and placed a specific number of eggs -only known to Him- into her ovaries. When a woman ovulates, and the egg is not fertilized, menstruation occurs. Menstruation is blood containing non-living tissue that used to line the uterus in preparation for the fertilized egg. During menstruation, the vaginal and cervical areas become irritated and prone to inflammation and growth of harmful bacteria. These harmful microbes may flourish or be transferred to the man if intercourse takes place during menstruation. Moreover, and due to hormonal changes, menstruation affects women and weakens their bodies; thus Allah permitted them to skip fasting and praying during this period.

The description of menstruation as "mild harm" requires the advice of how to mitigate its effects. Thus, Allah offers the following advice: "so keep apart from women during menstruation and do not approach them until they have purified themselves."

In other words, 'do not approach them' means do not enter from the place from which the harmful menstrual blood is exiting.

The verse continues: 'do not approach them until they have purified themselves. But once they have purified themselves, then go to them in the way that Allah has enjoined on you.' Here, we must take note of the Quranic expression 'until they have purified themselves.' Had the verse said 'do not approach them until they become pure,' it would have meant that you can resume intimate relations once the menstrual bleeding stops. However, Allah specified not to resume intimate relations 'until they have purified themselves' meaning that the bleeding had to stop and the woman has to bathe for purification afterward —also known as ghusl-. So for those who ask the question: Is it permissible for a man to have intimate with his wife the moment the menstrual bleeding stops? We answer that the Arabic words used in this verse are very clear and leave no room for ambiguity: Intercourse is not permissible until the woman has taken the ghusl shower after the bleeding had stopped. This is part of the beauty and wonder of the Quran where the words used —and sometimes even single letters- help clarify and illuminate the intended ruling.

The verse ends with "Allah loves those who turn back from wrongdoing and He loves those who purify themselves." Just as Allah asked you to purify yourself physically, He also asks you to purify yourself spiritually through prayer and repentance.

VERSE 223

Nisaaa'ukum harsullakum faatoo harsakum annaa shi'tum wa qaddimoo li anfusikum; wattaqul laaha wa'lamooo annakum mulaaqooh; wa bash shirilmu 'mineen

Your wives are the bearers of your seed; so, approach your tillage however you wish and send good ahead for yourselves. Act in due reverence for Allah, and know that you are to meet with Him; and give glad tidings to the believers

In this verse, Allah explains what is lawful when it comes to intimate relations between married couples. The key to the verse lies in the phrase "bearers of your seed" translated from the Arabic origin 'Harth.' 'Harth' is the fertile soil for sowing seeds. You may remember this word from an earlier verse. Allah says in the 205th verse:

And when he turns his back, he strives about the earth to foment disorder and corruption; destroying crops and future generations.

Allah is directing the believers to have sexual relations from the place of cultivation; more specifically, the place which results in continuity of the human race, and nowhere else. Some people have misunderstood this verse and used the phrase "so, approach your tillage however you wish' to prove that sexual intercourse is allowed in all parts a woman's body. We answer: read the verse closer, and study the phrase "so, approach your tillage' which specifically means that you can only enter into the place of germination and reproduction. The verse does not generalize; it specifies the location of intercourse.

Another proof to support this approach lies in the phrase "and send good ahead for yourselves." Allah is asking you to think of it as an investment in the offspring that will come from the intimate relation. Pleasure from intimate desire should be regarded as secondary while raising pious offspring should be the primary goal. Allah advises you to focus on the future. He says: "and send good ahead for yourselves."

How do you send good ahead for yourself, you may ask? More importantly: How do you avoid bringing on hardship and misery to yourself? We answer that you should choose your spouse carefully and based on the criteria of faith as Allah advised. You should also do as the prophet taught us to do. He –peace be upon him- advised that when you are about to have physical intimacy with your spouse, you should remember Allah and recite the following prayer: "O Allah, keep the devils away from us and keep the devils away from what You have blessed us with." In this manner, if your relations produce a child, he or she would start life in Allah's protection and aid. How could this be? We answer that if –at the time you sow your seed- you remember the One who creates, nourishes and protects; then He Almighty will protect your child. On the other hand, a child whose parents neglect to acknowledge Allah's blessings and bounty in marriage, sexual pleasure, and reproduction would have children that could easily fall prey to evil.

Allah –the All-Merciful- wants you to "send good ahead for yourselves" and have righteous children that comfort you and increase your good deeds. A righteous child will pray for you, and teach his or her children to pray for you. This chain will remain unbroken, and it is a wonderful way for your good deeds to continue well past your death. Prophet Muhammad –peace be upon him said-: "When the son of Adam dies, all his good deeds cease except for three: a charity that continues to bear fruit, knowledge that benefits people, and a righteous child who supplicates for him."

Even in awful circumstances the values of "and send good ahead for yourselves" still apply. Suppose that you kept Allah in mind while selecting a spouse, and during the marriage. Then you were blessed with the birth of a child that died soon after. Rest assured that Allah will reward you in return. In such case, your child will close a door of the doors of hellfire and be one of the reasons to bring you closer to paradise.

The verse ends with: "Act in due reverence for Allah, and know that you are to meet with Him; and give glad tidings to the believers." Allah is advising you to have reverence for Him in all your actions, even those that are done in private. As a believer, you are confident that you will meet Allah on the Day of Judgment, so you should always act accordingly at all times. Allah will reward you with paradise in return.

VERSE 224

Wa laa taj'alul laaha 'urdatal li aymaanikum an tabarroo wa tattaqoo wa tuslihoo bainan naas; wallaahu Samee'un 'Aleem

Do not, by your oaths, make Allah an obstacle in the way of doing good actions, being mindful of Allah, or putting things right between people. Allah is All-Hearing, All-Knowing.

There are three virtues listed in this verse: the first virtue is doing good deeds which is often hard and requires effort. The second is to be mindful of Allah in all your actions; this too is often hard and requires self-discipline. And the third is to reconcile disagreements between people and be a mediator. As you know, trying to solve disputes between people is hard work full of pitfalls and headaches.

Allah starts the verse with: "Do not, by your oaths, make Allah an obstacle in the way of doing good actions." An obstacle is a partition between two things. For example, you can put your hand over your eyes to block the sun. Your hand is the barrier between your eyes and the bright light. In essence, Allah is warning you against making your oaths a barrier between you and doing good deeds, being Allah-conscious, or helping people in your society. How can this be, you may ask? Perhaps the best way to explain this concept is through an example. Suppose that your cousin had borrowed money from you and never returned it. Then he fell ill. If your mother asks you to go and visit your sick cousin and bring him some food, you may say, "I had sworn to Allah that I would never do him any more favours." Thus, you have made your oath a barrier between you and doing a good deed.

Allah wants you to know that an oath in Him is not a permissible excuse for not doing good. Nor it is a permissible excuse to sever family ties or let disputes grow in society. If you swore to something, then found a better option, you should do two things: first you should go ahead and do the better option, and second, you should expiate for breaking your oath. Why? Because when you swear against doing good, you are putting Allah between you and righteousness. Allah is the source of all good and your actions and oaths –as a believer- should not contradict this fact. Allah is the one who commands righteousness, mindfulness, and reform among people. Isn't that the very essence of entering fully into Islam? Allah says:

You who believe, enter wholeheartedly into submission to Allah and do not follow in Satan's footsteps, for he is your sworn enemy. (2:208)

If you vowed not to do a good act, then Allah wants you to break your oath and be a mindful, righteous person who spreads equality in society. Take a moment to imagine a culture where every person does good, avoids sins, and when conflicts arise, he or she tries to reconcile between the disputing parties. Isn't this the very essence of a healthy and peaceful society? Allah wants you to leave the doors of good deeds open, and never to shut any of them with an oath.

People find many excuses to procrastinate and avoid doing good deeds. Most of us actively stay away from other people's disputes. We would rather do what gives us pleasure while pretending that we are obeying Allah's commands. Here the story of Mustah ibn Athatha comes to mind.

Ayesha, the wife of the Messenger (peace be upon him), joined the Prophet in the battle of Bani Al-Mustaliq. This was after the command of hijab –the head covering of Muslim women- was revealed. Therefore, Ayesha travelled in a canopy called Howdaj on the back of a camel. When the Prophet was about to return home after the battle, Ayesha lost her necklace and stayed behind to look for it. She was petite, so when the soldiers carried her Howdaj they did not realize that she was not in it. While Ayesha was looking for her necklace, she realized that the army had travelled far from her. She thought they would return to search for her. Another person that was left behind was a soldier named Safwan bin al-Mu'attal. When Ayesha recognized him as a man from the Muslim army, she accepted his help, embarked on his ride, and returned to Medina. Abdullah ibn Ubay Ibn Salul -the leader of the hypocrites- took this opportunity to slander her. He spread terrible rumours about Ayesha and Safwan.

Ayesha grieved for a long time. She was slandered with terrible accusations despite being the wife of the Messenger and the daughter of Abu Bakr –peace be upon them all-. Then Allah proved her innocence through verses of the Quran.

Mustah ibn Atatha was a poor relative of Abu Bakr; Abu Bakr used to help and support him. When Abu Bakr found out that Mustah was among those who joined in the slander of Ayesha, he vowed never to assist him again. Listen to what Allah says about the matter in the following verse:

Those of you possessing affluence and ample wealth should not make oaths that they will not give to their relatives and the very poor and to those who have migrated in the way of Allah. They should rather pardon and overlook. Wouldn't you love for Allah to forgive you? Allah is Ever-Forgiving, Most Merciful. (24:22)

Allah had cleared Aysha from any wrongdoing; moreover, He wants the Muslims to rise to higher moral standards. If you would like to be forgiven by Allah when you do wrong, then shouldn't you forgive those who have wronged you?

This brings us back to the verse: Allah says "Do not, by your oaths, make Allah an obstacle in the way of doing good actions, being mindful of Allah, or putting things right between people." So do not say: "I swore to Allah that I would not help this person; look for someone else to help," because Allah explains that breaking such an oath is better than withholding help from others. Allah –after all- is the Most Forgiving and All-Merciful.

Prophet Muhammad (peace be upon him) said: "He who takes an oath to do something and then finds something more beneficial should do what is better and make expiation for his oath." This is how Allah guards righteousness and promotes reform among people. When you make Allah a barrier between you and doing what is right, you contradict the very foundations of faith.

Allah concludes the verse with: "Allah is All-Hearing, All-Knowing." Allah is warning you that He hears the oaths you make and knows of your intention behind the oaths. He knows if you are deliberately making an oath to use it as an excuse against doing something good, or against fulfilling an obligation towards your family.

Here, a very important ruling should be clarified. When a person makes an oath, is it regarded as a true oath or is it a vain one? It is of Allah's mercy that only true intentional oaths are considered binding and accountable; not vain unintentional oaths. Common oaths in daily expressions and conversation are not binding. For example a mother scolding her child and saying: "I swear to Allah if you bother your sister one more time, I will take your phone away forever!!" Or a hungry man saying "I swear I can eat ten whole pizzas right now." Such expressions are not meant as true oaths as the people did not intend them as factual statements. These common vain oaths —while best to be avoided- are not held by Allah as binding.

VERSE 225

Laa yu'aakhi zukumul laahu billaghwi feee aymaa nikum wa laakiny yu'aakhi zukum bimaa kasabat quloo bukum; wallaahu Ghafoorun Haleem

Allah will not call you to account for what is vain in your oaths, but He will call you to account for what you mean in your hearts. Allah is most forgiving and forbearing.

In the previous ayat, we explained how oaths should not be used as a tool to justify evil or as an excuse to avoid doing good; we also touched on the issue of vain oaths used in common everyday expressions. The verse understudy follows directly to clarify which oaths you are held accountable for. Allah is telling you to nullify and expiate your oath if you see a better path towards good; Allah will accept that from you in exchange for better deeds and proper expiation. He says:

Allah does not call you to account for your inadvertent oaths; but He will take you to task for oaths you make intentionally. The expiation in that case is to feed ten poor people with the average amount you feed your family, or clothe them, or free a slave. Anyone without the means to do so should fast three days. That is the expiation for breaking oaths when you have sworn them. Keep your oaths. In this way Allah makes His Signs clear to you, so that hopefully you will be thankful. (5:89)

There is one kind of oath, however, that there is cannot be expiated for. It is called the immersive oath, or in Arabic 'Yameen Ghamoos.' The reason behind the name 'immersive oath' is that such oath will result in immersion in hellfire. It is an oath that you consciously and deliberately make as a lie to conceal the truth. The best example of such an oath is one taken in court in order to tell a lie. For example, a false witness comes forward, swears to tell the truth and then knowingly, he or she gives false testimony. There is no expiation for an oath purposely used to cause harm and injustice; the only remedy for it is immersion in hellfire. Prophet Muhammad –peace be upon him- asked his companions "would you like to know about the worst of major sins?" they replied, "tell us, messenger of Allah." He said: "there are three: associating partners with Allah; defying one's parents;" then he peace be upon him sat up straight and said "and giving false testimony; giving false testimony." He kept repeating it over and over until we wished he would stop. Allah says:

Allah will not call you to account for what is vain in your oaths, but He will call you to account for what you mean in your hearts.

The Arabic word for 'oaths' is 'yameen.' 'Yameen' which literally means the right hand is the word used for oaths because in the olden days when a person made an oath to a friend, he or she would place the right hand over the friend's right hand. Many of us do the same by shaking the other person's right hand after we make a deal or a promise. The right hand, after all, is the hand that performs most actions in life.

Keep in mind that the right hand possesses no power of its own; rather it is the dominant hand for most people because Allah created it so. Thus, when you find a person preferring to use his or her left hand as the dominant one, do not try to make him or her use the right hand instead. A person created to use his or her left hand cannot help but to do so. Our brains control our movements. As it is well-known, the brain is divided into two similar hemispheres, and each hemisphere controls the movement of one half of the body. Allah creates these connections.

Often, you will find that lefties have excellent artistic abilities and beautiful handwriting; something they can hardly do with the right hand. So do not ask a left-handed child to change and write with his right. There are a few people who are blessed with a brain that equally controls both hands to perform tasks well. Allah has absolute power, and He is capable of making the right hand operate, the left hand operate, making them work together, or making them both disabled. Everything is subject to His will.

Let's get back to the verse under study. Another word for oath in the Arabic language is 'Hilfan' from the root 'hilf.' 'Hilf' means an alliance or a pact. When you take an oath, you are in essence making a commitment to work with another person or group. You divide the work between the parties and assure the other person or group that you will live up to your word. So make sure to respect your word, and keep your oaths. You will be responsible for your word before people and before your Lord. Allah says:

Allah will not call you to account for what is vain in your oaths, but He will call you to account for what you mean in your hearts. Allah is most forgiving and forbearing.

VERSE 226

Lillazeena yu'loona min nisaaa'ihim tarabbusu arba'ati ashhurin fain faaa'oo fa innal laaha Ghafoorur Raheem

For those who vow abstinence from their wives there is a respite of four months. If they go back on their vow, then surely Allah is All-Forgiving, All-Compassionate.

In Arabia, before Islam, men used to employ a tactic to discipline and punish their wives. A man would abstain from having any intimate relations with his wife and deprive her of intimacy for a specified period. This would last for weeks, even months. To ensure that the man's will does not weaken, he would make an oath to avoid intimate relations for the period of his choosing. This oath would act as a further deterrent against his sexual desire. More often than not, at the end of the specified period, the man would make another oath to extend the sexual deprivation for a few more months. This led to the humiliation of the woman and the denial of her marital and sexual rights.

Islam came to restore balance to marriage. Allah did not want to tip the scales in one direction or the other, but to preserve the rights of both the man and the woman. Islam did not completely outlaw this practice because Allah is aware of His creation and common marital problems. Just as men abused their marital responsibilities, a woman might exploit the husband's desire for her to gain advantages and humiliate him. Thus, Allah permitted the husband to abstain from his wife for a maximum of four months during severe marital problems. He says:

For those who vow abstinence from their wives there is a respite of four months. If they go back on their vow, then surely Allah is All-Forgiving, All-Compassionate.

(Chapter 2: Verse 226)

Islam builds a married life on realistic basis, not extremes. It recognizes the power of sexual desires and channels them properly rather than suppress those desires or let them loose. There is a difference between control and suppression. Suppression bottles up the desire for a while, only to make it resurface as a psychological problem or as sexual promiscuity. On the other hand, correctly channeling sexual desires recognizes their force and uses this force towards building families and societies. Take for example our scientific progress that is mainly based on managing and channelling forces of nature. A steam pressure cooker creates pressure within the pot but manages it properly. A vent in the system relieves excess pressure and prevents the pot from exploding while allowing enough pressure to cook your food faster.

Allah has set a precise system to build families on a sound foundation. One of the cornerstones of a healthy family is the shared belief in One Allah and the commitment to follow His teachings. That is why Islam warned Muslims against marrying disbelievers. Allah says in the 221st of Surah Baqarah:

Do not marry the women who associate partners with Allah until they believe. A believing servant-girl is better than a free woman who associates partners with Allah, even though she pleases and attracts you. Nor give your women in marriage to men who associate partners with Allah until they believe. A believing slave is better than a free man who associates partners with Allah, even though he pleases and attracts you.

Another stone in the foundation is the proper channelling of sexual energy for reproduction first and enjoyment second. Allah says in the 222nd verse of Surah Baqarah:

And they ask you about menstruation. Say, 'It is a mild harm, so keep apart from women during menstruation and do not approach them until they have purified themselves. But once they have purified themselves, then go to them in the way that Allah has enjoined on you.'

Islam builds marriages not only on physical attraction and emotions that wane overtime; but also based on shared values and shared goals.

Allah knows that our human nature changes over time. Thus, it is crucial to enter marriage under the light of Allah's teachings. Emotions will cool, beauty will fade, and disputes between couples will inevitably rise. If the conflicts are severe and threaten the family unit, Allah allows for an outlet conducted by the husband to bring order back to the marriage. The husband is allowed to deny the wife from intimacy for a maximum of four months. If the man is unsure that he can resist the sexual urge, he can make an oath to strengthen his resolve. At the same time, Allah promotes love and compassion, not cruelty or score settling. He says: "if they go back on their vow, then surely Allah is All-Forgiving, All-Compassionate." In other words, if the couple resolves their issues and wish to restore intimacy before the end of the oath period, the man can expiate for his oath.

Why four months, you may ask? We answer that four months is a long enough period to solve problems and sort out complex matters, yet it is not too long to cause harm and loss of connection. If the husband exceeds this period, he will become a transgressor outside of Allah's limits. Allah is our Creator; He is best aware of our tendencies, emotions and instincts, and He set sound laws considering all aspects.

Once Omar ibn Al-Khatab –the 2nd Caliphate after the Prophet- was walking on a quiet street in the late hours of the night. He passed by a woman's house and overheard her reciting a poem expressing her loneliness and longing for her husband. Her emotions were about to push her to misbehave, but her fear of Allah held her back. When Omar heard the words of this woman, he was concerned for the well-being of the Muslims society. He went to his daughter Hafsah and asked her: how long can a woman stay apart from her husband? She replied: around four to six months. The next day, Omar issued a ruling stating that soldiers must not stay out on missions for more than four months. While the verse under study was revealed many years before this story, life's circumstances came to prove the wisdom and sound judgment of what Allah had prescribed.

For those who vow abstinence from their wives there is a respite of four months. If they go back on their vow, then surely Allah is All-

Forgiving, All-Compassionate. But if they are determined to divorce, remember that Allah hears and knows all

(Chapter 2: Verses 226

In the previous ayat we discussed how Allah had allowed the man to deprive his wife of intimacy and sexual activity for a maximum of four months when severe problems rock the marriage. The four months period would allow ample time to set things right and solve lingering issues. Moreover, if the underlying issues are solved, the man can reinitiate intimate relations sooner, even if that means breaking an oath. Allah, after all, wants us to have the priority of compassionate, healthy family.

But what if four months had passed and the husband continues to abstain from his wife? We answer that at that point the man would be a transgressor against Allah's teachings. He can be ordered by a judge to return to his wife or to divorce her. If the husband refuses to do so, then the judge can force a divorce.

VERSE 227

Wa in 'azamut talaaqa fa innal laaha Samee'un 'Aleem

But if they are determined to divorce, remember that Allah hears and knows all

There has been some disagreement among the scholars regarding the type of divorce forced by a judge when the husband refuses to restore marital relations after four months. Is it a revocable divorce that can be overturned if the issues are resolved? Or is it an irrevocable divorce? Revocable divorce means that the husband has the choice to restore the marriage if he chooses without the need for a new contract; while an irrevocable divorce requires a new marriage contract along with a dowry.

We answer that in cases where intimate relations have been cut off for more than four months, the divorce is irrevocable requiring a new contract with a dowry if the couple decides to reconcile. If a prior divorce had happened –meaning if the same couple has been divorced twice before the current problem- then this would be a third and final divorce in which the couple cannot remarry each other even with a new contract. The only way they can get back together after three divorces is for the woman to marry another man via a genuine contract. We say 'genuine contract' to discourage those who make a mockery of Allah's teachings by entering into a marriage contract with another man and divorce immediately in order to go back to the old husband. The ex-husband is only allowed to re-marry his thrice-divorced wife after he suffers jealousy of her marriage to another man. Allah explains:

If a husband re-divorces his wife after the second divorce, she will not be lawful for him until she has taken another husband; if that one divorces her, there will be no blame if she and the first husband return to one another, provided they feel that they can keep within the bounds set by Allah. These are Allah's bounds, which He makes clear for those who know. (02:230)

Islam is a practical religion that gives the Muslim couple time to calm anger and think through their problems. Islam provides the man with tools to bring order to the household. But it does not give the man a free-hand in discipline or allow him to be a tyrant at home.

When you study the position of Islam on divorce, you find it to be realistic and appropriate for the human condition. We are creatures of ever-changing emotions. And while a couple may enter into marriage guided by love and physical attraction; these feelings inevitably wane with time. Life will put the couple through situations that they did not consider at the time of marriage. Once the intimate desire is satisfied, the man and woman may realize that there is little compatibility between them. For example, the husband may find that his wife's ethics are lacking. Or the woman may find that her husband is looking outside the marriage for other relationships. We also see problems regarding greed and materialism where the wife demands more and more and does not care if the husband earns his livelihood form unlawful means. Sadly, there are also problems of the man being physically or verbally abusive towards the wife. Whatever the situation may be, a schism may arise that does not allow the couple to live harmoniously under one roof. It is for such reasons that Islam allows divorce and set up specific legislation to manage life's difficulties.

VERSE 228

Walmutallaqaatu yatarab basna bi anfusihinna salaasata qurooo'; wa laa yahillu lahunna ai yaktumna maa khalaqal laahu feee arhaaminhinna in kunna yu'minna billaahi wal yawmil aakhir; wa bu'oola tuhunna ahaqqu biraddihinna fee zaalika in araadooo islaahaa; wa lahunna mislul lazee alaihinna bilma'roof; wa lirrijjaali 'alaihinna daraja; wallaahu 'Azeezun Hakeem

Divorced women keep themselves in waiting for three menstrual cycles, and it is not lawful for them, if they believe in Allah and the Last Day, to conceal what Allah has created in their wombs. In such time their husbands have better right to take them back, if they desire a settlement. According to customary good and honourable norms, women have rights similar to those against them, but men have a degree above them. Allah is All-Mighty, All-Wise. (Chapter 2: Verse 228)

Let's start with the phrase: "Divorced women keep themselves in waiting for three menstrual cycles." Take note that this ruling did not come in the form of a command, rather it was in the form of a descriptive statement. In other words, Allah did not say that 'divorced women should wait for three menstrual cycles,' but He –The -All-wise- said: "Divorced women keep themselves in waiting for three menstrual cycles" as if the matter is already settled. This style of speech delivers a powerful command and places more emphasis on what Allah wants. How, you may ask? We answer that an informative statement means that when the Almighty commands, the command is accepted and implemented by the believers without any hesitation. The command instantly becomes a reality that can be used to describe the believers. Thus, instead of issuing an order for the newly divorced believing woman to wait 3 months before remarrying, Allah described how a believing woman behaves.

We can also look at the same statement from another angle: When Allah informs us that "Divorced women keep themselves in waiting for three menstrual cycles," we have a choice to follow Allah teachings and be faithful to Allah's words; or to go against Allah's description and suffer tremendous loss.

Let's take another example from the Quran where Allah issued a command in the form of a descriptive statement. He says:

Corrupt women are for corrupt men, and corrupt men are for corrupt women; good women are for good men and good men are for good women. The good are absolved of what has been said against them; they will have forgiveness and a generous provision. (24:26)

This verse, although delivered in an informative form, is a command that can be obeyed or disobeyed. So when Allah says "corrupt men are for corrupt women; good women are for good men," it does not imply that this is the way things are; instead it implies that this is the way the believers ought to behave. Here is another example from the Quran. Allah says in the 97th verse of chapter 3:

there are clear signs in it; it is the place where Abraham stood to pray; whoever enters it is safe.

Here, Allah is instructing the believers to make the Sacred Mosque in Mecca a safe sanctuary for people. However, some people disobey Allah and harm those who enter the Sacred House; such people are outside the realm of faith at that time.

This brings us back to the verse. The descriptive statement: "Divorced women keep themselves in waiting for three menstrual cycles" is a mandate which is obeyed by those who believe in Allah. Take note that Allah did not say 'Divorced women wait for three menstrual cycles'; rather He used the phrase "Divorced women keep themselves in waiting." What is the difference? We answer that the wording of "keep themselves in waiting" acknowledges an inner struggle within the woman where a part of her wants to prove herself as a desirable woman, while another part of her wants to follow Allah's teachings. In other words, a woman that ended a failed relationship or was rejected by her husband often has a need to feel wanted by other men, yet she has to fight that urge and wait the prescribed three months.

The phrase "for three menstrual cycles" is translated from the Arabic origin "thalathatu quroo." "Quroo" is the plural of "qar" which could mean either menstruation or the time between two menstrual cycles. So which one is it? We answer that the verse used the number 'three' 'thalathatu' which is a form only used when the subject being counted is masculine. Had the subject being counted been feminine, the proper number three to use would be 'thalathu.' In the Arabic language, menstruation 'Hyda' is grammatically feminine, while 'Tuhr' which is the period between menstruations is grammatically masculine. Hence, "for three menstrual cycles" is referring to three consecutive 'tuhr' purities between menstruations.

The long wait of three months ensures that the woman is not bearing children in her womb from the marriage; a three month-period also gives the couple time to rethink their situation. They may want to return to each other.

That is why Allah immediately warns: "and it is not lawful for them, if they believe in Allah and the Last Day, to conceal what Allah has created in their wombs." What is the meaning of creation? Creation is to produce something new which was non-existent. In the case of a woman's womb, something new which was non-existent may either be a pregnancy or menstruation. The woman is obligated to tell her divorcing husband in either case.

Allah specified the waiting period for pregnant women in the 65th verse of chapter 4:

the waiting period of those who are pregnant will be until they deliver their burden: Allah makes things easy for those who are mindful of Him.

So women who are in menopause and no longer have regular cycles must wait three months, and the same will apply to women who are not menstruating.

"and it is not lawful for them, if they believe in Allah and the Last Day, to conceal what Allah has created in their wombs" means that the woman is required to announce if she is pregnant or menstruating to her divorcing husband. Concealment of her status is a great sin especially in the case of pregnancy. A woman may be tempted hide her pregnancy so she would not have to wait nine months to marry another man. In such case, the child may be wrongly attributed to the new husband. Pregnancy typically lasts for nine months, but there are instances where a seven or even a six-month pregnant woman delivers. This variation gives the woman the opportunity to hide her pregnancy, get married and give birth claiming a short pregnancy, thus, maliciously attributing the child to the wrong man.

Here a story comes to mind. A woman was brought to the Caliph Othman (may Allah be pleased with him) because she gave birth after only being married for six months. Othman wanted to punish her for adultery. Ali Ibn Abi Talib intervened and said: You punish her for adultery just because she gave birth after six months? Haven't you heard what Allah has said? Othman asked: What did Allah say? Imam Ali recited:

Mothers suckle their children for two whole years, if they wish to complete the term, and clothing and maintenance must be borne by the father in a fair manner. No one should be burdened with more than they can bear: no mother shall be made to suffer harm on account of her child, nor any father on account of his. (from 02:233)

That is, a mother can breastfeed her newborn for twenty-four months. Then Imam Ali recited another verse:

We have commanded man to be good to his parents: his mother struggled to carry him and struggled to give birth to him- his bearing and weaning took a full thirty months. (from 46:15)

If we take the twenty-four months, which is the total duration of breast-feeding from the first verse, then we subtract them from the thirty months that combine pregnancy and breastfeeding in the second verse, we understand that pregnancy may be only six months. After hearing these verses, Othman (may Allah be pleased with him) said: "By Allah, I did not pay attention to this."

VERSE 228

Walmutallaqaatu yatarab basna bi anfusihinna salaasata qurooo'; wa laa yahillu lahunna ai yaktumna maa khalaqal laahu feee arhaaminhinna in kunna yu'minna billaahi wal yawmil aakhir; wa bu'oola tuhunna ahaqqu biraddihinna fee zaalika in araadooo islaahaa; wa lahunna mislul lazee alaihinna bilma'roof; wa lirrijjaali 'alaihinna daraja; wallaahu 'Azeezun Hakeem

Divorced women keep themselves in waiting for three menstrual cycles, and it is not lawful for them, if they believe in Allah and the Last Day, to conceal what Allah has created in their wombs. In such time their husbands have better right to take them back, if they desire a settlement. According to customary good and honourable norms, women have rights similar to those against them, but men have a degree above them. Allah is All-Mighty, All-Wise. (Chapter 2: Verse 228)

Let's start with the phrase: "Divorced women keep themselves in waiting for three menstrual cycles." Take note that this ruling did not come in the form of a command, rather it was in the form of a descriptive statement. In other words, Allah did not say that 'divorced women should wait for three menstrual cycles,' but He –The -All-wise- said: "Divorced women keep themselves in waiting for three menstrual cycles" as if the matter is already settled. This style of speech delivers a powerful command and places more emphasis on what Allah wants. How, you may ask? We answer that an informative statement means that when the Almighty commands, the command is accepted and implemented by the believers without any hesitation. The command instantly becomes a reality that can be used to describe the believers. Thus, instead of issuing an order for the newly divorced believing woman to wait 3 months before remarrying, Allah described how a believing woman behaves.

We can also look at the same statement from another angle: When Allah informs us that "Divorced women keep themselves in waiting for three menstrual cycles," we have a choice to follow Allah teachings and be faithful to Allah's words; or to go against Allah's description and suffer tremendous loss.

Let's take another example from the Quran where Allah issued a command in the form of a descriptive statement. He says:

Corrupt women are for corrupt men, and corrupt men are for corrupt women; good women are for good men and good men are for good women. The good are absolved of what has been said against them; they will have forgiveness and a generous provision. (24:26)

This verse, although delivered in an informative form, is a command that can be obeyed or disobeyed. So when Allah says "corrupt men are for corrupt women; good women are for good men," it does not imply that this is the way things are; instead it implies that this is the way the believers ought to behave. Here is another example from the Quran. Allah says in the 97th verse of chapter 3:

there are clear signs in it; it is the place where Abraham stood to pray; whoever enters it is safe.

Here, Allah is instructing the believers to make the Sacred Mosque in Mecca a safe sanctuary for people. However, some people disobey Allah and harm those who enter the Sacred House; such people are outside the realm of faith at that time.

This brings us back to the verse. The descriptive statement: "Divorced women keep themselves in waiting for three menstrual cycles" is a mandate which is obeyed by those who believe in Allah. Take note that Allah did not say 'Divorced women wait for three menstrual cycles'; rather He used the phrase "Divorced women keep themselves in waiting." What is the difference? We answer that the wording of "keep themselves in waiting" acknowledges an inner struggle within the woman where a part of her wants to prove herself as a desirable woman, while another part of her wants to follow Allah's teachings. In other words, a woman that ended a failed relationship or was rejected by her husband often has a need to feel wanted by other men, yet she has to fight that urge and wait the prescribed three months.

The phrase "for three menstrual cycles" is translated from the Arabic origin "thalathatu quroo." "Quroo" is the plural of "qar" which could mean either menstruation or the time between two menstrual cycles. So which one is it? We answer that the verse used the number 'three' 'thalathatu' which is a form only used when the subject being counted is masculine. Had the subject being counted been feminine, the proper number three to use would be 'thalathu.' In the Arabic language, menstruation 'Hyda' is grammatically feminine, while 'Tuhr' which is the period between menstruations is grammatically masculine. Hence, "for three menstrual cycles" is referring to three consecutive 'tuhr' purities between menstruations.

The long wait of three months ensures that the woman is not bearing children in her womb from the marriage; a three month-period also gives the couple time to rethink their situation. They may want to return to each other.

That is why Allah immediately warns: "and it is not lawful for them, if they believe in Allah and the Last Day, to conceal what Allah has created in their wombs." What is the meaning of creation? Creation is to produce something new which was non-existent. In the case of a woman's womb, something new which was non-existent may either be a pregnancy or menstruation. The woman is obligated to tell her divorcing husband in either case.

Allah specified the waiting period for pregnant women in the 65th verse of chapter 4:

the waiting period of those who are pregnant will be until they deliver their burden: Allah makes things easy for those who are mindful of Him.

So women who are in menopause and no longer have regular cycles must wait three months, and the same will apply to women who are not menstruating.

"and it is not lawful for them, if they believe in Allah and the Last Day, to conceal what Allah has created in their wombs" means that the woman is required to announce if she is pregnant or menstruating to her divorcing husband. Concealment of her status is a great sin especially in the case of pregnancy. A woman may be tempted hide her pregnancy so she would not have to wait nine months to marry another man. In such case, the child may be wrongly attributed to the new husband. Pregnancy typically lasts for nine months, but there are instances where a seven or even a six-month pregnant woman delivers. This variation gives the woman the opportunity to hide her pregnancy, get married and give birth claiming a short pregnancy, thus, maliciously attributing the child to the wrong man.

Here a story comes to mind. A woman was brought to the Caliph Othman (may Allah be pleased with him) because she gave birth after only being married for six months. Othman wanted to punish her for adultery. Ali Ibn Abi Talib intervened and said: You punish her for adultery just because she gave birth after six months? Haven't you heard what Allah has said? Othman asked: What did Allah say? Imam Ali recited:

Mothers suckle their children for two whole years, if they wish to complete the term, and clothing and maintenance must be borne by the father in a fair manner. No one should be burdened with more than they can bear: no mother shall be made to suffer harm on account of her child, nor any father on account of his. (from 02:233)

That is, a mother can breastfeed her newborn for twenty-four months. Then Imam Ali recited another verse:

We have commanded man to be good to his parents: his mother struggled to carry him and struggled to give birth to him- his bearing and weaning took a full thirty months. (from 46:15)

If we take the twenty-four months, which is the total duration of breast-feeding from the first verse, then we subtract them from the thirty months that combine pregnancy and breastfeeding in the second verse, we understand that pregnancy may be only six months. After hearing these verses, Othman (may Allah be pleased with him) said: "By Allah, I did not pay attention to this."

Divorced women keep themselves in waiting for three menstrual cycles, and it is not lawful for them, if they believe in Allah and the Last Day, to conceal what Allah has created in their wombs. In such time their husbands have better right to take them back, if they desire a settlement. According to customary good and honourable norms, women have rights similar to those against them, but men have a degree above them. Allah is All-Mighty, All-Wise. (Chapter 2: Verse 228)

In the previous session, we explained the wisdom behind Allah's instruction for divorced women to "keep themselves in waiting for three menstrual cycles, and it is not lawful for them, if they believe in Allah and the Last Day, to conceal what Allah has created in their wombs." Under no circumstance should a pregnant woman in the process of divorce claim that she is not pregnant in order to marry another man. Such a lie would attribute the child to the new husband and create many issues and injustices. Here are just a few examples: the child will not be able to inherit from his or her true father; the child's true relatives would be considered strangers, and strangers would be falsely considered relatives. In the future, this child might unknowingly marry someone who is a close blood relative —such as a biological brother or sister- and so on. As for the new husband, the child acquires illegitimate rights from him. He or she would inherit from him and so on. Allah says: "it is not lawful for them, if they believe in Allah and the Last Day, to conceal what Allah has created in their wombs." Allah wants life to be based on purity and honour where no one transgresses the right of another.

The issue of concealing what is in the womb does not only apply to childbearing; it also applies to menstruation. Why, you may ask? We answer that it is not permissible for a divorcing woman to conceal her menstruation in order to falsely put the man under the impression that she is pregnant. This would allow her to prolong the period of waiting in hopes of getting back with him.

Allah says: "if they believe in Allah and the Last Day." What do faith in Allah and the last day have to do with matters of pregnancy and menstruation? We answer that there is a close relationship between faith and Islamic laws because pregnancy and menstruation are hidden matters that cannot be governed by law; thus it is the woman's faith that governs her honesty in such private matters.

Allah continues: "In such time their husbands have better right to take them back, if they desire a settlement." The waiting period gives the husband the right to reconcile, take back his wife, and reunite the family. It is an implied part of the marriage contract that the woman should comply in such cases to preserve the family. Thus, Allah used the phrase 'better right' because it supersedes the rights of others. But in cases where the waiting period has expired, the woman and her guardians have the choice to accept or refuse. A new contract, dowry, and consent are required.

Perhaps the most crucial issue to note here is that Allah stipulated that "husbands have better right to take them back, if they desire a settlement." Allah made the desire for settlement and reconciliation a pre-condition for the couple to return to each other. Since intentions are unseen, this condition comes as a warning to the husband. If the husband, for example, plans to bring the woman back into marriage to cause her harm or prevent her from moving on with her life, Allah Almighty will punish him for being unjust to her. The husband has the right to return to his wife only if he is sincere in his desire to provide a healthy environment for a marriage. Under Islamic law, the judiciary gives the man the right to go back to his wife regardless of what he conceals within himself. But if he intends evil, then he will bear the heavy burden of his actions before Allah.

The verse then continues: "women have rights similar to those against them, but men have a degree above them." What rights is the verse referring to? We answer that married life is a life of shared rights and responsibilities according to the nature of women and men. There is the right of intimate relations which is equally shared between the man and the woman. Each has the right to this, and the responsibility of providing. The man has further responsibilities. He is to work, earn a living, and provide for his family according to his means; while the woman is required to provide a comfortable and peaceful home for the husband. Allah says:

And among His signs is that He has created for you, from yourselves, mates, that you may incline towards them and find rest in them, and He has engendered love and tenderness between you. Surely in this are signs for people who reflect. (30:21)

The phrase "find rest in them" is translated from the Arabic origin "Taskunu." The root "sakan" means stillness -the opposite of movement-. In other words, the man works and moves about to earn a living, then returns to his wife to rest. He is responsible for providing, and the woman has the right to be provided for. The woman has the responsibility of providing a comfortable home, compassion, and kindness, which the husband has a right to. Thus, life burdens are distributed equitably; your rights are the responsibilities of your spouse and vice-versa.

The verse continues: "But men have a degree above them," which is the degree of authority and guardianship. The degree of authority is something we need in all aspects of life. Any meeting of a group of people requires a person to preside over and organize. Similarly, any operation –regardless of how small- requires a person to manage it. This authority –if appropriately practiced- is a heavy burden. It is not a position to slack off, abuse, or dominate others.

In fact, it is perfectly reasonable for a husband to follow his wife's instructions regarding home duties and her personal affairs. The woman has her domain, so does the man. Aysha - may Allah be pleased with her- was asked: "What was the Prophet like at home?" She answered: "He was always in the service of his family. He would milk the goat, repair and wash his garments and shoes, and he would always serve himself."

The husband has a degree above the wife because of his work outside the home and his responsibility to provide for the family. Allah says in the 34th verse of chapter 4:Men are the guardians of women, because of the advantage Allah has granted some of them over others, and by virtue of their spending out of their wealth.

Here we should pay careful attention to the words Allah used to end the verse. He says: "Allah is All-Mighty, All-Wise." Within these terms is a warning to men. How, you may ask? We answer that Allah is the creator of men and women, and Allah takes care of His creation without discrimination. He is the All-Wise, and through His wisdom, he allocated rights and responsibilities. He granted men a degree over women through their spending, and their authority to manage the family unit. However, the man must always keep in mind that Allah is the Almighty who cannot be overcome. If the man abuses his authority or abuses his wealth to degrade and humiliate his wife, Allah –the Almighty- will retaliate for the woman. If the man practices his degree above the woman to be a tyrant, then Allah –the Almighty- has ultimate power and authority. Similarly, if the woman abuses her responsibilities or considers her sexuality and intimacy as a favour that she can use against her husband, then Allah –the Almighty- will penalize her for her actions.

VERSE 229

Attalaaqu marrataani fa imsaakum bima'roofin aw tasreehum bi ihsaan; wa laa yahillu lakum an taakhuzoo mimmaaa aataitumoohunna shai'an illaaa ai yakhaafaaa alla yuqeemaa hudoodallahi fa in khiftum allaa yuqeemaa hudoodal laahi falaa junaaha 'Alaihimaa feemaf tadat bihee tilka hudoodul laahi falaa ta'tadoohaa; wa mai yata'adda hudoodal laahi fa ulaaa'ika humuzzaa limoon

Divorce is twice; then, the wife may be retained honourably with courtesy or released with good will. It is not lawful for you to keep anything you have given them unless a couple fears that they will not remain within Allah's limits. If you fear that they will not remain within Allah's limits, there is no blame in the wife ransoming herself with some of what she received. These are Allah's limits, so do not overstep them. Those who overstep Allah's limits are wrongdoers.

In the previous verse Allah spoke of the waiting period and how the divorcing couple can get back together. In this verse, Allah informs us of the act of divorce and its rulings. The word divorce –translated from the Arabic origin 'talaq'- has the meanings of departure, liberty, and the undoing of a strong knot or a binding contract. This should alert you to the importance of the relationship of marriage.

Allah wants ease for us even in solving complex issues. He permitted the undoing of marriage contracts in a way different from initiating the contracts. Tying the knot in marriage requires a proposal from the man to the woman and her guardian –in most cases her father- and acceptance from them in the presence of witnesses. Allah has advised us to choose our life partners carefully and to take the consequences of this relationship into consideration. Think about your mate as the caretaker for your future children. But the process of divorce is different. Married life has its problems and stresses. Sometimes, people get worked up and overreact. A man may be unable to control himself and may divorce for a small and trivial reason only to regret it later. Allah wants people to be patient and careful before undoing the knot of marriage. Thus, He Almighty said: "Divorce is twice." But most of us know that for a divorce to be finalized, it has to happen three times. A man asked Prophet Muhammad: "the Almighty said: "divorce is twice," how come we have to do it three times?" He –peace be upon him- replied: "read the verse in its entirety. Allah said: "then, the wife may be retained honourably with courtesy or released with good will."

Thus, the phrase: "divorce is twice" means that the man has the say in the initial two divorces, but after the third divorce, the choice is not up to him anymore. Why? Because after the third divorce, the matter is irrevocable and the couple cannot get back together. Allah says:

If a man divorces her again, she becomes unlawful for him until she has married another man. (From 02:230)

Here, we should address a common problem. When a man says to his wife "I divorce you thrice" is it considered a single divorce or not? We answer that time is an essential element in the occurrence of divorce. When a man divorces his wife, a period of time has to pass before he can divorce her again, making it two divorces. Thereafter, a period of time has to pass yet again before the choice in this verse comes into effect: "then, the wife may be retained honourably with courtesy or released with good will." The verse makes the matter clear: A divorce pronounced threefold in one incident does not result in three divorces, rather, it is considered as one divorce. The wisdom behind spreading divorce over three episodes is to give the couple ample time to reconsider. If we accept a divorcing man's words "I divorce you thrice" as legitimate, then there would be no chance for reconciliation; marital life would be destroyed in a moment of rage. But the value of Allah's legislation lies in distributing divorce over a number of incidents, so the couple would have a chance to review their situation. Often the feelings of regret and the desire to return to each other prevail. Moreover, a single incident of divorce is a tool that can help correct significant flaws in behaviour. The fear of losing one's family in a second or third divorce is a great motivator to tackle serious problems. Allowing a man to issue divorce three times at once destroys the family and negates the wisdom of Allah's ruling.

The verse continues: "It is not lawful for you to keep anything you have given them." The husband must give a dowry at the time of marriage as a token for intimacy. If divorce occurs, the husband is not permitted to take back the dowry. Allah, however, made an exception in this matter; He says: "unless a couple fears that they will not remain within Allah's limits. If you fear that they will not remain within Allah's limits, there is no blame in the wife ransoming herself with some of what she received." Allah –the All-Merciful- wants to give the woman a way out if she was the subject of harm and abuse. Allah explained that the woman is allowed to ransom herself by giving some of the dowry money back if she is afraid that the man is not in observance of Allah's limits. It is discouraged, however, to increase the amount above the dowry unless the violation towards the woman is grave.

Here we recall the incident of Jamila, the sister of Abdullah ibn Ubay, at the time of the Prophet. She was married to of Abdullah bin Qais. She came to the Messenger –peace be upon him- and said: "I do not accuse my husband of any character flaw, any moral defects, or any violation of religion. But I do not like to live a lie in Islam." She meant to express that she did not have any emotional feelings towards her husband, and she was worried about not being able to fulfill his marital rights. Jamila was afraid of being an ungrateful partner to her husband. Prophet Muhammad enquired further to make sure he understood the underlying issue. She said: "I looked at him coming in the company of a few men. He had the darkest complexion, the shortest stature, and the ugliest face." The Prophet said to her: "Will you give his garden dowry back to him?" She said: "If he wants an increase, I will give him more." He peace be upon him answered: "there is no need to increase, but return his garden."

This event is an example of emancipation where the woman withdraws herself from the marriage when she fears that she would not hold true to her marital duties. She can divorce her husband by paying him back an amount –typically the dowry- to protect him from loss. He may want to marry another woman, and he may not have the means to pay a new dowry. Allah says: "It is not lawful for you to keep anything you have given them unless a couple fears that they will not remain within Allah's limits. If you fear that they will not remain within Allah's limits, there is no blame in the wife ransoming herself with some of what she received." Take note that Allah specified the "couple" in the first part of the verse, then said "If you fear" in the second part. Logically, the verse should have read: "if they fear." Instead, the phrase "If you fear" is referring to the responsibility of the parents, guardians, and the community as a whole in helping families going through difficulty.

Divorce is twice; then, the wife may be retained honourably with courtesy or released with good will. It is not lawful for you to keep anything you have given them unless a couple fears that they will not remain within Allah's limits. If you fear that they will not remain within Allah's limits, there is no blame in the wife ransoming herself with some of what she received. These are Allah's limits, so do not overstep them. Those who overstep Allah's limits are wrongdoers. (Chapter 2: Verse 229)

Allah's limits are the barrier between what is permissible and what is prohibited. Thus, Allah's limits come as prohibitions or as commands. It is interesting to note that when Allah talks about His limits after issuing a command, He says: "These are Allah's limits, so do not overstep them." But when Allah talks about His limits after issuing a prohibition, He says: "These are Allah's limits, so do not come near them." Why the difference, you may ask? We answer that Allah –the All-Merciful- wants to not only to protect you from sin, but also from the allure of sin. He knows that you have desires that may intensify if you approach what is prohibited, so He advises you not to even go near sin.

Prophet Muhammad –peace be upon him- explained this to us. He said: "That which is lawful is clear, and that which is unlawful is also clear. Between the two are doubtful matters. Whoever stirs away from these matters has guarded himself and his faith. And whoever wanders around them is bound to fall into prohibitions. Just like a shepherd who pastures around a king's sanctuary, grazing right on the king's borders. Verily, every king has a sanctuary, and Allah's sanctuary are His prohibitions."

So, Allah's limits include His prohibitions and commandments and these come in the form of "do" and "do not do." As a believer, you have the responsibility of keeping all your actions within these limits. Once you start doing what you are not supposed to do, or ignoring what you are supposed to do, your life goes out of balance. When more and more people ignore Allah's teachings, the balance of the entire society is disturbed. Injustice becomes common because people lose respect for the rights of others.

When it comes to social issues –such as divorce-, Allah's teachings are designed to prevent the society from falling into social diseases. Even if we assume that legislators have the best of intentions when they make family laws, we understand the limitations of their knowledge and experience. We -humans- can only look at our current circumstances and learn from our previous experiences; but what if something unpredictable occurs –which often does-? What will happen to the laws on the books? These deficient laws would need to be changed. In such cases, if the legislators are truly sincere, they would rise above their pride and say: "we will amend the law to address what we have missed in the past." Meanwhile, many people may suffer until the deficiency is recognized and corrected. If the legislators are stubborn and self-righteous, then the whole society would suffer.

We must understand the difference between our desire to do what is right, and our ability to do what is right. We legislate based on our limited knowledge and skills, and the society often suffers under conflicting theories and emerging social experiments.

When it comes to material sciences, all are in agreement. These sciences are proven in the lab with reproducible empirical evidence. Scientists toil and invest time and money testing different theories in the laboratory until they come up with scientifically reliable results. The entire society benefits from the hard work of a few. On the other hand, social and legal theories are often based on impulsive arguments. The prevailing unproven theory of the time is often implemented on an unsuspecting society through laws. It is the people and the society who suffer from the mistakes of a few lawmakers. This may go on for decades until a just legislator comes and makes adjustments to rectify the mishaps of the previous legislators.

Allah's law protects us from suffering because it frees us from the cycle of social theories and legal experimentation. The laboratories of material sciences are free from the influence of personal whims and desires. This is not true in social and legal opinions where there is a struggle for power, wealth, and influence. Thus, Allah took over the legislation of social matters to ensure that societies do not suffer from the mistakes and whims of a few. Our modern world is rife with problems stemming from greed. Dealing with such issues where people are exploited and marginalized often leads to violence and wars. Allah is our creator, He is free of need, and He does not benefit from the legislation. He has ultimate power and does not need anything from us. Thus, Allah's legislation is fair; it is for our benefit, and it does not require experimentation.

Someone asked:

Why didn't Islam prevail over all other religions as you claim in the Quran? He was implying that billions of people are not Muslim and referring to the following verses: Allah says:

He is the One Who has sent His Messenger with the guidance and the Religion of truth that He may make it prevail over all religions, however detested this may be to those who associate partners with Allah. (9:33)

He it is Who has sent His Messenger with the Divine guidance and the Religion of truth that He may make it prevail over all religions. Allah suffices for a witness (48:28)

The answer:

"You have to pay attention to the entire verse, not just part of it. Islam is not meant to be the sole religion of the world. The phrase: "however detested this may be to those who associate partners with Allah" suggests that Islam will always be at a time when non-believers and polytheists exist. Had there not been any disbelievers, the verse would be wrong. The real power of Allah's teachings is often observed when non-Muslim legislators resort to Islamic rulings when their system fails. They emulate Allah's teachings not as a religion but as a guide to set the laws right. Their application of Islamic disciplines further confirms the validity of Islam. Of course, if these rulings were adopted as religious teachings, the legislators would be accused of fanaticism. But despite their hatred for the religion of Islam, they are often forced by life's circumstances to mimic its teachings because they happen to be the best solutions.

I'll give you an example here. The Catholic Church did not allow divorce and considered it against a woman's right. But the circumstances of life and marital problems forced them to rethink the rulings related to divorce. Did they become lenient towards divorce because Islam had permitted it? Of course not, they became lenient because they found it to be the best solution. Hence, the verse "He is the One Who has sent His Messenger with the guidance and the Religion of truth that He may make it prevail over all religions, however detested this may be to those who associate partners with Allah" means that non-Muslims will have to resort to the Islamic system to resolve their issues, even if they do not accept Islam as a religion."

It is a testament to Islam's teachings that even non-believers who may hate and fight against it still take from its principles to reform corruption in their communities. These 14-century-old teachings are used to solve modern problems in modern societies. This is what is meant by Allah's words:

He is the One Who has sent His Messenger with the guidance and the Religion of truth that He may make it prevail over all religions, however detested this may be to those who associate partners with Allah. (9:33)

VERSES 230

Fa in tallaqahaa falaa tahillu lahoo mim ba'du hattaa tankiha zawjan ghairah; fa in tallaqahaa falaa junaaha 'alaihimaaa ai yataraaja'aaa in zannaaa ai yuqeemaa hudoodal laa; wa tilka hudoodul laahi yubaiyinuhaa liqawminy ya'lamoon

**If a husband re-divorces his wife after the second divorce, she will not be lawful for him until she has taken another husband; if the latter husband divorces her, there will be no blame if she and the first husband return to one another, provided they feel that they can keep within the bounds set by Allah. These are Allah's bounds, which He makes clear for those who know.
(Chapter 2: Verse 230)**

In verse 229, Allah mentioned that "divorce is twice" and continued: "then, the wife may be retained honourably with courtesy or released with good will." In verse 230, Allah is elaborating on the issue of "release with good will." He says: "If a husband re-divorces his wife after the second divorce, she will not be lawful for him until she has taken another husband."

This shows that when matters between the couple escalate into an on again, off again marriage, there is a point from which there is no return. In other words, they must be taught a harsh lesson by making it extremely difficult for the couple to get back together. Allah permitted reconciliation after the first and second divorces; He also allowed a reunion after the waiting period is over with a new contract and dowry. But the third divorce has no revocation. The only way to get back to each other would be for the woman to properly marry another man, live with him, and then get a divorce.

Some people try to go around Allah's teachings. They believe that a woman who has been divorced three times can ceremonially marry another man; this marriage is followed by a quick divorce so the woman can go back to her ex-husband. We answer that such practices are not recognized in Islam. Marrying another man with the intention of going back to re-marry the ex-husband is prohibited. This sort of sham marriage does not absolve the woman from the requirement to marry another man before returning to her former husband. Allah says: "she will not be lawful for him until she has taken another husband; if the latter husband divorces her, there will be no blame if she and the first husband return to one another."

A proper marriage with the full intention of living together is required. The marriage should be the result of the couple meeting under normal circumstances –not for ulterior motives-. If this marriage fails, and the divorce happens for legitimate reasons, then the woman and the ex-husband can get back together in a new marriage contract. Allah further stipulates: "there will be no blame if she and the first husband return to one another, provided they feel that they can keep within the bounds set by Allah." In other words, the couple can get back together given that the previous issues that lead to their divorce have been appropriately resolved.

VERSE 231

Wa izaa tallaqtumun nisaaa'a fabalaghna ajala hunna fa amsikoohunna bima'roofin law sarrihoo hunna bima'roof; wa laa tumsikoo hunna diraa rallita'tadoo; wa mai yaf'al zaalika faqad zalama nafsah; wa laa tattakhizooo aayaatillaahi huzuwaa; wazkuroo ni'matal laahi 'alaikum wa maaa anzala 'alaikum minal kitaabi wal hikmati ya'izukum bih; wattaqul laaha wa'lamooo annal laaha bikulli shai'in 'Aleem

When you divorce women and they have reached the end of their term, then either keep them in a fair manner or release them in a fair manner. Do not hold on to them with intent to harm them and commit aggression: anyone who does this wrongs himself. Do not make a mockery of Allah's revelations; remember the favour He blessed you with, and the Scripture and wisdom He sent to teach you. Be mindful of Allah and know that He has full knowledge of everything.
(Chapter 2: Verse 231)

Let's study the phrase: "and they have reached the end of their term." We ask: Once the term of the waiting period has ended, is there even an option of retaining according to honourable terms? Or is releasing the only option? We answer that the verb "reached" translated from the Arabic origin "balaghna can have one of two meanings: It could mean getting very close to the end -almost reaching your goal-, or it could mean that you have already reached the end and passed the finish line. For example, if you are traveling to visit a friend in Istanbul, you may send your friend a message stating that 'you have arrived' as soon as you enter the city borders, although you have not reached your friend's home yet. Here is another example from the Quran; Allah says in the 6th verse of chapter 5:

O you who have faith! When you stand up for prayer, wash your faces and your hands up to the elbows, and wipe a part of your heads and your feet, up to the ankles.

The intended meaning here is not to do ablution as you are in prayer, but to do it right before you pray. Similarly, in the verse under study, the phrase "When you divorce women and they have reached the end of their term" could mean 'as the waiting period is about to end,' or it could mean 'as the term have actually ended.' The intended meaning can be understood from the context of the verse.

Let's look at the context. Allah says "When you divorce women and they have reached the end of their term, then either keep them in a fair manner or release them in a fair manner." Here we understand that the man has divorced his wife, but her waiting period did not end yet; it is near completion. There is still a choice either to end the marriage on honourable terms or to get back together on honourable terms. Allah wants to keep the door of reconciliation open until the very last minute. The man can reconsider and bring back the family unit preserving a home for the children.

More importantly, Allah wants the couple to solve their own problems. In the very next verse He says: "When you divorce women and they have reached the end of their term, do not prevent them from remarrying their husbands if they both agree to do so in a fair manner." Allah leaves the decision for separation or getting back together exclusively in the hands of the couple with no outside interference. Why, you may ask? We answer that, more often than not, when a third party interferes, the situation is aggravated. People such as parents or siblings do not have the emotional connection the couple shares. They do not consider the intimacy and tenderness of the husband towards his wife, or the wife towards her husband. These emotional, psychological, and physical matters play a significant role in solving marital problems. A man who is attracted to his wife's beauty may forget about their problems. A woman may see something in her husband that she does not want to lose.

That is why I always advise for disputes to remain confined between the husband and wife. Allah made an emotional desire between them, and this desire is often the reason for reconciliation. Moreover, Allah has stipulated that divorce should not occur during menstruation because there is no intimacy at that time. In fact, divorce should happen between two menstrual periods where intercourse did not occur. In other words, the decision to divorce must occur when the couple has access to intimacy with each other.

When you divorce women and they have reached the end of their term, then either keep them in a fair manner or release them in a fair manner. Do not hold on to them with intent to harm them and commit aggression: anyone who does this wrongs himself. Do not make a mockery of Allah's revelations; remember the favour He blessed you with, and the Scripture and wisdom He sent to teach you. Be mindful of Allah and know that He has full knowledge of everything. (Chapter 2: Verse 231)

Allah issues a warning to men who are in the process of divorce: "Do not hold on to them with intent to harm them and commit aggression." Some men may pretend to be upright, while in reality, they want to harm and humiliate their wife. Let's take the example of a man who holds ill intentions and resentment towards his soon to be ex-wife. He may say to his family: "I do not want to divorce my wife, and I would like for my family to get back together." On the surface, this appears to be an act of goodwill to preserve a home, while in reality, the man has no interest in reconciliation or normalcy in daily life; His true intent is to abuse the wife either emotionally or physically. This is called 'Dirar,' and Islam forbids it. You may recall that the name 'Dirar' was used at the time of the prophet. There was a Mosque referred to as Masjid al-Dirar or the Mosque of Harm. On the surface, it was built as a house of worship, but the builders had ulterior motives to use it as a pulpit to divide the believers.

Allah warns men against 'Dirar'. He says: "Do not hold on to them with intent to harm them and commit aggression: anyone who does this wrongs himself." A divorcing husband should not fall under the illusion that he is only harming his wife by retracting the divorce for abuse; rather he is harming and abusing himself. How, you may ask? We answer that when you abuse another human being, whether physically, psychologically or financially, you move the Lord to his or her side. Allah –the All-Knowing, Almighty- responds to the prayer of the abused, and comes to his or her aid in this world and the next. By abusing others, you deprive yourself of Allah's help and set yourself in a position where Allah is your enemy. Is there a greater injustice to yourself than bringing the wrath of Allah upon you?

Allah further warns: "Do not make a mockery of Allah's revelations." Allah's teachings are meant to govern the movement of life in a fair and balanced manner. Those who ignore Allah's teachings, circumvent them, or pretend to follow them while doing the opposite are risking ruin.

The verse continues: "remember the favour He blessed you with, and the Scripture and wisdom He sent to teach you." Allah is reminding the Muslims of how His teachings transformed their society for the better. Before Islam, women had no rights and were often inherited as property. A man would divorce his wife and take her back tens of times with no repercussions. A man would refrain from having sexual relations with his wife for months at a time. If the husband dies, the woman would often be shunned by society and confined to her home. Thus, prior to Islam fathers often felt ashamed when they had a newborn daughter; some would go as far as killing their infant daughters to preserve the honour of the family. Now, with Allah's favour, clear rights and responsibilities are set in marriage, divorce and inheritance preserving the dignity and livelihood of women and men alike.

Allah is reminding the believers that before Islam, they were an ignorant, uncivilized nation; they worshiped idols and waged wars for the most trivial of reasons. Then Allah sent a system that raised the Muslim nation to the pinnacle of the world civilizations within a few decades. Allah says: "Do not make a mockery of Allah's revelations; remember the favour He blessed you with, and the Scripture and wisdom He sent to teach you." The scripture is the Noble Quran, and the wisdom is the teachings and practices –Sunnah- of our beloved prophet Muhammad.

The verse concludes with: "Be mindful of Allah and know that He has full knowledge of everything" as a reminder that all legislation in Islam are perfect because Allah is All-Knowing; He is aware of our needs and condition now and till the day of judgment.

VERSE 232

When you divorce women and they have reached their set time, do not prevent them from remarrying their husbands if they both agree to do so in a fair manner. Let those of you who believe in Allah and the Last Day take this to heart: that is more wholesome and purer for you. Allah knows and you do not. (Chapter 2: Verse 232)

The phrase "When you divorce women and they have reached their set time" means that the waiting has ended, and this is not the third and final divorce. At this point, the husband needs a new contract and dowry to return to his wife. Let suppose that the husband wants to get back together with his wife, and he is ready to renew the contract along with a dowry. Here, some of the relatives of the man or the woman may interfere to prevent the couple from getting back together. They get in the way of reconciliation without taking into account the emotional connection the couple share. Maybe the relatives are well-intentioned because they do not want to see a replay of old problems. We explain to them: if the couple have agreed to return, then you do not have the right to prevent them from doing so. Allah says: "When you divorce women and they have reached their set time, do not prevent them from remarrying their husbands if they both agree to do so in a fair manner."

We advise parents who prevent their sons or daughters from getting back together with their spouses that they are overstepping Allah's limits. Divorce is meant to be a gradual process with clear steps that have to be taken in succession. Do not ignore the Islamic system because you think you know better. The wisdom of legislating divorce on three separate occasions is to give a fresh chance for reconciliation every time.

Take note that the phrase " do not prevent them from remarrying their husbands" explicitly implies that Allah gave the marriage approval to the woman. In other words, returning to the husband requires the woman's consent. So, if the couple agrees to get back together and if they satisfy the condition mentioned in the verse: "to do so in a fair manner, then family members intending to oppose must stay away. Allah says: "Let those of you who believe in Allah and the Last Day take this to heart: that is more wholesome and purer for you." We trust in Our Lord; He is the All-Wise, the All-Knowing, and the provider of all good. Regardless of how bad the situation between the couple may be; regardless of what you think you know, always keep in mind that "Allah knows and you do not."

Verse 233

Walwaa lidaatu yurdi'na awlaada hunna hawlaini kaamilaini liman araada ai yutimmar radaa'ah; wa 'alalmawloodi lahoo rizqu hunna wa kiswatuhunna bilma'roof; laatukallafu nafsun illaa wus'ahaa; laa tudaaarra waalidatum biwaladihaa wa laa mawloodul lahoo biwaladih; wa 'alal waarisi mislu zaalik; fa in araadaa Fisaalan 'an taraadim minhumaa wa tashaawurin falaa junaaha 'alaihimaa; wa in arattum an tastardi'ooo awlaadakum falaa junaaha 'alaikum izaa sallamtum maaa aataitum bilma'roof; wattaqul laaha wa'lamooo annal laaha bimaa ta'maloona baser

Mothers should breastfeed their children for two full years – for those who wish to complete the full term of nursing, and clothing and maintenance must be borne by the father in a fair manner. No one should be burdened with more than they can bear: no mother shall be made to suffer harm on account of her child, nor any father on account of his. The same duty is incumbent on the father's heir. If, by mutual consent and consultation, the couple wish to wean the child, they will not be blamed, nor will there be any blame if you wish to engage a wet nurse, provided you pay as agreed in a fair manner. Be mindful of Allah, knowing that He sees everything you do. (Chapter 2: Verse 233)

Look at the beauty of Islam and the mercy of Our Lord. Here the Almighty talks about mothers nursing their newborns after divorce.

Divorce breeds discord between the couple, but the All-Merciful wants to shield the children from the parent's disagreements. He explains that no matter how ugly the divorce was, it should not be a source of misery for the innocent child.

The rulings in the verse are directed towards the divorced woman after she leaves the husbands' house. More specifically, in the Arabic origin, the phrase "and clothing and maintenance must be borne by the father in a fair manner" is in the feminine plural form which linguistically includes the mother and the child. If everyone lived under one roof, there would have been no need to mention that the man is required to fulfill the family's needs. Had the woman been divorced without a child, she would have to provide for herself. But in the situation under study, Allah imposes the rights of the infant over everyone else's. Both the infant and the nursing mother have to be provided for by the ex-husband. The mother would not have this right had it not been for the nursing infant. Some people misunderstood that providing livelihood and clothing is the man's duty for his ex-wife in general. But this ruling only applies to a divorced mother who is breastfeeding a child from the broken marriage. Allah cements this right for the infant so men do not think that they are free from their responsibilities after divorce. He says: "Mothers should breastfeed their children for two full years – for those who wish to complete the full term of nursing, and clothing and maintenance must be borne by the father in a fair manner." So the father is responsible for supporting the child and his mother who is nursing according to his ability.

The verse continues: "No one should be burdened with more than they can bear: no mother shall be made to suffer harm on account of her child, nor any father on account of his." Both parents are addressed here. It is not acceptable to exhaust the father with nagging demands beyond his financial ability. Similarly, the father must not harm the mother by leaving her to fend for herself and her baby. In either case, the child must not be used as a source of stress or a tool for revenge between the divorced couple. Allah sets a precise framework to guarantee the child's rights. This child has lost the warmth of living with two loving parents; he or she should not suffer any further.

The responsibilities of providing food and clothing do not stop if the father of the infant dies. In such a case, who would support the newborn and the mother? Allah answers: "The same duty is incumbent on the father's heir." Even though the infant may inherit a lot of money from the father's wealth, the care of the orphan and the nursing mother and the burden of managing the wealth still fall on the guardian of the child.

By setting these rules, Allah –the All-Merciful- guaranteed the rights of the child under the care of a loving family, under the care of a divorced family where the father is alive; and secured the same rights under the care of a divorced family where the father is dead.

The verse continues: "If, by mutual consent and consultation, the couple wish to wean the child, they will not be blamed." Allah wants to preserve the compassion and care between the divorced couple. Divorce should not mean that everything has ended and as a result, the children suffer. The phrase: "by mutual consent and consultation" indicates that a common bond remains between the man and the woman. This bond ensures that the children are not deprived of proper care. The father and mother must agree on how to best raise their children. They should not use hate and disagreement as obstacles in the way of caring for the children.

Neglect after divorce is a serious issue that produces children who often lead troubled lives. What is the fault of a child who is born into a dysfunctional family? Allah's teachings guide each parent on how to best provide for the child so the next generation would enjoy a better and more productive life.

At the beginning of the verse, Allah says: "Mothers should breastfeed their children for two full years – for those who wish to complete the full term of nursing," but what if circumstances prevent breastfeeding for the full two years? Allah answers: "If, by mutual consent and consultation, the couple wish to wean the child, they will not be blamed."

The verse continues: "nor will there be any blame if you wish to engage a wet nurse, provided you pay as agreed in a fair manner." When the father entrusts his child to his divorced wife for nursing, the child receives warmth and love from the mother. But in cases where she cannot nurse the child due to weakness or health issues, then the father can look for a wet nurse to breastfeed the newborn. Again, the father has the responsibility to provide the wet-nurse with whatever she requires for breastfeeding the child.

The verse ends with: "Be mindful of Allah, knowing that He sees everything you do." Allah is warning all parties against dishonesty and injustice. For example, a father who does not provide what he can; a mother who uses her newborn as an excuse to overburden her ex-husband, or a wet-nurse who does not care for the child properly. Allah issues a warning to all those involved in the child's care: remember, you are not dealing with the family, you are not dealing with your ex-wife or ex-husband, you are dealing with Allah who sees what you do and knows what you hold in your heart.

VERSE 234

Wallazeena yutawaffawna minkum wa yazaroona azwaajai yatarabbasna bi anfusihinna arba'ata ashhurinw wa 'ashran fa izaa balaghna ajalahunna falaa junaaha 'alaikum feemaa fa'alna feee anfusihinna bilma'roof; wallaahu bimaa ta'maloona Khabeer

If any of you die and leave widows, the widows should wait for four months and ten nights before remarrying. When they have completed this set time, you will not be blamed for anything they may reasonably choose to do with themselves. Allah is fully aware of what you do.
(Chapter 2: Verse 234)

'Iddah' is the waiting period Allah prescribed for the woman after the marriage ends in divorce or after the death of the husband.

The waiting period after divorce is three complete menstrual cycles. If the divorcee is in menopause or does not menstruate, then the waiting period is three months. After this period ends, the husband loses the right to get back together with his wife, unless there is a new contract and dowry. This applies to cases of first and second divorces. If all three divorces have been pronounced, then even the right of remarrying the ex-wife with a new contract and dowry is lost. It will not be allowed unless the woman marries another man properly -without the ulterior motive of getting back with her first husband-.

As for the 'iddah' waiting period of a widow, Allah set it at four months and ten days if she is not pregnant. If she is pregnant, then her 'iddah' is the longer of the two: either four months and ten days, or when she gives birth. To clarify this further, let's consider the example of a woman who is nine months pregnant, and her husband dies. If she delivers her baby a week later, does it mean that her waiting period has ended? No, rather the farthest term should be considered; in this case, it would be four months and ten days. As for cases of divorce, the waiting period ends when the divorced woman gives birth; even if she gives birth one day after the divorce is finalized.

Some people argue that the sole purpose of the waiting period is to determine if the woman is pregnant by the deceased husband. We answer that if the purpose of the 'iddah' was to determine if the woman is pregnant, then her waiting period would have been three menstrual periods, or when she is medically certified as not pregnant. But Allah – the All-wise- specified four months and ten days for many reasons, one of which is pregnancy. Other reasons, such as fulfilling the husband's rights and allowing time for emotional recovery also apply. The woman must not beautify herself, go out of her home for pleasure, or promise to marry. But when the four months and ten days have passed, the woman is free to adorn herself and accept marriage proposals. Allah says: "When they have completed this set time, you will not be blamed for anything they may reasonably choose to do with themselves."

Here, we should take careful note of the words Allah used in this verse. He says: "When they have completed this set time, you will not be blamed for anything they may reasonably choose to do with themselves." Logically, the verse should have read: 'When they have completed this set time, they will not be blamed for anything they may reasonably choose to do with themselves." In other words, when it came to assigning blame, Allah did not single out the grieving woman, He addressed the entire society. Why? We answer that each believing woman has a family and a guardian supporting her. Hence, if the family sees in her behaviour something contrary to Allah's commands, they have a responsibility and a right to intervene. For example, if a father sees his daughter beautifying herself or considering marriage proposals during her iddah waiting period, he should advise and question her about this behaviour. The guardian must not say : 'I have nothing to do with her,' or 'this is the way she is grieving.' The proper application of Allah's teachings is a communal responsibility. The Almighty says:

By the declining day! Indeed humankind is in loss, except for those who believe, do good deeds, urge one another to the truth, and urge one another to steadfastness.

(Chapter 103)

"urge one another to the truth" explains that each one of us is an adviser and each one us is a student who learns from the advice of others. So, if you see weakness in another person, then take a moment to advise him or her kindly. Likewise, if someone sees you making a mistake, then he or she should remind you of the right thing to do. You should receive the advice of others with an open mind. If we all advise one another, then each one of us will fare better.

Another lesson from the verse "except for those who believe, do good deeds, urge one another to the truth, and urge one another to steadfastness" is that all people are allowed to advise others and to listen to advice from others. Giving advice is not specific to a certain group of people, a government agency, or moral police because we all commit sins and errors. That is why, in the verse under study, Allah made the general statement: "When they have completed this set time, you will not be blamed for anything they may reasonably choose to do with themselves."

The verse concludes with: "Allah is fully aware of what you do." Allah is aware of our hidden actions, and He is aware of our deepest intentions even if no one in the community knows. Suppose that a woman secretly acted against Allah's teachings during her iddah waiting period and got away with it; she must know that Allah is fully aware of her actions.

Through all of the previous legislation, Allah protected the rights of the husband and the wife. Moreover, the waiting period preserves the dignity of the woman and provides her a shield of protection. How, you may ask? We answer that a woman —especially after a divorce- may have feelings of resentment and a desire for revenge, so she may rush to get married. Or perhaps other men want to take advantage of a woman while she is emotionally distraught after her husband's death. Overwhelming emotions often cloud her judgment. Thus, Allah imposed a mandatory waiting period –called Iddah- to protect the woman's interests.

VERSE 235

Wa laa junaaha 'alaikum feema 'arradtum bihee min khitbatin nisaaa'i aw aknantum feee anfusikum; 'alimal laahu annakum satazkuroonahunna wa laakil laa tuwaa'idoohunna sirran illaaa an taqooloo qawlamma'roofaa; wa laa ta'zimoo 'uqdatan nikaahi hattaa yablughal kitaabu ajalah; wa'lamooo annal laaha ya'lamumaa feee anfusikum fahzarooh; wa'lamooo annallaaha Ghafoorun Haleem

You will not be blamed whether you give a hint that you wish to marry these women, or keep it to yourselves- Allah is aware that you will keep them in mind. Do not make a secret arrangement with them; speak to them honorably and do not confirm the marriage tie until the prescribed period reaches its end. Remember that Allah knows what is in your souls, so be mindful of Him. Remember that Allah is most forgiving and forbearing.

In the previous verse, we highlighted how Allah preserved the rights and dignity of women by legislating a waiting period after divorce or after the husband's death. In this verse, Allah takes our emotions into consideration. He addresses the feelings of both sexes: the woman who may be looking to remarry and the man who may be interested in her. He says: "You will not be blamed whether you give a hint that you wish to marry these women or keep it to yourselves- Allah knows that you intend to propose to them. Do not make a secret arrangement with them; speak to them honourably and do not confirm the marriage tie until the prescribed period reaches its end."

The phrase "to give a hint" means to allude to something without clearly stating it. Allah gives both men and women an outlet for their emotions, so they are not bottled up or strained. During the Iddah waiting period, it is prohibited to express interest in marriage or engagement explicitly. But this prohibition may lead to missed opportunities, so Allah permitted the man to express his interest to marry implicitly. For example, a man can praise a woman in a way that does not contradict Islamic principles and social etiquettes. Such talk will let the divorced woman or widow know that this man is interested. If the man does not make his interest known, he may miss his chance as someone else may precede him.

Moreover, implicitly expressing interest in marriage allows the divorced woman or the widow to weigh her options rather than rush into a new relationship. Here, we see the real value of Allah's mercy in the Iddah waiting period. It acts as a shield for the woman while keeping her options open for future marriage.

The phrase "that you wish to marry" is translated from the Arabic origin 'khitbah.' The root of the word 'Khitbah' is 'kha' 'taa' 'baa.' This root is common to several words such as to give a sermon, to propose for marriage, and to describe an event of great importance. Take note that all of these expressions reflect crucial matters. The moment of the marriage proposal is what separates two lifestyles: a life of relative freedom, and a family life of intimacy, commitments, and duties.

The verse continues: "Allah is aware that you will keep them in mind." Allah, our creator, knows what we share with others and what we keep to ourselves. If a man likes a woman, and she gets divorced, or her husband dies, the man may see this as an opportunity to marry her. Allah does not want to put roadblocks ahead of forming a new family. Thus, He does not suppress the man's emotions but allows them to be expressed appropriately. Allah warns: "Do not make a secret arrangement with them" because making secret romantic arrangements and promises of future marriage are immoral acts; such actions also defeat the benefits of the Iddah waiting period. Allah says: "speak to them honourably and do not confirm the marriage tie until the prescribed period reaches its end." In other words, the man is not permitted to make promises for future marriage. He can only allude to the fact that he is interested in a proper manner. For example, he may say: "how lucky is the one who has a wife like you." This sort of speech can be made in a social setting, and the divorced woman or the widow would understand what is intended.

The verse continues: "do not confirm the marriage tie until the prescribed period reaches its end." This phrase clarifies that during the Iddah even tentative steps towards marriage are strictly prohibited. If mere steps towards marriage are prohibited, then the prohibition on tying the marriage knot is even stronger. All you can do is intend to marry, allude to this fact appropriately, and then stop. Do not take additional steps whatsoever during the waiting period. Put your trust in the Lord. Once the Iddah waiting period is over, you can move ahead with the proposal and marriage.

To clarify: the process of marrying a newly divorced or widowed woman goes through three stages: First, during the waiting period, the man can express his interest indirectly and honouArably. Second: commitment to marry is not permitted until the waiting period has ended, and the third and final stage is the marriage contract. Why such a strict schedule? Because Allah wants to give each party ample time to think deeply about this serious matter, especially when emotions are charged after death or divorce. If, after taking time to think and work through these emotions, both the man and the woman feel it is the right thing to do; then the marriage can happen after the iddah. It is a process that needs to run its course.

Moreover, the iddah waiting period and the stages mentioned earlier allow each party to back away for any reason. For example, if the woman discovers something she does not like about the man, she can just let her feelings be known or ignore his signals. Marriage holds many commitments and responsibilities; if it is not well thought through, it will most likely fail. We often see this happen when marriages are rushed based on urgent desires and soaring emotions that cloud the mind. This is one of the main reasons for the prohibition of the short-term marriage contract –known as Mut'a- where the participants do not intend to live a marital life, but only to be together for a short term for physical pleasure.

People should enter into marriage on a solid foundation, and should only divorce for serious reasons. When a person restricts the marriage to a specified period of time, he or she ignores all the foundations required for a healthy marriage in exchange for physical desire. Allah –who is fully aware of your weaknesses- warns you against such actions. He says: "Remember that Allah knows what is in your souls, so be mindful of Him. Remember that Allah is most forgiving and forbearing." More importantly, if you fall in error, Allah gives you a chance to repent because He Almighty is the All-Forgiving, All-Merciful.

VERSE 236

Laa junaaha 'alaikum in tallaqtumun nisaaa'a maa lam tamassoohunna aw tafridoo lahunna fareedah; wa matti'hoohunna 'alal moosi'i qadaruhoo wa 'alal muqtiri qadaruhoo matta'am bilma'roofi haqqan 'alalmuhsineen

You will not be blamed if you divorce women when you have not yet consummated the marriage or fixed a bride-gift for them, but make fair provision for them, the rich according to his means and the poor according to his – a provision according to customary and honourable practices - this is a duty for those who do good. (Chapter 2: Verse 236)

In the previous verses, we discussed matters related to married and widowed women. But what if a situation arises where a husband divorces his wife before the couple consummates the marriage? In this verse, Allah addresses such a situation.

First, we have to see if the couple had agreed upon dowry because divorce before consummation has two rulings: one for when the dowry was agreed upon, and one for when it was not agreed upon. In fact, from this verse we learn that agreeing upon dowry is not a requirement for a marriage contract. When a dowry is not specified, the marriage contract automatically assumes what is known as the customary dowry –Mahru Al Mithl-.

The phrase: "when you have not yet consummated the marriage" is translated from the Arabic origin 'Tamasoohun' from the root 'Mas.' Let's take a few moments to study this word.

There are three Arabic words related to this matter: 'Mas' which is the word used in the verse, 'Lams' and then 'Mulamasa.' Let's take them one by one: 'Mas' is to touch something briefly where you do not become fully aware of it. In other words, you cannot tell if it is soft or hard, cold or warm and so on. As for 'Lams', it is when you touch something and get a clear sense of what it is. Finally, 'Mulamasa' is when two things touch, interact or interlock for a period of time. So these three words give us three distinct stages of familiarity: first is 'Mas,' second is 'Lams' and the third is 'Mulamasa.'

In the verse under study, we understand that the intended meaning of the word 'Mas' is intimate relations. Why, you may ask? 'Mas' after all is the act of briefly and lightly touching something where you do not get a true sense of it! We answer that we take the word 'Mas' to mean sexual intercourse because it has been used in another verse to reflect the same meaning. Allah narrates to us the words of Virgin Mary:

She said, 'How can I have a son when no man has touched me, and I am not an unchaste woman?' (19:20)

The Quran explains through the dialogue of Mary that no one has touched her in a way that will make her pregnant. The expression –again using the word Mas- is very precise because Allah wants to relay to us that Mary did not have any relations with a man that could lead to pregnancy. Allah used the lightest of words to protect Mary's chastity against even the slightest suspicion. Similarly, in the verse under study, Allah expresses the meaning of sexual intercourse by hinting and using the most courteous of words.

The verse continues: "You will not be blamed if you divorce women when you have not yet consummated the marriage or fixed a bride-gift for them" indicating that there will be no blame upon a couple if they divorce before having sexual intercourse whether the dowry was specified or not. Take note that Allah used the conjunction "if" expressing possibility and doubt rather than using the conjunction "when" that expresses inevitability; as if Allah does not want you to take the matter lightly and resort to divorce easily. The Prophet (peace be upon him) said: "Among lawful things, divorce is most hated by Allah."

Allah continues: "but make fair provision for them, the rich according to his means and the poor according to his – a provision according to customary and honorable practices." If the divorce occurs before consummating the marriage and a dowry had not been set, then the man should give the woman what he can as a gift. The scholars said that the money due to the woman, or the value of the gift, should be half of what is customarily given to similar brides as dowry. Why? Because if a dowry had been set and divorce occurs before consummation, then the woman is supposed to receive half her dowry. The scholars argued likewise: if a dowry had not been set, then the man should research what brides in the same community customarily receive, and give his ex-wife a gift worth half that amount. This is called 'an equivalent dowry' or 'Mahru Al Mithl.' Allah says: "the rich according to his means and the poor according to his – a provision according to customary and honorable practices."

Keep in mind that when Allah commands the payment of half the equivalent dowry, the enforcement of such command does not only fall on the divorcing husband; it is the responsibility of the community. How, you may ask? We answer if the man who recently divorced his wife refuses to pay, or he spends far less than the required amount, then his family and the community should stand up for the woman's rights and ensure that proper payment is made. If you read the Arabic text of this verse, you will find that Allah –the All-Wise- had issued the command to 'make fair provision' in the plural form –rather than the masculine singular-indicating that the responsibility is shared among all members of the family.

VERSE 237

Wa in tallaqtumoohunna min qabli an tamassoohunna wa qad farad tum lahunna fareedatan fanisfu maa faradtum illaaa ai ya'foona aw ya'fuwallazee biyadihee 'uqdatunnikaah; wa an ta'fooo aqrabu littaqwaa; wa laa tansawulfadla bainakum; innal laaha bimaa ta'maloona Baseer

And if you divorce your wives before consummating the marriage but after fixing a bride-gift for them, then give them half of what you had previously fixed, unless they waive their right, or unless the one who holds the marriage tie waives the right. Waiving your right is nearer to Allahliness, so do not forget to be gracious towards one another: Allah sees what you do.
(Chapter 2: Verse 237)

In the previous verse, we discussed the situation of a couple divorcing before the marriage is consummated and where a dowry had not been set. In this verse, we look at a situation of a couple divorcing before the marriage is consummated where a dowry has been set. In such case, the woman should not receive the entire dowry; she would only get half of the agreed amount.

Here we should pause and study the difference between an order based on fairness and justice, and an order based on graciousness. To explain this better, we can learn from a story:

Two men went to a wise elder so he may judge between them about a disagreement. They said: We want you to be fair and to rule between us justly. He said: do you want me to judge with justice or with that which is better? They replied: Is there anything better than justice? He said: Yes, graciousness. Justice gives everyone their right, but graciousness allows people to waive their right or some of it for the betterment of society.

Therefore, when the All-Merciful issues legislation and sets the balances of justice, He does not deprive the faithful of the benefit of virtue. Allah gives you the just and fair ruling, and then He adds: "do not forget to be gracious towards one another.' Justice alone may be difficult on the soul, and often leaves traces of resentment or a desire to get even. On the other hand, when one party is gracious towards the other, all ill feelings are extinguished.

Here you may wonder, how can being fair leave some people bitter? We answer that when two people are in disagreement, each one is convinced that he is right and the other is wrong. It is possible that each party only sees circumstances that support his or her point of view. Thus, if we adhere to justice alone, one or both parties may feel that they were robbed of their right. There may be lingering doubt about the ruling. But when the parties treat each other with virtue and grace –in essence voluntarily waiving what they see is rightfully theirs- everyone becomes content and matters genuinely come to an end.

This brings us back to the verse. Allah says: "And if you divorce your wives before consummating the marriage but after fixing a bride-gift for them, then give them half of what you had previously fixed, unless they waive their right." So the ex-wife has the option to pardon the entire half of the dowry owed to her, or part of it if she sees fit.

The phrase: 'or unless the one who holds the marriage tie waives the right' is referring to the husband. Some scholars disagreed and said that the guardian –in most cases the father of the bride- is meant here, but the context of the verse actually refers to the husband. Keep in mind that the woman's guardian does not have the right to forgo the woman's dowry or any part of it. She alone has the right. This money is a source of wealth and a provision for the woman so she can move on and be compensated for the expenses she put into the marriage; it is money that is earned rightly and free of any doubt. That is why some women save their dowry for difficult times. For example, when a family member falls ill, the woman uses part of her dowry money to buy the medicine. It is considered lawful wealth that holds blessing within it.

My reply to those who claim that the phrase verse 'unless the one who holds the marriage tie waives the right' refers to ex-wife's guardian is the following: Why would Allah only burden the ex-wife and her guardian with the option of forgoing the dowry? It is only logical that both parties, the divorcing man and woman, have the opportunity to give more or forgive what is owed. It does not make sense that the woman and her guardians can pardon, while the man is not encouraged to do the same. I point to the last part of the verse as proof: Allah says: "so do not forget to be gracious towards one another." Being gracious happens between two people; it can go either way, and it can be reciprocal where each party offers something in return.

Then Allah advises: 'Waiving your right is nearer to Allahliness.' Isn't it better to let go of all these material attachments and forgive? It is closer to piety and a wonderful way to cleanse the soul. In such tough situations, remember Allah's words: 'so do not forget to be gracious towards one another: Allah sees what you do.' Take note that Allah wants you to be gracious and courteous to others even during the severe disagreements of separation and divorce. In other words, try not to hold grudges, seek revenge, or look to settle every score.

Allah says in the 216th verse of Surah Baqarah:

It may well be that you dislike something but it is good for you, and it may well be that you like something but it is bad for you. Allah knows, and you do not know.

Always leave room for kindness in your heart. Do not neglect the role of fate in your life. Allah may have a better plan for you. If you are angry at fate, you will open your heart up to hatred and resentment.

Allah concludes the verse by saying: "Allah sees what you do" to remind you that He knows what is in your heart, and He knows the real intentions behind your actions. Islam should be part of your daily living; so do not separate the acts of worship such as the daily prayers and fasting the month of Ramadan from other obligations such as treating others with grace.

VERSES 238

Haafizoo 'alas salawaati was Salaatil Wustaa wa qoomoo lillaahi qaaniteen

Maintain with care the prayers and in particular the middle prayer and stand devoutly before Allah. But if you are in danger, pray as you are out walking or riding; when you are safe again, remember Allah, for He has taught you what you did not know.

VERSE 239

Fa in khiftum farijaalan aw rukbaanan fa izaaa amintum fazkurul laaha kamaa 'allamakum maa lam takoonoo ta'lamoon

If ye fear (an enemy), pray on foot, or riding, (as may be most convenient), but when ye are in security, celebrate Allah's praises in the manner He has taught you, which ye knew not (before).

These two verses are very interesting; more specifically, their location in the chapter is fascinating. The preceding verses discussed the issue of divorce and family breakdown. The next verses return back to discussing widows, family and divorce. So at first glance, verses 238 and 239 look out of place. What is the wisdom behind the placement of these verses? We answer that Allah interjected the discussion of divorce and family breakdown with a reminder of prayers to encourage you to seek Him in prayers during hard times. Don't let worldly troubles overtake your life. Remember that matters of fate, such as death, and the legislation of social ties, such as marriage and divorce, are all from Allah. So make sure to maintain a strong connection with your creator at all times. Prayers are the best tool you have to be with your Lord and seek His guidance. Prayer gives you tranquillity when your life is breaking down. Prophet Muhammad -peace be upon him- used to stand in prayer whenever a matter troubled him.

Allah -who gives life and death and who legislated marriage and divorce- is your best refuge during difficult times. Only He can help relieve your worry and grief. Moreover, by remembering your Lord in prayers, you would also remember all His teachings that govern matters of death and divorce. Your faith will guide you to accept whatever Allah had destined for you humbly.

Allah says: "Maintain with care the prayers and in particular the middle prayer." We understand that the five daily prayers are intended in this verse. The phrase 'Maintain with care' is translated from the Arabic origin 'Hafizoo' which holds two meanings -both are appropriate for this verse-. 'Hafizoo' means to remember and not to forget.

If you skip and forget to perform your daily prayers, you have in fact wasted the prayers. And if you offer your prayers in haste while you are absent-minded, you have also wasted your prayers. Make sure to offer your prayers on time with mindful devotion. You will experience the sweetness of being close to your Lord.

Allah is reminding you to "Maintain with care the prayers" then emphasizes "the middle prayers" in particular. So, in essence, the middle prayer was mentioned twice, the first time it was included with all the prayers, and the second time it was singled out.

What is the reason for singling out the middle prayer in particular?

Well, let's start by defining what the middle prayer is.

Verses 238 & 239

The majority of scholars advised that the middle prayer is the `Asr prayer.

Imam Ahmad reported that `Ali narrated that Allah's Messenger (pbuh) said during the battle of Al-Ahzab (the Confederates):

(They (the disbelievers) busied us from performing the Middle prayer, the `Ar prayer, may Allah fill their hearts and houses with fire.)

To be devout is to be committed and loyal. Allah says:

What about someone who worships devoutly during the night, bowing down, standing in prayer, ever mindful of the life to come, hoping for his Lord's mercy? Say, 'How can those who know be equal to those who do not know?' Only those who have understanding will take heed. (39:09)

Allah is inviting you to compare two types of people: the first are those who worship Allah with love and devotion; they forgo sleep to be with their Lord in prayer and strive for His mercy and blessings. The second type are those who forget Allah in their daily lives until they are in trouble; only then, they turn to Him for help. Do those who honour Allah's rights equal to those who ascribe partners to Him or are too distracted to remember their Lord?

What is the best way to keep Allah in mind?

The best way to be close to your Lord is to maintain your daily prayers properly. Prayers are the firm connection you have with your Lord that renews five times a day. Prophet Muhammad asked: "If one of you had a river by his house and he bathed in it five times a day, would there be any dirt left on him whatsoever?" The companions answered: "None, oh Messenger of Allah, he would be perfectly clean." He –peace be upon him- replied: "So are the five daily prayers, Allah forgives and washes your sins with them."

The daily prayers are so critical that we are commanded to establish them even during battle. That is why Allah had legislated the 'fear prayer.' Allah advises: "But if you are in danger, pray as you are out walking or riding." So even if you fear for your life, you should not forget about your Lord; because, in that situation, you are in dire need of Him. Do not turn a situation where you should remember Allah –such as in the midst of a battle- into an excuse to forget Allah.

Likewise, when you are ill, you should remember Allah in prayers. Do not use your weakness as an excuse to forget Allah. There is no excuse to skip prayers. If you are too sick to pray standing, you must pray sitting. If you are too weak to pray sitting, you should pray lying down, and if that is not possible, then pray with eye movements.

In verse 239, Allah swt tells us about the Fear Prayer

Fa in khiftum farijaalan aw rukbaanan fa izaaa amintum fazkurul laaha kamaa 'allamakum maa lam takoonoo ta'lamoon

If ye fear (an enemy), pray on foot, or riding, (as may be most convenient), but when ye are in security, celebrate Allah´s praises in the manner He has taught you, which ye knew not (before).

Allah directs the Muslim soldier who is in danger to pray while walking, riding or driving. At the time of Prophet Muhammad –peace be upon him-, Allah commanded the Muslim soldiers to pray in two groups: the first group prays the first rak'ah –unit of prayer- with the Prophet and then complete their prayer individually; then a second group comes to pray the second rak'ah with the prophet and complete the prayer on their own. In this manner, the first group earns the blessings of starting their prayer with the Prophet and the second group earns the blessings of completing the prayer with him. Moreover, this arrangement allowed for a group of the Muslims to be on guard while their fellow soldiers pray.

Some are of the opinion that the 'fear prayer' as we just described was only for battles in which the Messenger of Allah was present. It was meant to guarantee that the entire Army had the honour of praying with the Prophet. But after the Messenger passed away, it is logical for both parties to pray at different times behind separate scholars or imams. There is no longer a need –after the prophet's passing- to split the prayer.

The phrase "But if you are in danger, pray as you are out walking or riding" reaffirms that the obligatory daily prayers are not to be dismissed even under fire. During war, when the time for prayer arrives, the believer must pray. If he or she can't perform the prayer physically, then he or she must say the words of the prayers and be in remembrance of Allah. He says "remember Allah, for He has taught you what you did not know." Had Allah not taught you how to be in His company, you would have been in a total loss.

LESSONS:

- Remember that all obligatory prayers are important and all of them should be performed at their appointed time with proper ablution and khushu [fear of Allah]. However, 'Asr prayer is the most important. It is because at this time, the day is coming to an end and people are busy in wrapping up their tasks. In hastening to finish off their tasks early, they often miss or delay the 'Asr prayer. For example, when the office day comes to an end, people rush to reach their homes. They delay the prayer that they will offer it upon reaching their destination, but they get stuck in traffic. Wouldn't it have been better had they performed their prayer before leaving?
- How many cases we have heard where people left their office and died on the way? What if they had delayed their prayer? They died while missing an obligatory prayer? If the Athan [call to prayer] has been given then the prayer becomes due.
- Earlier people used to talk during the prayer, Allah subhanahu wa ta'ala then revealed this ayah and prohibited speaking during prayer. He also said stand as qaniteen meaning like those who fear Him. One should not fidget, run their fingers through their hair, or fix their clothing during prayer. One should reach the prayer mat with preparation – after fixing their hair and clothing. One should also not raise their gaze or look at other people while in prayer. The gaze should be on the prayer mat in qiyam and on one's index finger during jalsa [sitting position].
- If we were truly concentrating on our prayer we would not be distracted by what is happening around us or by the whisperings of Shaytan. Whenever you feel daydreaming in prayer, recite tawuz [seeking protection from Allah against Shaytan] and spit on your left side.

- Obligatory prayers are not accepted without qiyam the only exceptions are for the old and disabled.
- If we are commanded to stand in prayer while being devoutly obedient, it also means that we should let others perform their prayer. There should be no disturbance or noise near them. Some people keep the television on while another person is offering prayer in the same room. Some people talk in loud voice while the Qur'an is being recited or someone is praying.
- It is because we have forgotten the etiquette of prayer that our prayers are not accepted. If we are offering prayers as they should be, with proper cleanliness and concentration at their appointed time, there is no reason why they will not be accepted.
- We should read the book, The Prophet's Prayer and learn the proper way of praying. We should not pray how our parents taught us but how the Prophet salAllahu 'alayhi wa sallam prayed and taught his Companions radhiAllahu 'anhum.

VERSES 240, 241 & 242

Wallazeena yutawaf fawna minkum wa yazaroona azwaajanw wasiyyatal li azwaajihim mataa'an ilal hawlighaira ikhraaj; fa in kharajna falaa junaaha 'alaikum fee maa fa'alna feee anfusihinna min ma'roof; wallaahu Azeezun Hakeem

Those of you who die leaving wives behind should make a bequest to their wives of maintenance for a year without them having to leave their homes. But if they do leave you are not to blame for anything they do with themselves with correctness and courtesy. Allah is Almighty, All-Wise.

Let's recall an earlier verse from the same chapter. Allah says:

If any of you die and leave widows, the widows should wait for four months and ten nights before remarrying. When they have completed this set time, you will not be blamed for anything they may reasonably choose to do with themselves. Allah is fully aware of what you do. (2:234)

So there are two rulings related to dying men and their widows. The first ruling —from verse 234- states that the widow should complete her 'iddah' waiting period of four months and ten days before moving on with her life. The second ruling is for the husband to make a proper will allowing his wife to remain in his house for one year without being expelled or even asked to leave. So the widow is obligated to stay for the first four months and ten days, and she should have the option -and the right- to remain in the family home up to one full year. Allah says: "Those of you who die leaving wives behind should make a bequest to their wives of maintenance for a year without them having to leave their homes." The will should come from the dying husband giving his wife the option to remain in the house beyond the mandatory 'iddah' for up to a year. No one has the right to ask her to leave the marital home.

The verse continues:

Wallazeena yutawaf fawna minkum wa yazaroona azwaajanw wasiyyatal li azwaajihim mataa'an ilal hawlighaira ikhraaj; fa in kharajna falaa junaaha 'alaikum fee maa fa'alna feee anfusihinna min ma'roof; wallaahu Azeezun Hakeem

Those of you who die and leave widows should bequeath for their widows a year's maintenance and residence; but if they leave (The residence), there is no blame on you for what they do with themselves, provided it is reasonable. And Allah is Exalted in Power, Wise.

And for divorced women is a provision according to what is acceptable - a duty upon the righteous.

For every social situation, Allah made a suitable ruling. We have studied a few examples in regards to financial suapport for divorced and widowed women. Allah says:

You will not be blamed if you divorce women when you have not yet consummated the marriage or fixed a bride-gift for them, but make fair provision for them, the rich according to his means and the poor according to his – a provision according to customary and honourable practices - this is a duty for those who do good. (2:236)

And in the 237th verse

And if you divorce your wives before consummating the marriage but after fixing a bride-gift for them, then give them half of what you had previously fixed

So every Muslim man must take care of his family according to his means and ability. Allah says:

In this way, Allah makes His revelations clear to you, so that you may grow in understanding. (Chapter 2: Verse 242)

Allah always invites you to use your intellect, because when the clear mind ponders issues, such as divorce and marital support, it will reach the same sound rulings Allah provided for us. The mind will logically confirm Allah's wisdom in the legislation He prescribed.

Perhaps, the best examples of the wisdom of Allah's legislation can be seen in those who do not follow them. How, you may ask? We answer that, more often than not, people who abandon Allah's teachings end up in courts bearing great financial and social costs. When people do not abide by the laws of the Creator, it is only logical that problems arise. Otherwise, people would say: "Look, such and such is doing as he likes and he has no problems." I have seen many examples of people who rebelled against Allah's teachings in regards to family matters only to become the most vocal supporters of these teachings after they suffered severe family problems. They realized, through experience, that the best family rules come from the One who created families.

LESSONS:

- Though today we are not called for battles, we have many battles going on in our homes. When a couple fights, the first thing that they should do is strengthen their bond with their Creator – turn to Him with humility. Do not abandon your prayers. For the men, it is obligatory to pray in the mosque. If the husband is punctual, he will leave the argument and go to the mosque. At the mosque, he will be distracted. He will meet and greet other Muslims, talk to the Imam and his mood will change. While the husband is away, the wife too will pick up her prayer mat and offer her prayers. When she will stand before Allah subhanahu wa ta'ala and cry out to Him, He will change the state of her heart and give her comfort. [The Virtue of Patience and Prayer]

- But how many of us think like this? We keep on arguing, name calling and miss our obligatory prayers. The tempers are iron hot and both the parties do not wish to speak with one another. They are waiting to draw others in their private matter but do not share with Allah subhanahu wa ta'ala. We take pride in throwing out our dirty laundry. It seems we have lost the virtue of self-respect. We can preserve our family honour, if we learn to conceal our private matters and only share them with Allah subhanahu wa ta'ala.

- We learn that prayer cannot be skipped under any circumstance. When people are going through trials in their lives, they get depressed and withdraw from life. If we have a regular habit of praying, we will know there is before and ask for help. [What is the Best Way for treating Anxiety? a Rabb that we can talk to, cry]

- In the Qur'an, some people will enter Hellfire because of their abandoning of the prayers. Let us not become of them. No matter what the situation in our life is – happiness or sorrow – hold on to your prayer and your relationship with your Creator.

- When giving our daughters in marriage, how many of ask the groom-to-be whether he prays? Why is it that we focus more on worldly education and financial status or looks, than one's relationship with their Creator? If one cannot maintain a strong relationship with their Creator then there is no guarantee they will maintain good relations with fellow human beings. One who does not gives the Right of Allah subhanahu wa ta'ala has no respect for the rights of others. May Allah subhanahu wa ta'ala protect us and our families from abandoning prayers. May He not make us of those who pay more attention to the fleeting joys of this world and little to the life to come. May He make us of the musaaleen and qaniteen.

Ameen.

VERSE 243

Alam tara ilal lazeena kharajoo min diyaarihim wa hum uloofun hazaral mawti faqaaala lahumul laahu mootoo summa ahyaahum; innal laaha lazoo fadlin 'alannaasi wa laakinna aksarannaasi laa yashkuroon

Didn't you see those who abandoned their homes, though they were in the thousands, for fear of death? Allah said to them: "Die." Then He restored them to life. Truly, Allah shows real favour to people, but most of them are ungrateful.

After Allah addressed the social issues of the Muslim family, whether in marriage, divorce, or death, He turns our attention to matters concerning every individual in the entire Muslim nation. The Muslim nation is the one entrusted with carrying Allah's message to humanity till the end of time. There is no prophet after our beloved Muhammad. So it is essential for every Muslim to understand that there is no escape from Allah except to Allah himself. It is vital for every Muslim to study history and learn all the lessons of the previous nations, all the difficulties they faced, and all the hardships they put their Prophets through. We, as a nation, and as individuals, should not repeat the mistakes of the past. These are not abstract theoretical lessons; they are lessons from real life and past historical events.

We start at the very core of creed: Allah is the only One who gives life; He is the One who takes it away. People cannot give life or create life. We can preserve life through food, drink, and healthcare; but it is ultimately Allah's domain when life ends.

Allah reminds us of this lesson through the story of Prophet Moses and his people –the Israelites-. In fact, the story of Moses and the children of Israel is the most told story in the Quran. Why, you may ask? We answer that the Israelites were the last nation that received a message from the heavens before Islam. More importantly, due to their defiance and materialism, the children of Israel put their prophets through hardships; Allah wants us to avoid such trouble. Thus, it was necessary to review these events and learn from them.

The story starts with a question: "Didn't you see those who abandoned their homes, though they were in the thousands, for fear of death?"

Ibn Abu Hatim related that Ibn 'Abbas *radhiAllahu 'anhu* said that these people were the residents of a village called Dawardan – a place several miles away from Wasit, Iraq.

Explaining this *ayah* Ibn 'Abbas said that they were four thousand people who escaped the plague (that broke out in their land). They said, "We should go to a land that is free of death!" When they reached a certain area, Allah said to them: **Die.** And they all died. Afterwards, one of the prophets passed by them and supplicated to Allah *subhanahu wa ta'ala* to resurrect them and He brought them back to life.

Other scholars among the Salaf said that these people were the residents of a city during the time of the Children of Israel. The weather in their land did not suit them and an epidemic broke out. They fled their land fearing death and took refuge in the wilderness. They later arrived at a fertile valley and they filled what is between its two sides. Then Allah *subhanahu wa ta'ala* sent two angels to them, one from the lower side and the other from the upper side of the valley. The angels screamed once and all the people died instantly, just as the death of one man. They were later moved to a different place, where walls and graves were built around them. They all perished, and their bodies rotted and disintegrated.

Long afterwards, one of the prophets of the Children of Israel, whose name was Hizqil [Ezekiel], passed by them and asked Allah *subhanahu wa ta'ala* to bring them back to life by his hand. Allah *subhanahu wa ta'ala* accepted his supplication and commanded him to say, **"O rotted bones, Allah commands you to come together."** The bones of every body were brought together. Allah *subhanahu wa ta'ala* then commanded him to say, **"O bones, Allah commands you to be covered with flesh, nerves and skin."** That also happened while Hizqil was watching.

Allah *subhanahu wa ta'ala* then commanded him to say, **"O souls, Allah commands you to return, each to the body that it used to inhabit."** They all came back to life, looked around and proclaimed, "All praise is due to You (O Allah!) and there is no deity worthy of worship except You." Allah *subhanahu wa ta'ala* brought them back to life after they had perished long ago.

LESSONS:

The lesson for us is that no living being can escape death by running away from it. If a certain area has been struck by plague or an epidemic, do not leave the place. Because your running away will cause the epidemic to spread and result in more deaths. Stay where you are and take precautionary measures to remain protected.

It also indicates that no caution can ever avert destiny and that there is no refuge from Allah subhanahu wa ta'ala, but to Allah Himself. These people departed from their land fleeing the epidemic and seeking to enjoy a long life. What they earned was the opposite of what they sought, as death came quickly and instantaneously and seized them all.

We should remember that death comes at an appointed time; it can neither be earlier nor later. At the time of someone's death, people who say, **"I wish he had not taken that bus or train,"** *or* **"I wish he had not gone to that area,"** *need to be corrected. These are all asbaab of death. We will all die, on a date decided by Allah subhanahu wa ta'ala and in a manner decreed by Him. Therefore, when someone dies accept it as a Divine decree and don't fall for kash [saying "if"]. And don't wail over their death or tear clothes, this is not the Islamic conduct. We ask Allah subhanahu wa ta'ala to teach us the best manners, aameen. Our loved ones have passed and soon we will be joining them.*

VERSE 244

Wa qaatiloo fee sabeelil laahi wa'lamooo annal laaha Samee'un 'Aleem

And fight in Allah's cause and remember that He is all hearing and all knowing.

Then fight in the cause of Allah, and know that Allah Heareth and knoweth all things.

Abandoning Jihad does not Alter Destiny.

When the need arises to defend one's home and faith, fear of death should not be part of what a Muslim says or thinks. Allah grants life and takes it away. He is fully aware of what you say, think and do. The same concept that applies to life and death also applies to wealth and loss. Allah grants wealth and takes it away. He says:

As for those who stayed behind, and said of their brothers, 'If only they had listened to us, they would not have been killed,' tell them, 'Ward off death from yourselves, if what you say is true.' (3:168)

VERSE 245

Man zal lazee yuqridul laaha qardan hasanan fayudaa 'ifahoo lahoo ad'aafan kaseerah; wallaahu yaqbidu wa yabsutu wa ilaihi turja'oon

Who will lend Allah a good loan, which He will increase for him many times over? It is Allah who withholds and Allah who gives abundantly, and it is to Him that you will return (Chapter 2: Verse 245)

In the previous verses, Allah spoke of life, death, and war. Now, He turns our attention to wealth. Let's start with the phrase: "Who will lend Allah a good loan." When you lend your money to help a friend, you are in fact lending Allah. How, you may ask? We answer that you are supporting the needy as Allah commanded. Allah brought each one of us into existence; thus He is responsible for providing for us.

Similarly, when you invite a guest into your home, you —as the host- become responsible for providing him or her with food and a place to rest. Allah brought us to life, and He provides us with our basic needs. He does not ask you to take over the responsibility of providing for others. He only asks you for a loan to help others. Allah will repay you in full and will increase you in reward.

Here you may ask: Why wouldn't Allah provide for the poor directly? Perhaps the answer is best given with an example. Say that a wealthy father gave each of his children a large sum of money. If one of the children falls on hard times, the father would not go to the children and say 'give me back my money to help your brother', rather he would say 'lend me some of your money and I will return it to you with a handsome reward once your brother is out of trouble.' In this manner, the father would not only preserve each child's wealth, but he would also foster love and compassion between the brothers.

There are many instances where you do not give to a particular person; instead, you spend in Allah's cause and for the general benefit of society. Here again, you are dealing directly with Allah, and He will compensate you for your efforts.

Through the use of the word 'loan,' Allah is alerting you that He is aware of the difficulty of the task. He knows our nature and knows that giving money in His cause is a burden. The word 'loan' is translated from the Arabic origin 'Qard' which means to bite something with your front teeth. So when you take money from your savings to give to others in need, it is as if you are taking a bite out of your own wealth. In the verse under study, Allah assures you that difficult deeds are rewarded handsomely. Say for example that you are planning to move to a new apartment. When you find a worker to help you move, you would say to him: "Listen, I know the furniture is big and heavy, but don't worry." In essence, you have informed the worker that you are aware the job is difficult and that you will pay him well for it.

The fact that you are lending Allah directly, regardless if you are helping a single person or helping Islam in general, should make you feel very secure about your loan. This is because any time you loan money, you loan it in the hopes of getting it back. However, the person you lend to may not be able to pay you back. He or she may lose a job, get disabled, die or renege on the promise to repay. But the Almighty is the truth; He is the All-Giving, the Ever-Providing. Allah will not only repay your loan, but He will return it multiplied many times over. Your capital is preserved, invested and grown. Allah says: "Who will lend Allah a good loan, which He will increase for him many times over? It is Allah who withholds and Allah who gives abundantly." Rest assured that your loan will be multiplied many times over by the standards and ability of Allah, not by our standards and abilities as human beings.

The expression 'good loan' suggests that the source of the money you lend must be lawful. That is why we say to a person who gives charity out of the money earned from theft or bribery: "It would have been better to never have earned this money, and to never have given it to charity."

It is said that the reward for a loan is higher than the reward for charity. This is despite the fact that when giving to charity, you completely let go of the money, while when lending you would be getting your money back later. The scholars explained that when you give to charity, you feel the pain of letting go of your money once then you forget about it. On the other hand, when you lend money, you keep thinking about it; you anticipate repayment and worry about missed and late payments. The more patience you exhibit, the more rewards you attain.

Allah is well aware of your anxiety when helping and lending to others. He knows the emotional pain of seeing your wealth decrease. Thus, He –the All-Generous- grants you rewards multiple times over. That is precisely what is meant by "It is Allah who withholds and Allah who gives abundantly." Allah is also assuring you that "it is to Him that you will return" to find your reward in the hereafter.

Now we are going to learn about a story that Allah swt is telling us. These are contained in verses 246 to 251.

Before we go to the Tasfeer of the verses, let us look at the story.

This story starts with the Israelites started committing a lot of sins and even became idolaters. Just imagine, this was a nation whose forefathers had witnessed so many miracles and now they are committing the worse unforgiveable sin.

So let us begin this story with their evil king who mistreated them and shed their blood. They fought many battles. They will take their Ark of the Covenant to these wars because they believe it brought them luck. The Ark of the Covenant was a chest containing relics from the time of the people of Prophet Musa. They won every war they went to. But there came a time when they lost the war against the Philistines and their Ark was snatched from them. When the king heard what happened he had a heart attack and died instantly. The Israelites now were without a king and were like sheep without a shepherd. There was no one to rule the country.

It was then that Allah sent Prophet Shammil (Sammuel) to guide the people of Israel. As time goes by, they requested that the prophet appoint a leader. They wanted to go into battle with the Philistines and win back their Ark. One day Prophet Shammil prayed to Allah to help him choose a king. His prayers were answered, and Allah gave him signs of the chosen person. There was a young boy name Talut (Saul), who lived far away with his father in a farm. One day Talut and his servant were out looking for their missing donkeys. They spent several days looking without any luck. Eventually, Talut decided they must return home as his father will be worried about them and had no help in his farm.

However, his servant informed him that as Prophet Shammil lived in this land, they should pay him a visit and asked whether he can shed any light about the missing donkeys. As they were walking they met a group of women who directed them to the prophet's house. When they arrived, they saw a large gathering in front of the prophet's house. People had assembled there with the hope that they will be the chosen one for the leadership of Israel. Talut greeted the prophet with much respect and asked about his missing donkeys. He was assured that all his donkeys were on their way home. Talut was relieved. Prophet Shammil immediately recognised him as the chosen one. The prophet told Talut there and then. He is going to be the King of Israel. The crowds protested at the Prophet's choice. They objected because they felt that Talut was a descendant of Benyameen and was very lowly without much wealth. But the Prophet had made his choice informing everyone that it was by the will of Allah. Talut's role will be to unite the Bani Israel and protect them from their enemies. He was worried about taking on such a big responsibility and felt he knew nothing about leadership and was just a poor shepherd. But when Prophet Shammil told him that it was the will of Allah, he accepted the role. King Talut started his duties. An army was organised to fight the Philistines to win back their Ark of Covenant. He only chose those who were free from responsibilities. He did not accept anyone who was building homes, recently got married, and who was engaged in business affairs. He prepared his army for battle by putting them through strenuous training. When he felt that they were ready he started putting his plan in action. They travelled for many days and nights until they came to a stream. King Talut decided to test his army and commanded them only to drink amounts of water to quench their thirst. Not all of them follow his instructions. Some were gulping down like there was no tomorrow. The king was very disappointed and dismissed the greedy ones from his army. He needed his army to be sincere. During the journey he put his army through many tests and by the time they reached the land of the Philistines, there were only 30 soldiers. But Talut was not scared. He preferred an army of small believers rather than a large army of unreliable men. The Phillistines army was a large one. The soldiers were well equipped with their weapons. Their leader was a giantlike soldier name Jalut. When faced with such a large army some of the Israelite soldiers ran away. Rather than the whole army fighting, it was their custom to send one soldier from each side to fight with each other. Hence, Talut asked his army who will volunteer for this position. No one did. They were all scared. He even offered his daughter's hand in marriage to the one who will fight Jalut. Yet no one volunteered. Talut was very disappointed with his army. But then a young boy from his army came forward and volunteered. When the soldiers from the Philistines saw him, they roared with laughter. They thought it was a done deal that they will win the battle. His name was Dawood (David) and was from Bethlehem. His brothers were all soldiers and he was the youngest. He came to the battlefield to update his family of the news on the warfront. His father told him that he must not take part in any fighting. Talut admired young Dawood's courage but felt that he was no match for the strong giantlike Jalut. Indeed, Dawood was a very courageous young man and related that he had killed a lion and a tiger all by himself. Talut was impressed and asked the soldiers to dress young Dawood in battle clothes and to give him a sword. Dawood refused because he had a plan, a very good plan. He collected pebbles and put it in his pouch and took his slingshot out. By now Talut was getting very worried and wondered how a few pebbles and a slingshot can help their victory against this huge army. As he approached Jalut the roar of laughter from the opponent army grew louder and louder. With a sword in his hand, Jalut was ready to cut off Dawood's head. Dawood said to him:

"I face you in the name of Allah whose laws you have mocked, l am not scared of you. I believe in Allah". With that he took a pebble, put it in his slingshot and hit Talut's head with extreme force. Blood was gushing out from his forehead. Talut fell dead to the ground. The shocked army upon seeing the death of their leader ran away.

THE ISRALITIES HAD WON THE WAR.

Their sufferings from the Philistines had finally come to an end. Victory were theirs. Dawood was a hero and the soldiers fetched him on their shoulders back to the palace. King Talut kept his word and Dawood and his daughter were married. Despite becoming the most famous man in Israel he remained humble. He went to the desert to glorify Allah. Dawood was chosen to be a prophet of Allah. And revealed the Zabour (Psalms) to him. Allah also blessed Prophet Dawood to understand the language of the birds and animals. Prophet Sulayman was his son.

TAKEN FROM THE BOOK: TOWARDS UNDERSTANDING THE MESSAGE OF QURAN BY SERENA YATES

VERSE 246

Alam tara ilal malai mim Baneee Israaa'eela mim ba'di Moosaaa iz qaaloo li Nabiyyil lahumub 'as lanaa malikan nuqaatil fee sabeelillaahi qaala hal 'asaitum in kutiba 'alaikumul qitaalu allaa tuqaatiloo qaaloo wa maa lanaaa allaa nuqaatila fee sabeelil laahi wa qad ukhrijnaa min diyaarinaa wa abnaaa'inaa falammaa kutiba 'alaihimul qitaalu tawallaw illaa qaleelam minhum; wallaahu 'aleemum bizzaalimeen

Have you not seen the elders of the Children of Israel who came after Moses, when they said to one of their Prophets, 'Appoint a king for us and we shall fight in Allah's cause.' He said, 'Is it not possible that if fighting were prescribed for you, you would not fight?' They said, 'How could we not fight in Allah's cause when we have been driven out of our homeland and our children?' Yet when they were commanded to fight, all but a few of them turned away: Allah has full knowledge of the unjust. (Chapter 2: Verse 246)

The verse starts with the phrase 'Have you not seen?' asking you if you have witnessed an event that happened thousands of years ago. The Quran is Allah's word, and to the believer, what Allah says is as true and certain as one's own eyesight. We believe in what Allah tells us with the same certainty as if we were present witnessing the event first hand.

So what do we see?

Allah says:

'Have you not seen the elders of the Children of Israel who came after Moses, when they said to one of their Prophets, 'Appoint a king for us and we shall fight in Allah's cause.' The word 'elders' translated from the Arabic origin 'Malaa' refers to the leaders, elites, and nobles of a society. The tribe of the Israelites in this verse could be from the era of Joshua, Ezekiel, or any period after the prophet Moses. The exact period does not concern us because the Quran did not specify a time. What is important is they were after Moses, peace be upon him.

The nobles and leaders from the children of Israel gathered in discussion, and then they went to their Prophet. They asked him to appoint a king. We understand the presence of a prophet and the absence of a king. What is the significance? We answer that Prophets at that time played the role of advising and monitoring, but the Prophet did not lead projects or initiate actions. That was left to kings. The wisdom behind separating the two matters is that the person who leads projects and takes action often becomes a target for disputes and hatred. Had the prophet been in charge, then the failure of one project would have been blamed on Allah. That, in turn, would negatively affect people's perception of faith and the prophet. By having a king, such matters and disputes are handled differently. Therefore, the elders of the Israelites asked their Prophet to appoint a king who would deal with such issues. In this manner, the prophet would remain the moral compass to which the tribe turns.

Let's consider the situation of this tribe. Their elders gathered, saw a clear need to fight, and decided to ask their prophet to appoint a king to lead them into war. They have been driven out of their town; some families were separated from their loved ones. They were humiliated by losing their homes and children to the enemy. Despite these dire reasons, the Prophet was worried. He asked them: "Is it not possible that if fighting were prescribed for you, you would not fight?" He knew that appointing a king to lead them to war would make fighting —which is not compulsory at the moment- a religious duty. And when Allah makes fighting obligatory, you might lose your nerve and fail to obey His command and thus fall in sin.

They answered: 'How could we not fight in Allah's cause when we have been driven out of our homeland and our children?'

Let's take a moment to examine their statement. While they claimed to want to fight "in Allah's cause," the real reason behind their decision was worldly and material. They wanted to fight because they were driven from their homes and their children! They only considered fighting when they were personally going through a hard time. It was not for Allah's sake. However, since they sought Allah as their refuge, He accepted their request and considered their fight in His path.

The verse continues: 'Yet when they were commanded to fight, all but a few of them turned away.' The critical point to remember is that the elders and nobles of the tribe asked to fight, and requested a leader to take them to battle. They studied the matter and came up with the solution. Even when their prophet questioned them, they insisted: 'How could we not fight in Allah's cause when we have been driven out of our homeland and our children?' Allah only made fighting obligatory upon them based on their request. It was not imposed haphazardly. Sadly, their prophet was proven right when he predicted their true willingness to fight. Most of them changed their minds, but not all. There were a few who obeyed the mandate of their Lord to fight.

Here we should address an important issue. When it comes to life's tough struggles, the majority of people will often turn away from confrontation. But you should not say:

"We are only a few; we don't stand a chance" because true results are not attained through numbers, they are attained through Allah's support. You may be up against overwhelming odds, but if you have the grace and support of your Lord on your side, the odds do not matter. In the verse under study Allah says: 'Yet when they were commanded to fight, all but a few of them turned away.' The expression "all but a few of them" was mentioned for a reason.

Allah says in the 249th verse of 'The Cow':

"Many a times has a group of a few defeated a much bigger group by Allah's command; Allah is with the steadfast."

Victory comes through the will of Allah. Each one of us sees matters according to the strength of his or her faith. Here is an example: two soldiers standing shoulder to shoulder before battle. They can both see that the enemy far outnumbers them, but their thoughts differ. One soldier sees the enemy and thinks: "we are few, and they are many; we cannot fight them." The other soldier sees the enemy and thinks: "Unlike our enemy, we are fighting for the truth; Allah is with us." Allah says:

When they had crossed it, and those who believed with him, they said: "We have no strength to combat Goliath and his forces today. But those who believed they have to face their Lord, said: "Many a time has a small band defeated a large horde by the will of Allah. Allah is with those who are patient" (from 2:249)

The verse ends with: "Yet when they were commanded to fight, all but a few of them turned away: Allah has full knowledge of the unjust."

Take note that Allah described those who disobeyed Him as unjust. Injustice in its purest form is to transfer a right to someone other than its owner. The Israelites who turned away from fighting were unjust on three levels. First, by not fighting for their homes and their children, they gave up their rightful ownership to their enemies. They were unjust towards their families and property. Second, they were unjust towards their fellow fighters as they robbed them of the morale of a strong army. Lastly, and most importantly, they were unjust towards themselves. Why, you may ask? Because by disobeying Allah's command, they earned themselves the punishment of Hellfire and robbed themselves of the rewards of paradise.

VERSE 247

Wa qaala lahum Nabiy yuhum innal laaha qad ba'asa lakum Taaloota malikaa; qaalooo annaa yakoonu lahul mulku 'alainaa wa nahnu ahaqqu bilmulki minhu wa lam yu'ta sa'atamminal maal; qaala innallaahas tafaahu 'alaikum wa zaadahoo bastatan fil'ilmi waljismi wallaahu yu'tee mulkahoo mai yashaaa'; wallaahu Waasi'un 'Aleem

Their Prophet said to them: "Allah has sent Saul for you as king." They said: "How can he have kingship over us when we are more deserving of kingship than him, seeing that he has not been given abundance of wealth?" He said: "Allah has chosen him over you and increased him abundantly in knowledge and physical power. Allah bestows kingship on whomever He wills, and Allah is All-Encomapssing, All-Knowing. (Chapter 2: Verse 247)

In the previous session, we explained how the Israelites had asked their prophet to appoint a king to help them fight for their families and homes. They knew their prophet well; they trusted and respected his ability to deliver. Since it was their idea and their request, it should have been enough for the Prophet to choose a person and appoint him king. But the Israelites complicated matters and put up obstacles.

The prophet presented the appointed man in a clear, respectful manner. He said: "Allah has set up Saul for you as king." The prophet reassured the tribe that he was not the one who chose Saul, rather it was Allah. So what was their response? They said, "How can he have kingship over us when we are more deserving of kingship than him, seeing that he has not been given abundance of wealth?" They argued with their prophet and based their argument on materialistic worldly matters. They looked for prestige and wealth. Rather than appreciating Allah's favour, they considered Allah's choice a personal insult to them. We understand from the statement "how can he have kingship over us" that Saul was not of the elites. Normally, during elections and appointments, people have a few candidates in mind. But Saul was not from the leaders, so the divine decision was unexpected.

It was customary among the Israelites to look at the lineage of a person. In particular, they looked for the descendants of two progenies. The progeny of

Allah wants to teach us a valuable lesson: Leadership and kingship should not come from pride and arrogance. Lineage and social status should not deceive you. You should choose the most experienced and most suitable person to manage the task at hand. What was the task at hand for the Israelites? It was leading an army to regain lost homes and reunite families. To properly perform this task, a king needs to have two qualities: strength and knowledge. Saul had both of them.

Take note of the divine etiquette when presenting the chosen king. At the beginning of the verse, Allah said to the Israelites: "Allah has sent Saul for you as king." This simple and straightforward presentation should have eliminated any objections or feelings of inferiority. But when the elites showed stubbornness and displeasure, Allah said to them: "Allah has chosen him over you" informing the quarrelling nobles that Allah choice was better than them in every way. He had knowledge and strength; two qualities lacking in your ranks. Allah "increased him abundantly in knowledge and physical power."

The verse ends with: "Allah bestows kingship on whomever He wills, and Allah is All-Encomapssing, All-Knowing." As if the Almighty says to them: don't think that you are the ones who recommend the right king to us. It is sufficient for you to request, and for me to send you a king. Allah is all-Encompassing, so He has the choice of the entire creation to select a king from. He is not limited by a few candidates or specific lineage. Allah is all-Encompassing, so He considers every task, every situation and every skill needed to do the job properly. He is not limited by the knowledge or desire of the Israelites. Allah is all-Knowing of who fits all the criteria for this task.

Fatima —the prophet's daughter- (peace and blessings be upon her) presents an excellent example for us. Once, our beloved Prophet came into her room and found her cleaning and burnishing a coin into a shine. He asked: 'Fatima, what are you doing?' She replied: I am polishing this coin before I give it to charity. He asked: 'why?' She said: 'because I know that charity passes through Allah's hand before it falls into the hand of the poor.'

VERSE 248

Wa qaala lahum Nabiyyuhum inna Aayata mulkiheee ai yaatiyakumut Taabootu feehi sakeenatummir Rabbikum wa baqiyyatummimmaa taraka Aalu Moosa wa Aalu Haaroona tahmiluhul malaaa'ikah; inna fee zaalika la Aayatal lakum in kuntum mu'mineen

Their prophet said to them, 'The sign of his authority will be that the Ark will come to you. In it there will be tranquillity from your Lord and relics of the family of Moses and Aaron. It will come to you carried by the angels. There is a sign in this for you if you believe.'

In the previous verse, we explained how the elites of the Israelites objected to Allah's choice for a king. They saw themselves as more worthy of kingship because of their wealth and lineage. Thus, and in order to put an end to pointless discussions, a miracle was necessary. More specifically, a material miracle for people obsessed with materialism.

A sign accompanied King Saul proving that Allah selected him. The prophet said to them: "The sign of his authority will be that the Ark will come to you." This gives us a clue that the Ark had been lost. It was a precious relic that the Israelites longed for.

What is the Ark of the Covenant? It is a wooden chest that is mentioned in the Quran twice. Once in the verse under study, and another in the following verses:

We inspired your mother, saying: "Put your child into the ark, then place him in the river. Let the river wash him on to its bank, and he will be taken in by an enemy of Mine and his." I showered you with My love and planned that you should be raised under My watchful eye. (20:38-39)

Hence, we know about the wooden chest from the days of Moses' infancy. His mom placed him in it and left it in the water out of fear for his life. So this Ark had a long history starting from the infancy of Moses up to the kingship of Saul and the prophet of the Israelites.

From this verse, you should also understand an important point: we —as Muslims- must take care of objects that have historical religious value. Caring and seeking these objects should not be considered a sign of infidelity or practice of idolatry. These objects serve as a reminder of significant historical events and a link to our faith and history. Consider the fact that Allah had the chest of Moses, which contained remnants of the family of Moses and Aaron delivered by the Angles. This proves that it is something special. As if the Almighty is advising us: Take care of such objects because they remind you of sacred events and of Allah's prophets.

Most likely the chest went missing because of an occupier that took over the towns of the Israelites. When an enemy overtakes a country, the first thing they do is obliterate the sacred sites that possess religious and historical value.

Allah reassured the Israelites that the sign of Saul's kingship is to bring the chest which they longed for, and along with it, bring them tranquillity. Not only did the Ark represent a connection to their homeland, but it also represented a spiritual connection that symbolized the survival of their great Prophet Moses against all the odds. Such objects can be great motivators and lifters of spirit.

Allah says: 'The sign of his authority will be that the Ark will come to you. In it there will be tranquillity from your Lord and relics of the family of Moses and Aaron' indicating that the family of Moses and Aaron had preserved part of the material history of their Prophets. The ark and all the objects in it were of such value that Allah had them handled with the utmost care and delivered 'by the angels.'

Take note of the accuracy of the Quranic expression. Allah says regarding the chest: "It will come to you carried by the angels." Allah attributed the action of coming to the chest itself. What does that mean, you may ask? We answer that we as humans cannot see angles, thus when the angles delivered the Ark, it would have appeared to the Israelites as if it is floating in thin air. Therefore, the Almighty attributed the action of coming to the chest itself. This scene would make the heart shiver and would lay aside all doubts of the stubborn Israelites. In fact, the Quran does not mention what happened after the Ark was delivered, because such a miracle does not leave any room for doubt. Saul was proven as Allah's choice and appointed as king.

People often want to know the contents of the ark and the preserved keepsakes of Moses and Aaron. Some scholars said that it was Moses' staff. This sounds reasonable because it was one of the tools of Moses' miracle. Moses or the believers would not neglect such a priceless tool. Allah says:

'Moses, what is that in your right hand?' "It's my staff," he answered; "I lean on it, and fell leaves for my goats with it, and I have other uses for it." Allah said, 'Throw it down, Moses.' He threw it down and- lo and behold!- it became a slithering snake. He said, 'Pick it up and do not fear: We shall turn it back into its former state.' (20:17-21)

VERSE 249

Falammaa fasala Taalootu biljunoodi qaala innal laaha mubtaleekum binaharin faman shariba minhu falaisa minnee wa mallam yat'amhu fa innahoo minneee illaa manigh tarafa ghurfatam biyadih; fashariboo minhu illaa qaleelamminhum; falammaa jaawazahoo huwa wallazeena aamanoo ma'ahoo qaaloo laa taaqata lanal yawma bi Jaaloota wa junoodih; qaalallazeena yazunnoona annahum mulaaqul laahi kam min fi'atin qaleelatin ghalabat fi'atan kaseeratam bi iznil laah; wallaahuma'as saabireen

When Talut set forth with the armies, he said: "Allah will test you at the stream: if any drinks of its water, He goes not with my army: Only those who taste not of it go with me: A mere sip out of the hand is excused." but they all drank of it, except a few. When they crossed the river,- He and the faithful ones with him,- they said: "This day We cannot cope with Goliath and his forces." but those who were convinced that they must meet Allah, said: "How oft, by Allah's will, Hath a small force vanquished a big one? Allah is with those who steadfastly persevere."

When Saul parted with the army, he said, 'Allah will test you with a river. Anyone who drinks from it is not with me. But anyone who does not taste it is with me – except for him who merely scoops up a little in his hand.' But they drank from it – except for a few of them. Then when he and those who had faith with him had crossed it, they said, 'We do not have the strength to face Goliath and his troops today.' But those who thought that they were going to meet Allah said, 'How many a small force has triumphed over a much greater one by Allah's permission! Allah is with the steadfast.' (Chapter 2: verse 249)

The phrase "parted with the army" is translated from the Arabic origin 'fasal.' It means to separate something from something else. Here is another example from the Quran. Allah says:

And when the caravan parted, their father said: "You may think I am senile, but I find Joseph's scent" (12:94)

We also use the term 'fasl' when dividing the contents of a book into chapters. The same word, fasl, is also used to describe a group of students in one class. So in the verse under study, the phrase "When Saul parted with the army" means when he left the camp and marched out to battle; it also means that he separated the soldiers, organized them into formation and divisions, and assigned each one a task.

The verse continues: "When Saul parted with the army, he said, 'Allah will test you with a river.'" Take note that Saul started immediately with his mission as king and military leader. He wanted to test his troops early because they were the same people who objected to his leadership and appointment as a king earlier. He wanted to make sure that he had a solid base of followers. Saul said to them narrating Allah's command: "Allah will test you with a river. Anyone who drinks from it is not with me. But anyone who does not taste it is with me – except for him who merely scoops up a little in his hand." Saul explained to his army: 'you are on a mission on Allah's path. He, Almighty, will test you; and the test will be appropriate for our mission. I am only responsible for the implementation of Allah's command.'

We had explained earlier that the word 'test' is often received negatively. That should not be the case because a test is only a negative experience for the person who is not prepared. It would be quite a different experience if you were prepared and passed with flying colours.

Saul's army was tested with a river. We understand that they must have been very thirsty; otherwise, the test would be pointless. The fact that they were very dehydrated means that the moment they see water, they would rush to quench their thirst. Allah wanted to test their resolve, so He asked them to refrain from drinking. It was an exercise in discipline and self-control. Why, you may ask? We answer that a person who rushes to satisfy a desire and puts his or her needs ahead of Allah's command is not worthy of being in the army of Allah. As for the soldier who sees water and refrains from drinking despite his or her thirst, He or she is indeed worthy of carrying the banner of Allah.

Nevertheless, Allah did not make their test too difficult. He permitted them to drink a small amount that would keep them alive. Allah did not completely deprive them of their needs. The purpose of the test was to prepare the soldiers for battle. During war, soldiers are exposed to all sorts of difficulties such as scarcity of food and water. Their enemy may besiege them for weeks. In such situations, the fighter who has control over his or her desires and can survive on minimum rations is a fighter that can win wars.

How did Saul's soldiers fair in their test? Allah says: "But they drank from it – except for a few of them." It was a process of filtration where the good got separated from the bad. Recall that initially only a few of the Israelites joined the army and agreed to fight. Allah said in the 246th verse: "Yet when they were commanded to fight, all but a few of them turned away." Now, only a few of the few refrained from drinking. This is how Saul ended up with the crème of the crop: The best believers for the task ahead. They had the strongest faith, the most discipline, and the toughest bodies. Allah had selected the people best suitable to carry His banner.

The verse continues: "Then when he and those who had faith with him had crossed it, they said, 'We do not have the strength to face Goliath and his troops today.'" So after they crossed the river and passed all the previous tests, some of them became afraid. Allah interjects: "But those who thought that they were going to meet Allah said, 'How many a small force has triumphed over a much greater one by Allah's permission! Allah is with the steadfast."

Here we should take a few moments to examine how two groups of soldiers saw the same thing, yet came to entirely different conclusions. After crossing the river, Saul's soldiers stood opposite of Goliath's massive army. The first group of Saul's soldiers saw the enemy, recognized their considerable disadvantage in numbers and equipment, and decided out of fear, that they could not logically win this fight. They said: 'We do not have the strength to face Goliath and his troops today.' The second group also saw the enemy, recognised the large disadvantage in numbers and equipment, but they did not fear. Why, you may ask? We answer that the second group included Allah in their calculations of power. They saw themselves plus Allah against Goliath and his army. Once you have Allah on your side, every opponent appears weak and insignificant. As for the soldiers who isolated themselves from their Lord, they saw themselves few against a large army. Allah says: "But those who thought that they were going to meet Allah said, 'How many a small force has triumphed over a much greater one by Allah's permission! Allah is with the steadfast.'"

Take note that the mere thought that they will meet their Lord made them fearless. Many battles in history were won –with Allah's help- by the most faithful and steadfast. Allah says:

Remember when you said to the believers, 'Will you be satisfied if your Lord reinforces you by sending down three thousand angels? Indeed, if you are steadfast and mindful of Allah, your Lord will reinforce you with five thousand swooping angels if the enemy should suddenly attack you!' and Allah arranged it so. (03:124, 125)

So, Allah's help started with three thousand angels, and that number increased to five thousand as the faithful remained steadfast and mindful. Allah's support comes according to the amount of patience and effort you put in. Allah's compassion increases the moment He sees you bearing hardships patiently in His path. As your strength is depleted, Allah's help increases. He says: 'How many a small force has triumphed over a much greater one by Allah's permission! Allah is with the steadfast.'

VERSES 250

Fahazamoohum bi iznillaahi wa qatala Daawoodu jaaloota wa aataahul laahulmulka Wal Hikmata wa 'allamahoo mimmaa yashaaa'; wa law laa daf'ullaahin naasa ba'dahum biba'dil lafasadatil ardu wa laakinnal laaha zoo fadlin 'alal'aalameen

And when they met Goliath and his warriors, they said, 'Our Lord, pour patience down on us, make us stand firm, and help us against the disbelievers,'
(Chapter 2: Verse 250)

Listen to the supplication of the faithful during difficulty.

They called out:

'Our Lord, pour patience down on us.' Take note that they used the call "Our Lord," not "Our Allah" or "O Allah." What is the difference, you may ask? We answer that the Lord is the Caretaker, the Provider, and the Protector. The Lord is the one who nourishes and provides; while the call of Allah is a call of worship and duties. Let's clarify this with an example. The word "Dad" describes the person who cares for you and gives you food and shelter; while the word "father" describes the person who teaches you, asks you to help around the house, and disciplines when necessary. The two words 'Dad' and 'father' refer to the same person, but different roles. Likewise, a believer in difficulty calls out 'My Lord, help me!' not 'My Allah, Help me!'

The believers who were with Saul said:

"Our Lord, pour patience down on us, make us stand firm, and help us against the disbelievers."

When we contemplate what they asked for, we find that they wanted hearts filled with patience, and feet firmly on the ground, because these are the conditions required to receive Allah's help.

LESSONS

River mentioned in the ayah symbols the blessings of the world.

Allah subhanahu wa ta'ala has offered has many blessings and attractions.

We are permitted to use and enjoy within permissible means but refrain from "indulging" in them. The one who gets deluded by the charms of this world and exhausts himself in their chase will not be working on his Hereafter. Victory is with the patient ones meaning those who can see the delusions of this world but do not lose their path. They keep themselves in check from straying away. The Israelites who remained with Saul thought that they were few in the face of their enemy who were many then. So, their knowledgeable scholars strengthened their resolve by stating that Allah's promise is true and that triumph comes from Allah Alone, not from the large numbers or the adequacy of the supplies. They said to them, "How many a small company has overcome a large company by permission of Allah. And Allah is with the patient."

Allah subhanahu wa ta'ala tests everyone. The wisdom behind these tests is to make us come out of mediocrity and recognize our special talents. You don't find blocks of gold or diamond in a mine. These precious stones are mixed with other material and must go through a rigorous process to be refined. Likewise, a human being goes through trials to become a refined person. But there are not many who would stay firm in their hour of trial. The weakness shown by these people becomes contagious making others panic as well. Allah subhanahu wa ta'ala willed that such people be pruned out. This purpose is accomplished by tests. Whenever you face a blockade in your life, instead of complaining remind yourself that Allah subhanahu wa ta'ala has a different plan for you. A life that is free of challenges is a boring life. Be patient when you are tested and connect yourself to Allah subhanahu wa ta'ala. Ask Him to show you your special talents and take the task that He wants to take from you. He who has the help of Allah subhanahu wa ta'ala can never lose. Some people when they are angry they explode on others. And then there are those who distract their mind be picking up productive tasks. Make yourself productive. And remember this is not Jannah. Things won't be as we desire them.

Allah subhanahu wa ta'ala teaches us a du'a to ask for patience.

"Rabbana afrigh alayna sabran wa tawaffana muslimin" which translates to "Our Lord, pour upon us patience and let us die as Muslims" - found in the Quran, Surah Al-Araf, verse 126.

ALLAH SAYS IN VERSE 251:

Tilka Aayaatul laahi natloohaa 'alaika bilhaqq; wa innaka laminal mursaleen (End Juz 2)

and so with Allah's permission, they defeated them. David killed Goliath and Allah gave him sovereignty and wisdom and taught him what He pleased. If Allah did not drive some people back by means of others, the earth would be completely corrupt, but Allah is bountiful to all. (Chapter 2: Verse 251)

Here the Almighty informs us that He aided the believers. The opposing army retreated in escape. Sometimes retreat is a strategy used to gain a more favourable ground or to lure the attackers into an ambush, but when withdrawal happens out of fear, then it is an escape in defeat. Allah indicated that not all of the enemy soldiers escaped. Some of their leaders and prominent warriors were killed.

Allah says: "David killed Goliath."

Goliath was the fearsome warrior of the disbelievers. As they retreated, David followed and killed him. This is the first time the name of David –peace be upon him- appears. In a later chapter, Allah introduces David to us:

We graced David with Our favour.

We said, 'O mountains, echo Allah's praises together with him, and you birds, too.'

We softened iron for him, saying,

'Make coats of chain mail and measure the links well.' 'Do good, all of you, for I see everything you do.' (34:10-11)

David came into the picture after killing Goliath. He was the youngest of ten brothers. Before the battle, the Israelites' Prophet-Shammil, said to his people:

"in order to fight with Saul, you have to fit into the armor of Moses. So the father of David had all his sons try on Moses' vest. It did not fit any of them except for the youngest: David. So David joined the army of Saul and eventually killed Goliath, the leader of the idolaters.

It was of Allah's wisdom that He had the youngest believer kill the head of the army of the disbelievers.

It was this battle –and the killing of Goliath- that brought David into prominence. Allah blessed him with kingship and wisdom and made the mountains and birds echo David's praises of Allah. Naturally, David fell in love with the armour of Moses –peace be upon them all- and asked Allah to teach him the craft of making armour. David made it his life's work. Allah made iron mouldable for him so he can shape it as he wanted.

Allah says:

And We taught him the art of making coats of mail to shield you from each other's violence. Will you not be grateful even then? (21:80)

The verse continues: "If Allah did not drive some people back by means of others, the earth would be completely corrupt, but Allah is bountiful to all."

LESSONS

This Ayat teaches us that injustice does not last forever. If a person holds on to the commands of Allah subhanahu wa ta'ala then he will certainly be helped. But to receive justice, first be patient. You cannot fight your oppressor unless first you work on yourself. We want the world to change but do not change ourselves. One's condition does not change unless first they change themselves.

And so with Allah's permission, they defeated them. David killed Goliath and Allah gave him sovereignty and wisdom and taught him what He pleased. If Allah did not drive some people back by means of others, the earth would be completely corrupt, but Allah is bountiful to all. (Chapter 2: Verse 251)

Let's study the phrase:

"If Allah did not drive some people back by means of others, the earth would be completely corrupt."

Allah gave us the example of a conflict between the Israelites and their enemies who drove them out of their homes and separated them from their families. The elders of Israel realized that the only way to regain what is rightfully theirs is to fight. So, they went to their prophet and asked Allah for permission to fight. Allah sent them a king to lead them into battle, and He supported His choice with the clear sign of the chest filled with relics of Prophet Moses and his family.

Then came the lesson that any wise person understands -even without heavenly revelations-: When you are about to embark on a mission, you must prepare for it properly using all the resources at your disposal. Always remember that Allah is the one who made resources available to you. Thus, you must utilize these resources before you turn to Allah for help. Do not abandon Allah's gifts and ask Him to help you directly. Instead, take all the means He made available to you first; only then you can ask for His help.

Another lesson we can learn from the story of the Israelites is how to scrutinize and properly vet those who defend the truth. A person who fights in Allah's way should be strong, steadfast, and able to control his or her desires. Many people boast about their abilities, but when the time comes for action, they weaken and make excuses. Only a select few have the strength and determination to stand up for the truth. After Saul put his troops through rigorous tests, he ended up with the believing few who were able to defeat their enemies; one of them was David who killed Goliath.

This story was an example of how Allah drives back some people by means of others. He says: "If Allah did not drive some people back by means of others, the earth would be completely corrupt, but Allah is bountiful to all."

This concept applies to battles of ideas and principals, and to battles of war. Allah urges the believers to stand up for the truth and fight the disbelievers. Fighting is not meant as a tool for aggression; rather, it is meant to restore balance and peace. Take note that Allah only allowed the Israelites to fight after they were kicked out of their homes and had their families torn apart; these conditions justified fighting. It is a general principle, not just an Islamic one. Allah says:

Those who have been driven unjustly from their homes only for saying, 'Our Lord is Allah.' If Allah did not repel some people by means of others, many monasteries, churches, synagogues, and mosques, where Allah's name is much invoked, would have been destroyed. Allah is sure to help those who help His cause- Allah is strong and mighty- (22:40)

and in another verse:

Fight them: Allah will punish them at your hands, He will disgrace them, He will help you to conquer them, He will heal the believers' feelings (9:14)

We find a similar example in the early Muslims who were forced to leave their homes and property in Mecca and join their believing brothers in Madina. They later returned to Mecca victorious without a fight.

Both stories share the common fact that the believers should fight back. In the case of the Israelites, they were large in numbers and went into battle shortly after there were driven out. In the story of the early Muslims, their defense was to migrate, spread their message and build a healthy society that could overcome the influence of Quraysh and overtake Mecca without a fight. Here you may be wondering: How could retreating and leaving your home behind be a way of fighting? We answer that had the early Muslims remained in Mecca; their opponents would have killed them all. So they went to Madina to build a healthy Islamic society then returned as victorious conquerors. Allah says:

When Allah's help comes and He opens up the way before you; When you see people embracing Allah's faith in crowds, celebrate the praise of your Lord and ask His forgiveness: He is always ready to accept repentance. (Chapter 110)

So the core message of both stories is one: the believers have to use the means at their disposal to stand up for the truth and fight the disbelievers. Otherwise the earth would turn into a corrupted mess. Allah says: "If Allah did not drive some people back by means of others, the earth would be completely corrupt." There will always be people who enrich themselves and benefit from corruption. They are more than willing to fight for their cause against whoever stands in their way. They are the enemies of moral people –regardless of their faith-. Allah says in the 40th verse of chapter 22:

If Allah did not repel some people by means of others, many monasteries, churches, synagogues, and mosques, where Allah's name is much invoked, would have been destroyed.

Churches and monasteries are both Christian houses of worship that serve different types of worshippers. Christians who fulfill the mandates of worship attend churches weekly, while those who commit themselves to a higher level and seclude themselves for worship attend monasteries. Synagogues are the Jewish houses of worship, while mosques are for Muslims. These houses of worship maintain peoples' connection with their creator and instill humbleness before Allah. Without such places, people often forget their Lord and are overtaken by greed.

Houses of worship are the protectors of moral values. They are not the only source of moral values, but they are the foundation. Similarly, we say that Islam is built on the foundation of the five pillars: faith in Allah and His messenger, prayer, fasting, almsgiving and pilgrimage. That does not mean that Islam is limited to these five pillars; rather, these pillars are required for the structure of Islam to stand correctly. Allah wants the houses of worship to be the moral compass of our society. A mosque, when properly utilized, should be the place from which the light of Allah shines upon the entire neighbourhood.

Let's take a moment to compare verse 251 of 'The Cow' with verse 40 of chapter 22. More specifically, let's compare these two phrases:

In chapter 2: If Allah did not drive some people back by means of others, the earth would be completely corrupt

In chapter 22: If Allah did not drive some people by means of others, many monasteries, churches, synagogues, and mosques, where Allah's name is much invoked, would have been destroyed.

Take note that Allah –the All-Wise- equated the destruction of religion and houses of worship with the spread of corruption in the land. This is because the forces of evil constantly try to distract you from your Lord and the values of faith. Thus, as believers, we have to adhere to Allah's teachings properly; only then would our battle with evil and corruption become short. Allah says:

And say: "The truth has come, and falsehood has vanished. Surely falsehood is ever bound to vanish by its very nature." (17:81)

And so with Allah's permission, they defeated them. David killed Goliath and Allah gave him sovereignty and wisdom and taught him what He pleased. If Allah did not drive some people back by means of others, the earth would be completely corrupt, but Allah is bountiful to all. (Chapter 2: Verse 251)

Here is a fact: Conflict and war will never break out between two forces of the truth because there are no two truths in existence; there is only one. So you can never say: 'well both sides are right.' If a conflict occurs, it could happen between the truth on one side and falsehood on the other, or it could happen between two forces of falsehood.

Moreover, the battle between the truth and falsehood does not last long. Only those battles which are between two falsehoods prolong because neither of them is worthy of Allah's support. Allah allows the forces of corruption to destroy one another. Then, when people tire of corruption and return to His path, they prosper in peace.

If you look at conflicts around the world today, you will see that each party –regardless of its declared ideology- has a different worldly desire. Allah does not support either side; He leaves them to quarrel with each other for years and decades. But if either of them fought while keeping Allah in mind, then they would earn His support.

Listen to the following verse: Allah says:

If two groups of the believers fight, you should try to reconcile them; if one of them is oppressing the other, fight the oppressors until they submit to Allah's command, then make a just and even-handed reconciliation between the two of them: Allah loves those who are equitable. (49:09)

When a fight breaks out between two sects of the believers, the Almighty commands a third party of the believers to resolve the conflict. If one transgresses over the other and refuses to reconcile, then Allah instructs the believers to fight the transgressing party until they return to His path.

The tragedy of our modern era is that conflicts and fights rage for years and decades because the warring parties have different worldly desires; even third parties who claim to be arbitrators intervene for the sake of their worldly desires. No one has justice in mind, and no one has Allah in mind. Our world will remain in turmoil until people seek truth and justice for the sake of the truth and justice. Otherwise, we will continue to waste time and resources. We will deprive ourselves of Allah's help until we realize that the only way to end these problems is to set aside greed and return to the shared teachings of Our Creator.

Would you like to see how things run under the command of your Creator?

Take a moment to look at nature that has not been spoiled by man. Gaze into space, the moon, the sun, planets, and stars. Everything runs with beautiful precision. The lifecycle takes its due course. Nothing is wasted, everything is recycled, and everyone flourishes. Allah says: 'If Allah did not drive some people back by means of others, the earth would be completely corrupt.'

Every place where man has interfered, there is corruption. When modern governments want to preserve the beauty and resources of an area, they declare it a natural protected area. In other words, they set laws to keep human and commercial activities out, because they realize that these activities equal corruption. Any human activity that is not governed by Allah's law will result in corruption. He says:

He erected heaven and established the balance (55:7)

The Almighty is the One who elevated the sky and set the balance. Everything functions like clockwork; everything runs in perfect harmony. If you want your life to run in harmony and precision, then you need to align your actions with Allah's teachings just as the heaven and earth do. Let the Creator be the standard for your deeds. Allah says:

He erected heaven and established the balance; that you should not violate the harmony and balance. And observe the balance with full equity, and do not fall short in it. (55:7-9)

Wouldn't it make sense to follow the teachings of the One who set everything in perfect balance? Haven't we learned enough from our own mistakes that caused corruption and conflict? Life can be upright and beautiful similar to the divine creation in the universe.

Remember Allah's words:

He erected heaven and established the balance; that you should not violate the harmony and balance. (55:7-8)

If you keep these words in mind, you will aim for a higher balance in your life. The earth does not spin away from its orbit because it is governed by the system Allah created for it. Allah says:

Neither can the sun overtake the moon, nor the night outpace the day: Each of them keeps coursing in its orbit. (36:40)

Allah created you and gave you freedom of choice; He also guided you through prophets and scriptures. The seal of the prophets is our Beloved prophet Muhammad, and the crown of the scriptures is the

Noble Quran. The following verse gives you a perfect summary. Allah says:

We sent you the Scripture with the truth, confirming the Scriptures that came before it, and with final authority over them: so judge between them according to what Allah has sent down. Do not follow their whims, which deviate from the truth that has come to you. We have assigned a law and a path to each of you. If Allah had so willed, He would have made you one community, but He wanted to test you through that which He has given you, so race to do good: you will all return to Allah, and He will make clear to you the matters you differed about. (5:48)

VERSE 252

Tilka Aayaatul laahi natloohaa 'alaika bilhaqq; wa innaka laminal mursaleen (End Juz 2)

These are the revelations of Allah which We recite to you with the truth, and you indeed are one of the messengers.

Allah —the All-Merciful- addresses Prophet Muhammad, peace be upon him. The words: 'these are' are referring to the preceding verses that highlighted Allah's power and majesty. Allah says earlier in the chapter:

Didn't you see those who abandoned their homes, though they were in the thousands, for fear of death? Allah said to them: "Die." Then He restored them to life. Truly, Allah shows real favor to people, but most of them are ungrateful. (02:243)

Allah controls life and death, and that is a sign of His power and majesty. When the Israelites asked for a leader to fight with, Allah appointed for them a king and sent with him the lost chest containing the relics of Moses and Aaron. Were these not great signs of Allah? Allah gave David —a young man- the power to kill the great warrior Goliath. Isn't that another sign of Allah's majesty?

Moreover, with Allah's help, a group of few believing men who were ill-equipped and exhausted won a battle over a much larger and far superior enemy. Isn't that another great sign of Allah's power? Allah says:

'How many a small force has triumphed over a much greater one by Allah's permission! Allah is with the steadfast.'

Prophet Muhammad, peace be upon him, was not aware of any of these stories before. He was an illiterate man, a fact well known to everyone, especially his disbelieving enemies. They knew him since he was a young boy. He never sat down to learn from a teacher or a friend. No one took the time to teach him history. Even on his trading trips, where he was accompanied by many merchants, he never sat down to learn. Had any man of Quraysh saw him learn or sit with a teacher, he would have loudly announced it to others to discredit the prophet.

But isn't illiteracy a shame, you may ask? We answer that yes, for you and me illiteracy is an embarrassment. But for our beloved prophet Muhammad, it was an honour.

Why?

Because it was a sign that all the knowledge that he brought us, all the revelations of the Quran and the wisdom he speaks are taught to him directly by Allah. He was not taught by any great teacher; he did not sit down with any philosopher of the east or west. He, peace be upon him, could not even read a book. So everything he brought to us is from Allah alone.

The very first verses revealed from the Quran to Prophet Muhammad:

Read! In the name of your Lord who created: He created man from a clinging clot. Read! Your Lord is the Most Bountiful One. Who taught by the pen, who taught man what he did not know. (96:1-5)

Likewise, when it came to the Israelites, Allah informed our beloved prophet of their stories. If Prophet Muhammad(pbuh) had learned from a teacher, people would have used that against him. Thus, every fact and every story the Prophet brought us is, in of itself, a miracle.

Some of the enemies of the prophet conspired to make up a story that he used to sit down with a teacher in the town of al-Marwa to learn. Allah revealed the following verse to prove their fabrications.

The verse says:

We know very well that they say, 'It is a man who teaches him,' but the language of the person they allude to is foreign, while this revelation is in a clear Arabic tongue. (16:103)

The Almighty answered that the man they claimed to have taught the prophet was not even an Arab.

Allah says: 'These are the revelations of Allah which We recite to you with the truth, and you indeed are one of the messengers.' (2:252)

"We recite to you" means we teach you word after word; and 'the truth' refers to facts that took place and would not ever change.

Let us look at the following scenario:

Suppose a car accident occurred right in front of you. No matter how many times you are asked about the accident, your answer would be the same because you are telling the truth. But if the accident was a lie, or if the accident was something you heard about but did not witness, then your story would change with time. You would forget the details you told a month ago. When you tell the story the third time, it would be different again. Isn't that the same technique investigators use to catch crooks and criminals? They ask a suspect on several occasions about the details of a crime or event. A person with an ever-changing story is a liar. The truth never changes.

Allah says: 'These are the revelations of Allah which We recite to you with the truth.' Allah is the one who is narrating the verses. Thus, they are the ultimate truth.

Allah says:

This is an account of things beyond your knowledge that We reveal to you: you were not present among them when they drew lots to see which of them should take care of Mary, you were not present with them when they argued. (28:44)

And in another chapter

Accordingly, We have revealed a spirit to you by Our command: you knew neither the Scripture nor the faith, but We made it a light, guiding with it whoever We will of Our servants. You give guidance to the straight path (42:52)

The Quran is Allah's revelation and the light that guides the believers to their Lord. Our beloved prophet Muhammad(pbuh) calls to the straight path. Every event in the Quran that starts with "you were not present" is a reminder that whatever is revealed to you is from Allah through the angel Gabriel. We teach you O Muhammad in the most exceptional way, even though you did not ever read a book or learn from a teacher. And when your enemies hear a story that matches what they already know —and hide in their books-, they realize that the one who taught you is Allah Almighty.

The words of the Quran are primarily divided by chapter (surah) and verse (ayah). The chapters vary in length and are generally arranged from longest to shortest. To make the reading process easy, the Quran is additionally divided into 30 equal sections; each called a Juz. These divisions make it easier for you to pace the reading of the entire Quran over a one month period: reading a fairly equal amount of one Juz each day. It is particularly helpful during the month of Ramadan when it is recommended to complete one full reading of the Quran from cover to cover.

Verse 252 of marks the end of the second Juz of the Nobel Quran.

LESSONS:

Allah subhanahu wa ta'ala tests everyone. The wisdom behind these tests is to make us come out of mediocrity and recognize our special talents. You don't find blocks of gold or diamond in a mine. These precious stones are mixed with other material and must go through a rigorous process to be refined. Likewise, a human being goes through trials to become a refined person. But there are not many who would stay firm in their hour of trial. The weakness shown by these people becomes contagious making others panic as well. Allah subhanahu wa ta'ala willed that such people be pruned out. This purpose is accomplished by tests. Whenever you face a blockade in your life, instead of complaining remind yourself that Allah subhanahu wa ta'ala has a different plan for you. A life that is free of challenges is a boring life. Be patient when you are tested and connect yourself to Allah subhanahu wa ta'ala. Ask Him to show you your special talents and take the task that He wants to take from you. He who has the help of Allah subhanahu wa ta'ala can never lose. Some people when they are angry they explode on others. And then there are those who distract their mind be picking up productive tasks. Make yourself productive And remember this is not Jannah. Things won't be as we desire them.

Injustice does not last forever. If a person holds on to the commands of Allah subhanahu wa ta'ala then he will certainly be helped. But to receive justice, first be patient. You cannot fight your oppressor unless first you work on yourself. We want the world to change but do not change ourselves. One's condition does not change unless first they change themselves.

VERSE 253

Tilkar Rusulu faddalnaa ba'dahum 'alaa ba'd; minhum man kallamal laahu wa rafa'a ba'dahum darajaat; wa aatainaa 'Eesab na Maryamal baiyinaati wa ayyadnaahu bi Roohil Qudus; wa law shaaa'al laahu maqtatalal lazeena mimba'dihim mim ba'di maa jaaa'athumul baiyinaatu wa laakinikh talafoo faminhum man aamana wa minhum man kafar; wa law shaaa'al laahu maq tataloo wa laakinnallaaha yaf'alu maa yureed

Those are the messengers - We preferred some above others. Allah spoke to some; others He raised many degrees in rank; We gave Jesus, son of Mary, Our clear signs and strengthened him with the Holy Spirit. If Allah had so willed, their successors would not have fought each other after they had been brought clear signs. But they disagreed: some believed and some disbelieved. If Allah had so willed, they would not have fought each other, but Allah does what He will.

A Messenger is the one who is charged with delivering a message. The message is speech that has a specific goal. Allah used the plural 'Those Messengers' to alert you that no matter how many different prophets and messengers were sent, they were all from One Allah carrying the same core message.

Allah is reminding our beloved Prophet Prophet Muhammad(pbuh) of the prophets and messengers who are mentioned in the Quran. Earlier verses in this chapter spoke of Adam, Abraham, Ishmael, Jacob, Moses, and Jesus (peace be upon them all). Take note that this reminder comes right after the verse that said to Prophet Muhammad(pbuh):

These are the revelations of Allah which We recite to you with the truth, and you indeed are one of the messengers. (2:252)

So our beloved Prophet Prophet Muhammad(pbuh)(belongs to a long procession of prophets and messengers. But there is a distinction between the prophets: Each has his status and degree in virtue. They are all messengers of Allah, but the Almighty has preferred some over others.

Those are the messengers - We preferred some above others. Allah spoke to some; others He raised many degrees in rank; We gave Jesus, son of Mary, Our clear signs and strengthened him with the Holy Spirit. If Allah had so willed, their successors would not have fought each other after they had been brought clear signs. But they disagreed: some believed, and some disbelieved. If Allah had so willed, they would not have fought each other, but Allah does what He will. (Chapter 2: Verse 253)

In the previous session, we discussed how Allah blessed Prophet Moses with His speech and blessed Prophet Jesus –son of Mary- with the continuous presence of the Holy Spirit Gabriel by his side. Take note that Allah interjected His speech about Moses and Jesus with the following statement: 'others He raised many degrees in rank.' This statement is referring to our beloved Prophet Prophet Muhammad(pbuh).

Here you may wonder, why was Prophet Prophet Muhammad(pbuh) mentioned between Moses and Jesus –peace be upon them all-? Wasn't Prophet Muhammad(pbuh) sent as the final messenger hundreds of years after Jesus? We answer that Prophet Prophet Muhammad(pbuh)(pbuh) came between Moses and Jesus because the religion of Islam came as a moderate middle religion between Judaism and Christianity. Judaism was heavily weighted towards materialism, and it focused on the physical over the spiritual. Christianity was heavily weighted in spirituality over the physical. And the world needs a balance between the material and the spiritual. Thus, Prophet Prophet Muhammad(pbuh) and the Nobel Quran came to bring balance. Allah says in the 143rd verse of Surah Baqarah:

Thus have We made you a middle balanced nation, to be witnesses over men, and that the prophet may be a witness over you.

Let's look at some of the ways Prophet Prophet Muhammad(pbuh) (pbuh), peace be upon him, was raised in rank over other prophets and messengers:

All previous messengers were sent to a limited number of people in a certain place for a specified period of time. Prophet Lot, for example, was sent to one town. Prophets Jesus, Moses and Isaac were sent to the children of Israel. Prophet Prophet Muhammad(pbuh) (pbuh), on the other hand, was sent to all humanity and Jinn with a message that will endure until the end of time.

Another example of how our beloved prophet was raised in rank is his miracle: the Nobel Quran. Allah reveals miracles to support his messengers and prove the authenticity of their message to the people. We find that all of the miracles before Prophet Muhammad (pbuh) were tangible physical miracles. The miracles of the previous prophets were like a flame that lit brightly. Whoever saw that flame had witnessed the miracle, but once the flame extinguished, its power and light could only be felt by storytelling. For example, whoever saw Moses' staff parting the sea into two huge mountains of water had witnessed Moses' miracle; and whoever saw Jesus heal the leper and the blind had also witnessed Jesus' miracle. But do these miracles have any presence now? They do not. You might say that Jesus is the prophet of Allah, but you cannot point and say: 'this here is his miracle.'

The miracle of Prophet Muhammad (pbuh), peace be upon him, is not like any other miracle of previous prophets. Allah sent Prophet Muhammad (pbuh) as a messenger to all humanity until the last hour. Thus, his miracles had to be ever present and tangible to all humanity until the last hour. Any Muslim man or woman should be able to say -at any point in time- that Prophet Mohammed (pbuh) is the messenger of Allah and this here –The Quran- is his miracle.

Moreover, since the miracle of the Quran is ever-present until the last day, its treasures should also continue until the end of time. It is the gift that keeps on giving. This means that the Quran could not be fully explained at the time of the prophet. Each generation of humanity from the time of the prophet until the last day will continue to discover hidden treasures and wondrous meanings within the Holy book.

The Quran is Allah's word. It holds within it the power of Allah. Since the power, wisdom, and knowledge of Allah are infinite, so is the richness of His words. The treasures of the Noble Quran are infinite, and they will continue to be discovered until the end of time. Allah says:

We shall show them Our signs in every region of the earth and in themselves until it becomes clear to them that this is the Truth. Is it not sufficient that your Lord witnesses everything? (41:53)

Let's examine another area Allah blessed Prophet Mohammad with. If you look at all the previous heavenly message, you will find that the mission of the messengers was to deliver the religious teachings and act as an example for others to follow. In other words, previous prophets and messengers did not come to legislate; rather they only conveyed what Allah had legislated. As for the Prophet Muhammad (pbuh), peace be upon him, he was the only messenger that Allah entrusted to legislate. Allah says in the 7th verse of chapter 59:

Whatever the Messenger gives you accept it willingly, and whatever he forbids you, refrain from it. Keep from disobedience to Allah in reverence. Surely Allah is severe in retribution.

Allah, the All-Wise, gave our beloved prophet the freedom to legislate. Isn't this the pinnacle of rank? So the phrase 'others He raised many degrees in rank' applies only to Prophet Muhammad(pbuh), peace be upon him.

All of Allah's actions are actions of flawless wisdom and complete knowledge. Allah has no whim, desire, nor does He look for personal benefit. We are all Allah's creation, and we are all the same to Him. Thus, when He Almighty grants someone a bounty or a virtue, it is through His wisdom.

Allah says: 'Those are the messengers - We preferred some above others. Allah spoke to some; others He raised many degrees in rank; We gave Jesus, son of Mary, Our clear signs and strengthened him with the Holy Spirit.' When you hear the phrase 'Allah spoke to some,' Moses, peace be upon him, comes to mind. He was blessed with the amazing honour of speaking with Allah. Some people imagine that Allah's speech is a voice that requires vocal cords and so on. We answer: No, you should not measure Allah against your knowledge. Always take matters concerning Allah within the context of "there is nothing whatever like Him." We take every description of Allah exactly how He intended it, and we do not attribute it to our understanding, or compare it to our attributes as humans.

Allah also mentions the virtues He blessed Prophet Jesus with: 'We gave Jesus, son of Mary, Our clear signs and strengthened him with the Holy Spirit.' Whenever Prophet Jesus is mentioned in the Quran, Allah reaffirms that he was supported with the Holy Spirit, the Archangel Gabriel. This is because of the great challenges Jesus faced from day one.

Allah says:

She pointed at him. They said, 'How can we converse with an infant?' He said: 'I am a servant of Allah. He has granted me the Scripture; made me a prophet; made me blessed wherever I may be. He commanded me to pray, to give alms as long as I live, to cherish my mother. He did not make me domineering or graceless. Peace was on me the day I was born and will be on me the day I die, and the day I am raised to life again.' (19:29,33)

From the day Jesus was born, he and his mother faced accusations and hostilities. Prophet Jesus was sent to a people who were immersed in materialism. Their hearts were far from spirituality, and they did not believe in the unseen. Such people necessitated a messenger whose entire life revolved around the unseen in order to turn their hearts and minds to the Lord.

He, unlike any other human being, was born to a mother and no father. Allah Almighty kept the Holy Spirit in his company at all times for protection and support. The challenges continued until his enemies conspired to capture and kill him. It was through the archangel Gabriel that Jesus, peace be upon him, was rescued and raised to the heavens. Allah says:

and because they disbelieved and uttered a terrible slander against Mary, and said, 'We have killed the Messiah, Jesus, son of Mary, the Messenger of Allah.' They did not kill him, nor did they crucify him, though it was made to appear like that to them; those that disagreed about him are full of doubt, with no knowledge to follow, only doubt: they certainly did not kill him- Allah raised him up to Himself. Allah is almighty and wise.

(4:156-158)

LESSONS

The first lesson for us is to respect and honour all the prophets of Allah *subhanahu wa ta'ala* without making any comparisons between them.

-Allah *subhanahu wa ta'ala* has honoured His Messengers differently, however, for us, as the followers, it is mandatory for us to believe in all the Messengers and in the Books that were revealed to them. Our *emaan* [faith] would be incomplete, if we believe in some and reject others. This is because, in Surah Al-Baqarah we have read, **"And who believe in what has been revealed to you, [O Muhammad], and what was revealed before you..."** (2: 4)

-Being from the Ummah of Prophet Muhammad *salAllahu 'alayhi wa sallam* should not make us arrogant. It was Allah's decision to raise us from his Ummah. The real work for us is to emulate the Sunnah of the Prophet *salAllahu 'alayhi wa sallam,* live by it and spread its message to others. We should not go on arguing with people of other faiths regarding who is better than who, Allah *subhanahu wa ta'ala* knows best.

[Learn Some of the Sunnahs of the Prophet]

– Allah *subhanahu wa ta'ala* informs us that differences are part of His planning, had He willed He would have created all of us from the same Ummah. When the Jews refused to believe in Jesus *'alayhi salaam*, they not only rejected him but were so intense in their hatred for him that they agreed to kill him. We need to be conscious of our thoughts and feelings – and think before engaging in arguments with other people. If Allah *subhanahu wa ta'ala* and His Messenger *salAllahu 'alayhi wa sallam* has prohibited us from making comparisons or belittling others then we should hold on to their command.

VERSE 254

Yaa ayyuhal lazeena aamanoo anfiqoo mimmaa razaqnaakum min qabli ai yaatiya yawmul laa bai'un feehee wa la khullatunw wa laa shafaa'ah; walkaa firoona humuz zaalimoon

O you who believe! Spend some of what We have provided for you before a Day arrives on which there is no trading, no close friendship and no intercession. And the faithless—they are the wrongdoers.

When you hear any verse starting with "O you who believe," you should know that whatever follows is a command from Allah to the believers. Allah does not issue commands of 'do' and 'do not do' to all mankind, He only addresses those who willingly believed and declared their faith in Him. Once you declare your faith in Allah, you entrust Him as your Lord, the All-Wise, All-Knowledgeable. Only then, does He address you with 'do so' and 'do not do so.'

This concept is the very essence of every act in religion. We fast the month of Ramadan not because it makes us experience the hunger of the poor, but because Allah, our trusted Lord, instructed us to do so. I perform ablution before prayer not to cleanse my skin, but because Allah, my Lord, instructed me to do so. I entrust my Lord with my affairs and follow His commands even when –at times- I may not understand the wisdom behind these commands.

Allah says: 'O you who believe! Spend some of what We have provided for you.' Your earnings come from your work in life. Work requires a thinking mind; a mind that Allah provided for you. It requires a skill; a skill performed by the hands Allah provided for you. It requires energy such as oil, coal or sunrays; all provided by Allah. Any materials you use are also from Allah. So how much of your work is really from you, and how much is from Allah? All is from our Lord. He says:

Consider the seeds you sow in the ground- is it you who make them grow or We? (56:63, 64)

Allah is not asking you to give back what is His. He is not asking you to take over the responsibility of providing for others. He is only asking you to allocate a small portion of your wealth to help your brothers and sisters in need. He says:

I want no provision from them, nor do I want them to feed Me- Allah is the Provider, the Lord of Power, the Ever Mighty. (51:57,58)

Here you may ask: Why wouldn't Allah provide for the poor directly? We answer that Allah wants to foster the spirit of cooperation, support, and love in society. Here we should stress that the weak and the needy are those who are overwhelmed by life's circumstances, not those who are too lazy to work, or those who are professional beggars.

Do not ever say: "Why should I be concerned with the poor? Can't they work hard just like I did?" I like to remind you that poverty is a circumstance, and like many circumstances it is subject to change. Do not assume that you will always be OK, or that your job, income, or health is secure and guaranteed. Allah advises you: give to the poor out of your wealth today, because, in the future, if you happen to run into trouble.

Imagine how a person in financial trouble would feel when he or she sees wealthy Muslims taking time, effort and money to help. In a society where the rich help the poor and the strong help the weak, there are no feelings of hate and resentment. When you help a person in need, he or she would love to see you do better in your business.

Take note that when Allah asks you to: "Spend some of what We have provided for you." He is appreciating your work, and the effort you put in to earn money. Allah will repay you in full. He says:

Who will lend Allah a good loan, which He will increase for him many times over? It is Allah who withholds and Allah who gives abundantly, and it is to Him that you will return (2:245)

Allah is advising you to 'Spend some of what We have provided for you before a Day arrives on which there is no trading.' The word spend is translated from Arabic origin 'Anfiqoo.' The linguistic root 'Na Fa Qa' means a market that is all sold out of good. When you and I trade, we exchange goods for money. Goods are what directly benefits to you, while money cannot directly benefit you. Say, for example, that you are very hungry, and you have a pile or Gold. Does that pile do your hunger any good? It does not. But if you had a loaf of bread, you would benefit directly. Likewise, if you had millions in cash and you were dying of thirst in the desert, would your cash offer you any direct benefit? No, but a bottle of water would save your life. In other words, true benefit and value come from the goods that you have, whether food, drink, or clothes; not from money.

Allah, the All-Wise, is alerting and warning you not to have pride in wealth. He says: 'O you who believe! Spend some of what We have provided for you before a Day arrives on which there is no trading, no close friendship and no intercession. And the faithless—they are the wrongdoers.' There will come a day where money can no longer be exchanged for any goods. Your wealth will not help you or anyone else. So make sure to use your wealth now to secure your salvation on the Day of Judgment.

Not only will your wealth be useless, but even your close family and friends would be unavailable to help on the Day of Resurrection. There will be no one to intercede on your behalf. Allah says:

The Day man will flee from his own brother, his mother, his father, his wife, his children: each of them will be absorbed in concerns of their own on that Day- (80:34-37)

All doors of help and aid will be closed before you on the Day of Judgment. Your wealth will be worthless and the door of trade is closed. There will be no friends around to help either. The door of friendship and personal connections is also closed. There is no one to intercede on your behalf. Allah Almighty holds all the keys of intercession on that day. He is the only one to offer mercy and forgiveness. Wouldn't it then, make sense to listen to His advice now? Allah is advising you to spend out of your wealth today to help the needy and, more importantly, to help yourself on the Day of Resurrection.

Allah, the All-Merciful, has given you ample warning. He informed you in detail of how to avoid the terrible calamities of the Day of Judgment. He outlined what you can do now to earn salvation and success. Thus, if you find yourself in trouble on the day of Judgement, you only have yourself to blame. Allah did not wrong anybody. He says: 'And the faithless—they are the wrongdoers.'

LESSONS:

-Why does Allah subhanahu wa ta'ala keep encouraging us to spend in His cause? One reason is that it washes away the sins we committed.

[Where Should We Spend Our Money]

-Make a commitment to regularly spend in the way of Allah not just your spare change but an amount that will make you proud in the Hereafter and raise your scales with Allah. Word of caution: Do not advertise your charity. Let it be a secret between you and Allah.

VERSE 255

Allahu laaa ilaaha illaa Huwal Haiyul Qaiyoom; laa taakhuzuhoo sinatunw wa laa nawm; lahoo maa fissamaawaati wa maa fil ard; man zal lazee yashfa'u indahooo illaa bi-iznih; ya'lamu maa baina aydeehim wa maa khalfahum wa laa yuheetoona bishai'im min 'ilmihee illaa bimaa shaaa'; wasi'a Kursiyyuhus samaawaati wal arda wa laa Ya'ooduhoo hifzuhumaa; wa Huwal Aliyyul 'Azeem

Allah! There is no Allah but He,-the Living, the Self-subsisting, Eternal. No slumber can seize Him nor sleep. His are all things in the heavens and on earth. Who is there can intercede in His presence except as He permitteth? He knoweth what (appeareth to His creatures as) before or after or behind them. Nor shall they compass aught of His knowledge except as He willeth. His Throne doth extend over the heavens and the earth, and He feeleth no fatigue in guarding and preserving them for He is the Most High, the Supreme (in glory).

We start with the phrase "Allah: there is no Allah but Him." Allah is the ever-present. Everything around you points to his presence: From the majestic moon and stars, to the beauty of plants, animals, and the exquisite creation of people. Look at the largest star or the smallest atom: each is working to perfection in an orderly manner. The fine arrangement of crystals in gemstones, the intricate geometry of individual snowflakes, and everything in existence points to the absolute existence of a creator.

Allah informed us of some of his names; the most prominent of these names is Allah. When you hear someone say Allah, your mind exclusively recalls Allah the creator. Allah, however, did not share with us all of His names; We know this fact from the supplication of our beloved prophet Muhammad. He –peace be upon him- taught us say the following whenever we feel any sadness or grief in life: "Dear Allah, I am your servant, son of your servants, within your hand is my fate, and your judgment is my destiny. I ask you by any name you named yourself with, whether you revealed it in your book, or taught it to one of your creation, or kept it in the knowledge of the unseen, to make the Quran the spring of my heart, the light of my chest, and the relief of my sorrow, sadness and grief."

Most of Allah's names that He revealed to us are descriptive attributes such as the All-Hearing, the All-Merciful, and the Almighty. You may note that we as humans share some of these attributes. You and I have the ability to hear, the ability to see, and the ability to show mercy. But Allah's attributes are of absolute perfection. You may be able to see, but is your sight like Allah's? Of course not. You are alive and present. Is your presence like Allah's? No. He says in the 11th verse of chapter 42:

There is nothing whatever like Him.

Some of Allah's names have antonyms or opposites; Names that indicate an action and its opposite such as the Giver and the Taker, The Enricher and the Withholder. Take note that these types of names and attributes are actions that affect Allah's creation. He enriches us and withholds from us; He gives us life and causes us to die. The rest of Allah's names are His alone. They are descriptions of Himself, and thus they do not have opposites. He is The Majestic, the Almighty, and the Most High with no antonyms. The name that combines all Allah's attributes of perfection is: Allah.

Thus, Allah started this verse with His name: Allah. Then He immediately gave us the most critical attribute: "there is no God but Him." The first part of the phrase excludes everyone from being a God or deity, and the second part of the phrase affirms that Allah alone is the deity and no one else. What should you learn from this statement? You should learn to first clear your heart from any distraction and purify it before you turn to Allah and receive His love.

Since the beginning of time, Allah has loudly and repeatedly announced: 'Allah: there is no God but Him.' He is the creator, and He is the sustainer. Let's take a moment to think about creation: If someone else had created the universe, then where are they? If someone else created, didn't they hear Allah's repeated announcements? If they did not hear then they are not suitable to be Allahs. If they heard and did not challenge the announcement, again, they are not suitable to be Allahs. Allah says:

Say: "Had there been other Allahs with Him, as they assert, they would surely have sought a way against the Lord of the throne." (17:42)

The fact that Allah and Allah alone proclaimed to be the creator of the universe and no one challenged Him is evidence that 'there is no God but Him.'

This brings us back to the phrase: 'Allah: there is no Allah but Him.' Allah supported His message with Prophets, miracles and heavenly books. Let's look at the false Gods people set for themselves over the ages. People worshiped idols, they worshiped the sun and the moon, and they worshiped trees, stones, and much else. Did any of those false Gods send a miracle, a prophet or a book? Did the sun ask its worshipers to do such and such or avoid such and such? The answer is No. Allah, on the other hand, claimed creation and supported His claim over and over again. Thus, the statement: 'Allah: there is no Allah but Him' is self-evident and it is further supported by a procession of prophets, messengers, heavenly books and miracles.

"Allah: there is no God but Him" is the only deity to be worshipped. But what is the true meaning of worship? By definition, worship means to obey Allah's commands and avoid His prohibitions. Hence, when Allah says: 'do' then I must do, and when He says: 'do not do' then I must not do.

Keep in mind that Allah only asks you to do what is well within your ability. Some people try to confine worship to rituals such as prayer, fasting, going to the Hajj pilgrimage and giving the Zakat almsgiving. We answer that worship in Islam encompasses all aspects of life. Yes, faith, prayer, fasting, Hajj and Zakat are the foundation of Islam, but they are not the whole of Islam. Performing the rituals of worship alone is like laying a foundation with no building on top. The purpose of laying a foundation is to build a building. Allah says in the 61st verse of chapter 11:

'My people, worship Allah. You have no God other than Him. It was He who brought you into being from the earth and asked you to thrive in it'

In order to thrive on earth, we need to work.

We ask the people who claim that worship is only prayers and fasting: How long do your prayers take each day? An hour at the most? How about fasting? A month out of the year? Hajj? A few days out of your life? What do you plan to do with the rest of your time? Perhaps the more important questions to ask are: Can you pray without clothes? Can you break your fast without bread and vegetables? If our only purpose in life is to do the rituals of worship, then who will make us clothes, farm the land and bake bread? We answer that since you and I cannot pray without food and without clothes, then making food and making clothes is a requirement of worship. The believing man or woman who farms the land is performing an act of worship. The truck driver who delivers grains to the mill is performing an act of worship. The same goes for the baker, store owner and street cleaner. Allah says:

O you who believe, when the call to prayer is made on the day of congregation, hasten to remember Allah, putting aside your business. — —that is better for you, if only you knew— then when the prayer is finished, disperse in the land and seek out Allah's bounty. Remember Allah often so that you may prosper. (62:9,10)

Take note that Allah did not only order you to pray your Friday congregation prayers, but He also ordered you to go out and earn a living after the prayer is done. Both are acts of worship and obedience to Allah. It is your duty as a believer, not only to work, but to excel at your job. All of your actions in life should fall under the banner of: 'Allah: there is no God but Him.'

Allah started the verse with the proclamation of His Lordship alone. Then, He stated the first requirement of being a God: 'the Ever Living,' because with life comes the power to do, and the knowledge to do. Here we should ask: What is life? There have been endless discussions among philosophers about the meaning of life. Some said that life is awareness: if you are aware of yourself and your surroundings then you are alive. Others said that life is movement and so on. All these definitions are based on our life and our existence. We answer that the broadest and most comprehensive meaning of life is the ability and the fitness to perform your intended task. Take a tree for example. As long as it is growing and producing fruit, it is alive. Once it stops growing, or producing, it no longer performs its task and it is dying. A man is alive as long as he can perform his duties and tasks in life. We refer to a man in a coma as a vegetative state because he can no longer do any tasks. You can apply the same to inanimate objects. Go to the beach and look at the smooth pebble stones. You will see that each has a different shape and size. Some are big, others very small. This indicates change. Even the largest stone, with time, will turn into grains of sand. This is the lifecycle and function of a stone. If you remove a pebble from its natural environment, change will stop and the stone is no longer performing its intended task. So each being and each object is alive as long as it can perform its intended task in life. Allah says in the 42nd verse of chapter 8:

it happened so that Allah could settle a matter whose result was preordained: so that those who perished would perish with clear proof, and those who lived would live with clear proof. Allah is All-Hearing, All-Knowing.

Take note that Allah used the verb "to perish" as opposite to the verb "to live." Then we read the following verse:

Do not call out to any other God beside Allah, for there is no God but Him. Everything will perish except His Face. His is the Judgement and to Him you shall all be brought back. (28:88)

"Everything will perish except His Face" refers to all beings such as people, angels and jinn; it refers to all plants, animals, planets, stars, all objects and matter. Since all these things will perish, it means that each was alive before. Each had a life –it may not be like yours and mine- but it was a life suitable for its purpose. Modern science showed us that individual atoms are full of movement and change. A drop of water is full of living bacteria. Even when matter drastically changes, such as when we make sand into glass, it simply moves from one form of life and function to another.

This brings us back to the verse: 'Allah: there is no Allah but Him, the Ever Living.' Allah has the supreme life. It is an ever-existing life, because Allah is the first and the last. Allah is ever present, ever watchful over His creation. No one gave Him life, and no one takes it away. It is a principal of the Divine self.

The next attribute in the verse is 'the Ever Watchful' translated from the Arabic origin 'Al Qayyum' 'القيوم' which is in the superlative exaggerated form of the word 'Qa'em. قائم' Here we should ask, Do Allah's attributes change? We answer that Allah's attributes do not change or oscillate between strength and weakness. Rather they are attributes of absolute perfection at all time. For example, in the Arabic language: 'راحم' Rahem means the merciful. Allah chose to use the names "Most Merciful" and "Most Benevolent" in the hyperbole form indicating the vastness of his Mercy. Allah's mercy does not change; the only change is to whom His vast mercy applies. Allah is the Most Merciful in this world because of the large number of those whom he includes under His mercy. Allah's Mercy envelops all -the believer, the disobedient and the disbeliever-. He provides everyone with the essentials of life, and pardons many regardless of their faith or disbelief. On the other hand, in the hereafter, Allah will only extend His mercy to the believers while the rest will be expelled from it. Here you may ask: Why do we still use the form of hyperbole "the most Merciful" when

Allah's mercy in the hereafter is only limited to the believers? We answer; Allah's mercy in this world is general and widespread to all his creation. And while his mercy is specific for the believers in the hereafter, it is far greater in its quantity and everlastingness. Allah was the Most-Merciful even before any creation existed to seek His Mercy; and Allah will ever be the Most-Merciful even after all the creation perishes.

Let's examine this concept in two examples from the Quran. Allah says:

Allah does not wrong any one, not even the equal of an atom (4:40)

This verse negated all unjustness from Allah; but then we encounter the following verse:

and your Lord is not tyrannical to the slaves (03:182)

In this verse, we notice the use of the word "tyranny", which means extreme unjustness. So, at first glance, there seems to be a contradiction: Verse 182 of chapter 3 does not negate Allah being unjust; it only negates him being extremely unjust or a tyrant, while the 40th verse of chapter 4 negates all unjustness from Allah. We answer that when you take a closer look at the nuances of the language, you will find the answer.

The first verse negates all unjustness from Allah with regard to a single being. The second verse did not mention unjustness in regard to a single person; rather it mentioned the plural word 'slaves', meaning all of Allah's creation. Given the enormous number of Allah's creation, if each person is inflicted even with an atom's weight of unjustness, the total unjustness would be massive, and this adds up to tyranny. Thus, both verses negate all unjustness from Allah, but the expression of hyperbole "tyranny" is used for the large number of people to whom the verse applies. Allah does not treat anyone unjustly; his fairness, just like his mercy, is absolute and consistent.

This brings us back to the verse. Allah is the 'The Ever Watchful' translated from the Arabic origin 'Al Qayyum' 'القيوم'. The word 'Qa'em 'قائم' means to manage. A man manages and keeps a close eye on his household. A principal manages his or her school. The word 'Al

Qayyum' 'القيوم'also shares the root with the word 'Qam' which means to stand up. In other words, Allah is actively managing and watchful over the entire universe and creation. This management is not by delegation, rather Allah himself is every watchful. He says:

He has the keys to the unseen: no one knows them but Him. He knows all that is in the land and sea. No leaf falls without His knowledge, nor is there a single grain in the darkness of the earth, or anything, fresh or withered, that is not written in a clear Record. (6:59)

And in another verse:

Who is it who stands over every soul marking its action? Yet they ascribe partners to Allah. Say, 'Name them,' or, 'Can you tell Him about anything on earth He does not know? Or is this just a display of words?' Rather the plotting the disbelievers devise is made alluring to them and they are barred from the right path: no one can guide those Allah leaves to stray. (13:33)

Have any of the idols or false Gods people assigned for themselves ever create anything? Are they able to manage or watch over even the smallest of operations? Allah is the Creator, the manager and the Ever-Watchful over the entire universe, over every human being, and every creation. Those who seek any Allahs other than Allah have truly gone astray. Allah is Qayyom who need no help. Allah is ever Qayyoum even before any creation was there to watch over and will always be Qayyoum even after all creation has perished. It is a principal of the divine self.

Allah: there is no god but Him, the Ever-Living, the Ever Watchful. Neither drowsiness nor sleep overtakes Him. All that is in the heavens and in the earth belongs to Him. Who is there that can intercede with Him except by His leave? He knows what is before them and what is behind them, but they do not comprehend any of His knowledge except what He wills. His seat encompasses the heavens and the earth; it does not weary Him to preserve them both. He is the Most High, the Tremendous. (Chapter 2: Verse 255)

We discussed how Allah, the one and only, is ever-living and ever-present. But is that enough to oversee the creation? An essential part of managing the creation is to be ever watchful and aware where 'Neither drowsiness nor sleep overtakes Him.'

The children of Israel asked Prophet Moses: 'Does our Lord sleep?' Allah directed Moses to bring two glasses filled with water and give them to the strongest man in the group to hold. He was to hold them for as long as he can without spilling. Naturally, after a while, the man got tired and nodded before he fell asleep. The two glasses fell, broke, and water spilled everywhere. There was the answer: If the caretaker of the heavens and the earth got tired or fell asleep, everything would go to ruin.

Isn't that the most beautiful reassurance you can get from your Lord? Isn't that the highest honour you can hope for? Allah is telling you: sleep well my servant, sleep with no care in the world because I am always watchful. I am always in charge, so you do not have to worry.

While you sleep, everything is taken care of. The universe runs like clockwork; Your lungs, digestive system, and heart do their job; All under the watchful eye of your Lord. Indeed being a servant of Allah brings you the highest degrees of honour.

Take note that Allah did not just specify sleep, He mentioned drowsiness first. What is drowsiness? It is the state of feeling dull, sluggish and sleepy. It is what you feel after a long day, right before you fall asleep. Your eyes feel heavy; your eyelids start drooping, and your energy is drained. Allah mentioned both, drowsiness and sleep so you do not assume that He can resist sleep, but may feel tired or dozy. Allah the Ever-Living is also Ever-Aware, Ever-Watchful.

When you read 'Allah: there is no Allah but Him, the Ever-Living, the Ever Watchful. Neither drowsiness nor sleep overtakes Him,' you are reassured that your Lord who created everything is in charge of everything, and nothing whatsoever is out of His control. Thus, Allah says right after: 'All that is in the heavens and in the earth belongs to Him.'

The verse continues: "Who is there that can intercede with Him except by His leave?" Allah created all of us, and he provides for all of us regardless of our faith. The sun rises on all humanity, the earth yields crop for everyone, and livestock serve the believer and disbeliever alike. If you work hard and utilize the resources Allah put at your disposal, you will get results even if you are a disbeliever. But on the Day of Judgment, things are different. Allah says:

They worship those besides Allah who cannot do them harm or bring them gain, and say: "These are our intercessors with Allah." Say: "Do you want to inform Allah of things in the heavens and the earth He does not know?" Glorious is He, and exalted above what they associate with Him! (10:18)

So anyone who associates partners with Allah in the hopes of receiving their help on the Day of Judgment is deeply mistaken. Sadly, if he or she is counting on their intersession, there is only Hellfire awaiting. Allah says:

But the deeds of those who disbelieve are like a mirage in a desert: the thirsty person thinks there will be water but, when he gets there, he finds only Allah, who pays him his account in full- Allah is swift in reckoning. (24:39)

Allah is above taking any partners, spouses or children. He says: 'All that is in the heavens and in the earth belongs to Him. Who is there that can intercede with Him except by His leave?'

By associating partners with Allah, a person loses all hopes of forgiveness and forgoes any chance that Allah would allow anyone to intercede on his or her behalf. Allah says:

Your Lord is Allah who created the heavens and earth in six Days, then established Himself on the throne, governing everything; there is no one that can intercede with Him, unless He has first given permission: this is Allah your Lord so worship Him. How can you not take heed? (10:3)

And in another chapter:

And beware of a Day when no soul can stand in for another. No compensation will be accepted from it, nor intercession be of use to it, nor will anyone be helped. (2:123)

Allah: there is no god but Him, the Ever-Living, the Ever Watchful. Neither drowsiness nor sleep overtakes Him. All that is in the heavens and in the earth belongs to Him. Who is there that can intercede with Him except by His leave? He knows what is before them and what is behind them, but they do not comprehend any of His knowledge except what He wills. His seat encompasses the heavens and the earth; it does not weary Him to preserve them both. He is the Most High, the Tremendous. (Chapter 2: Verse 255)

We begin with the phrase: 'He knows what is before them and what is behind them.' Scholars explained this phrase from different angles. Let's look at a couple of explanations. Usually, you can see what is before you –or in front of you-, and you are not aware of what is behind you. In other words, Allah knows what we know, and He knows what we do not know. Others explained that 'what is before them' refers to the future, while 'what is behind them' refers to the past. So Allah knows the past and the future.

We answer that Allah knows all: He knows what we know and what we do not; He knows what is in our world and what is beyond our world, and He knows the past, present, and future. He says:

He has the keys to the unseen: no one knows them but Him. He knows all that is in the land and sea. No leaf falls without His knowledge, nor is there a single grain in the darkness of the earth, or anything, fresh or withered, that is not written in a clear Record. (6:59)

Allah's knowledge is comprehensive and complete, while our knowledge is limited and deficient. In fact, we cannot even imagine the vastness of Allah's knowledge, because if we understood how vast His knowledge is, it means that His knowledge has limits. He says: 'but they do not comprehend any of His knowledge except what He wills.'

Let's look at the sources of our knowledge: First, we can research and draw conclusions. For example, a student who is given a math problem can use the information in the problem and his or her prior knowledge to reach the answer. Scientists can use the information they already know, plus the materials in the lab, to run experiments and learn something new. Even this type of knowledge falls under the rule: 'but they do not comprehend any of His knowledge except what He wills.'

Another source of knowledge is gifts from Allah. How, you may ask? We answer that Allah has set a preordained birth date -or reveal date- for every piece of knowledge given to humanity. Just like each one of us has a set birthday; each piece of knowledge has a set birthday. Sometimes, this birthday coincides with scientists researching and exploring. Other times, the birthday of a certain piece of knowledge falls during a time when no one is looking. This is when scientists trip over a great discovery by chance. In fact, most of humanity's major discoveries happened by chance. Let's look at a few examples: The discovery of penicillin, one of the world's first antibiotics and a turning point in human history, happened by pure chance. In September of 1928, Dr. Alexander Fleming, a bacteriologist, returned from a summer vacation to very a messy lab bench. Upon examining some bacterial colonies, Dr. Fleming noted that a mold called Penicillium Notatum had contaminated his Petri dishes. He was amazed to find that this particular mold prevented normal bacterial growth. Here are Dr. Fleming's own words in his journal: "When I woke up just after dawn on September 28, 1928, I certainly didn't plan to revolutionize all medicine by discovering the world's first antibiotic, or bacteria killer. But I guess that was exactly what I did." There are countless other stories of accidental discoveries: Medical x-rays, plastics, heart pacemakers, cooking with microwaves, and much more. Allah holds all the knowledge of the unknown, and He gives humanity —by research or by chance- a few gems. He says:

We will show them Our signs in every region of the earth and within themselves until it becomes clear to them that this is the Truth. Is it not enough that your Lord witnesses everything? (41:53)

The revelation of knowledge and secrets of the unseen are not limited to science. Allah —the Most Generous- also gives from His knowledge and blessings to His close servants who excel in devotion. He says:

He is the One who knows the unseen and does not divulge His Unseen to anyone – except a Messenger with whom He is well pleased, and then He posts sentinels before him and behind him (72:26, 27)

More importantly: Allah holds all the keys to His knowledge. He may grant us knowledge now and then, even if we are not actively looking. But He does not grant the master key to anyone. Allah says:

He has the keys to the unseen: no one knows them but Him. He knows all that is in the land and sea. No leaf falls without His knowledge, nor is there a single grain in the darkness of the earth, or anything, fresh or withered, that is not written in a clear Record. (6:59)

The word "any" in the phrase: 'they do not comprehend any of His knowledge except what He wills' refers to even the smallest and most trivial pieces of knowledge. Indeed, Allah has control over everything.

Allah: there is no god but Him, the Ever-Living, the Ever Watchful. Neither drowsiness nor sleep overtakes Him. All that is in the heavens and in the earth belongs to Him. Who is there that can intercede with Him except by His leave? He knows what is before them and what is behind them, but they do not comprehend any of His knowledge except what He wills. His seat encompasses the heavens and the earth; it does not weary Him to preserve them both. He is the Most High, the Tremendous. (Chapter 2: Verse 255)

We begin with the phrase: 'He knows what is before them and what is behind them.' Scholars explained this phrase from different angles. Let's look at a couple of explanations. Usually, you can see what is before you –or in front of you-, and you are not aware of what is behind you. In other words, Allah knows what we know, and He knows what we do not know. Others explained that 'what is before them' refers to the future, while 'what is behind them' refers to the past. So Allah knows the past and the future.

We answer that Allah knows all: He knows what we know and what we do not; He knows what is in our world and what is beyond our world, and He knows the past, present, and future. He says:

He has the keys to the unseen: no one knows them but Him. He knows all that is in the land and sea. No leaf falls without His knowledge, nor is there a single grain in the darkness of the earth, or anything, fresh or withered, that is not written in a clear Record. (6:59)

Allah's knowledge is comprehensive and complete, while our knowledge is limited and deficient. In fact, we cannot even imagine the vastness of Allah's knowledge, because if we understood how vast His knowledge is, it means that His knowledge has limits. He says: 'but they do not comprehend any of His knowledge except what He wills.'

Let's look at the sources of our knowledge: First, we can research and draw conclusions. For example, a student who is given a math problem can use the information in the problem and his or her prior knowledge to reach the answer. Scientists can use the information they already know, plus the materials in the lab, to run experiments and learn something new. Even this type of knowledge falls under the rule: 'but they do not comprehend any of His knowledge except what He wills.'

Another source of knowledge is gifts from Allah. How, you may ask? We answer that Allah has set a preordained birth date -or reveal date- for every piece of knowledge given to humanity. Just like each one of us has a set birthday; each piece of knowledge has a set birthday. Sometimes, this birthday coincides with scientists researching and exploring. Other times, the birthday of a certain piece of knowledge falls during a time when no one is looking. This is when scientists trip over a great discovery by chance. In fact, most of humanity's major discoveries happened by chance. Let's look at a few examples: The discovery of penicillin, one of the world's first antibiotics and a turning point in human history, happened by pure chance. In September of 1928, Dr. Alexander Fleming, a bacteriologist, returned from a summer vacation to very a messy lab bench. Upon examining some bacterial colonies, Dr. Fleming noted that a mold called Penicillium Notatum had contaminated his Petri dishes. He was amazed to find that this particular mold prevented normal bacterial growth. Here are Dr. Fleming's own words in his journal: "When I woke up just after dawn on September 28, 1928, I certainly didn't plan to revolutionize all medicine by discovering the world's first antibiotic, or bacteria killer. But I guess that was exactly what I did." There are countless other stories of accidental discoveries: Medical x-rays, plastics, heart pacemakers, cooking with microwaves, and much more. Allah holds all the knowledge of the unknown, and He gives humanity —by research or by chance- a few gems. He says:

> We will show them Our signs in every region of the earth and within themselves until it becomes clear to them that this is the Truth. Is it not enough that your Lord witnesses everything? (41:53)

The revelation of knowledge and secrets of the unseen are not limited to science. Allah —the Most Generous- also gives from His knowledge and blessings to His close servants who excel in devotion. He says:

> He is the One who knows the unseen and does not divulge His Unseen to anyone – except a Messenger with whom He is well pleased, and then He posts sentinels before him and behind him (72:26, 27)

More importantly: Allah holds all the keys to His knowledge. He may grant us knowledge now and then, even if we are not actively looking. But He does not grant the master key to anyone. Allah says:

> He has the keys to the unseen: no one knows them but Him. He knows all that is in the land and sea. No leaf falls without His knowledge, nor is there a single grain in the darkness of the earth, or anything, fresh or withered, that is not written in a clear Record. (6:59)

The word "any" in the phrase: 'they do not comprehend any of His knowledge except what He wills' refers to even the smallest and most trivial pieces of knowledge. Indeed, Allah has control over everything.

> Allah: there is no god but Him, the Ever-Living, the Ever Watchful. Neither drowsiness nor sleep overtakes Him. All that is in the heavens and in the earth belongs to Him. Who is there that can intercede with Him except by His leave? He knows what is before them and what is behind them, but they do not comprehend any of His knowledge except what He wills. His seat encompasses the heavens and the earth; it does

not weary Him to preserve them both. He is the Most High, the Tremendous. (Chapter 2: Verse 255)

Let's examine the phrase: 'His seat encompasses the heavens and the earth.' When you read the Quran, you come across many words used to describe Allah that can also apply to us. For example: Allah is alive, and you are alive. But is your life similar to His? Allah has knowledge and so do you. Is your knowledge like His? Allah sees and hears, and you see and hear, but do your hearing and sight resemble His? Of course not! Thus, when you read any description of Allah, whether in attributes or actions, do not compare it to your attributes and actions. Do not regard these descriptions with your human logic and worldly understanding, rather, always remember the following verses:

'There is nothing whatever like Him' (from 48:10)

And in another chapter:

Glory be to your Lord, the Lord of Might, beyond anything they describe. (37:180)

When you read a verse talking about 'Allah's hand' then remember, just as Allah's life is not like yours, just as Allah's knowledge is nothing like yours, so is His hand; it is nothing like yours. Similarly, when you read: 'His seat encompasses the heavens and the earth,' think of it in the frame of 'There is nothing whatever like Him.' Do not say that Allah has a chair and He sits in it as you and I do.

Even time and place do not apply to Allah. How, you may ask? We answer that a place is where an event happens, and time is how long an event or action takes. For example, if I tell you that I ate a sandwich, then you can ask: 'when and where did you eat?' You can ask about time and place when an event happens and something changes. Allah, on the other hand, is ever-constant. His attributes never change. Allah is ever-existent; He is the ever-living; there is neither a beginning nor an end to Allah. Thus, time and place do not apply to Him. Time and place are two of Allah's creations. And since there is no time or place for Allah; you cannot explain the phrase 'His seat encompasses the heavens and the earth' based on your understanding of a place to sit, or a time to sit.

Some scholars tried to avoid the topic of Allah's physical attributes all-together. For example, verses such as: 'Those who pledge loyalty to you are actually pledging loyalty to Allah Himself- Allah's hand is placed on theirs' (from 48:10) were explained as Allah's ability and power rather than Allah's hand. We answer that since Allah used the description: 'Allah's hand,' then we should accept it as He intended. Allah is best aware of His divine being and the words He uses in the Quran. We accept these descriptions just as Allah intended and within the frame of: 'There is nothing whatever like Him.'

In the verse under study, the word 'seat' carries many meanings. A seat or a chair indicates power and control. We sit after our work is done, and everything is just as we want it to be. We do not sit if there is chaos around, or if there are tasks still need to be done. A chair or a seat also represents authority. We use the expression 'The Seat of Power' to refer to the highest government or corporate positions. A seat also represents structure and stability.

The verse continues: 'His seat encompasses the heavens and the earth.' To encompass something is to contain it and surround it from all directions. Take a moment to look around you, look at your city, and look at the sky, the sun, the moon, and all the stars. The universe is the largest thing we know. Allah says:

The creation of the heavens and earth is greater by far than the creation of mankind, though most people do not know it. (40:57)

Yet, all that you see and everything the science of astronomy has revealed are well within Allah's seat. He says: 'His seat encompasses the heavens and the earth.' Prophet Muhammad gave us some clues of the unimaginable vastness and majesty of Allah's creation. Abu Thar –one of the Prophet's close companions- asked Prophet Muhammad about Allah's words: 'His seat encompasses the heavens and the earth.' He, peace be upon him, answered: 'O Abu Thar. The seven heavens in relation to the seat of Allah are like a ring in a desert. And the seat of Allah in relation to the throne of Allah is like a ring in a desert.'

Even with all the recent leaps in modern science, we are still in the immediate vicinity of earth. When we measure distance in space, miles and kilometers are too small to use. A light-year is the unit astronomers use to measure distance. It is the distance a beam of light travels in one year. One light-year equals about six trillion miles. The moon is mere light-seconds away from the earth. Mars and the sun are a few light-minutes away. That is as far humanity has traveled. But we know that there are stars that are thousands, hundreds of thousands, and even millions of light-years away. Keep in mind that all the stars that you see, study and know about are in the lowest heaven. Allah created seven heavens. The vastness of His creation is beyond comprehension.

Here is something interesting to consider. Allah says:

So race for your Lord's forgiveness and a Garden as wide as the heavens and earth, prepared for those who believe in Allah and His messengers: that is Allah's bounty, which He bestows on whoever He pleases. Allah's bounty is infinite. (57:21)

Paradise, which Allah has prepared for you, is as wide as the heavens and earth. As you well know, width is the lesser of two dimensions. Length is longer. How long is paradise? Only Allah knows. This is the ultimate reward that is worth working hard for day in and day out.

The verse continues: 'it does not weary Him to preserve them both.' To weary is to tire or to be overburdened. For example, if you can carry 15Kgs, and I give you 17Kgs to hold, you may feel a little strained. But, if I give you 30Kgs to carry, then you would feel overburdened; your back would arch, and you may drop the weight. Allah, on the other hand, does not tire nor strain with the care of the heavens and earth. He says:

Indeed Allah sustains the heavens and the earth lest they should fall apart, and if they were to fall apart there is none who can sustain them except Him. Indeed He is all-forbearing, all-forgiving. (35:41)

Allah is the One —the only One- who holds the universe in its magnificent balance. He alone keeps the universe, and He alone is capable of ending existence. Thus, with all that we learned in this verse, it is only logical to end with Allah's words: 'He is the Most High, the Tremendous.'

Allah: there is no Allah but Him, the Ever Living, the Ever Watchful. Neither drowsiness nor sleep overtakes Him. All that is in the heavens and in the earth belongs to Him. Who is there that can intercede with Him except by His leave? He knows what is before them and what is behind them, but they do not comprehend any of His knowledge except what He wills. His seat encompasses the heavens and the earth; it does not weary Him to preserve them both. He is the Most High, the Tremendous. (Chapter 2: Verse 255)

This marvellous verse in the Nobel Quran is known for its high value and blessings. The verse of the seat, or Ayatu Al Kursi, is mentioned in many narrations of our beloved prophet Muhammad. He said: "Within 'The Cow' –Surat Al Baqara- is a verse. This verse is the pinnacle of the Quran. Whoever reads it in his or her house builds a shield between the devil and his or her family."

Imam Ali heard the prophet say: "Whoever reads Ayatu Al Kursi before sleep is blessed by Allah's protection, so are his family and his neighbours." Lastly, Abu Munthir, one of the prophet's close companions, narrates: Prophet Muahmmad, peace be upon him, asked me: "O Abu Munthir, do you know which verse of the Book of Allah holds tremendous value?" I replied: "Allah and His Messenger know best." Prophet Muhammad repeated the question: "O Abu Munthir, do you know which verse of the Book of Allah holds tremendous value?" I answered: "Allah: there is no Allah but Him, the Ever Living, the Ever Watchful. Neither drowsiness nor sleep overtakes Him." The messenger of Allah then patted my chest and said: "May Allah bless your knowledge and grant you more."

Scholars have poured over this verse to unlock its secrets. Some attributed the verse's blessings to its name. It is the verse of the seat, the seat of absolute power, the seat of Lordship, the seat of grand majesty. Allah is the one. 'there is no Allah but Him, the Ever Living, the Ever Watchful. Neither drowsiness nor sleep overtakes Him.' He has full knowledge of the heaves and the earth, and He is beholden to no one. 'Who is there that can intercede with Him except by His leave?'

Other scholars attributed the value of the verse to the number of times the Almighty was referenced in it. We find sixteen mentions of the Divine in this single verse. Let's count together:

'Allah' mentioned at the very beginning is the ultimate name of the Divine.

Second, we find the reference 'Him' in the phrase: 'there is no Allah but Him'.

Third, He is 'The ever living'

Then, 'the Ever Watchful.'

Fifth we read the reference 'Him' in 'Neither drowsiness nor sleep overtakes Him.'

Again, the reference 'Him' in 'All that is in the heavens and in the earth belongs to Him.'

Seventh and eighth 'Who is there that can intercede with Him except by His leave?'

Ninth, tenth and eleventh in the following: He knows what is before them and what is behind them, but they do not comprehend any of His knowledge except what He wills.'

Another reference to the divine in the following phrase: 'His seat encompasses the heavens and the earth.' And we are up to twelve.

The thirteenth is mentioned here: 'it does not weary Him to preserve them both.'

The pronoun 'He' is the fourteenth mentions.

And lastly, 'the Most High, the Tremendous' complete the fifteenth and sixteenth.

Some scholars pointed to the verb 'to preserve them both' as another reference to Allah, making the total seventeen.

Prophet Muhammad peace be upon him, said: "Nothing stands between the person who recites Ayatu Al Kursi after each prayer and paradise expect death."

Allah: there is no Allah but Him, the Ever Living, the Ever Watchful. Neither drowsiness nor sleep overtakes Him. All that is in the heavens and in the earth belongs to Him. Who is there that can intercede with Him except by His leave? He knows what is before them and what is behind them, but they do not comprehend any of His knowledge except what He wills. His seat encompasses the heavens and the earth; it does not weary Him to preserve them both. He is the Most High, the Tremendous.

VERSE 256

Laaa ikraaha fid deeni qat tabaiyanar rushdu minal ghayy; famai yakfur bit Taaghooti wa yu'mim billaahi faqadis tamsaka bil'urwatil wusqaa lan fisaama lahaa; wallaahu Samee'un 'Aleem

There is no compulsion in religion: The right course has become distinct from error, so whoever rejects the powers of evil and believes in Allah has grasped the firmest hand-hold, one that will never break. Allah is all hearing and all knowing.

In the previous verse, 'Ayatul Kursi', Allah gave us the core of Islamic creed; a creed that each one of us can be proud of and honoured by. Allah, our Lord, there is no God but Him. He is 'the Ever-Living, the Ever Watchful. Neither drowsiness nor sleep overtakes Him. All that is in the heavens and in the earth belongs to Him. Who is there that can intercede with Him except by His leave?' Isn't that a Lord who is worthy of worship? If you follow the Highest, doesn't that bring you honour? If you obey the Ever-Living, the Ever Watchful, who owns the heavens and earth, doesn't that bring clarity and security to every aspect of your life?

Thus, after presenting us with the solid foundation of faith and the compelling case of Allah's Lordship, it was logical for Allah to follow with: "There is no compulsion in religion." Because if you force someone to believe in you, it means that you have a weak case. If, on the other hand, you have a solid case, smart people would naturally come to you.

This brings us back to the verse; compulsion is to force another person to do an action that he or she does not want to do, or does not value. When it comes to faith in Allah "There is no compulsion in religion: The right course has become distinct from error."

Allah did not compel us to abide by faith as He compelled the heavens, the earth, the animals, the plants and the non-living to do. All creation, except humans and Jinn, are compelled to obey Allah. Allah gave us intelligence. He says in the 31st verse of chapter 13:

Do those who have faith not know that if Allah had wanted to He could have guided all mankind?

And in another chapter:

It is Allah who subjected the sea for you—ships sail on it by His command so that you can seek His bounty and give Him thanks— He has subjected all that is in the heavens and the earth for your benefit, as a gift from Him. There truly are signs in this for those who reflect. (45:12,13)

Allah wants you to come to Him willingly out of conviction, not out of fear or coercion. Compulsion proves power but does not prove love. Allah did not use the power of compulsion because He, Almighty, wants the power of love and reason. By extension, the prophets and messengers sent by Allah were not sent to compel people. They were sent to inform and act as a living example of compassion for others to follow. Had Allah wanted to force people into belief, there would have been no reason to send any messengers. He says:

And had your Lord willed, those on earth would have believed - all of them entirely. Then, O Muhammad, would you compel the people into belief? (10:99)

The Prophet is only required to convey Allah's message, not to force anyone into faith.

Here we should pause and address a common misconception: There is a difference between the compulsion over religion and compulsion over the requirement of religion. You ask a Muslim: why don't you pray?

He or she is quick to quote the Quran: "there is no compulsion in religion." 'I can do whatever I see fit.' Here, you should tell him that the proper meaning of the verse is that there is no compulsion in selecting or entering into religion. However, once you have voluntarily declared your belief in Allah, then you have joined the Muslim community, and you must abide by the rules of faith. You cannot pick and choose what you like and do not like. If you violate Islamic rules, there are consequences. You are free to believe or disbelieve, but when you commit to the faith, you become obligated to implement your faith as required. If you are a disbeliever and you drink wine, you are free to do so. But if you are a believer and you drink wine, you have overstepped Allah's limits, and there are consequences.

We should also address another misconception, often propagated by the enemies of Islam: They claim over and over that Islam was spread by the sword. We say to them: look at the history of Islam. Islam started very weak. For well over a decade, early Muslims suffered all kinds of persecution, torture, loss of property and life. They were driven out of their home, wealth and families, and were not able to defend themselves. Allah had wisdom behind this initial period of weakness and persecution of early Muslims. We ask those who claim that Islam was spread by the sword: who oppressed and forced the early Muslims into faith? For 13 years in Mecca, a person would lose all protection and become a target of violence when he or she became Muslim. In other words, everything was used –including the sword- to force people out of Islam.

Here is another fact to refute the claim of the sword. Saying that Islam was spread by the sword implies that when the Muslims won battles, they forced their enemies into Islam. Yet, the same people who make this accusation criticize Islam for imposing a tax –called Jezya- on the nonbelievers under their rule. These charges are frail and, in fact, contradictory. By imposing a Jezya tax on the non-believers, Islam officially recognizes their faith and their right to practice it. If Muslims had forced people to embrace Islam, then there would have been no need to legislate the Jizya tax. Hence, Islam did not impose faith on anyone; to the contrary, Islam freed the people from the powers which dominated them. The Jezia tax guarantees the right of non-Muslims to practice their faith freely and guarantees them the protection of the state. It is worth noting that non-believers are exempt from paying almsgiving –zakat- which is obligatory for the believers.

Here you may ask: if that was the case, then why did the Muslims go to war to begin with? We answer that the Islamic wars were fought for two reasons: The first was to defend the community from outside aggression. And the second was to stand against those who oppressed and imposed a dictatorial rule on others. Islam fought to give people the freedom to decide the most appropriate religion for themselves. Why? Because the believers were confident that when people were free to choose, and when they saw the mercy of our Lord and the exemplary life of the Muslim society, they would naturally find the truth in Islam. Allah says: 'There is no compulsion in religion: The right course has become distinct from error.'

There is no compulsion in religion: The right course has become distinct from error, so whoever rejects the powers of evil and believes in Allah has grasped the firmest hand-hold, one that will never break. Allah is all hearing and all knowing.

Let's start by exploring the phrase: 'The right course has become distinct from error.' The 'right course' is the path of salvation, and "the error" is the path to destruction. Allah clarifies further in the following verse:

I will keep distracted from My signs those who behave arrogantly on Earth without any right, and who, even if they see every sign, will not believe in them; they will not follow the right course if they see it but will take the way of error if they see that. This is because they denied Our signs and paid them no heed (7:146)

The opposite of the 'right course' is the 'the way of error' translated from the Arabic origin 'Al-ghay.' When a traveller in the desert loses his path, we use the verb 'ghawa' which not only means that the man is lost but also means that he in danger. Allah teaches us that arrogance and injustice will be rewarded with misguidance and ruin.

The verse continues: "so whoever rejects the powers of evil and believes in Allah has grasped the firmest hand-hold, one that will never break." Take note that Allah mentioned renouncing 'the powers of evil' before He mentioned belief in Allah. Why, you may ask? We answer that purifying your heart from all evil is a prerequisite to faith in Allah. You must let go of all other beliefs first, and then embrace faith into your heart. We wash our clothes from all dirt first, and only then, we iron them and put them on.

'The powers of evil' is translated from the Arabic origin 'Taghoot.' The translation 'powers of evil' does not embody the full meaning of 'Taghoot,' so let's take a moment to explain the word further. 'Taghoot' is derived from the root 'tagha', and the word 'Taghoot' is in the superlative exaggerated form.

'The powers of evil' refer to Satan and to those who use their whims and desires to legislate and declare who is a proper believer, and who is not. They trade faith for temporary worldly power. "Taghoot' is used for sorcerers and fraudsters. It is also used for anyone who transgresses and exceeds his or her boundaries. 'The powers of evil' cover a wide spectrum from tyrants to demons and witch doctors, and especially, to Satan because he is the origin of transgression.

Another distinctive attribute of a 'Taghoot' is the one who increases in tyranny if he is obeyed. You often see that in the early years of a dictator, he tests the people with small transgressions. If he sees that the people have followed, or turned a blind eye, he transgresses and terrorizes further and so on. Allah says describing Pharaoh:

So he incited his people to levity, and they obeyed him: surely they were perverse people. (43:54)

A tyrant incites people to transgress over the rights of others one small step at a time. He continues until he becomes a dictator. No one became a dictator overnight; it is a gradual process, and often a large portion of the population act as enablers until it becomes a system of 'taghoot.' It is obedience that makes the 'taghoot' increase in transgression.

There are also corrupt priests and imams who abuse their knowledge and power to serve tyrants in the name of religion. Many media moguls abuse their powers to instill fear and foment hate among people. 'Taghoot' encompasses all of these meanings.

Allah wants you to cleanse your heart from all types of evil, and then turn to Him in pure worship. He says: 'so whoever rejects the powers of evil and believes in Allah has grasped the firmest hand-hold, one that will never break.' The word 'grasped´ is translated from the Arabic origin "istmsaka" which is an exaggerated form of 'to hold' or "masaka." "Istamsaka" means to grasp firmly because adhering to Allah's teachings is a struggle for the soul. Why? Because as long as you are on Allah's path, satan would not leave you alone. You will also face much opposition and temptation from many elements of society. Thus, it is not sufficient to hold; rather you have to grasp firmly to your faith. Allah says narrating satan's words:

He said, 'By Your misguidance of me, I will lie in ambush for them on your straight path. I will come at them- from their front and their back, from their right and their left- and You will find that most of them are ungrateful.' (7:16,17)

The verse continues: "whoever rejects the powers of evil and believes in Allah has grasped the firmest hand-hold, one that will never break." The 'Firmest Handhold' translated from the Arabic origin 'Al Urwatul wuthqa' which has a reference from the desert environment. It is a tightly-wound heavy-duty rope commonly used to tie the bucket which is lowered down into the well to draw water. It is the most important rope because it represents our link to the source of life and sustenance in the desert. Likewise, Allah's teachings are our link to the source of life and sustenance for the soul.

VERSE 257

Allaahu waliyyul lazeena aamanoo yukhrijuhum minaz zulumaati ilan noori wallazeena kafarooo awliyaaa'uhumut Taaghootu yukhrijoonahum minan noori ilaz zulumaat; ulaaa'ika Ashaabun Naari hum feehaa khaalidoon

Allah is the ally of those who believe: He brings them out of the depths of darkness and into the light. As for the disbelievers, their allies are the power of evil who take them from the light into the depths of darkness, they are the inhabitants of the Fire, and there they will remain.

Allah is the ally of any person who 'rejects the powers of evil and believes in Allah.' This is a direct benefit of the faith Allah described in the previous verse. He says: 'whoever rejects the powers of evil and believes in Allah has grasped the firmest hand-hold, one that will never break.' In other words, if you are faithful, Allah will be right there by your side.

The word 'ally' is translated from the Arabic origin 'Wali.' The word "Wali' has many derivatives such as 'Welaya' and 'Mawla.' In general, it refers to something that closely follows something else, or comes right after it without any separation. It means that the two parties are closely related. When you are in trouble, you lean on the closest one to you. If you are walking with your best friend and you trip, your friend's hand instinctively reaches out to break your fall. Your friend is usually the first one you would call for help. When it comes to Allah, however, you do not even need to ask. Allah is fully aware of your condition, your needs, and your vulnerabilities. Do you remember how Allah ended the previous verse? He says: 'Allah is all hearing and all knowing.' Those who believe receive Allah's help without the need to call out for Him as He is the All-Hearing, All-Knowing.

The words 'Wali' and 'Mawla' hold another meaning. They refer to someone who governs and overlooks the affairs of others. Historically, the word "Wali" was used as a title for the governor of a city. 'Mawla' is sometimes used to address a master and sometimes to address a servant. The two meanings are complimentary because a master is there to aid a servant in trouble, and the servant is there to follow the master's lead.

Take note that Allah offered His aid to 'those who believe' as a group, not as individuals. This is because in all the believers should share one faith and one outlook. Allah says:

Hold fast to Allah's rope all together; do not split into factions. Remember Allah's favour to you: you were enemies and then He brought your hearts together and you became brothers by His grace; you were about to fall into a pit of Fire and He saved you from it- in this way Allah makes His revelations clear to you so that you may be rightly guided. Let there be a community among you who call to the good, and enjoin the right, and forbid the wrong. They are the ones who have success. And do not be like those who, after they have been given clear revelation, split into factions and fall into disputes: a terrible punishment awaits such people. (3:103-105)

What is the benefit of Allah's guardianship? The answer comes in multiple levels. The guardianship of Allah started when He provided humanity with the clearest evidence of His lordship. He sent us prophets and messengers; He gave us scriptures and instilled signs in every creation.

Allah did not leave you wandering aimlessly; He brought the evidence right to your doorstep. Then after you believed, He became your ally and supporter. Allah loves you, responds to your prayers in a manner most appropriate for your condition. He says:

Allah has increased the guidance of those who follow the right path and given them piety and protection from sin (47:17)

When a conflict arises between the faithful and their enemies, Allah is with the faithful.

Lastly, and most importantly, Allah is your ally in the hereafter. The All-Merciful will reward you in full for your efforts, and then increase you more. Allah's guardianship is present in all stages of life. Is there a better ally than this? Allah is your guardian and ally through evidence before faith. He is your ally in support against your enemies during faith. And in the Hereafter, Allah is your ally with love and mercy.

The verse continues: "Allah is the ally of those who believe: He brings them out of the depths of darkness and into the light." Allah brings the believers out of the darkness of ignorance into the light of faith. Darkness, whether material or spiritual, obstructs your vision and blunts your senses, making you unable to find your way.

"As for the disbelievers, their allies are the power of evil who take them from the light into the depths of darkness, they are the inhabitants of the Fire, and there they will remain." Here, the phrase 'the power of evil who take them from the light into the depths of darkness' makes you wonder: Were the disbelievers guided by the light before they were misguided? Or is the verse referring to those who were prevented from seeing the light of Allah to begin with? We answer that both meanings apply to the verse understudy. Let's explain using two examples. In the first example, a friend may say to you: 'Did you not know that my father took me out of his will?' Meaning that your friend was included in the father's inheritance until the father removed him from the will. Likewise, the phrase 'the power of evil who take them from the light into the depths of darkness' is referring to people who saw the light of Allah, and then decided to leave it for worldly desires.

For the second example, listen to the following verse narrating the words of Prophet Joseph –peace be upon him-:

Indeed I left behind the creed of the people who have no faith in Allah and who disbelieve in the Hereafter. (12:37)

Was our Prophet Joseph amongst the disbelievers and then left to embrace faith? No, he was never of the disbelieving people. These people were all around him, but he rejected their ways and chose the religion of Abraham. The expression 'I left behind the creed of the people who have no faith in Allah' reflects how Prophet Joseph exercised his freedom of choice. Likewise, the phrase 'the power of evil who take them from the light into the depths of darkness' is referring to people who never saw the light of Allah to begin with.

The verse continues: "As for the disbelievers, their allies are the power of evil who take them from the light into the depths of darkness." In the previous session, we explained in detail the meanings of the 'power of evil' or 'Taghoot' from satan, to dictators, sorcerers, and corrupt clergymen. Allah says:

Verily you and those you worship other than Allah will be fuel for Hell; and come to it you will. (21:98)

May Allah protect you and me from this punishment.

AMEEN

VERSE 258

Alam tara ilal lazee Haaajja Ibraaheema fee Rabbiheee an aataahullaahul mulka iz qaala Ibraaheemu Rabbiyal lazee yuhyee wa yumeetu qaala ana uhyee wa umeetu qaala Ibraaheemu fa innal laaha yaatee bishshamsi minal mashriqi faati bihaa minal maghribi fabuhital lazee kafar; wallaahu laa yahdil qawmaz zaalimeen

Didn't you see the man who argued with Abraham about his Lord, because Allah had given him the power to rule? When Abraham said, 'It is my Lord who gives life and death,' he said, 'I too give life and death.' So Abraham said, 'Allah brings the sun from the east; so bring it from the west.' The disbeliever was dumbfounded: Allah does not guide those who do evil. (Chapter 2: Verse 258)

In the previous three verses, Allah the Ever-Living, the Ever-Watchful gave you ample evidence of His Lordship. He laid before you the case for faith and worship and explained the benefits of having Him as your ally and guardian. But how about a real-life example? That's what Allah gives us in the verse under study.

By asking 'Didn't you see?' Allah is drawing your attention to a strange event that happened. It is like how we sometimes say: "didn't you see what Keyaan did in the classroom?" When you here such an expression, you know that what Kryaan did was unexpected. It entices you to listen to the events attentively.

The verse starts with: "Didn't you see the man who disputed with Abraham about his Lord, because Allah had given him the power to rule?" Take note that Allah did not specify the identity of the person who argued with Abraham. Identifying the person does not concern us, whether it was Nimrod —as some scholars speculated- or someone else. What concerns us is that this ruler entered into an argument with the Messenger Abraham -peace be upon him-. By keeping the identity of the ruler anonymous, Allah made the story applicable to all rulers who are deluded by temporary power and influence. Had this particular ruler been identified, most people would think that the lessons of the story were only relevant to that particular king.

Similarly, some scholars spend an inordinate amount of time trying to answer questions about the story of the people of the cave from chapter 18 of the Quran. They want to know where and when the events took place? How many believers were involved? Who were they? We answer that if any of the answers were specified, it would take away from the moral of the story. For example, if the time of the events was specified, a person may say: it makes sense that these events happened so long ago, but they do not apply to modern times. And if the identity of the believers was determined, people may say that such personalities are capable of such behaviour, but we cannot match their strength of faith. Hence, Allah, the All-Wise, left these matters unknown. The lessons of the story apply to all believers at all times in any land.

Allah describes this man as the one whom 'Allah had given him the power to rule.' Abraham -peace be upon him- said: 'It is my Lord who gives life and death.' Take note of the literary brilliance of the Quran as it does not mention the original question. He left it to the listener to make that connection. In other words when you hear our beloved prophet Abraham saying: 'It is my Lord who gives life and death,' you conclude that he was asked by the king: "Who is your lord?"

Abraham's answer brought forth the main issue that cannot be disputed by anyone: The issue of life and death. Even the most ardent disbeliever cannot claim creation. No one ever said that he or she creates life or can cause natural death. Allah is the Creator. However, the king wanted to enter into a sterile philosophical argument with Abraham. He answered: 'I too give life and death.' The king ordered two prisoners to be brought before him and sentenced one of them to death, and the other to go free.

Prophet Abraham understood the trick and decided not to fall into the trap of endless argument of the true meaning of life on one hand, and the difference between death and killing on the other. Abraham wanted to get to the core of the matter, so he replied with a statement which would end the controversy. He said: 'Allah brings the sun from the east; so bring it from the west.'

Let's take a few moments to explain the difference between killing – which is what this king did- and death. It is true that death and killing share one thing: the departure of the soul from the body, but they are inherently very different. Allah says:

Muhammad is but a Messenger, and Messengers passed away before him. If, then, he dies or is killed, will you turn back on your heels? Whoever turns back on his heels can in no way harm Allah. But Allah will reward the grateful. (3:144)

Take note that Allah mentioned death and killing as separate events. It is true that they both end life, but there is a difference between taking the soul without the destruction of the physical body and causing death by destroying the body. The soul is subject to certain laws. It can only reside within a matter of very specific characteristics. If the physical characteristics are violated, the soul departs. Killing violates the physical characteristics of the body. Allah, the grantor of life, is the only one who can cause death without changing the physical. Many of us have seen footage of a young, perfectly healthy athlete suddenly drop dead for no reason at all. This is death.

Here is an example to clarify the interaction between the soul and the body: suppose that you have a lit light bulb. What is causing the light bulb to emit light? It is the electricity flowing through it. If you break the glass, the bulb goes dark, but is the electricity gone? No, the electricity is still there, but it only shines as light under certain physical conditions – such as the vacuum inside a bulb-. Likewise, the soul manifests as life only in a structure that has special characteristics. Hence, the killer does not take the soul away; rather he or she only destroys the physical structure making it inhospitable to the soul. Allah made it clear: death cannot come to anyone without His permission, and the time of each person's death is written in a preordained register. Keeping that in mind, the king who disputed Abraham did not give life to the freed prisoner, nor did he cause death to the prisoner he killed.

Allah wants to alert you to an important fact about prophets and messengers. The goal of the prophets when they dispute with their nations is not to triumph in argument; it is not to score points and boast. The one goal of prophets and messengers is to convey the truth. Thus, Prophet Abraham -peace be upon him- did not prolong the discussion about life and death, he only wanted to show the king who the true master of the universe is.

The phrase "the man who argued with Abraham about his Lord, because Allah had given him power to rule' explains that the source of the king's stubbornness and tyranny was his power and authority. Allah has blessed you with countless bounties. Do you make your kingdom a means of transgression against the One who has bestowed upon you this kingdom? Do you show your gratitude to Allah by opposing Him? What made this ruler so ungrateful? It was pride.

In order to deliver Allah's message, Abraham changed the topic from the unseen soul to something apparent and visible. He said: 'Allah brings the sun from the east; so bring it from the west.' The verse continued: 'The disbeliever was dumbfounded' translated from the Arabic origin 'Buhita.' 'Buhita' means to be overwhelmed and become speechless. The king went through three stages: first, he was surprised that Abraham changed the argument from life and death to the sun making further dispute impossible. Second, he was perplexed as he could not find a way out of this dilemma. Lastly, he was speechless and defeated.

Here you may wonder: why didn't the king ask Abraham to bring the sun from the west? To answer this question, you should recall the previous verse. Allah says:

Allah is the ally of those who believe: He brings them out of the depths of darkness and into the light. As for the disbelievers, their allies are the power of evil who take them from the light into the depths of darkness

You should not be surprised by the weakness of the king's case. As long as he is a disbeliever, he will not receive Allah's help. As for Abraham, he was the friend of the Most Merciful. Allah is the ally of the believers; He did not inspire the king to argue further. Either the king's mind froze and became speechless, or deep inside, he knew the truth and feared that Abraham's Lord would bring the sun from the west to support His prophet. Either way, Allah is truly the ally of those who believe. Moreover, 'Allah does not guide those who do evil' to His signs, nor does he support them in an argument.

VERSE 258

Aw kallazee marra 'alaa qaryatinw wa hiya khaawiyatun 'alaa 'urooshihaa qaala annaa yuhyee haazihil laahu ba'da mawtihaa fa amaatahul laahu mi'ata 'aamin summa ba'asahoo qaala kam labista qaala labistu yawman aw ba'da yawmin qaala bal labista mi'ata 'aamin fanzur ilaa ta'aamika wa sharaabika lam yatasannah wanzur ilaa himaarika wa linaj'alaka Aayatal linnaasi wanzur ilal'izaami kaifa nunshizuhaa summa naksoohaa lahmaa; falammaa tabayyana lahoo qaala a'lamu annal laaha 'alaa kulli shai'in Qadeer

Or take the man who passed by a village which had fallen into ruin. He said, "How will Allah bring this town to life after its death?" So Allah caused him to die for a hundred years; then He revived him. He said, "How long have you remained?" The man said, "I have remained a day or part of a day." He said, "Rather, you have remained one hundred years. Look at your food and your drink; it has not changed with time. And look at your donkey; We will make you a sign for the people. Look at the bones - how We raise them and then cover them with flesh." When it became clear to him, he said, "I know that Allah is over all things competent."

In the previous verse, a dispute erupted between an arrogant king and Prophet Abraham. The subject of who truly controls life and death was brought up. Rather than engaging in pointless debate, Abraham, peace be upon him, moved the argument form life and death to the creation of the sun.

Allah does not want you to think that a true discussion of life of death was marginalized or avoided. Thus, the Almighty immediately addressed this issue in multiple stories starting with the verse understudy.

The verse starts with the conjunction "or" which means that both the example in this verse and the example in the prior verse could equally serve to prove the case that "Allah: there is no Allah but Him, the Ever-Living, the Ever Watchful. Neither drowsiness nor sleep overtakes Him. All that is in the heavens and in the earth belongs to Him." The same examples also prove the case that "Allah is the ally of those who believe: He brings them out of the depths of darkness and into the light. As for the disbelievers, their allies are the power of evil who take them from the light into the depths of darkness."

Let's examine the story. A 'village" is a small place where a group of people lives together. The person who passed by it was an outsider-a traveller-. We note that Allah did not specify the town or the name of the traveller. Some believe that the town was Jerusalem and the person's name was Armiya the son of Hilkiah, or maybe he was al-Khidr or Uzair. We discussed earlier that had Allah willed, he would have identified the person and the town. He, the All-Wise, left the names unidentified and so should we. The verse is general because the events could have happened to anyone, and the lessons from the story are universal.

BUT THE MOST POPULAR OPINION IS THAT IT WAS PROPHET UZAIRS.

This will feature later in this discussion.

The phrase 'had fallen into ruin' means the town was empty. It may have had buildings and houses, but no inhabitants. It also means that the structures were damaged, and ceilings had collapsed over foundations. A ghost town abandoned in ruin must have been an eye-catching scene. Naturally, a question came to the mind of the traveller: "How will Allah bring this town to life after its death?" As if the traveller was wondering about the revival of the village and, more specifically, the revival of its people. Here is another example from the Quran where a town is mentioned, but its people are intended. Allah says:

'ask the town in which we were, and the caravan in which we came, and indeed we are truthful.' (12:82)

When the children of Jacob, peace be upon him, returned from Egypt and left their younger brother behind, they said to their father: send someone to ask the people of the town in Egypt, and they will corroborate that our brother is there. So the phrase 'ask the town' means to ask its people. Likewise, the question "How will Allah bring this town to life after its death?" was about its people.

It is clear that the traveller who asked this question was a believer because he did not question: 'Who will bring this town to life?' He did not doubt that Allah alone is capable of resurrecting people from death. His only question was 'how?' A similar question was asked by Prophet Abraham. Allah says:

When Ibrahim said, 'My Lord, show me how you bring the dead to life.' He asked, 'Why, Do you not believe?' He replied, 'Indeed I do! But so that my heart may be at peace.' He said, 'Take four birds and train them to yourself. Then put a part of them on each mountain and call to them; they will come rushing to you. Know that Allah is Almighty, All-Wise.' (02:260)

Abraham did not doubt that Allah gives life to the dead, but he wanted to see how it is done. When you see a remarkable object or a complex machine, you often wonder how it's made. When you see the pyramids of Egypt, you know who made them, but wonder how such a feat was built? How did the ancient Egyptians move these monstrous stones to the top with no scaffolding or mechanical levers? Indeed, such questions are a healthy branch of faith. Allah does not stop you from asking such questions nor prevent you from searching for the answers. In fact, when you ask 'how,' rather than 'who', it indicates that you have full faith in the maker.

For example, when you see an exquisite wedding dress, you turn to the designer and say: 'You have to tell me: how did you do this?' It is an expression of admiration to both, the designer and the product.

Is there anything more wondrous than the creation of our Lord? Our beloved Prophet Abraham had no doubt about who gave life after death; he was amused by resurrection and wanted to witness the craft and see how it is done.

This brings us back to the village in ruin. The traveller wanted to see the village come back to life with its people. Human beings are the driver of movement and construction, and they bring life to towns and villages. Thus, when people die, so does their village. So, when the traveller asked: '"How will Allah bring this town to life after its death?" Allah wanted the answer to be a real-life experience for the questioner, not mere theories. 'So Allah caused him to die for a hundred years; then He revived him.' In essence, Allah's answer was 'Why the village? Let's do you!'

The verse continues: 'So Allah caused him to die for a hundred years; then He revived him. He said, "How long have you remained?" The man said, "I have remained a day or part of a day." It could be that Allah spoke to the traveller as He spoke to Moses, or the man could have heard a voice. It could be that an angel revealed Allah's message to the man, or simply that a passer-by witnessed the event and asked. What is important is that there was a question and an answer. Allah narrates the conversations.

The man's answer to the question: "How long have you remained?" suggests that he had doubt. It seems that he could not determine how much of the day had passed just by looking at the sun, so he replied: "I have remained a day or part of a day." Here we ask: Was he truthful or not? We answer that he was truthful to the best of his abilities because the changes that he saw were mixed. For example, he did not notice any changes in his beard, nor to the colour or length of his hair, yet his donkey was a pile of bones. What was Allah's answer? He said: "Rather, you have remained one hundred years."

Or take the man who passed by a village which had fallen into ruin. He said, "How will Allah bring this town to life after its death?" So Allah caused him to die for a hundred years; then He revived him. He said, "How long have you remained?" The man said, "I have remained a day or part of a day." He said, "Rather, you have remained one hundred years. Look at your food and your drink; it has not changed with time. And look at your donkey; We will make you a sign for the people. Look at the bones - how We raise them and then cover them with flesh." When it became clear to him, he said, "I know that Allah is over all things competent." (Chapter 2: Verse 259)

In the previous verses, we heard two different answers to the same question. The traveller who had wondered how Allah brought things back to life awoke. He was asked: "How long have you remained?" The man said, "I have remained a day or part of a day." Allah said: "Rather, you have remained one hundred years." So which was it?

Let's break down this puzzle. The man who thought that he was out for about a day could not offer much proof. He had a donkey that was carrying his rations of grapes, figs, and drink. Allah said: "Look at your food and your drink; it has not changed" This seems to support the claim that the man was out for about a day, as his fruit did not rot. Allah continued: "And look at your donkey; We will make you a sign for the people. Look at the bones - how We raise them and then cover them with flesh." It was something wondrous. Allah wanted to show the man that a hundred years had passed. When the man looked at his donkey, he found that it was a pile of dry bones. It took years for the donkey to grow old, die, and for his flesh to decompose, and his bones to dry out.

How could this be, you may ask? We answer that Allah is The Expander and The Restrictor. He is not governed by the laws of physics, the flow of time, or the rules of the universe; rather He is the one who governs. Allah set the rules, and He can overrule them. He can fold time in regards to the food, and extend time in regards to the donkey, while both coexist right next to each other. This can only be done by the One who possesses all the power. He says: 'Look at your food and your drink; it has not changed with time. And look at your donkey; We will make you a sign for the people. Look at the bones - how We raise them and then cover them with flesh." When it became clear to him, he said, "I know that Allah is over all things competent."

Allah showed the traveller the bones of his long gone donkey rise to come together, then they were covered with flesh, and his donkey came back to life. He witnessed first-hand the process of resurrection. And in that was the answer to the question: "How will Allah bring this town to life after its death?" The man saw the answer in himself and his donkey. Then, he then looked up to see the abandoned village full of life.

Let's examine the phrase "We will make you a sign for the people." Who are the people Allah referring to? We answer that the most authentic narrative seems to point out that the traveller in this story was a righteous man named Uzair. He was one of only four people who had fully memorized the Torah. The other three who knew it by heart were prophets Moses, Jesus, and Yoshah –peace be upon them all-.

The story goes that when Uzair awakened and witnessed the miracle of resurrection, he returned to his home village. Of course, when he arrived, everything had changed. Everyone he knew had died. People gathered around to see who this stranger was. He told them that he was Uzair, a resident of the village. The villagers took him to an elderly woman who was blind and bedridden. They told her that a man who claims to be Uzair of this village has arrived. She replied: 'Uzair left us a hundred years ago and never returned.' He said: "I am 'Uzair." She answered: 'I recognize this voice....But Uzair was a righteous man whose prayers were always answered.' Uzair supplicated Allah to give the woman her sight back. She looked up, saw him and said: 'This is Uzair exactly as I remember him from my childhood.'

The story of Uzair spread quickly until it reached his son –who was now a man over a hundred years old-. He came to see his father –a man of fifty years-. The son said: I heard that my father had a distinct birthmark between his shoulders. Uzair lowered his garment revealing his shoulder and a birthmark exactly as his son described.

The last piece of evidence came as the villagers told Uzair about the fall of Jerusalem, and how Nebuchadrezzar had burned all copies of the Torah. There was only one that survived, but they were not sure about its authenticity. That copy was brought forth, and Uzair started reciting from memory verbatim as written in the copy. Now, there was no question of who this man was. The villagers marvelled at watching a son over one hundred years old standing next to his father of fifty. Allah says: 'We will make you a sign for the people.' Uzair said, "I know that Allah is over all things competent." As a young man, he knew, through contemplation and faith, that Allah has the attributes of absolute perfection. Now, as a resurrected man, he knew through first-hand experience that Allah has the attributes of absolute perfection. "I know that Allah is over all things competent" was a confirmation of his faith.

Allah, the Almighty, extends time and restricts it. He gives life and takes it away. He gives us clues and signs from our daily lives. Time almost stops for a hibernating bear as its heart slows to a few beats a minute while life goes on normally around it. We see a similar story to Uzair's in the people of the cave. Allah says in the 19th verse of Chapter 18:

In time We woke them, and they began to question one another. One of them asked, 'How long have you been here?' and one answered, 'A day or part of a day,' but then another said, 'Your Lord knows best how long you have been here.

Allah says:

And they had remained in their cave three hundred years, and they were increased nine (18:25)

The story of the resurrection of Uzair, the alteration of the flow of time, and the story of Prophet Abraham's argument with the king who claimed to give life and death affirm the core of Islamic creed:

Allah: there is no God but Him, the Ever-Living, the Ever Watchful. Neither drowsiness nor sleep overtakes Him. All that is in the heavens and in the earth belongs to Him. Who is there that can intercede with Him except by His leave? He knows what is before them and what is behind them, but they do not comprehend any of His knowledge except what He wills. His seat encompasses the heavens and the earth; it does not weary Him to preserve them both. He is the Most High, the Tremendous. (Chapter 2: Verse 255)

VERSE 260

Wa iz qaala Ibraaheemu Rabbi arinee kaifa tuhyil mawtaa qaala awa lam tu'min qaala balaa wa laakin liyatma'inna qalbee qaala fakhuz arba'atan minat tairi fasurhunna ilaika summaj 'al 'alaa kulli jabalin minhunna juz'an summad'uu hunna ya'teenaka sa'yaa; wa'lam annal laaha 'Azeezun Hakeem

And when Abraham said: "My Lord, show me how You will restore life to the dead!" Allah said: "Why? Do you not believe?" Abraham said: "Yes, but that my heart may be at peace." He said: "Then take four birds of different kinds, and tame them to yourself to know them fully. Then chop them into pieces, mix them, and put on every one of the hills a piece from each. Then summon them, and they will come to you walking in haste. And know that Allah is Almighty and All-Wise

Prophet Abraham asked the Lord: How do you give life to the dead? Did he doubt resurrection? Of course not. He, peace be upon, was fascinated by Allah's power, and wanted to see how it is done. He did not question revival; he simply wanted to witness it. Abraham had unshakable faith, and his question did not involve creed at all. Say for example that you saw an amazingly beautiful building. You may go to the architect who designed it and say in wonder: "Would you show me how you designed this building?" You are not questioning who designed the building; you have no doubt. You just want to see how it was done because you are fascinated by it.

Here you may ask: If Abraham had unshakable faith, then why did he say: "but that my heart may be at peace." Didn't he have peace in his heart? We answer that Prophet Abraham had faith in Allah, faith in resurrection and the last day. In fact, he had so much faith that he was preoccupied not with questioning resurrection, but in how resurrection was done. Abraham wanted to see resurrection so he can stop wondering about it and put his curious mind to rest.

And what better way to explain resurrection than an experiment? Rather than words, Allah wanted Abraham to see it first-hand. He said: "Then take four birds of different kinds, and tame them to yourself to know them fully." Some scholars said that Abraham chose a crow, a peacock, a rooster, and a pigeon: Four very different birds he raised and got to know intimately, so there would be no doubt. Then Allah said: "Then chop them into pieces, mix them, and put on every one of the hills a piece from each."

It is interesting to note that Allah used the phrase: "summon them, and they will come to you walking in haste." As you know, birds fly, so why wouldn't they come flying? Because Allah did not want to leave any room for doubt; the birds would come walking to Abraham so he can closely examine each one and make sure they are his pet birds. It was not a quick fly-by.

Here we should take a few moments to examine the phrase: "Then summon them, and they will come to you walking in haste." Abraham, as a human being, is unable to give life, but the Almighty gave him the ability to call the birds back to life. Keep in mind the difference between the absolute ability of Allah the creator, and the relative ability of the creation –in this case Prophet Abraham-. Allah's power and ability are absolute, ever-present and ever-lasting. No one can take away Allah's ability, nor will His abilities waiver or change.

On the other hand, we as humans, have relative abilities. A person may have an ability that is absent in others. You, for example, can help a disabled person carry a chair up a flight of stairs. An artist can help a person decorate his or her house. The most important point to remember is that these abilities are not inherent within us. Allah can change our abilities at any moment. You are physically healthy today, but may be disabled tonight. A writer maybe famous today, but lose his or her talent tomorrow. Allah is the only one who gives from His power to the powerless. He says: "be, "and it becomes.

This brings us back to the verse. When Allah said to Abraham: "summon them, and they will come to you walking in haste," He gave Abraham the ability to raise the birds from death. Allah can grant His power to whomever He wills because His power is inherent and absolute. You and I cannot grant our power to others, because our power is a gift. In fact, you and I cannot even guarantee to keep the abilities that we have.

Let's look at an example from the Quran. Listen to Allah's words about Prophet Jesus son of Mary -peace be upon him-:

And a Messenger to the Children of Israel: 'Assuredly, I have come to you with a clear proof from your Lord: I fashion for you out of clay something in the shape of a bird, then I breathe into it, and it becomes a bird by Allah's permission. And I heal the blind from birth and the leper, and I revive the dead, by Allah's permission. And I inform you of what things you eat, and what you store up in your houses. Surely in this is a clear proof for you, if you are sincere believers (03:49)

We understand that Allah granted Prophet Jesus (peace be upon him) two types of miracles. The first type were abilities given to Jesus so he can perform certain miracles by himself, such as knowing what people ate, and what they store and hide in their homes. The second type of miracles were those that were not inherent to Jesus; rather, they required Allah's direct permission and power every single time. Miracles like resurrecting the dead, and breathing life into objects. These miracles could not be done without Allah's will and cannot be exclusively attributed to the Prophet Jesus.

Similar was the experience of our beloved Abraham. Thus, Allah said to him: "And know that Allah is Almighty and All-Wise." Allah is Mighty so no one can overcome Him, and He is wise in granting and withholding powers and abilities.

And when Abraham said: "My Lord, show me how You will restore life to the dead!" Allah said: "Why? Do you not believe?" Abraham said:

"Yes, but that my heart may be at peace." He said: "Then take four birds of different kinds, and tame them to yourself to know them fully. Then chop them into pieces, mix them, and put on every one of the hills a piece from each. Then summon them, and they will come to you walking in haste. And know that Allah is Almighty and All-Wise." (Chapter 2: Verse 260)

In the previous few verses, Allah gave us one example after another of stories of life, death, and resurrection. The last example was a physical experiment to reassure the heart of our beloved Prophet Abraham. Why such an emphasis on resurrection? Because those who lived in the era of Prophet Muhammad's call to Islam were sceptical about the afterlife. Listen to their words as narrated in the Quran:

they say, 'What? When we die and turn to dust and bones, shall we really be resurrected? (23:82)

and in another chapter:

He draws comparisons for us, and forgets his own creation. He says, 'Who shall revive the bones when they have decayed?' Say, 'He who created them in the first place will give them life again: He has full knowledge of every act of creation. (36:78-79)

Allah is the originator of life, and He is the Resurrector. He says:

He is the One who originates creation and will do it again- this is even easier for Him. He is above all comparison in the heavens and earth; He is the Almighty, the All-Wise. (30:27)

Allah Almighty can start creation from nothing without an example, then, restore it after everything perishes. To revive after death is certainly easier than to create from scratch. To Allah, it is a simple matter of "Be," and it becomes. Even for us humans, once you make something like a chair, it only becomes easier and easier to make other chairs.

The issue of resurrection is central to Islamic creed because it is directly related to the Last Day and, and more importantly, to accountability for one's actions. When you have faith in the Last Day, you watch over your actions to ensure your salvation. When you know that you will face your Creator and be questioned about your deeds, you become aware of the consequences of your decisions. There is no escaping death, resurrection, or meeting Allah. This inevitable moment of accountability should be ever present in your mind.

But what exactly is your responsibility in life? Allah says:

To Thamud, We sent their brother Saleh. He said, 'My people, worship Allah! You have no Allah apart from Him. He brought you into being from the earth and made you thrive in it. So ask His forgiveness and then repent to Him. My Lord is Close and Quick to Respond (11:61)

Allah wants you to be his successor on earth; in order to be a worthy successor, you need to thrive using your talents. Allah distributed different talents and abilities amongst people. No single person has all the talents. We all need one another. If you have a special skill that I do not possess, then I am forced to seek your help. Likewise, you would seek my help in matters I excel at. This sort of cooperation builds societies and progress.

On the other hand, if each one of us possessed all talents, we would fight. For this reason, there is no real progress in a society unless talents are diverse and complementary. Thus, you should never look down on a hard working person, even if his or her job is less than socially admirable.

Take the example of a wealthy doctor who is highly respected within the community. He has a mansion and a fleet of luxury cars. He comes home late at night to find that the master bathroom has flooded and the bedroom reeks of sewage. This doctor calls the local plumber to come and fix the toilet urgently. But the plumber declines because he does not work weekends. The respected doctor would plead with the plumber and offer to pay him extra and to pick him up from his house personally. Suddenly, the plumber is the most important person in the world. Similarly, if the minister of health does not show to his or her job for three months, people would hardly notice. But if the garbage man does not show up for one week, the whole neighbourhood would be miserable.

Allah presents life as a system based on social and economic issues. Why? Because man is firstly occupied with his or her own survival, then by the survival of the family and society. We preserve our life through work and sustenance and preserve humankind through marriage. Allah highly appreciates your work and asks you to extend the preservation of life to the less fortunate, the weak and the overwhelmed by life's circumstances. He says:

If you give charity openly, it is good, but if you keep it secret and give to the needy in private, that is better for you, and it will atone for some of your bad deeds: Allah is well aware of all that you do. (2:217)

and in another verse:

Who will give Allah a good loan, which He will increase for him many times over? It is Allah who withholds and Allah who gives abundantly, and it is to Him that you will return. (2:245)

Allah explains: some of you are deprived, and some are capable; I will take care of the deprived by borrowing from the capable. Always keep in mind that strength, ability, wealth, poverty, and weakness are all circumstances that are subject to change. When a rich person sees a poor person, he or she should remember that wealth is not inherent or guaranteed. Wealth, health and ability are all gifts from Allah that may be taken away at any moment. Those who are less fortunate around you are your wake-up call. When you see a blind man, you suddenly become aware of your eyes and instinctively rub them to make sure they are OK. When you see a woman going into a dialysis centre, you start thinking about your kidneys.

Allah does not abandon the poor or the disabled. He, the All-Wise, safeguards their basic needs and security by asking their more able brothers and sisters to help.

VERSE 261

Masalul lazeena yunfiqoona amwaalahum fee sabeelil laahi kamasali habbatin ambatat sab'a sanaabila fee kulli sumbulatim mi'atu habbah; wallaahu yudaa'ifu limai yashaaa; wallaahu Waasi'un 'Aleem

The example of those who expend their wealth in the way of Allah is that of a grain of corn from which grow seven ears, each ear containing a hundred grains. Truly Allah multiplies for whomsoever He will, for Allah is infinite and all-wise.

After clarifying the issues of life, death, and resurrection, Allah turns our attention to social and economic matters.

All money and property belong to Allah. He says in the 33rd verse of Chapter 24:

and give them some of the wealth Allah has given you.

You earn your living through work, and Allah respects and values your effort. He attributes the money that you earn to you. It is your property. It is of Allah's bounty that when the time comes to help the needy, He asks you for a loan from what you have earned and promises to repay you many times over. Had Allah wanted, he could have taken this money away from you. All belongs to Him. So do not grieve nor fear over what you spend in Allah's cause because you have given it to the Most Capable and Knowledgeable. He gives back according to your intention and effort.

The verse under study addresses the issue of stinginess in humans. Most people have something extra above their basic needs, but they are stingy and fearful of giving it away to help others. In such situations, faith steps in to tell you: Do not worry; your wealth will not decrease; to the contrary, Allah will increase it for you many times over. Look how the earth increases your crop when you invest in it. If you sow a single seed, does the earth give you one seed back? No. One planted seed sprouts many stems, and in each stem, there is a large number of fruits and seeds. So, if the earth -which is a creation of Allah-, can multiply what you give it many times over, think about what the Creator of the earth can do for you.

Consider the example of a farmer who takes one bag of wheat grains out of his stock and sows it into the field. Does that mean he or she has reduced the amount of wheat in stock? Of course not. By planting this one bag, the farmer would probably double his or her entire stock. In fact, the farmer who keeps all the seeds and does not plant any is the one who is depleting his or her reserves. Allah, the All-Generous, All-Encompassing, teaches you:

The example of those who expend their wealth in the way of Allah is that of a grain of corn from which grow seven ears, each ear containing a hundred grains. Truly Allah multiplies for whomsoever He will, for Allah is infinite and all-wise. (Chapter 2: Verse 261)

Allah attributes the wealth spent to you. He did not say: 'give me back my money,' instead, He says: "The example of those who expend their wealth in the way of Allah."

"The way of Allah" is a general term that spans everything from sharing a small meal to caring for orphans, helping the traveller, and helping equip those who defend the society. Always remember that when a poor person finds him or herself surrounded by a supportive society, he or she would not feel any resentment or anger towards the rich. There was a story of a farmer who used to walk his cow in the neighbourhood during the hot summer days. He would give a small amount of milk to each neighbour. Everyone along his path would pray for the protection of this cow, and ask Allah to increase this man in wealth and health. Why? Because each person felt that he or she has a personal stake in the man's cow. A world where the weak enjoy the support of the strong is a happy, peaceful world. There is no room for hatred or anger. The rich also feel assured that if one day he or she loses all his wealth, others would be there to help. Wealth and strength are conditions that can change in a blink of an eye.

The verse: "The example of those who expend their wealth in the way of Allah is that of a grain of corn from which grow seven ears, each ear containing a hundred grains" is a divine law by which Allah fights our stinginess. He says to each one of us: 'look and think carefully: the earth does not decrease your stock when you spare it a few seeds. Don't be fooled when you temporarily have few fewer seeds in your silo, because in a short few months, you will reap hundreds –if not thousands– of seeds in return.' Imagine the return Allah –the All-generous– has in store for you when you spare some of your wealth.

VERSE 262

Allazeena yunfiqoona amwaalahum fee sabeelillaahi summa laa yutbi'oona maaa anfaqoo mannanw wa laaa azal lahum ajruhum 'inda Rabbihim; wa laa khawfun 'alaihim wa laa hum yahzanoon

hose who spend their wealth in Allah's cause, and then do not follow their spending with reminders of their benevolence or hurtful words, will have their rewards with their Lord: no fear for them, nor will they grieve.

Allah is warning you: when you spend your money in His cause, beware of thinking that you are doing the poor and needy a favor. Beware of bragging to others of what you did. Most importantly, do not remind the person you helped of your deed.

It is from the etiquettes of faith to completely forget that you gifted something to someone in need or spent money to help. You should act as if your charity never happened to begin with. You should not tell family members about your help, especially your children and the children of the poor man or woman.

Allah is making it clear to you not to follow your help –whether it was financial or otherwise- with bragging, reminders of your favour, or hurtful words. Allah wants to foster the spirit of cooperation and love not that of resentment and anger. If you help your friend with money and then make him or her feel burdened or humiliated, he or she will not only hate that money, but he or she will also resent you.

I have had many people come to me and complain: "Can you believe this! I have helped so and so many times and now look how he treats me." My answer to those people is: "it serves you right that he would deny the good that you did! Had you done it for Allah's sake, you would have reaped the full reward. But since you did your favour to be remembered and recognized by others, then this is what you get."

In the previous verse, verse 261, Allah opened the hearts of the believers to giving. He, the All-Wise, gave you the example of one good seed sprouting a plant carrying over 700 seeds. Allah assured you that your wealth would not decrease by giving; rather, it increases just as a farmer's crop increases when he or she plants seeds in fertile ground.

In the verse under study, Allah clarifies the pitfalls that could spoil your harvest: this happens when you accompany your charity with reminders of your favour, and hurtful words whether in public or private. Such actions rob the poor of the feelings of solidarity and appreciation and foster the feelings of hate and resentment. Allah says:

Those who spend their wealth in Allah's cause, and then do not follow their spending with reminders of their benevolence or hurtful words, will have their rewards with their Lord: no fear for them, nor will they grieve. (Chapter 2: Verse 262)

Here we should study the intricacies of the Quranic text; more specifically, the use of the word "then." The verse would have read perfectly fine if it said 'Those who spend their wealth in Allah's cause, and do not follow their spending with reminders of their benevolence or hurtful words.' But Allah chose to include the word "then" so the verse now reads: "Those who spend their wealth in Allah's cause, and then do not follow their spending with reminders of their benevolence or hurtful words." What is the significance, you may ask? We answer that Allah is alerting you to be careful with your words and actions not only at the time of your gift, but days, weeks, or even years later. Spending must never be accompanied with or followed by hurtful words or reminders of the favour. With time, you may learn something new about the person you helped; you may see him or her do something you disapprove, but that should not be an excuse to spoil your gift. The poet Shawqi wrote:

Have you ever held a debt in your life?

Have you felt resentment in your heart?

Have you had someone remind you

of the favour by day and throughout the night?

That is life and these are its burdens

It makes carrying a load of steel and iron feel light

So do not burden those you helped with reminders and hurtful words. Allah, the All-Generous, assures you that if you help others for His sake, and without harm, you will be rewarded very handsomely. He alone, the ever-present and the most Competent will take care of you.

As for those who follow their charity with reminders and harms, it shows that they did not have Allah at heart. They sought their reward from the weak, and not from the Lord of the weak. Allah is the One who brought us into existence, and He is the One who grants us wealth and takes it away. Allah is the ultimate provider, not you or the rich. So when you help the weak and distressed, you are, in fact, giving on behalf of Allah.

Once, our beloved Prophet came into his daughter's room and found her cleaning and burnishing a coin into a shine. He asked: 'Fatima, what are you doing?' She replied: I am polishing this coin before I give it to charity. He asked: 'why?' She said: 'because I know that charity passes through Allah's hand before it falls into the hand of the poor.'

The verse ends with another assurance for the believers. Allah says: "no fear for them, nor will they grieve." Fear usually comes from external sources. Allah explains that there is often a third party involved in charity. It is usually a person who has a genuine concern for the giver. He or she may say: "You know, you should think about your family first. Save your money for the dark days ahead. Leave something for your children." Keep in mind that if you spend in Allah's cause, Allah guarantees you prosperity, blessing, and protection. You should not fear the present, and you should feel assured that you will not grieve about your charity in the future.

Here I want to take a few moments to discuss true prosperity, blessing, and protection. People often think about prosperity in the form of wealth and income. If you make a lot of money, people see you as prosperous and lucky. This is what I call 'positive income.' However, most people overlook the true blessings of 'negative income' which often far exceed those of earning more money.

This is best explained by a real-life example. Suppose a man –who is not very honest in his dealings- earns £50 a day, and he just got a raise of another £10. He goes home happy, only to find his daughter suffering from high fever. His wife is worried because she just heard about an outbreak of Typhoid fever on the news. Allah throws worry and doubts into the father's heart. He rushes his daughter to the doctor who does blood tests and x-rays that cost over £190. The tests are inconclusive. The kid returns home, goes to sleep and she wakes up the next day with no fever.

Another man, who is God conscious, earns £25 a day; he goes home to find his daughter suffering from high fever. Allah throws tranquillity into the father's heart. He asks his wife to make some hot tea and lemon for the child, and give her some Aspirin. The kid goes to sleep, and she wakes up the next day with no fever.

Allah cured both kids, but it cost the first man over 3 days of income and a sleepless night; while the second man got away with a few pennies and peace of mind. Who is the richer man? Which man provided his daughter with true security? Superficial people believe the first man to be lucky and fortunate, where –in reality- the second man is the one who is truly blessed. Allah, the All-merciful, can get you out of hardship without the need to spend, worry or grieve. Allah guarantees you prosperity and protection in this world and the next if you keep Him first and foremost in your mind. He says:

Those who spend their wealth in Allah's cause, and then do not follow their spending with reminders of their benevolence or hurtful words, will have their rewards with their Lord: no fear for them, nor will they grieve. (Chapter 2: Verse 262)

VERSE 263

Qawlum ma'roofunw wa maghfiratun khairum min sadaqatiny yatba'uhaaa azaa; wallaahu Ghaniyyun Haleem

Kind words and the covering of faults are better than charity followed by injury. Allah is free of all wants, and He is Most-Forbearing.

In the previous verses, Allah spoke of charity and aid for the weak. He also warned against following your charity with hurtful words and constant reminders. But what if you do not have money to spare? Allah reminds you that generosity is not exclusive to material wealth. You can donate your time, effort, or share your knowledge. You can be charitable with something as simple as a smile or a kind word. Prophet Muhammad -peace be upon him- said: 'Guard yourself against Hellfire even by sharing a slice of fruit. And if you do not have a slice, then share a nice, pleasant word.'

What is meant by "kind word" you may ask? The word "kind" is translated from the Arabic origin 'Ma'aroof' which means common or communal. Its antonym is 'Munkar' which means repulsive or rejected. As if good is naturally recognized and approved by the community, while evil is detested and rejected. In a healthy society, acts of good are done publicly, while acts of evil are hidden.

So if someone comes to you asking for help, make sure to treat him or her with kindness and respect. Treat others in a way that does not leave room for hatred and resentment. Even if the person in need came at you with persistence and rudeness, try to pardon and understand. Why? Because a person in dire need is generally blinded by his or her condition; he or she perceives that all the people around can help and save the day. A person in dire need may be harsh in language, so be patient and understanding.

How many times have you personally stepped over the boundaries of your Lord in sin? Yet Allah forbears and forgives, and He gives you one chance after another. He does not respond to your harshness and transgression in-kind, rather, Allah, the All-Merciful, shows you patience and forgiveness. He says:

Those who have been graced with bounty and plenty should not swear that they will not give to their relatives, the poor, those who emigrated in Allah's way: let them pardon and forgive. Wouldn't you like for Allah to forgive you? Allah is most forgiving and merciful. (24:22)

Listen to the story of our beloved prophet Abraham and his guest. He, peace be upon him, was very generous and hospitable. It is said that he did not eat dinner unless there was a guest at his table. One day a tired traveller walked in asking for rest and food. Prophet Abraham welcomed him, and after conversing for a while, he found out that this man was an atheist. Abraham got angry and told the man "I cannot have you at my table if you deny Allah." The man picked up his belongings and left. Shortly after, the Arch Angel Gabriel came to Prophet Abraham and said: "Allah is displeased with you Abraham, He says to you: 'This man has been a disbeliever for forty years, and for forty years I have been patient with him; I gave him food and provisions, yet you could not tolerate him for one evening at your table?'" Prophet Abraham ran after the man until he caught up with him. He said: 'forgive me. Please come back to my table.' The traveller asked: 'what happened!?' Abraham replied: 'My Lord scolded me for my inhospitality.' The man marvelled and said, "I am a disbeliever, and you are a prophet, yet your Lord scolded you for my sake!? Indeed this is a Lord that deserves to be worshipped. I bear witness that there is no Allah but Allah."

We all want Allah to forgive us and treat us with kindness. Shouldn't we forgive others, especially those in need?

The verse ends with: "Allah is self-sufficient, forbearing" to remind you that Allah is free of need. So when you deny help to others, you are not depriving Allah of anything, you are in fact depriving yourself of the reward of the All-Generous. Allah says:

Ah! There you are, being invited to spend in the way of Allah; yet among you, there are those who are stingy; and whoever is stingy is stingy only to himself. Allah is the All-sufficient, and you are the ones truly in need, and if you turn away He will replace you with another people, and they will not be like you. (47:38)

VERSE 264

Yaaa ayyuhal lazeena aamanoo laa tubtiloo sadaqaatikum bilmanni wal azaa kallazee yunfiqu maalahoo ri'aaa'an naasi wa laa yu'minu billaahi wal yawmil aakhiri famasaluhoo kamasali safwaanin 'alaihi turaabun fa asaabahoo waabilun fatara kahoo saldaa; laa yaqdiroona 'alaa shai'im mimmaa kasaboo; wallaahu laa yahdil qawmal kaafireen

You who believe, do not nullify your charitable deeds with reminders and hurtful words, like someone who spends his wealth showing off to people and not believing in Allah and the Last Day. Such a person is like a smooth rock coated with soil: heavy rain falls and leaves it completely bare. Such people get no rewards for their works: Allah does not guide the disbelievers.

Sadly, a person who follows his or her charity with bragging, hurtful words or reminders has wasted the reward. In fact, the loss is twofold: the first loss is financial where his or her wealth is decreased because Allah will not replenish it. The second loss, which is much worse, is deprivation of the reward in the hereafter.

If you do good deeds so people would say: 'look how generous; what a good person,' then make sure to collect your reward from these people. If you do good deeds purely for Allah's sake, then expect your reward from the All-Generous. Ask yourself: Where do I want my reward to come from? Prophet Muhammad, peace be upon him, said: 'A person whom Allah had given riches will stand before Allah on the day of Judgment. He will be shown his wealth, and he will recognize it. The Almighty will ask: And what did you do with your wealth? The man will answer: I left no path in which you like money to be spent without spending for your sake. Allah will say: "You have lied - you spent so people would say: 'He is generous.' And so it was said." Then he will be ordered to into Hell-fire.

Another pitfall charitable people often fall into is the false expectation that Allah's reward should show up immediately. In other words, beware of saying: 'I have spent in Allah's cause, but He did not replenish or increase my wealth!' We ask: Did you give to charity because you wanted more wealth, or did you purely give for Allah's sake? He almighty may test you by delaying your reward or may reserve your entire reward for the Hereafter when you would need it and benefit from it the most.

This brings us back to the verse. Allah says: "Such a person is like a smooth rock coated with soil: heavy rain falls and leaves it completely bare." The words "smooth rock" are translated from the Arabic origin "Safwan." It is the same word we use to describe the head of a bald man. A large smooth rock covered with fertile soil may fool you into thinking that it will sprout all kinds of plants and crops. But as soon as the wind blows or rain falls, the rock is stripped, and all that soil washes away. So are the charitable deeds of people who spend for show, or who spend while looking down at others. They may think that their deeds would amount to something in the hereafter, but they will be sorely disappointed. Allah says: "Such people get no rewards for their works: Allah does not guide the disbelievers. "

VERSE 266

Ayawaddu ahadukum an takoona lahoo jannatum min nakheelinw wa a'naabin tajree min tahtihal anhaaru lahoo feehaa min kullis samaraati wa asaabahul kibaru wa lahoo zurriyyatun du'afaaa'u fa asaabahaaa i'saarun feehi naarun fahtaraqat; kazaalika yubaiyinul laahu lakumul aayaati la'allakum tatafakkaroon

Would any of you like to have a garden of palm trees and vines, graced with streams flowing from underneath and all kinds of produce, which, when you are afflicted with old age and feeble offspring, is struck by a fiery whirlwind and burnt down? In this way Allah makes His messages clear to you, so that you may ponder.

In the previous verses, Allah gave us examples of those who give money to charity out of faith and sincerity, and of those who give to brag and feel superior to others. In the verse under study, Allah gives you yet another example. However, in this instance, He makes you part of the story, so you can live the emotions of giving first and then wasting your gift.

Have you dreamt about owning a great piece of land? Would you like your land to have palm trees and grape vines? Do you want your large property to have its own rivers and wells? What type of fruit and crop would you grow? Close your eyes for a moment and picture the perfect land and how you and your family would enjoy it.

Let's look at how Allah described this land. He started with: 'Would any of you like to have a garden of palm trees and vines.' Allah mentioned palm trees and grape vines in particular because they are cherished by growers and farmers. He says:

Tell them the example of two men: to one of them We gave two gardens of grape vines, surrounded them with date palms, and put fields in between; both gardens yielded fruit and did not fail in any way; We made a stream ?ow through them, and so he had abundant fruit. One day, while talking to his friend, he said, 'I have more wealth and a larger following than you.' He went into his garden and wronged himself by saying, 'I do not think this will ever perish, or that the Last Hour will ever come- even if I were to be taken back to my Lord, I would certainly find something even better there.' (18:32-36)

The gardens mentioned in the verses above had many types of plants, but Allah specified two in particular: date palms, and grapevines.

Allah continues the description: "with streams flowing from underneath." This phrase is usually mentioned in the Quran in a couple of variations with subtle differences. Let's examine the differences. Allah says describing paradise:

Allah has prepared for them Gardens graced with rivers flowing from underneath, and there they will stay. That is the supreme triumph. (09:89)

And in another verse, He says:

The forerunners – the first of the immigrants and those who supported them – and those who have followed them in doing good: Allah is pleased with them and they are pleased with Him. He has prepared Gardens for them with rivers flowing underneath them, remaining in them timelessly, for ever and ever. That is the great victory. (09:100)

Take note that in the first verse, Allah says: 'with rivers flowing from underneath,' while in the second He says: 'rivers flowing underneath them,' omitting the preposition 'from.' What is the difference, you may ask? We answer that when the preposition 'from' is used, it suggests that the source of the spring or river is located on the property, making it fully self-sufficient. It is more enjoyable to see springs gushing from the ground.

When the phrase 'with rivers flowing underneath them' is mentioned without the preposition 'from,' it means that the springs of these rivers are located somewhere else, not on the property. However, do not think that the flow of the rivers would ever be interrupted in paradise. Allah is just describing different levels of pleasure and enjoyment.

This brings us back to the verse, Allah says:

Would any of you like to have a garden of palm trees and vines, graced with streams flowing from underneath and all kinds of produce, which, when you are afflicted with old age and feeble offspring, is struck by a fiery whirlwind and burnt down? In this way Allah makes His messages clear to you, so that you may ponder. (Chapter 2: Verse 266)

Remember that perfect piece of land you dreamed about? You worked very hard all your life for this property. You secured water for irrigation, grew crops for food, and fruits for enjoyment. But you are getting older and weaker by the day. Now, you rely on the yield of this garden more than ever before; not only for yourself but also for your weak children. This represents the height of dependence on this piece of land. It is your family's security blanket: Two vulnerable generations are living off of it.

How would you feel, in your weak old age, if a storm hits the land that is supporting your helpless children? How would you feel if your crops were burned to the ground from thunder strikes? Would you feel extreme sadness? Anger? Desperation? This is exactly how you would feel if you gave money to charity and then wasted the immense rewards by bragging, hurtful words and harm. High hopes come crashing down on bad intentions.

Thus, every time you spend to help others, you should pause and think about your true motivation. Imagine that perfect piece of land, and do not do anything to destroy it.

VERSES 267

Yaaa 'ayyuhal lazeena aamanooo anfiqoo min taiyibaati maa kasabtum wa mimmaaa akhrajna lakum minal ardi wa laa tayammamul khabeesa minhu tunfiqoona wa lastum bi aakhizeehi illaaa an tughmidoo feeh; wa'lamooo annal laaha Ghaniyyun Hameed

You who believe, give charitably from the good things you have earned and that We have produced for you from the earth. Do not give away the bad things that you yourself would only accept with your eyes closed: remember that Allah is self-sufficient, worthy of all praise.

During the time of our beloved Prophet Muhammad, the residents of Medina used to hang containers of dates by the entrance of the mosque. The poor and the travellers could eat from it without the need to ask or beg. Sadly, the hypocrites and some Muslim residents used to bring in whatever old or rotting dates they had and pretend they were helping the poor. Allah warns us against such behaviour. You should not give to charity what is worn and torn, or what is old and spoiled. Allah says: "You who believe, give charitably from the good things you have earned."

Your Zakat almsgiving and charity should satisfy two conditions: First, spending must be from wealth you earned lawfully. Allah is good and pure, and He only accepts that which is good and pure. Second, spending should not be given from low-quality or damaged items.

Allah also reminds you that all you have is from His bounty. He says: 'and that we have produced for you from the earth.' Do not fall under the illusion that working and earning is your true source of sustenance.

Rather, working is a gift from Allah. You can only move around because Allah granted you the energy to do so. He gifted you a thoughtful mind and an able body. He subjected the earth and many animals to your will. These are just a few of the countless instruments Allah has blessed you with; none of them are inherent to you. But Allah respects your effort and hard work. He says: "You who believe, give charitably from the good things you have earned."

So do not use charity as a cover to get rid of subpar items that you hate. Allah says: "Do not give away the bad things that you yourself would only accept with your eyes closed." In other words, before you give anything to charity, ask yourself: would I give these clothes to my kids to wear? Would I put this food on my table? If you are ashamed to give such items to your family, then you should be ashamed of giving them away. Remember that giving to charity is for your own good because 'Allah is self-sufficient, worthy of all praise;' He does not need anything you have.

Let's take a moment to review what Allah taught us in the last few verses in regards to charity and almsgiving:

Spending in Allah's path does not reduce your wealth in any way; it actually increases your reward by seven hundredfold or more.

You should not nullify your charity with hurtful words or reminders of your favour.

A pleasant smile and a good word are better than a charity which is followed by harm or constant reminders.

You should not brag about giving charity, or give damaged or subpar items.

Remember that charity is not a favour to the poor. It is cleansing for your soul.

Now, contrast these teaching to what Allah says in the next verse in,

VERSE 268

Ash Shaitaanu ya'idukumul faqra wa ya'murukum bilfahshaaa'i wallaahu ya'idukum maghfiratam minhu wa fadlaa; wallaahu Waasi'un 'Aleem

The devil promises you poverty and commands you to self-gratification. Allah promises you forgiveness from Him and abundance. Allah is All-Encompassing, All-Knowing.

When you are about to give charity, the devil steps in and whispers to you to withhold your gift. Why risk poverty? Why give your money away to someone who may waste it? Don't you want that new car? Don't you want to insure the future of your kids? The devil scares you with poverty and tries to distract you from spending in Allah's path...

When the rich refrain from helping the needy, the hearts of the poor become filled with hatred and resentment. The rich become the enemy, and the society turns on itself. In a community where indifference and selfishness prevail, all sorts of evils become widespread. Allah addresses these issues in the following verses:

The present, worldly life is nothing but a play and a pastime. If you truly believe and keep from disobedience to Him in reverence for Him and piety, He will grant you your rewards, and will not ask of you your wealth. You would be grudging if He were to ask you and press you for them, and He would bring your resentment to light- (47:36-37)

Allah does not ask you to give back the money he blessed you with. He only asks you to purify your money and your soul, by spending a small percentage for His sake. In return, He will not only increase you in wealth, but He will also remove hatred from the community.

On the other hand, when injustice becomes widespread, social unrest follows, and the entire community –rich and poor-suffers. Allah says: The devil promises you poverty and commands you to self-gratification. Allah promises you forgiveness from Him and abundance. Allah is All-Encompassing, All-Knowing. (Verse 268)

A person who responds to Satan's whisper and ignores Allah's promise is preferring the enemy of Allah over Allah Himself. May Allah protect you and me from such behaviour. Any time the devil is followed, man ends in ruin. And anytime Allah is followed, mercy and immense gifts await. Wisdom requires you to know which path to choose.

VERSE 269

Yu'til Hikmata mai yashaaa'; wa mai yu'tal Hikmata faqad ootiya khairan kaseeraa; wa maa yazzakkaru illaaa ulul albaab

He gives wisdom to whoever He will. Whoever is given wisdom has truly been given much good, but only those with insight bear this in mind.

Wisdom is to place each matter in its rightful place. It is translated from the Arabic origin: 'Hikma.' The word 'Hikma حكمة' originated from the 'bridle' which is the piece of leather and iron placed in a horse's mouth so the rider can control and aim the animal towards the desired destination. Without it, the animal may wonder aimlessly and stray from the rider's goal. Similarly, wisdom sets a proper goal for each action and then steers the person in the right direction. Allah, the all Wise, is the one who identifies for each creation its bounds and mission. Who is better than your creator, the one who knows you best, in determining your goal in life? Allah's teachings are the essence of wisdom because they insure your security and the security of your children in this world, and paradise in the Hereafter. So when you follow the teachings of your creator, you have -in fact- applied wisdom and put matters in their rightful place.

Here we should take a few moments to learn a very valuable lesson about our children; more specifically, a lesson of how to raise them wisely and insure their future against calamities. There will be a period in every person's life where he or she is more preoccupied by the needs of the children than his or her own needs. A father may starve in order to feed his family. A mother would wear old torn clothes so she can buy her children something new for school.

Take the example of our beloved Prophet Abraham. He, peace be upon him, was tested in his youth and in his old age. But the tests were different. The Almighty tested Abraham in the early stages of his life by putting his health and wellbeing on the line for faith. When Abraham was captured by his enemies, they threatened to throw him in the fire. When he refused to worship their Gods, they pushed him into the raging flames. Allah protected His prophet as narrated in the following verses:

Abraham said: "How do you worship, instead of Allah, that which cannot benefit you in any way, nor harm you? "Shame on you and on all that you worship apart from Allah! Will you not reason and understand?" They said, 'Burn him and avenge your Gods, if you are men of actions.' "O fire," We ordered, "Be cool and peaceful for Abraham!" (21:66-69)

Contrast that to the test Allah put Abraham through at his old age. He tested him with a command to slaughter his son. As Abraham and Ishmael got ready to obey their Lord, Allah redeemed Ishmael with a great ram. From Abraham's tests, we learn that a man in the latter stages of his life is far more concerned for his children's wellbeing than his own.

But how do you protect your children? How do you insure their wellbeing if you die? Should you leave them a lot of money? Or will money spoil them and send them down a dark path? Allah teaches you the wisdom that offers the best insurance policy for your kids. He says:

Let those who would fear for the future of their own helpless children, if they were to die, show the same concern for orphans; let them be mindful of Allah and speak out for justice. (04:09)

In other words, Allah wants you to secure the future of your children with good deeds and just words. Take good care of those less fortunate around you, and Allah will take good care of your kids.

Let's look at examples from the Quran of how this insurance policy pays out. We start with the story of Moses and the righteous servant, Al-Khidr, -peace be upon them-. Allah says:

So they went on until when they came upon the people of a township, they asked its people for food, but they refused them hospitality. They found there a wall which was on the verge of tumbling down, and he restored it. Moses said: "If you had wished, you could have taken payment for it." (18:77)

Moses did not know that there was a treasure belonging to two orphans buried under the wall by their father. The people of this village were rude. They refused to help when Moses and Al-Khidr asked for food –which is the most basic of human needs-. Such people would have robbed the orphans' treasure if they found it. Thus, it was necessary to erect the wall so the treasure would be concealed from the villagers until the kids reached maturity. But why did Allah protect the orphans and their wealth from the villagers?

This answer can be found from verse 82 of chapter 18:

The wall belonged to two young orphans in the town and there was buried treasure beneath it belonging to them. Their father had been a righteous man, so your Lord intended them to reach maturity and then dig up their treasure as a mercy from your Lord.

Allah teaches us that the future of the two orphans was secured because of the good deeds of their father. This is true wisdom and it can only be appreciated by the thoughtful mind.

We find another example of how the wisdom of a parent protects their children in this surah, Surah Baqarah. If you recall, among the children of Israel lived a very poor but righteous man. All he had in this world was a small calf. On his deathbed his last words were: "O Allah, I entrust my wife, my little boy, and my only possession, a calf, to your care." He knew that his wife could barely take care of the household, so he entrusted this calf to Allah's care and let it loose right before he died.

After a few years, the mother told her grown son: 'Your father left you a little fortune: A calf; it should be a grown cow by now." The son was surprised and asked his mother where it was. She replied: "Your father entrusted it to Allah and set it free. Be like him and say: 'I put my trust in you Lord, please guide me to my cow.'" The young man supplicated then he set out to search for it. Barely a day had passed and a cow came towards him and stopped submissively. As he lead it to his house, a group of the Israelites –who were quarrelling over the murder of a relative- saw the cow and realized that it fit perfectly the cow Allah described for them to slaughter. They offered to buy it for 3 gold coins, but the young man's mother refused. The Israelites increased their bid to 5 coins, then 10, but the mother kept refusing. Finally, they urged the son to speak to his mother to be reasonable. He told them: "I will not sell without my mother's approval, even if you offer me its skin-fill in gold!" The mother smiled and said: "Let that be the price: The cow's skin-fill of gold."

Again, the story teaches us that parents' righteousness plays the main role in the protection of their children. Through the wisdom and good deeds of the father and mother, Allah facilitated the affairs of this child and enriched him beyond the wealthiest people of the town.

I would also like to give the example of the wisdom of Hasan Al-Basri. When a needy person would come to him asking for charity, he would say: 'I welcome the one who will carry my supplies to the hereafter free of charges.' Through his great wisdom, Hasan Al-Basri realized that true success is beyond worldly riches and instant gratification. He invested his time, effort and wealth in the ever-lasting benefits of the hereafter.

In our daily lives, we have all seen the example of the student who strives and works hard to be successful, while his or her classmates rest and waste time on games and television. The student who works hard will rise in society, while others would struggle for the rest of their lives. Allah says:

He gives wisdom to whoever He will. Whoever is given wisdom has truly been given much good, but only those with insight bear this in mind. (Chapter 2: Verse 269)

VERSES 270

Wa maaa anfaqtum min nafaqatin aw nazartum min nazrin fa innal laaha ya'lamuh; wa maa lizzaalimeena min ansaar

Whatever you spend, or vow to do, Allah knows it well, and those who do wrong will have no one to help them.

In the previous session, we covered matters of charity and giving. But what is the issue of a vow? To vow –translated from the Arabic Nuthr- is to make a promise to yourself, or assign yourself a duty of a specific good deed beyond what Allah has obligated you with. For example, you can vow to pray every night a specific number of prayers. This goes above and beyond the five obligatory prayers. By vowing to pray more, you make it incumbent upon yourself to perform these extra prayers nightly.

When you make a vow, it shows that you have tasted the sweetness of worship and you love to get closer to the Lord. It is an acknowledgment that Allah is worthy of far more than what He obligated you with. Allah has been extremely generous and merciful because if He had imposed what He deserved from us, no one could have fulfilled His right. He says:

Can He who creates be compared to one who cannot create? Why do you not take heed? And should you attempt to count Allah's blessings, you could not compute them. Allah is indeed All-Forgiving, All-Compassionate (16:17, 18)

You have the freedom to make a vow or not. However, if you choose to make a one, it becomes an obligation. Why? Because you freely made that choice. Thus, it is wise not to get carried away and make a vow that is difficult to abide by.

Righteous people who have true knowledge of Allah say to those who violate a vow: Didn't you find Allah worthy of your continuous love? There is no one among us who has any doubt that Allah is deserving of deep affection. Therefore, it is better to take your time and think deeply before making a vow.

Take note of the ending of the verse. Allah says: 'and those who do wrong will have no one to help them.' Wrongdoers are those who have been unjust to themselves. Allah explains:

Allah does not wrong people at all- it is they who wrong themselves. (10:44)

Some of the more serious ways you can do injustices unto yourself are to brag about helping others, to spend your money in sin, or to fail to fulfil a vow. Be careful, because the consequences of such actions are dire.

VERSE 270

If you give charity openly, it is good, but if you keep it secret and give to the needy in private, that is better for you, and it will atone for some of your bad deeds: Allah is well aware of all that you do. (Chapter 2: Verse 271)

When you give charity openly, it is good because it may serve as an example for others to follow. And when you give to the poor privately, Allah will expiate your sins. Allah is the only One who knows the true intention behind the declaration or concealment of your charity.

We generally advise that if you are rich, it might be better for you to give to charity openly now and then. This will help protect you from society's gossip. When people see that someone is rich, they should also see him or her spending on the poor. Otherwise, they will hold grudges in their hearts. People would often gossip that so and so has much wealth but he or she does not help anybody. However, if a person is not outwardly rich, we generally advise concealing charitable donations.

Either way, if you give openly to be a good role model, then that is praiseworthy. Allah says: "Allah is well aware of all that you do."

VERSE 271

In tubdus sadaqaati fani'immaa hiya wa in tukhfoohaa wa tu'toohal fuqaraaa'a fahuwa khayrul lakum; wa yukaffiru 'ankum min saiyi aatikum; wallaahu bimaa ta'maloona Khabeer

If you give charity openly, it is good, but if you keep it secret and give to the needy in private, that is better for you, and it will atone for some of your bad deeds: Allah is well aware of all that you do.

To close the pathways of stinginess before the human soul, Allah asks you to meet the basic needs of your family first, and only then, give a small portion of your excess wealth to the poor. This is only possible if you work to your capacity, not just to meet your basic needs. If everyone worked just to put food on the table, then how will those who are unable to work survive?

Here you may ask: Why wouldn't Allah make the helpless capable of working rather than ask others to help them? We answer that Allah created an integrated and harmonious universe and subjected the means to our will. The earth responds to our work; so do plants and livestock. Sadly, over time people mistakenly think that the means are inherent to them. Let's clarify this point. A farmer may think that the crops grow exclusively because he sows seeds and irrigates. When the earth responds to him, the farmer thinks that he is the one who makes things happen in the universe.

To save us from our arrogance, Allah occasionally makes the means at our disposal inconsistent. For example, Allah may occasionally cause drought or vermin to hit the farmer's crops. If the farmer were truly in control, he would never have a bad year. Put simply, just because you can produce today, does not mean that you will be able to produce tomorrow. The presence of helpless people around you should make you realize that you are not in control. The One who grants the ability can take it away. Allah can make the helpless yesterday capable today, and the capable yesterday helpless today. Allah is the only constant.

This realization is one of the critical differences between the believer and the non-believer. Both work hard to earn their livelihood. Both use the means at their disposal to get ahead in life. However, when the believer earns and provides for his or her family, he or she puts aside some of the excess to help the needy and seek Allah's reward. Allah says:

And keep up the prayer and pay the prescribed alms. Whatever good you store up for yourselves, you will find it with Allah: He sees everything you do. (02:110)

By making the Zakat Almsgiving a pillar of faith, Allah made giving to the poor a goal for the believer. But what stops us from giving?

The main source of stinginess is the fear that charity will decrease wealth. Allah made it clear: Your wealth will never decrease from charity; Allah will reward you many times over. Take a moment to think about what you earn through your work and investments compared to what Allah has in store for you through your charity. Compare your power to Allah's power. Who do you trust with your wealth? Allah says:

The example of those who expend their wealth in the way of Allah is that of a grain of corn from which grow seven ears, each ear containing a hundred grains. Truly Allah multiplies for whomsoever He will, for Allah is infinite and all-wise. (2:261)

A smart farmer invests and sows seeds in his or her land. In return, the land will more than triple or quadruple the investment. A stupid farmer keeps all the seeds in the silo, because he or she is afraid that planting some will decrease the amount in storage. If the earth, which is one of Allah's creations, gives abundantly once you invest in it, then think about the grant of the Lord, the Creator of the earth. Through this example, Allah closed the main door of stinginess for the human soul. Prophet Muhammad, peace be upon him, said "Beware of doing injustice, for it is darkness upon darkness on the Day of Judgment; and beware of stinginess because it doomed those who were before you. It incited them to shed blood and transgress over the rights of others."

Here is another pitfall Allah addresses in this chapter: A wealthy person may feel annoyed when people ask him for money. He or she may be under social pressure to give to charity. At that point, there is a struggle between greed and stinginess on one side, and social status on the other. What happens next? The wealthy individual may give with resentment, and follow this gift by scolding or reproaching the beggar. The Almighty says: stop. He advises us in the Quran:

A kind word and forgiveness is better than a charitable deed followed by harm. Allah is self-sufficient, forbearing. (2:263)

Constant reminders are a sure way to invalidate the rewards of giving. It is of our human nature to seek recognition and praise. However, by reminding the poor of your favour, you foster the feelings of humiliation and resentment. Allah warns you that such actions would cause you to be the ultimate loser. How? The poor would still get the benefit of your money, while you lose the reward. So be careful not to waste both your money and reward with a few hurtful words.

Later, Allah addressed another aspect of stinginess. It happens when a generous person finds it hard to give from the best of what he or she owns. In other words, you keep the best to yourself and give the worn, torn or already spoiled to others. Allah says:

You who believe, give charitably from the good things you have earned and that We have produced for you from the earth. Do not give away the bad things that you yourself would only accept with your eyes closed: remember that Allah is self-sufficient, worthy of all praise. (2:267)

Do not give something that you would not accept if it were given to you.

Then, Allah warns that the devil can exploit all these avenues of stinginess. He says:

The devil frightens you with poverty and commands you to self-gratification. Allah promises you forgiveness from Him and abundance. Allah is All-Encompassing, All-Knowing. (2:268)

Lastly, in the verse under study, Allah addresses the issue of giving charity secretly or publicly, and more importantly, the true intention behind it. If you are an affluent person, then guard your family against prying eyes and wondering minds by spending openly so people would not talk ill about you. However, you should also volunteer and give secretly so that your left-hand does not know what your right is doing. Ibn Abbas narrated that giving voluntary charity –also known as Sadaqa- in secret is seventy times more rewarding than giving it publicly. However, giving the obligatory Zakat publicly is twenty-five times more rewarding than giving it in secret.

Through the verses we reviewed, Allah had opened all the doors of giving before you and closed all the doors of stinginess. He protected the weak by asking their strong believing brothers and sisters to step up. Always keep in mind that while Allah is asking you to help the weak and poor today, He would also ask everyone to help you if you fall on hard times. In an ever-changing world, if you become poor, Allah's commands are an asset on your side, not the burden that you may see them to be today.

VERSE 272

Laisa 'alaika hudaahum wa laakinnal laaha yahdee mai yashaaa'; wa maa tunfiqoo min khairin fali anfusikum; wa maa tunfiqoona illab tighaaa'a wajhil laah; wa maa tunfiqoo min khairiny yuwaffa ilaikum wa antum laa tuzlamoon

It is not for you to guide them; it is Allah who guides whoever He will. Whatever charity you give benefits your own soul, provided you do it for the sake of Allah: whatever you give will be repaid to you in full, and you will not be wronged.

Look at the bounties of Islam, benefiting even those who do not believe in it. Allah asks you to give the obligatory Zakat almsgiving to your believing brothers and sisters, then He gives you the opportunity to increase your reward by giving a voluntary Sadaqa to the needy regardless of their faith. Allah says: It is not for you to guide them; it is Allah who guides whoever He will. Whatever charity you give benefits your own soul, provided you do it for the sake of Allah.

Here you may ask, why was there a shift in the subject? Where did the issue of 'It is not for you to guide them; it is Allah who guides whoever He will' come from? The preceding verses discussed charity and giving, and the next verses continue to discuss charity and giving. So why did Allah, the All-Wise, interject with guidance?

Here is the story behind this verse: At the time of the Prophet, there were many Muslims who had poor non-believing relatives. They wanted to help their relatives financially, yet they were unsure if it is OK to assist a non-believer. So they went to the Prophet to ask. One of the believers was Asma, the daughter of Abu Bakr. Her mom, a non-believer, was in need. She went and asked the prophet: 'Should I help my Mom?' He, peace be upon him, replied: 'Of course you should!'

There were also some Muslims who withheld financial help from their relatives to pressure them into Islam. To stop such practices, Allah revealed: 'It is not for you to guide them; it is Allah who guides whoever He will. Whatever charity you give benefits your own soul.'

Allah prioritized the care of your fellow humans over pushing any belief system on them. Allah is the Lord of every human being, even if He is not the deity of every human being. Let me explain this further. Allah is the creator; He brought everyone into existence. You and I had no say whether to be born or not. Thus, Allah takes on the responsibility of providing for each one of us regardless of our belief. Allah, Our Lord, provides the believer and non-believer alike with air, water, food and all the necessities of life. Allah, Our Lord, shows the believer and non-believer alike His path of guidance. Whether you accept Allah as your deity and entrust Him with your affairs is up to you.

Another reason behind the revelation of this verse is to encourage the believers to give well. Some had been giving substandard items, such as food that was about to spoil or worn and torn clothes.

Islam came to curb the whims of the ego. Your faith should be a counterweight against your greed and self-indulgence. Thus, Islam repeatedly addressed moral issues in faith. Allah says: 'It is not for you to guide them; it is Allah who guides whoever He will. Whatever charity you give benefits your own soul.' Our beloved Prophet Muhammad used to feel sorrow if he saw the believers unenthusiastic about implementing Allah's commands. Allah explained to Prophet Muhammad (pbuh) that his job was only to convey the message, not to chase after each person to accept and implement it.

Here, we should take time to address a critical issue. Some people quote verses such as 'It is not for you to guide them; it is Allah who guides whoever He will' and say: 'since Allah guides whoever He wills, then our job is done. We do not have to talk to people about Islam.' Or they claim: "I cannot help myself from doing sin. If Allah wants me to be good, He will make me good. Allah guides whoever He will." We answer that to truly understand the issue of guidance, you have to study all the Quranic verses that address this issue, not just one. Allah says in the 82nd verse of chapter 4:

Why do they not ponder over the Quran!?

The Quran is the Devine word of Allah. It should not be taken lightly or glanced over. Allah is asking you to read, ponder, and examine the Quran inside and out. Keeping that in mind, let's look into the issue of guidance.

If guidance was exclusively Allah's domain where He chooses who is guided and who is not, then there would have been no punishment or reward in the hereafter. You cannot punish someone for an act he or she had nothing to do with. Having paradise as a reward for the righteous and hellfire as punishment for the sinner indicates freedom of choice.

So how do we reconcile these two issues: the issue of 'It is not for you to guide them; it is Allah who guides whoever He will' on the one hand and the issue of freedom of choice on the other? Let's examine the Quran. Allah says:

As for the tribe of Thamood, We gave them guidance, but they preferred blindness, so they were struck by a blast of humiliating punishment for their misdeeds. Yet We saved those who believed and were mindful of Allah. (41:17-18)

Allah guides all humanity towards His path. More specifically, Allah calls everyone to faith; He sends prophets and messengers and supports them with miracles and scriptures to deliver his message to everyone. Allah clarifies the outcome of those who follow His path and those who abandon it. So whoever wants to follow the right path can do so, and whoever chooses to abandon it can do so. This is summarized by the phrase: 'We gave them guidance, but they preferred blindness.'

Here is another example. In this verse Allah addresses the Prophet and says:

"and you certainly guide them to the right path" (42:52)

Now listen to a second verse, where again, Allah also addresses the prophet and says:

You cannot guide the ones you love to the truth; it is Allah who guides whoever He will: He knows best those who will follow guidance. (28:56)

At first glance these two verses are in contradiction: One verse affirms that the prophet guides, while the other denies him guidance even to his loved ones. How can this be? We answer that our beloved prophet Muhammad is the means of delivering Allah's book and general guidance to humanity. He lit the path towards heaven for everyone. Allah confirms: 'and you certainly guide them to the right path.' On the other hand, Prophet Muhammad cannot force anyone into faith. The phrase 'Surely you cannot guide whom you love' ensures that every person has the freedom to believe or not.

We say to people who use verses such as 'It is not for you to guide them; it is Allah who guides whoever He will' to absolve themselves from the responsibility of faith and deed: you are wrong. You cannot blame Allah for your disbelief or shortcomings. Allah has sent you prophets and scriptures. He filled the universe around you with sign after sign of His Lordship. Moreover, if you choose to follow Allah's guidance, the Lord will support you with his divine guidance; He will endear faith and piety to your heart and facilitate for you the actions that lead to paradise. Allah says:

As for those who follow true guidance, He leads them far ahead in their right ways and grants them piety and restraints from evil suited to their condition. (47:17)

This brings us back to the verse. Allah says addressing our stinginess: 'Whatever charity you give benefits your own soul.' People do not want to give because they like to keep what they have. Allah assures you that if you give your time or money to help others while keeping Allah in mind, you are in fact benefiting yourself. He says: 'provided you do it for the sake of Allah: whatever you give will be repaid to you in full.'

Hasan Albasri, a famous righteous man, used to rejoice when someone would come and ask him for charity. He would say: 'I welcome the one who will carry my good deeds to the hereafter free of charge.' Another righteous man was asked by his friend: 'How many people have you helped today?' He answered: 'none.' The friend replied: 'But I saw you give money to a poor family, aid an elderly woman, and visit a sick child.' The righteous man said: 'I was doing good to help myself.'

Allah wants you to turn your thoughts about charity upside down: You are not helping others; you are helping yourself. You are not spending your money on charity; you are saving it for later. Your wealth is not decreasing; it is being invested with a guaranteed return by the Lord of the Worlds. He says: 'whatever you give will be repaid to you in full, and you will not be wronged.'

Whatabout when people complain about the ill treatment they received from poor relatives they helped: 'You deserve what you got. When you helped your relatives, you were expecting thanks and praise from them. Had you helped them for Allah's sake –and for His sake alone- you wouldn't have been disappointed.' Allah says: 'whatever charity you give benefits your own soul, provided you do it for the sake of Allah: whatever you give will be repaid to you in full, and you will not be wronged.'

VERSE 273

Lilfuqaraaa'il lazeena uhsiroo fee sabeelil laahi laa yastatee'oona darban fil ardi yah sabuhumul jaahilu aghniyaaa'a minat ta'affufi ta'rifuhum biseemaahum laa yas'aloonan naasa ilhaafaa; wa maa tunfiqoo min khairin fa innal laaha bihee 'Aleem

To the poor who are held back in the Way of Allah, unable to move about in the land. The uninformed presume them rich because of their dignified discretion. You will recognize them by their characteristics: They do not ask from people insistently. Whatever good you give away, Allah knows it.

Perhaps the first question that comes to mind in this verse is: what is 'to' in the phrase 'to the poor' referring to? The verse starts with a preposition 'to' seemingly unrelated to anything else. We answer that 'to' is referring to charity. To whom should you give? 'To the poor who are held back in the Way of Allah, unable to move about in the land.'

When you hear the phrase 'held-back,' you may wonder: What is holding them back? We answer that a person can be held back by circumstances from within or from without. For example, if you wanted to travel, but on the day of travel you fell ill, then, you were held back by your illness —a personal issue-. If, on the other hand, you were able to travel, but the border agent prevented you from leaving the country, then you were held back by an external issue.

Similarly, those who were 'held back in the Way of Allah, unable to move about in the land' could have been held back by personal or external matters. On a personal level, a person who is dedicated to serving Allah may decide to stay in an area where he or she cannot make a good living. He or she may forgo a good job opportunity in exchange for helping the community grow and fight for their rights. On an external level, a person who is dedicated to serving Allah may be oppressed by corrupt authorities benefiting from robbing others of their rights.

We are all required to move about in the land to earn a living. To be a productive human being requires constant work. Farming the land requires movement; manufacturing requires movement, and raising a family requires movement. Allah says:

It is He who made the earth subservient to you that you may travel all around it, and eat from His provisions, and to Him will be your resurrection. (67:15)

if you are restricted in your movement, then you are limited in earning a living.

Allah described those who have been harmed on his path with the phrase: 'The uninformed presume them rich because of their dignified discretion.' In other words, despite their need, they do not ask others for help. Yet, the very next sentence says: 'You will recognize them by their characteristics.' So, if you pay attention, you would notice small signs in their appearance, clothes, and possessions indicating that they are in need and can use some help.

Allah says: 'The uninformed presume them rich because of their dignified discretion. You will recognize them by their characteristics: They do not ask from people insistently.' The question that comes to mind here is: Which is it? Are they discreet and do not ask others for help? Or do they 'not ask from people insistently'? If they asked for help –even discreetly-, then you would know them, not by their characteristics, but by their asking for help.

On the other hand, if they did not ask, then why the phrase 'They do not ask from people insistently'? We answer that there are two types of people here. The first type is the general poor who Allah allows to ask for help but discourages them from insisting or nagging others. The second type relates to 'the poor who are held back in the Way of Allah, unable to move about in the land.' This type has dedicated themselves to the straight path, and they do not ask anyone for help. They are recognized by their condition.

This puts the social burden on wealthy believers. How, you may ask? We answer that it is essential for the believer to be socially astute and pay close attention to his or her community. Allah wants you to be aware of those around you: your relatives, neighbours, and friends. Pay attention to their circumstances and be ready to help when you see signs of trouble.

Here, a story comes to mind: A neighbour in need knocked the door of a righteous man and asked him for help. The righteous man rushed inside, gathered some money and gave it to him. After the neighbour left, the man's wife saw him crying. She asked: 'what happened?' He replied: 'My neighbour came to me in need.' She said: 'and you rushed to his aid, so what's wrong?' He answered: 'I was so ignorant of his condition that he had to knock on my door and ask....' This righteous man felt the burden of guilt because he was not proactive in noticing which of his neighbours and friends needed help.

VERSE 274

Allazeena yunfiqoona amwaalahum billaili wan nahaari sirranw wa 'alaaniyatan falahum ajruhum 'inda Rabbihim wa laa khawfun 'alaihim wa laa hum yahzanoon

Those who give, out of their own possessions, by night and by day, in private and in public, will have their wage with their Lord: no fear for them, nor will they grieve.

The questions that come to mind after reading this verse are: Why did Allah mention spending by day and by night? Is there any other time than night or day? We answer that Allah mentioned day and night because he does not want you to withhold your charity at any time. In other words, do not say: "it is too late in the evening; I will give tomorrow." If you intend to help the poor, help them right now! Do not procrastinate or make excuses.

Take note that the All-Wise did not say: 'by night or by day," He said: "by night and by day." As long as you have the purity of motive in your heart, spend today, tonight and tomorrow. Help the needy publicly and privately. If you do not constrain your gift by time or place, Allah, the All-Generous, will take care of your reward. He says: "Those who give, out of their own possessions, by night and by day, in private and in public, will have their wage with their Lord."

Here, the scholars often mention the story of Imam Ali, may Allah be pleased with him. There was a time when he had only four coins to his name. Despite his need, he gave one to the poor during the day, one during the night, one in public, and one in private. The verse under study was revealed to our beloved Prophet Muhammad after that. However, the verse and the rewards of giving are general to all those who give not just to Imam Ali.

The word "wage" should give us some insight into the reward of the believer because a wage is usually given for work and effort. When you buy something, you do not give a 'wage,' rather you pay a 'price.' You only give a wage to someone who did work for you. So why is Allah giving you a wage for your work, not a price for what you have donated? We answer that when you work, you use your intellect which is a gift from Allah; you use your hands and tools which are also granted by Allah. Whether you farm the land, work at a factory, or on a computer, you are using materials made available to you by Allah. So Allah owes you nothing for the materials you use or produce. He, the All-Wise, will give you a very handsome wage for your work, not a 'price' for what you donate. Your fellow man pays you a price for a product, but your Creator –who owns everything in existence-, rewards you for your effort.

The verse ends with "no fear for them, nor will they grieve." To fear is to worry about the future, while to grieve is to regret the past. So what could you fear? You could fear yourself. For example, you fear that you would fail a test.

You could also fear others. For example, you fear that a stronger person would hurt you, or that the government would harass you. Allah will protect you from both, the constant worry of poverty and failure, and from the harm of others.

Be aware that when you spend to help the needy, some people may advise you to hold back, to save for the future, and to set aside more for your kids. The Messenger of Allah, peace be upon him, said, "Never has a wealth of a person decreased due to charity; If you forgive another, Allah will increases you in honour, and if you humble yourself for the sake of Allah, Allah will raise you in status." Allah says:

Allah deprives interest of any blessing, and blights it, but blesses charitable deeds with multiple increases. He does not love the ungrateful sinner. (02:276)

The phrase: "nor will they grieve" means that on the day of judgment when the generous donor meets his or her Lord, he or she will find Allah's reward so vast that it will leave no room for regret or sadness. Allah says:

The semblance of those who expend their wealth in the way of Allah is that of a grain of corn from which grow seven ears, each ear containing a hundred grains. Truly Allah increases multiples for whomsoever He will, for Allah is infinite and all-wise. (2:261)

Suppose that people withheld their Zakat and charity, who will support the poor? If a person is unable to meet the basic needs of his or her family, and no one steps up to help or offer a good loan, this person would be forced to steal, or take out usurious loans. Such actions would lead the entire society down a very dangerous path.

Allah, the All-Knowing, All-Wise, has put in place the system of Zakat –almsgiving- that sufficiently meets the needs of the poor. If you see a person in dire need, then rest assured that there is a wealthy person out there who withheld his or her almsgiving. If you see an Islamic society filled with usury and interest dealings, then rest assured that people have long left the path of their Lord.

VERSE 275

Allazeena yaakuloonar ribaa laa yaqoomoona illaa kamaa yaqoomul lazee yatakhabbatuhush shaitaanu minal mass; zaalika bi annahum qaalooo innamal bai'u mislur ribaa; wa ahallal laahul bai'a wa harramar ribaa; faman jaaa'ahoo maw'izatum mir rabbihee fantahaa falahoo maa salafa wa amruhooo ilal laahi wa man 'aada fa ulaaa 'ika Ashaabun naari hum feehaa khaalidoon

Those who devour interest will not rise but like a person possessed by the devil and demented. That is because they say, 'Trade is the same as usury.' But Allah has permitted trade, and He has forbidden usury. Whoever is given advice by his Lord and then desists, may keep what he received in the past and his affair is Allah's concern. But all who return to it will be the Companions of the Fire, remaining in it timelessly, forever.

On the Day of Judgement, each group of sinners will be distinguished by its specific sin. Allah says:

The sinners will be recognized by their marks and seized by the forelock and their feet. (55:41)

People who have neglected their prayers will have their distinguishing mark, so will those who did not pay their Zakat almsgiving. What is the mark of those who deal with usury and interest? Allah answers, "but like a person possessed of the devil and demented." So they will appear possessed, frantic, and tormented by the devil.

Allah wants to present usury to us in a repulsive manner, so he describes the condition of those who deal in usury not only in the hereafter, but also in this world. Perhaps the word that stands out the most in the verse is "devour." Eating is one of the essential needs of life, but "devouring" is something beyond what is needed for sustenance. So is usury and interest, they are a transgression beyond what is needed for healthy economic life. Allah says: 'Those who devour interest will not rise but like a person possessed by the devil and demented.'

The words: 'Satan' and 'the devils' refer to the disobedient Jinn. The Jinn have believers just like humans have believers, and the Jinn have disbelievers known as the devils who spread corruption just as disbelieving people. We believe in the devils, not because we can see them, but because Allah informed us of their existence. Matters that you can see, hear or touch do not require belief. You cannot say: "I believe in my shirt," or "I believe that I am listening to you right now." Belief is only in matters of the unseen, such as the angles and the devils.

Allah gives us a mental image of the devils. He says:

This tree grows in the heart of Hell's blazing Fire, and its fruits are like devils' heads. (37:64, 65)

The tree being described is the tree of 'Zaqqum' which only exists in hellfire. So how is that any help? Why would Allah describe something we cannot see –like devils' heads- with something else we cannot see – like the Zaqqum tree-? We answer that Allah used this metaphor so your mind would imagine the ugliest most repulsive thing possible. In other words, Allah left it to each one of us to imagine the vilest scene. Isn't that exactly how we picture the devil? If you announced a contest of who could draw the devil, all participants, regardless of their background, would compete in drawing a hideous foul creature. Each would express ugliness according to his or her personal view.

This brings us back to the verse. Allah says: "Those who devour interest will not rise but like a person possessed by the devil and demented." To be possessed and demented is to act frantically irrational.

This is because any human who has contact with the devil is harmfully afflicted. Allah says:

"Indeed some men from the humans would seek the protection of some men from the jinn, thus only adding to their vileness". (72:6)

As if any contact with a devil would throw the human off balance. You are probably wondering: How is this all related to usury? We answer that just as this unnatural contact between a human and a devil creates chaos, so is dealing with usury. It throws all economic affairs into frantic chaos.

Allah created us and gave each a talent different from others. Someone might be good in math and engineering, while another is good at manual work. Another might be talented in fixing cars, whilst some can excel in sales. This is how the economy thrives. We trade talents, and we all enjoy the fruits of our work. Some areas are rich in oil and minerals, while other areas have fertile land and livestock. Allah created earth to be enjoyed by all. He says:

He laid out the earth for all living creatures (55:10)

So it is the earth –the entire earth- for all, with no borders, walls, or restrictions. Borders cause a massive imbalance between demand and supply. Some people are drowning in resources, while others are starving.

Keep in mind that goods and talents are what directly benefits you, while money cannot. Money is just a medium of exchange. Say, for example, that you are very hungry, and you have a pile of Gold. Does the pile do your hunger any good? It does not. But if you had a loaf of bread, you would benefit directly. Likewise, if you had millions in cash and you were dying of thirst in the desert, would your cash offer you any direct benefit? No, but a bottle of water would save your life. In other words, true benefit and value come from the goods and services that you have, whether food, drink, or clothes; not from money.

In the past century, humanity made incredible strides in technology and manufacturing. We enjoy daily comforts that were not available to kings a few decades ago. Our phones allow us to see and speak to people in other continents. We can fly; we can wash our clothes, heat our food, and research any topic with the click of a few buttons. Yet, even in the most advanced economies, people are stressed, and depression and despair are rampant. There are migrant crisis, wars, and famine. The world seems out of balance, and human affairs are frantic. But why? We touched earlier on the issues of borders and restriction of movement. We see many examples today of a developing country full of workers with no work available. Yet at the same time, another country has an abundance of rich businessmen who are ready to invest but cannot find real opportunities. Both sides can benefit if they had no borders or restrictions on the movement of money and labour.

The second reason is money, which is no longer a medium of exchange; it is being treated as the ultimate goal of life. Usury enriches the rich and plunges the poor deeper into poverty. Money is transferred from the poor to the rich, not in exchange for goods, services, or talent; rather, it is in exchange for more debt and poverty. This leads to corruption and the widespread of evil. Allah says:

Those who devour interest will not rise but like a person possessed of the devil and demented. That is because they say, 'Trade is the same as usury.' But Allah has permitted trade and He has forbidden usury.

It is fascinating to watch the same countries that exported the interest usury-based banking system to the entire planet resort to zero interest policies when they run into trouble. This is not done to comply with the Lord's teachings, but it is done because they see it as the best way to bring the financial life back into balance.

Those who devour interest will not rise but like a person possessed of the devil and demented. That is because they say, 'Trade is the same as usury.' But Allah has permitted trade and He has forbidden usury. Whoever is given advice by his Lord and then desists, may keep what he received in the past and his affair is Allah's concern. But all who return to it will be the Companions of the Fire, remaining in it timelessly, forever.

(Verse 275)

If you examine any usurious or interest-based contract, you will find it to be an invalid contract. Why? Because a contract should be a balanced legal document that protects the rights of both parties; while the usurious transaction is unfair at its core. It protects and guarantees the rights of one party only: the rich lender.

Take a moment to think about this inherently despicable transaction. The person who is poor, in need, and can barely feed his or her family is seeking a loan; yet he or she is the one burdened with guaranteeing the enrichment of the lender who is -by definition- not in need. This injustice fosters resentment and hatred in society. It weakens the spirit of charity and cooperation. Imagine the feelings of the poor who toil in debt just to see their situation worsen because they have to give the wealthy more and more. It would have been sufficient for the rich to help the poor with a good loan that requires the return of the principal amount without any addition.

Here we should stop and answer people who falsely claim that the following verse allows interest: Allah says:

You who believe, do not consume usurious interest, doubled and redoubled. Be mindful of Allah so that you may prosper- (3:130)

Some people use the phrase "do not consume usurious interest, doubled and redoubled" as an excuse that they can charge interest on loans as long as it is not outrageous. In other words, they falsely claim that lending with interests is allowed as long as it is not predatory lending. We say to them: rather than look through the Quran to find a loop-hole in Allah's teaching, why don't you study the Quran properly? Let us study the following verses:

Allah says:

O believers, fear Allah and forego the interest that is owed, if you really believe. And if you do not, then be warned of war from Allah and

His messenger. And if you repent, then you will have your principal, neither harming others, nor suffering harm. (2:278, 279)

Take note that Allah did not allow any interest whatsoever; He directed those who repent to get back their original principal and nothing more. Allah did not allow them to keep any increase, even a small one.

Other people use the contract as an excuse to deal with interest and usury. They falsely claim that since both parties agreed on the terms of a clear contract, then the transaction is permissible. We answer that there is a higher authority directing our affairs. Allah's teachings overrule any contract you and I may concoct together. Take the example of an unmarried man and woman agreeing to have sexual relations. Does their agreement overrule Allah's teachings against adultery? Of course not. A contract where both parties agree is only valid on matters that do not contradict heavenly teachings. Another main requirement of a contract is that the agreement does not cause harm to the society at large. A contract that involves usury and interest violates both conditions.

Let's look into a practical example from everyday life. There are two adjacent stores in a market. The owner of the first store has a thousand dollars. He buys good quality merchandise to sell in the store. He will need to earn enough money to make a living and keep the store running. The owner of the second store is poor. He does not have any capital to work with, so he borrows a thousand dollars to buy merchandise. The loan contract stipulates that he has to return the original thousand dollars plus $100 in interest after six months. This man also needs to earn enough money to make a living and keep the business running. So where would the $100 of interest come from? If the 2nd merchant tries to sell his goods at a higher price than the first one, no one will buy from him. If he sells the goods at a lower price, he would barely make a living, would not be able to pay back the loan, or stay in poverty forever. Most likely, and in order to make a living, run the business, and pay back the interest on the loan, the 2nd merchant would have to get lower quality goods and sell them at a price similar to the better goods. He or she would have to trick the customer into buying these goods. Thus, the society in general would suffer. In effect, the society has to pay the price for the usurious loan.

Allah is the creator and the provider. He wants to foster the spirit of cooperation and charity in society. If Allah blessed you with more than you need, make sure to share some and help others. When the rich pay the prescribed alms –Zakat-, and come to the aid of those who fell on hard times, the entire society is lifted. A poor man would pray to Allah to increase the wealth of the wealthy because he knows that he would get a share from it too. Contrast that to a poor man who feels that the entire world is against him exploiting his weakness and need. What kind of prayer would he ask Allah for?

Allah, the All-Wise, set economic relations on three pillars: First, is the pillar of social solidarity. Allah wants the needy and the poor to find generosity from their wealthy counterparts. Ideally, the rich should give for the sake of giving, not under the obligation of social pressure. Second, is the pillar of –Zakat- almsgiving, an obligation on the rich and a right for the poor. And lastly is the pillar of a good loan where no interest is involved. These three pillars, if properly applied, would leave no poverty in a Muslim society.

Contrast that to a society based on usury. Allah says: "those who devour interest will not rise but like a person possessed by the devil and demented. That is because they say, 'Trade is the same as usury.'" It is interesting to note the order of the words such people use. They say: 'Trade is the same as usury.' Was the main topic of discussion trade, or was it usury? Of course, the main topic was usury. So logically, they should have said: 'usury is the same as trade.' Why the flip flop? We answer that this backward argument is a perfect reflection of their condition. They are 'like a person possessed of the devil and demented' not only in their dealings but in their arguments. Ibn Masood narrated that our beloved Prophet Muhammad(pbuh) cursed both the lender and borrower in usury.

The people who deal in interest argue that lending first then collecting interest is just like buying first then selling with profit; so if you prohibit one as unlawful, you should also prohibit the other. Allah gives the definitive answer: 'But Allah has permitted trade, and He has forbidden usury. Whoever is given advice by his Lord and then desists, may keep what he received in the past and his affair is Allah's concern. But all who return to it will be the Companions of the Fire, remaining in it timelessly, forever.'

When you receive advice from someone, you should first look if he or she is benefiting from it. In other words, does the person giving you advice have hidden motives? Is he or she self-serving? Our Lord is the All-Sufficient. He does not need anything, nor does He benefit form anything you and I do. Thus, when you are 'given advice' from Allah, you should accept it and act on it immediately because it is exclusively for your benefit. Allah created you, and He takes care of His creation. In fact, the words 'his Lord' are translated from the Arabic origin 'Rabehe.' 'Rab' or 'Lord' is the one creates, cares, and nourishes. In the Arabic language, the father is called the Rub of the family, while the mother is called the Rubat of the home. The same word 'Rub' is the root of the word 'tarbia' which means to raise and educate a child.

Our Lord is our –Rab- the creator, He is the Caretaker and Educator. He created us from nothing and put the entire universe at our service. Shouldn't we be the least bit appreciative and listen to His advice? He says: 'Whoever is given advice by his Lord and then desists, may keep what he received in the past and his affair is Allah's concern.' Our Lord is the Most-Merciful even in his warning. He did not issue a retroactive ruling and will not punish those who did not know. Allah will only punish those who heard His advice and neglected it.

If you happen to be dealing with interest and usury, this is your chance to stop and reorganize your financial affairs. Allah, who knows best, will take care of you. He says: 'his affair is Allah's concern.' So, if you depend on usury and interest for your livelihood, do not think to yourself: 'it is too late, I cannot stop now. I will lose everything. My family will starve.' Listen to your Lord's advice and stop. He, almighty, will be in your corner taking care of your affairs. You will be moving from the material bounties of Allah to the company of Allah. Still have a doubt? Look at Allah's words:

Do not sell for a small price any pledge made in Allah's name: what Allah has is better for you, if you only knew. What you have runs out but what Allah has endures, and We shall certainly reward those who remain steadfast according to the best of their actions. (16:95, 96)

Usury is one of the major sins. Prophet Muhammad, peace be upon him, said: "Avoid the seven ruinous sins." We said: "What are they, O Messenger of Allah?" He said: "Polytheism, witchcraft, the killing of the soul that Allah has forbidden except for due cause, devouring usury, devouring the wealth of orphans, and abandoning the armed forces on the day of battle."

Now let's take a closer look at the dire warning Allah gave those who ignore His advice. Allah says at the end of the verse: 'But all who return to it will be the Companions of the Fire, remaining in it timelessly, forever.' This phrase is interesting because it would have been sufficient to say that a believer who deals with interest and usury will be punished in hellfire, but what was the reason behind adding: 'remaining in it timelessly, forever'? We answer that this type of punishment is usually reserved for those who are outside the fold of faith. In other words, a believer dealing with interest will be treated as a non-believer. This is important to know because there are two types of sinners when it comes to usury: first, there are believers who, after knowing that usury is prohibited, deal with it anyway. They acknowledge that usury is wrong, but may say that they deal with interest because of life circumstances. Such believers will be punished for their sin, but they will not remain in hellfire indefinitely. Second, there are believers, who after learning Allah's teachings, go back and argue that 'Trade is the same as usury.' They deal with usury and interest claiming that they are not prohibited. Such people who reject Allah's teachings are no longer believers. Allah says about them: 'But all who return to it will be the Companions of the Fire, remaining in it timelessly, forever.'

Here, I want to take a moment to caution those who deal with interest: "Do not rationalize what you are doing as permissible. Rather, admit that usury is wrong and that you are weak in stopping yourself." In this manner, you are a sinner, but still within the folds of faith.

To better understand the difference, think about Adam and Satan. Both had disobeyed Allah, but only Satan was expelled from Allah's mercy, while Adam was forgiven and granted another chance. Why? The answer lies in the fundamental difference between the two sins. The sin of Satan reached the height of disobedience as he denied a direct command from Allah and argued that it did not apply to him. He said: "Never will I prostrate nor would I obey you because I have been created from fire while he has been created from clay." Adam, on the other hand, acknowledged his shortcomings and said: "My Lord, your command is the truth, your word is the truth, and your path is the truth, but I was weak and unable to bring myself to carry your order. So, my Lord, pardon my weakness." Thus, Allah forgave Adam and cursed Satan out of His mercy.

VERSES 276

Yamhaqul laahur ribaa wa yurbis sadaqaat; wallaahu laa yuhibbu kulla kaffaarin aseem

Allah blights usury, but blesses charitable deeds with multiple increases: He does not love the ungrateful sinner.

The word 'Usury' is translated from the Arabic origin 'Riba' which means to grow. Allah is warning you not to be deceived by the name. Just like, in the English language, the word 'interest' may deceive you into believing that dealing in usury is to your benefit.

Superficially, it may seem that earning interest or 'riba' increases your money while giving charity or paying almsgiving decreases it. But the truth is quite different. Allah says:

Allah blights usury, but blesses charitable deeds with multiple increases: He does not love the ungrateful sinner. (Chapter 2: Verse 276)

The word 'blights' means 'to wither.' In other words, if you deal in interest, Allah will not suddenly erase your wealth; rather, he will gradually take it away. He, the All-Wise, will open door after door of expenses and troubles that would constantly drain your finances. You may think that you are rich, but you are blind to the countless road bumps ahead. Allah says:

What you give with usurious intent, aiming to get back a greater amount from people's wealth, does not become greater with Allah. But anything you give in almsgiving, seeking the Face of Allah – all who do that will get back in multiples (30:39)

Take note that Allah mentioned 'multiples' meaning many times over. Here, I would like to remind you that when you hear of someone doing an action, you have to realize that the action is proportional to the doer. For example, if I tell you that a 2-year old child is angry and coming to hit you, you would feel differently than if I told you that the world heavyweight champion boxer is mad and coming to hit you. Similarly, if the one who is promising you multiples back on your investment is Allah Almighty, you should expect a reward befitting The-All-Generous. And if the warning that your wealth will be wiped out is coming from Allah Almighty, then rest assured that you will have nothing left.

Always remember that 'Allah blights usury, but blesses charitable deeds with multiple increases' is part of the Nobel Quran. It is a miracle brought forth to support the message of Prophet Muhammad (pbuh) till the end of time. It is as true today as it was the day it was revealed. Allah Almighty made it part of His doctrine. Would Allah have mentioned it and included it in the Quran if it was not true at all times? Allah says:

We have sent down the Quran Ourself, and We Ourself will preserve it. (15:9)

Part of preserving the Quran is preserving what it stands for. Allah will afflict the wealth of every person who deals in interest until the end of time.

The verse ends with: "He does not love the ungrateful sinner" translated from the Arabic origin 'Kaffar Atheem' both in the exaggerated superlative form. Why the exaggeration? We answer that the sin of usury is a double sin because it involves the sin of usurious dealing and the sin of claiming that 'Trade is the same as usury.' The sin of usury is also a compound sin because it tears the fabric of society at its core. The poor are victimized by the rich.

But do not get too caught up with the ugliness of this sin, take a moment to consider the beauty of virtue. Allah says in the very next verse:

VERSE 277

Innal lazeena aamanoo wa amilus saalihaati wa aqaamus salaata wa aatawuz zakaata lahum ajruhum 'inda rabbihim wa laa khawfun 'alaihim wa laa hum yahzanoon

Those who believe, do good deeds, keep up the prayer, and pay the prescribed alms will have their wage with their Lord: no fear for them, nor will they grieve.

The word "wage" should give us some insight into the reward of the believer because a wage is usually given for work and effort. When you buy something, you pay a price, not a "wage." You give a wage to someone who does work for you. So why is Allah giving you a wage for your work, not a price for what you donated? We answer that when you work, you use your intellect, which is a gift from Allah; you use your hands and tools, which are also granted by Allah. Whether you farm the land, work at a factory or on a computer, you are using materials made available to you by Allah. In other words, Allah owes you nothing for the materials you use or produce. He, the All-Wise, will give you a very generous wage for your work. Your fellow man pays you a price for a product, but your Creator —who owns everything in existence- rewards your effort.

Here is a further guarantee that you will be handsomely rewarded: The verse states that you will have your 'wage with your Lord.' If a boss owes you money for work, he or she may not pay, may pay you less, or he or she may die before paying. Allah, on the other hand, is the All-Generous, All-Giving, and Ever-Living. You have absolutely nothing to worry about. He says: 'Those who believe, do good deeds, keep up the prayer, and pay the prescribed alms will have their wage with their Lord: no fear for them, nor will they grieve.'

VERSES 278

Yaaa ayyuhal lazeena aamanut taqul laaha wa zaroo maa baqiya minar ribaaa in kuntum mu'mineen

You who believe, be mindful of Allah: give up any outstanding dues from usury, if you are true believers. If you do not stop, then be warned of war from Allah and His Messenger. You shall have your capital if you repent, and without suffering loss or causing others to suffer loss.

The phrase "You who believe," is the master key of faith. How, you may ask? We answer that Allah does not issue commands of 'do' and 'do not do' to all mankind; He only addresses those who have willingly believed and declared faith in Him. When you declare your faith in Allah, you entrust Him as your Lord, the All-Wise, All-Knowledgeable. Only then, does He address you with 'do so' and 'do not do so.' This is the essence of every act in religion. I fast in the month of Ramadan, not because it makes me experience the hunger of the poor, but because Allah, my trusted Lord, instructed me to do so. I perform ablution before prayer, not to cleanse my skin, but because Allah, my Lord, instructed me to do so. I entrust my Lord with my affairs and follow His commands even when –at times- I may not understand the wisdom behind these commands.

So, if someone asks you: 'Why do you pray five times a day?' do not fall into the trap of explaining the reason behind prayers, or the reason behind abstaining from Alcohol. The simple answer is: 'My Lord instructed me to do so.' Your faith in Allah is the answer. You may know a few reasons behind certain acts of worship, but Allah, your creator, knows all the reasons.

Should you stay away from gambling only after you and your family are hurt by addiction? Or should you entrust your Lord when He tells you not to gamble? We obey Allah's commands even if the wisdom behind them is not immediately apparent. When you see entire communities suffering from the financial and social ills of gambling and addiction, you thank your Lord who protected you from the very beginning.

This brings us back to the verse. Allah says: "You who believe, be mindful of Allah: give up any outstanding dues from usury." Allah's command to the believers is: "be mindful of Allah" translated from the Arabic origin "Itaqoo Allah." The word 'Itaqoo' is very rich in meaning, and the translation "be mindful" does not quite do it justice. In fact, If you were to look up this word in a dictionary you will find it encompassing all the following meanings: to be mindful of, to shield yourself from, to guard yourself, to be vigilant, and to fear. It is mentioned numerous times in the Quran. Let's look at two examples:

O you who believe! Guard yourselves and your families against a Fire whose fuel is human beings and stones (66:6)

and twice in the following verse:

You who believe! Be mindful of Allah, and let every soul consider carefully what it sends ahead for tomorrow; and fear Allah, for Allah is well aware of everything you do. (59, 18)

Here we have two verses, one is asking us to be mindful and shield ourselves from hellfire, and the other is asking us to shield ourselves from Allah, both translated from the same word 'Itaqoo.' How can this be? How can the same word apply to both Allah and hellfire?

The answer is simple. To shield yourself from hellfire, you would avoid that which angers Allah. Mindfulness and good deeds are your best tools to build this shield between you and the fire.

The second verse advises 'to be mindful of, and to fear Allah.' How do you shield yourself from Allah while you are connected to Him? How do you fear and shield yourself from the one you love? We answer that

Allah Almighty has both the attributes of majesty and the attributes of beauty. His attributes of majesty are apparent in His names: the Mighty, the Compeller, the Avenger and so on. On the other hand, the attributes of beauty are apparent in his names: the Most-Forgiving, the Most-Compassionate, the Most-Merciful and many more. Hence, you should fear Allah's attributes of majesty because they could result in punishment in hellfire. And you should seek Allah's attributes of beauty through mindfulness and good deeds.

The verse continues: 'give up any outstanding dues from usury.' To 'give up' means to leave behind, to stop, and completely forget about usury. A person dealing in usury should stop now and ask Allah to replace it with something better.

In the 275th verse, Allah gave us a ruling about past earnings from usury. He says: 'Whoever is given advice by his Lord and then desists, may keep what he received in the past and his affair is Allah's concern.' In the verse under study, Allah is commanding us to cease and desist any future dealings. He says: 'You who believe, be mindful of Allah: give up any outstanding dues from usury, if you are true believers.' Do not say: 'I signed a contract before I was aware of this ruling; I have to honour my contract first, then I will stop.' Allah made it very clear: such a contract is not acceptable, and any future usury is forbidden. He says: 'give up any outstanding dues from usury.'

Allah continues

VERSE 279

Fail lam taf'aloo faazanoo biharbim minal laahi wa Rasoolihee wa in tubtum falakum ru'oosu amwaalikum laa tazlimoona wa laa tuzlamoon

If you do not stop, then be warned of war from Allah and His Messenger. You shall have your capital if you repent, and without suffering loss or causing others to suffer loss.

Within the 279th verse is a universal law that many people wilfully neglect. It is a law protecting the weak from the overreach of the strong. It was set after the poor and disadvantaged were exploited by the rich and powerful through interest bearing and predatory loans. The Quran came to set the scales of justice, stop the exploitation, and give the rich back their capital without any increase.

Allah issued a warning about usury; He says 'If you do not stop, then be warned of war from Allah and His Messenger.' When you do something counterproductive at home or work, you may be warned by your boss or parents. However, your parents may not come through with their warning even if you do not stop. Your boss may not have full authority to punish you, or may be overruled by a higher manager. However, when the warning comes from Allah, rest assured that He, Almighty, will come through and you will suffer dire consequences.

Allah's soldiers are infinite and unknown. He says in the 31st verse of chapter 74:

No one knows the soldiers of your Lord but Him.

So you cannot evade Allah's punishment. The war of the Prophet is more evident because it is a brought on by the believers who are tasked with fighting corruption in society. Allah is threatening those who deal with usury and interest with a full assault on their affairs from all sides.

Take note that Allah is warning of a war for justice, not a war of aggression or humiliation. The phrase: 'You shall have your capital if you repent, and without suffering loss or causing others to suffer loss,' clarifies that the lender has no right in doubling, or tripling his or her money. In fact, he or she has no right to even a 1% increase. Any increase is considered unjust as it causes the poor to suffer a loss.

It is important to pause and point out a pitfall many societies and revolutions fall into. When an oppressor is stopped and the rights of the oppressed are restored, people should not overreach and start oppressing their previous tormentors. Just as Allah gave you the power to overcome your oppressors, make sure you respect His words that say: 'You shall have your capital if you repent, and without suffering loss or causing others to suffer loss.' It is the only way to stop the cycle of oppression and corruption. Everyone is equal before Allah and before the law.

So, a just fight against corruption should have two clear goals: First, to stop the oppressor; and second to restore the rights of the oppressed. Sadly, often, the result of fighting corruption and oppression is revenge and reverse oppression. The old oppressed become the new oppressors and the pot begins to slowly boil again. We always say that the best punishment for those who wronged us is to treat them justly. Allah says: 'You shall have your capital if you repent, and without suffering loss or causing others to suffer loss.'

VERSES 280

Wa in kaana zoo 'usratin fanaziratun ilaa maisarah; wa an tasaddaqoo khairul lakum in kuntum ta'lamoon

If the debtor is in difficulty, then delay things until matters become easier for him; still, if you were to write it off as an act of charity, that would be better for you, if only you knew.

The phrase "If the debtor is in difficulty" recognizes the lender's right in getting back the principal of the loan. Allah, however, is asking the rich for consideration and common courtesy. If the borrower is going through hardship, the lender is advised to be patient and allow for a grace period. Each extra minute of waiting will be rewarded by Allah.

It is said that the reward for a loan is higher than the reward for charity. This is despite the fact that when you give to charity, you completely let go of your money, while when lend you eventually get it back. The scholars explained that when you give to charity, you feel the pain of letting go of your money once, and then you forget about it. On the other hand, when you lend, you keep thinking about your money; you anticipate repayment and worry about missed and late payments. The more patience you exhibit, the higher the reward you attain.

Of course, patience is only required when the borrower is in true hardship. He or she should be doing all that is reasonably possible to pay back the loan in a timely manner. If the borrower is lying, or procrastinating, then he or she has fallen into sin.

The Lender might ask: "How would I know if the borrower is procrastinating or not?" I would advise the lender to look into his or her heart. If it is preoccupied with worry about the loan, then most likely the borrower is procrastinating and giving excuses. If the heart is at ease, then most likely the borrower is truthful in his or her distress. I would like to remind you of a narration of our beloved prophet. He, peace be upon him, said: "Whoever borrows money from others with the intent of paying it back on time will receive Allah's full support in repayment. And whoever borrows money from others with the intent of laying it to waste will be wasted by Allah."

When you borrow money, Allah looks into your heart and intention. If you sincerely plan to pay back the lender, Allah will support you. If you are scamming people, then Allah will lay you and your wealth to ruin.

During the time of the prophet, a man who was heavily indebted passed away. Prophet Muhammad asked his companions to perform the Janaza funeral prayer for the man, but he, peace be upon him, did not join them. Why? Because the man was a procrastinator who always delayed paying back his debts.

Our beloved Prophet wanted ease and gentleness to prevail in society. He said: "Whoever is patient with a borrower in difficulty and whoever forgives a debt, will be shaded by Allah's shade on the day where there is no shade but the shade of the Almighty." Being patient means to give the borrower extra time without constant reminders and harassment. The righteous used to avoid even passing by the home of the person who owes them money. They did not want the borrower to feel uncomfortable or pressured. At even a higher level, the lender would just forgive the debt and make it a gift. Allah says: "if you were to write it off as an act of charity, that would be better for you, if only you knew." The phrase "better for you" is a promise from Allah for a great reward.

So if you happen to be in a position to lend someone money, you have three options: First, you can collect your debt in full on time, regardless of the borrower's circumstances. Second, you can choose to be a bit higher on the piety scale and give the borrower in hardship a grace period. Third, at the highest level, you can forgive part of the loan or the entire loan. You have the freedom to do whatever you like, but keep Allah's reward in mind.

You can attain a level of piety called 'Ihasn.' 'Ihsan' means to go beyond obligation and expectations. Prophet Muhammad –peace be upon him- explained: "Ihsan is to worship Allah as if you see Him; for if you cannot see Him, then rest assured that He sees you." Allah gives us a detailed description of those who attained 'Ihsan' in the following verses:

The righteous will be in Gardens with flowing springs. They will receive their Lord's gifts because of the Ihsan they did before: sleeping only little at night, praying at dawn for Allah's forgiveness, giving a share of their wealth to the beggar and the deprived. (51:15-19)

Did Allah ask you to stay up at night to pray? No, He did not. You can fulfil your obligation by praying the night Isha prayer and then go to sleep. If you want to enter the realm of Ihsan, however, then you would pray additional prayers after Isha and into the night.

Did Allah ask you to wake up before Dawn and pray for forgiveness? No, He did not. You can fulfil your obligation by sleeping till the morning Fajr prayer. But if you want to enter the realm of Ihsan, you would wake up a little earlier to spend some time with your Lord in prayer.

How about charity? Allah asked you for a small percentage of your excess wealth ranging from 2.5% to 20% as Zakat almsgiving. He says:

Those who are regular in their prayers, who give a due share of their wealth to the needy and the deprived (70:23-25)

Did you notice the difference between obligation and 'Ihsan'? When Allah spoke about obligation He said: 'those who give a due share of their wealth.' However, when He spoke about Ihasn, He said: 'those giving a share of their wealth' omitting the work 'due' because when you practice 'Ihasn' you choose to give more that what is due.

Here we should pause and take note of the beauty of Islamic legislation compared to man-made laws. When legislators write laws and constitutions, they write them in a dry manner. For example, the punishment for murder is death, and the punishment for manslaughter is 20 years in prison and so forth. Allah, on the other hand, legislates based on both justice and courtesy. Let us look to the verse regarding murder, the most heinous of crimes. Allah says:

You who believe, fair retribution is prescribed against you in cases of murder: the free man for the free man, the slave for the slave, the female for the female. But if the perpetrator is pardoned by his aggrieved brother, this shall be adhered to fairly, and the perpetrator shall pay what is due in good will. This is easing from your Lord and an act of mercy. If anyone then exceeds these limits, grievous suffering awaits him. (2:178)

Likewise, when it comes to debt and money, Allah says:

If the debtor is in difficulty, then delay things until matters become easier for him; still, if you were to write it off as an act of charity, that would be better for you, if only you knew. (Chapter 2: Verse 280)

VERSE 281

Wattaqoo yawman turja'oona feehi ilal laahi summa tuwaffaa kullu nafsim maa kasabat wa hum laa yuzlamoon

And be mindful of the day in which you will be brought back to Allah. Then every soul shall be paid fully for what it has earned, and they will not be wronged.

Allah warns you: "be mindful of the day in which you will be brought back to Allah" translated from the Arabic origin "Itaqoo Yauman." The word 'Itaqoo' is very rich in meaning, and the translation "be mindful" does not quite do it justice. It encompasses all the following meanings: to be mindful of, to shield yourself from, to guard yourself, to be vigilant, and to fear.

Usually a day or a week or a month is nothing to be afraid of. You may fear an event, but not a day. However, the Day of Judgment is so packed with horrifying events, one after the other, that it should be feared in its entirety.

Take note of the accuracy of the Quranic expression: 'you will be brought back to Allah.' More specifically, the phrase 'brought back' indicates that meeting the Lord on that day is not by your choice or mine, rather, it is Allah's. However, when Allah speaks about the righteous, the expression changes.

Look at the following verses:

Seek help with steadfastness and prayer- though this is hard indeed for anyone but the humble, who know that they will meet their Lord and that it is to Him they will return.

(2:45, 46)

The believers who did well in life look forward to meeting their Lord: 'To Him they return.' As for the sinners and disbelievers, they 'will be brought back to Allah' against their wishes. Allah says:

Woe on that Day to those who deny the Truth, who amuse themselves with idle chatter: the Day they are shoved roughly into the Fire of Hell (52:11-13)

VERSE 282

Yaa ayyuhal lazeena aamanoo izaa tadaayantum bidaiynin ilaa ajalimmusamman faktubooh; walyaktub bainakum kaatibum bil'adl; wa laa yaaba kaatibun ai yaktuba kamaa 'allamahul laah; falyaktub walyumlilil lazee 'alaihil haqqu walyattaqil laaha rabbahoo wa laa yabkhas minhu shai'aa; fa in kaanal lazee 'alaihil haqqu safeehan aw da'eefan aw laa yastatee'u ai yumilla huwa falyumlil waliyyuhoo bil'adl; wastash hidoo shaheedaini mir rijaalikum fa il lam yakoonaa rajulaini farajulunw wamra ataani mimman tardawna minash shuhadaaa'i an tadilla ihdaahumaa fatuzakkira ihdaahumal ukhraa; wa laa yaabash shuhadaaa'u izaa maadu'oo; wa laa tas'amooo an taktuboohu sagheeran awkabeeran ilaaa ajalih; zaalikum aqsatu 'indal laahi wa aqwamu lishshahaadati wa adnaaa allaa tartaabooo illaaa an takoona tijaaratan haadiratan tudeeroonahaa bainakum falaisa 'alaikum junaahun allaa taktuboohan; wa ashidooo izaa tabaaya'tum; wa laa yudaaarra kaatibunw wa laa shaheed; wa in taf'aloo fa innahoo fusooqum bikum; wattaqul laaha wa yu'allimu kumul laah; wallaahu bikulli shai'in 'Aleem

You who believe, when you contract a debt for a stated term, put it down in writing: have a scribe write it down justly between you. No scribe should refuse to write: let him write as Allah has taught him, let the debtor dictate, and let him fear Allah, his Lord, and not diminish the debt at all. If the debtor is feeble-minded, weak, or unable to dictate, then let his guardian dictate

> justly. Call in two men as witnesses. If two men are not there, then call one man and two women out of those you approve as witnesses, so that if one of the two women should forget the other can remind her. Let the witnesses not refuse when they are summoned. Do not disdain to write the debt down, be it small or large, along with the time it falls due: this way is more equitable in Allah's eyes, more reliable as testimony, and more likely to prevent doubts arising between you. But if the merchandise is there and you hand it over, there is no blame on you if you do not write it down. Have witnesses present whenever you trade with one another, and let no harm be done to either scribe or witness, for if you did cause them harm, it would be deviancy on your part. Be mindful of Allah, and He will teach you: He has full knowledge of everything.

This is the longest verse in the entire Quran. It starts with the phrase: 'You who believe' informing the believers that a command or prohibition is to follow. Why? Because our faith in Allah is the main reason we –as believers- follow His commands and prohibitions. Allah does not issue any commands to non-believers. He only invites them to faith. But once you freely accept faith, then you should follow what Allah commands you to do, even when you do not fully understand the wisdom behind the command.

Take the example of a man who is diagnosed with cancer. He is free to use his intellect to research the best doctor and hospital for his treatment. However, once he chooses a doctor and entrusts him or her to treat the disease, he would follow the doctor's orders even if some of them do not make sense. If the doctor orders the man not to drink any orange juice, then the man should not drink any because the command came from his trusted doctor. If the man argues and wants to know the exact reason behind each and every doctor's order, then he has no faith in his doctor. The only person who can argue with the doctor is someone who holds the same medical degree.

Here we ask: Do you have full faith in your Lord? Do you have the same level of knowledge and wisdom as your Lord? Your belief and trust in Allah should be more than enough reason to follow each and every command. Allah is the All-Wise; He is free of any need. He only commands what is best for you. We follow our Lord's commands, and often come to appreciate their true benefits months or years later.

So what is Allah's command in this verse? He says: 'You who believe, when you contract a debt for a stated term, put it down in writing.' Take note of the phrase 'stated term,' wouldn't it have been enough to say 'when you contract a debt for a term'? We answer that Allah wants to emphasize the importance of specifying a term. For example, you may lend someone money and say to him or her: pay me back when your father returns from his trip. But this leaves much to chance. What if the father extends his trip? What if he dies abroad and never comes back? The terms of the contract become vague. Allah wants clarity, not ambiguity. It is more proper to state a term on a specific date and time.

The phrase 'put it down in writing' is meant to ease social pressures. For example if you lend your cousin some money and she says: 'we are family, we don't have to write this down.' You may feel pressured not to write. But when the command comes from Allah, it helps to alleviate all these pressures. What if your cousin dies? Do her heirs know about the loan? They have to take your word. Life is easier when things are properly documented.

Many people assume that writing the terms of a debt down is specifically designed to protect the lender. We answer that this is not true. In fact, regulating lending is designed to protect the weak and needy. How, you may ask? We answer that writing the debt down puts pressure on the borrower to pay back on time. That, in turn, allows the borrower to have access to money again when a need arises. If the borrower does not pay the initial debt back, then no one will lend him or her again. In fact, if a wealthy lender loses money once because of a deadbeat borrower, he or she may not lend anyone again. The entire society suffers. By regulating the debt contract, Allah assures that the poor can find help when they need it. He says: 'You who believe, when you contract a debt for a stated term, put it down in writing.'

But who writes the contract? The lender or the borrower? Neither. Allah answers: 'have a scribe write it down justly between you. No scribe should refuse to write' Look at the wisdom of Allah's teachings: By having a third party, who has no vested interest in either the lender or the borrower write the contract, Allah protects the interest of both parties. Allah makes it a duty for any person who knows how to write a contract to do so without hesitation. If a person who can write is present, he or she should volunteer to write even if he or she is not asked. This ensures that Allah's teachings are followed properly leaving no room for ambiguity. If you are riding in a car, and the driver falls asleep, would you take over immediately? Of course. You would not leave things to chance hoping that it will work out.

We should learn from the example of our beloved prophet Joseph. Look at the following verses:

Joseph said, 'You will sow for seven consecutive years as usual. Store all that you reap, left in the ear, apart from the little you eat. After that will come seven years of hardship which will consume all but a little of what you stored up for them (12:47, 48)

There was a national emergency of drought and famine in Egypt. Joseph had the knowledge and experience to manage such a situation. He, peace be upon him, did not leave such a critical issue to chance, so he volunteered to take the job as the following verses show:

The king said, 'Bring him to me: I will have him serve me personally,' and then, once he had spoken with him, 'From now on you will have our trust and favour.' Joseph said, 'Put me in charge of the nation's storehouses: I shall manage them prudently and carefully.' (12:54, 55)

Likewise, when a matter as important as a loan arises, a competent writer should volunteer to put things into a contract, even if he or she is not asked. Allah says: 'have a scribe write it down justly between you. No scribe should refuse to write: let him write as Allah has taught him.'

You who believe, when you contract a debt for a stated term, put it down in writing: have a scribe write it down justly between you. No scribe should refuse to write: let him write as Allah has taught him, let the debtor dictate, and let him fear Allah, his Lord, and not diminish the debt at all. If the debtor is feeble-minded, weak, or unable to dictate, then let his guardian dictate justly. Call in two men as witnesses. If two men are not there, then call one man and two women out of those you approve as witnesses, so that if one of the two women should forget the other can remind her. Let the witnesses not refuse when they are summoned. Do not disdain to write the debt down, be it small or large, along with the time it falls due: this way is more equitable in Allah's eyes, more reliable as testimony, and more likely to prevent doubts arising between you. But if the merchandise is there and you hand it over, there is no blame on you if you do not write it down. Have witnesses present whenever you trade with one another, and let no harm be done to either scribe or witness, for if you did cause them harm, it would be deviancy on your part. Be mindful of Allah, and He will teach you: He has full knowledge of everything. (Chapter 2: Verse 282)

In the previous ayat, we explained the importance of writing down any loan in a clear contract, and the duty of a writer to step up and document the terms of the debt.

We continue with the phrase: 'let the debtor dictate.' Why should the borrower, and not the lender, dictate to the writer? The answer is twofold. First, it is an acknowledgment from the borrower of his or her responsibilities in repayment. Second, and more importantly, it is because the borrower is in the position of weakness. Let's clarify with an example.

For example, I need to borrow £2000. I agree to repay it back to you in six months. In this situation, I am in need, and you have the stronger position. When the writer comes to write the terms of the contract, you –the strong lender- dictate to him that you agreed to lend me £2000 to be repaid in full in three months. You made a mistake regarding the length of the loan. I may feel embarrassed to say anything because l will not be able to make that repayment in that time. I am afraid that if I object, you would cancel the entire loan. On the other hand, if I was dictating to the writer and I made a similar mistake, you –in the position of power- would feel comfortable to jump right in to make the correction. Thus, Allah, the All-Wise, teaches us that the borrower should be the one dictating the terms of the loan.

But what if the borrower was a young child, an elderly, a disabled person, or someone who is illiterate? Allah answers: 'If the debtor is feeble-minded, weak, or unable to dictate, then let his guardian dictate justly.'

To keep both parties honest and to further ensure the validity of the contract, Allah commands witnesses to be present. He says: 'Call in two men as witnesses. If two men are not there, then call one man and two women out of those you approve as witnesses.' By having witnesses on one hand, and the borrower dictating the terms to a scribe on the other, the rights of both parties are guaranteed. The economy runs smoothly because the rich feel comfortable lending and those in need have access to capital. And when the economy runs smoothly, peace and security prevail as each person is able to provide for his or her family.

Keep in mind that there is a condition for someone to be accepted as a witness. Allah says that we should choose: 'those you approve as witnesses.' In other words, the man or woman should be known to be honest, trustworthy and of good character.

Let's look in to the phrase: 'If two men are not there, then call one man and two women out of those you approve as witnesses' as it has caused much controversy. Some men who are ignorant use such phrases as an excuse to mistreat women, or to support false claims that women are not as intelligent. They argue that one man is equal to two women. We answer that these false arguments highlight such men's true ignorance of the Quran. Allah the All-Wise clearly gave us the reason behind this substitution. He says: 'If two men are not there, then call one man and two women out of those you approve as witnesses, so that if one of the two women should forget the other can remind her.' In other words, because the majority of women do not routinely deal with contracts, terms of loans, and financial jargon, they may easily forget or overlook a specific aspect of the transaction. Allah advices that in such situations, where a trust-worthy man who routinely deals with financials is not available as a witness, two women can substitute.

The verse continues: 'Let the witnesses not refuse when they are summoned.' Just as Allah commanded the writer to perform his or her duty in documenting the terms of the loan without hesitation, Allah is commanding the witnesses to do the same. Here we should note that a witness bears two responsibilities. The first is to attentively witness the contract, and the second is to tell the truth if called upon on a later date. The duty of a witness to perform without hesitation applies to both situations: on the day of the contract, and later on if there is a dispute.

Yet, Allah wants to assure that this obligation is not misused to pressure or inconvenience a witness. People have families and jobs, and they should not be abused. Allah says: 'and let no harm be done to either scribe or witness.' Both, witnesses and scribes, should be treated with courtesy, and their circumstances should be taken into consideration. In fact, personal circumstances are one of the criteria of the witness selection process. If a witness or scribe is going to miss work, then he or she should be compensated. If travel is required, then the travel expenses should be covered by the lender and borrower. Allah, who is protecting the rights of the lender and borrower, is not about to overlook the rights of witnesses and scribes.

To summarize, a person who is versed in writing contracts should do his or her job by writing the contract accurately without falsification. A person who is trustworthy should do his or her job as a witness and pay close attention to the details of the contract; and later he or she should bear true testimony if needed in a dispute. The lender and borrower should treat both the scribe and the witnesses with respect and compensate them if they incur any inconvenience. Allah warns all the parties involved –whether the borrower, lender, witness or scribe-: He says: 'for if you did cause them harm, it would be deviancy on your part.'

Oh you who believe, when you contract a debt for a stated term, put it down in writing: have a scribe write it down justly between you. No scribe should refuse to write: let him write as Allah has taught him, let the debtor dictate, and let him fear Allah, his Lord, and not diminish the debt at all. If the debtor is feeble-minded, weak, or unable to dictate, then let his guardian dictate justly. Call in two men as witnesses. If two men are not there, then call one man and two women out of those you approve as witnesses, so that if one of the two women should forget the other can remind her. Let the witnesses not refuse when they are summoned. Do not disdain to write the debt down, be it small or large, along with the time it falls due: this way is more equitable in Allah's eyes, more reliable as testimony, and more likely to prevent doubts arising between you. But if the merchandise is there and you hand it over, there is no blame on you if you do not write it down. Have witnesses present whenever you trade with one another, and let no harm be done to either scribe or witness, for if you did cause them harm, it would be deviancy on your part. Be mindful of Allah, and He will teach you: He has full knowledge of everything. (Chapter 2: Verse 282)

In the previous Ayats, we explained how the lender and the borrower should treat both the scribe and witnesses with respect, and compensate them for any inconvenience. We also explained how the scribe and witnesses should do their job to the best of their abilities without taking sides. Allah says warning all parties: 'for if you did cause them harm, it would be deviancy on your part.'

What does the word 'deviancy' mean? To understand the meaning, we should look at the Arabic origin of the word. The word 'فُسُوقٌ Fusuq' originated from the desert environment where the Arabs lived at the time of the prophet. When a date ripens on a palm tree, its skin stays attached to the body of the fruit and acts as a protecting barrier from the elements. As the date ages, the skin separates from the fruit, making it easy to peel. The word 'Fasaqa فسق' describes the detachment of the protective skin from its natural place, exposing the fruit to harm and causing it to spoil. Similarly, Allah used the same word 'Fasaqa فسق' to describe a person who distances him or herself from Allah's teachings; thus exposing him or herself to harm and ruin.

The verse continues: 'Be mindful of Allah, and He will teach you: He has full knowledge of everything.' The advice to 'be mindful of Allah' is common in this chapter. To be mindful is to be steadfast on Allah's path, and to avoid taking unnecessary risks that may cause harm in this world and the next. When you implement Allah's teachings, you shield yourself and your family against harm.

Some people have questioned the Quranic verses that ask us to 'be mindful of Allah' and the verses that ask us to 'be mindful of hellfire.' How can this be? How can the same word apply to both Allah and Hellfire? We answer that in order to shield yourself from hellfire, you would avoid that which angers Allah. Mindfulness and good deeds are the best tools to build this shield between you and the fire.

Let's take a moment to study the phrase, 'and He will teach you.' It is an Islamic principle that you should keep in mind in all matters related to religion. When people set the rules, you should not follow them unless you trust the wisdom and knowledge of the persons setting the rules. Why? Because these people are your equal. They have the same abilities as you. Why would you follow any person unless you are convinced that he or she knows much more than you do? Otherwise, maybe you should be the leader! None of us is perfect, and none of us has superpowers.

However, when the legislation comes from Allah, things are different. As a Muslim, you have declared faith in Allah and have conviction in His ultimate wisdom and perfect knowledge; you entrust that Allah is free of need and that He has your best interest at heart. Thus, there is no need to understand the wisdom behind His teachings fully. You follow Allah's teachings first and come to understand the wisdom behind them later.

For example, when Allah legislated fasting the month of Ramadan, He did not try to convince you of the benefits. He, the All-Merciful used your faith in him as the main reason to fast, Allah says: 'You who believe, fasting is prescribed for you.' Your belief in Allah is why you fast. However, when you fast properly, you slowly discover the benefits of fasting one after another. Allah wants you to follow His teachings first and then enjoy their immense benefits. He says:

O you who believe! If you remain mindful of Allah, He will bestow upon you the criterion with which you will separate the truth from falsehood, and He will unburden your misdeeds and forgive you; Allah's favour is indeed immense. (8:29)

Allah promises you clarity of vision and the ability to see right from wrong, but only if you follow His teachings first. Allah is All-Knowledgeable, All-Wise.

You who believe, when you contract a debt for a stated term, put it down in writing: have a scribe write it down justly between you. No scribe should refuse to write: let him write as Allah has taught him, let the debtor dictate, and let him fear Allah, his Lord, and not diminish the debt at all. If the debtor is feeble-minded, weak, or unable to dictate, then let his guardian dictate justly. Call in two men as witnesses. If two men are not there, then call one man and two women out of those you approve as witnesses, so that if one of the two women should forget the other can remind her. Let the witnesses not refuse when they are summoned. Do not disdain to write the debt down, be it small or large, along with the time it falls due: this way is more equitable in Allah's eyes, more reliable as testimony, and more likely to prevent doubts arising between you. But if the merchandise is there and you hand it over, there is no blame on you if you do not write it down. Have witnesses present whenever you trade with one another, and let no harm be done to either scribe or witness, for if you did cause them harm, it would be deviancy on your part. Be mindful of Allah, and He will teach you: He has full knowledge of everything. (Chapter 2: Verse 282)

Religion came to organize the people's affairs in a just manner. Islam aims to support the basic needs of the poor and preserve the society as a whole. A poor person in need can get help in one of three ways: First is charity —or Sadaqa- where money is freely given to help. Second is the religious obligation of Zakat almsgiving. And third, a loan can be extended where money is given with the expectation of repayment.

We had mentioned before that the reward for giving a loan is higher than the reward for giving to charity. This is despite the fact that when you give to charity, you completely let go of the money, while when you lend, you eventually get your money back. The scholars explained that when you give to charity, you feel the pain of letting go of your money once, and then forget about it. On the other hand, when you lend, you keep thinking about your money; you anticipate repayment and worry about missed and late payments. The more patience you exhibit, the higher the reward you attain.

Let's take a few moments to study the transactions of charity, Zakat, and loans from two perspectives. First, let's look from the perspective of the wealthy. The primary goal of regulating these transactions is to protect the wealth and property of the rich and assure their continued investment in society. Had Islam allowed interest earnings, the wealthy would not invest in any projects; they would leave their money in the bank to earn interest, or they would exploit the poor through predatory lending. Had Islam left loans unregulated, without guarantees to preserve capital, a rich person may hold on to his or her money for fear of loss. The lack of regulation would also bring the entire economy to a halt. By outlawing interest and imposing Zakat almsgiving on savings, Islam encouraged investment.

Take the example of a man who has a large sum of money saved. If he leaves this money uninvested –and not earning interest-, he would have to pay the Zakat almsgiving annually. No one likes to see their wealth decrease. If he invests the money, he would not have to pay Zakat on the working capital. Thus, this man starts thinking about ways to invest. He decides to construct a small apartment building to rent out. He dreams and calculates how much he will receive each month in rental income. He may only be thinking of earning a profit for himself; however, by starting the project, this man would benefit many members of the society. Before he earns a single penny, he would have to hire and pay an architect, an engineer, a project manager, many labourers, carpenters, blacksmiths, plumbers, and others. Impoverished members of the society will benefit from this man's money before he does.

The second perspective we should consider is that of the poor. Allah guaranteed their wellbeing by encouraging work, encouraging charity and obligating Zakat almsgiving. Allah also legislated and regulated interest-free lending. The legislation is designed to protect the borrower from him or herself. How, you may ask? We answer that if you borrow money, and the loan is documented and witnessed by people you trust, you would not slack on repayment. The loan document and the society as a whole act as an incentive for you to work, produce and repay. This too, assures a vibrant economy. If, on the other hand, you take the responsibility of the loan lightly, and start procrastinating, you would hurt yourself and the society. A rich person would say: 'look at my friend, he lent so and so money and never got it back, I will never lend my money to anyone.' Every poor person would suffer from the action of a few who discard their responsibilities.

Thus, we find that Allah, the All-Wise, had emphasized and then reemphasized the necessity of proper documentation of a loan. The Arabic word for 'to write down' is 'Kataba.' When you examine the Arabic text of verse 282 of 'Al Baqarah,' you will find that the root Kataba is repeated nine times. The emphasis on writing down and documenting the loan transaction is designed to protect people's affairs. A written document does not forget and does not change its mind under pressure. Allah says: 'Do not disdain to write the debt down, be it small or large, along with the time it falls due: this way is more equitable in Allah's eyes, more reliable as testimony, and more likely to prevent doubts arising between you..'

VERSE 283

Wa in kuntum 'alaa safarinw wa lam tajidoo kaatiban farihaanum maqboodatun fa in amina ba'dukum ba'dan falyu'addil lazi tumina amaa natahoo walyattaqil laaha Rabbah; wa laa taktumush shahaadah; wa mai yaktumhaa fa innahooo aasimun qalbuh; wallaahu bimaa ta'maloona 'Aleem

If you are on a journey, and cannot find a scribe, something should be handed over as security, but if you decide to trust one another, then let the one who is trusted fulfil his trust; let him be mindful of Allah, his Lord. Do not conceal your testimony: anyone who does so has a sinful heart, and Allah is fully aware of everything you do.

As you well know, travelling is the opposite of being a resident. When you are on a trip, things are not readily available. You are not as familiar with your surroundings as you are in your hometown. If you fall into trouble, who will lend you money? None of your friends are around. Who can you trust? More importantly, who would trust you? Can you find someone to write a loan contract? Can you get witnesses that you trust? Allah gives you the answer. He says: "If you are on a journey, and cannot find a scribe, something should be handed over as security." Note that Allah wants to guarantee the rights of all parties under all circumstances. In a loan contract, collateral should be handed over during travel where a scribe and witnesses are hard to come by.

Yet, Allah, the All-Merciful, allows room for kindness and trust. He says: "but if you decide to trust one another, then let the one who is trusted fulfil his trust." Allah wants generosity and altruism to rise above obligation. If both the lender and borrower trust one another, then the obligations of a scribe and witnesses can be bypassed.

Most people assume that when it comes to trust, it is the borrower who is in doubt and has to be trusted. We answer: No, there are two issues to consider. The first is the actual debt, and the second is the security deposit, which is held against the debt. Hence, one party is entrusted with the security, while the other is entrusted with the debt. When we rise to this level in our dealings, it is not the scribe or witnesses that are the guardians of the transaction; it is the faith within the lender's and borrower's hearts. Each person holds him or herself accountable.

Here, many questions come to mind. Can you trust all people? Do you know what's in my heart? Can you guarantee life's circumstances? The simple answer is No. I want to direct your attention to a very critical point: there is a big difference between trust at the time of bearing the responsibility, and at the time of performing the duty of the responsibility. I will explain with an example. A friend may come and ask: "I have ten thousand pounds; can I trust you keep it safe until I come back from my journey? I will be going overseas for four years." This is what we call 'Amanah.' It means that there is no written record or witnesses. It is a matter of trust between two people. Your friend is counting on trust and your faith to safeguard his savings. You may accept the responsibility and have full intention to safeguard your friend's money. But life is not predictable. What if, during the next two years, you fall on hard times, and need money for a critical medical operation for your child? You may feel the need to spend some of your friend's money to save your child's life. Would you tell your friend? Or would you procrastinate in giving the money back? That is the difference between bearing the responsibility of trust and fulfilling the responsibility of trust.

The issue of trust and bearing responsibility is not specific to this verse, or to financial dealings. It is a common pitfall for all human beings. In fact, this very issue has to do with the origin of our humanity as trustees in the universe. Allah says:

We offered the Trust to the heavens, the earth, and the mountains, yet they refused to undertake it and were afraid of it; humankind undertook it- they have always been unjust and ignorant. (33:72)

The entire universe feared to bear the trust of free will. It understood the difference between bearing the responsibility of faith and fulfilling that responsibility. No one can guarantee to properly fulfil the trust when the time comes. Hence, the universe declined Allah's offer and chose to keep its will in the hands of Allah the Creator. What is the result? A universe performing its duties as Allah intended; working like clockwork. There is, however, one exception: humankind. Man accepted the trust and thought: 'I am intelligent, I will always choose what is best between alternatives.' Look around you, where does corruption come from? It comes from the places where people had interfered in nature.

Always remember: You may be strong at the moment of bearing the trust, but what about at the time of fulfilment? Allah says: 'humankind undertook it- they have always been unjust and ignorant.' If you commit yourself to something and do not do it properly, you have wronged yourself. It is unjust. Similarly, if you commit yourself to something without fully appreciating the time and effort it will take to fulfill, then you are ignorant.

This brings us back to the verse, more specifically, to the issue of trust and responsibility in loan dealings. Allah gave you the option to forgo documenting a loan and rely on trust. But remember: you and your circumstances are subject to change. Thus, I remind you of Allah's words. He says in Ayat 282:

'Do not disdain to write the debt down, be it small or large, along with the time it falls due: this way is more equitable in Allah's eyes, more reliable as testimony, and more likely to prevent doubts arising between you.' Documenting the loan transaction in writing is a great opportunity for all parties to protect themselves against weakness at the time of fulfillment. It is the perfect tool to assure the rights of both parties and to protect them against the ever-changing circumstances of life. Allah wants you to document the matter, so it is not solely the burden of your religious conscious.

If you are on a journey, and cannot find a scribe, something should be handed over as security, but if you decide to trust one another, then let the one who is trusted fulfil his trust; let him be mindful of Allah, his

Lord. Do not conceal your testimony: anyone who does so has a sinful heart, and Allah is fully aware of everything you do. (Chapter 2: Verse 283)

Allah advises you: "do not conceal your testimony." If you have witnessed something firsthand, then you know it is the truth, and the truth can never change. Suppose a car accident occurred right in front of you. No matter how many times you are asked about the accident, your answer would be the same because you are telling the truth as it occurred in front of you. But if the accident were a lie, then your story would change with time. You would forget some details that you told a month ago, and when you tell the story a third time, it would be different again. Isn't that the same technique investigators use to catch crooks and criminals? They ask a suspect on several occasions about the details of a crime or event. A person with an ever-changing story is a liar. The truth never changes. Thus, we always hear the adage: "No man has a good enough memory to be a successful liar."

This brings us back to the verse; the word 'testimony' points to something that has been seen. It is of our human nature to be eager to tell others if we witness an interesting event. It takes effort to conceal and lie, because the innate nature of faith pushes the person to share what he or she had witnessed.

The verse continues: 'Do not conceal your testimony: anyone who does so has a sinful heart.' Here you may wonder: Are lying and concealing traits of the heart or traits of the mind? A poet said:

Speech is truly in the heart,

the tongue is merely a display

All your body parts are subject to what is within your heart. Prophet Muhammad, peace be upon him, said: "But there is in the body an organ, if it is upright the whole body is upright, and if it is corrupt, the whole body is corrupted. That organ is the heart." Allah reminds you that regardless of what you say, or you do not say, He 'is fully aware of everything you do.' Concealing your testimony will not change anything because Allah is All-Aware; it will only hurt you. Prophet Muhammad –

peace be upon him- asked his companions, "would you like to know about the worst of major sins?" they replied, "tell us, O' messenger of Allah." He said: "there are three: associating partners with Allah; defying one's parents;" then he peace be upon him sat up straight and said, "and giving false testimony; giving false testimony." He kept repeating it over and over until we wished he would stop.

All these arrangements, from writing down the loan contract to giving collateral during travel, and the witnesses' obligation to be truthful are designed to guarantee each hardworking person an honourable and dignified life. Because if trust is lost, contracts become worthless, then the whole economy grinds to a halt. What would a person who is unable to provide for his family do if no one helps or lends? He would either cheat, steal, or his heart would fill with hatred towards the rich. He would resent every bounty other people have, and in return, the bounty itself would resent him. How? We answer that Allah's bounty loves a person who has a thankful heart, not a hate-filled one. Whoever detests a blessing which is granted to someone else is distancing him or herself even further from this blessing. In other words, if you hate to see your neighbours enjoying the bounties of Allah, then the bounties of Allah would hate to come into your life. As if Allah's bounty says: as long as you resent me, you will never receive any good from me.

When a poor person is not able to find anyone who would lend a good loan or give Zakat, he or she will resort to an interest-bearing usurious loan. Such a community lacks solidarity. When the rich prey on the poor with usury, the society enters into war with the Almighty Allah, can anyone endure war against Allah? Never.

Our beloved Prophet Muhammad during the farewell pilgrimage said: "Allah has forbidden you to take usury; therefore, from this moment on, all interest obligations shall be waived. Your capital, however, is yours to keep. You will neither inflict nor suffer any inequity. Allah has judged that there shall be no interest. All interest due to Abbas Ibn Abd al Muttalib shall be waived."

This is the hallmark of heavenly legislation. Abbas Ibn Abd al Muttalib was the prophet's uncle. Legislators often shield their family, kin, and friends from the law. They set hidden loopholes to allow their family and friends to amass power and wealth. Not heavenly legislation! Allah and the Prophet impose heavenly laws on the family and companions of the prophet first, then on everyone else.

Take the example of Omar ibn al-Khattab, a close companion and the second Khaliph after the Prophet. When Omar wanted to announce new legislation, he would gather his family, close friends, and the public. He would say to his family: "I will set such and such laws, and I swear by the One in whose hand is my soul, if any of you violates the law, I will make of his punishment an example for all Muslims." Why would Omar do such a thing? Because most people are courteous and sometimes afraid of their leaders and their families. For example, when the son of a city mayor enters a local bank or a government agency, his presence may stir fear and awe in the employees; they may facilitate his affairs or look the other way if he does something wrong. The mayor may not even be aware of his son's behaviour.

But when the leader declares to the people that his relatives are equal under the law, and may even be under more scrutiny than the general public, everyone respects the law and justice prevails. No one would dare take advantage of his or her position of authority, and people would have no fear of reporting abuses of power. A proper Muslim ruler should demonstrate that the laws apply to him first and to his close family and friends second even in matters of life and death.

In the Battle of Badr, our beloved Prophet Muhammad brought his family and relatives to fight along with him. Had he not done that, the enemies of Islam would have said: 'Of course He protects his family! He does not even believe in the reward of martyrdom. Doesn't he claim paradise for Muslims who die in battle?' But the Messenger of Allah stationed his family next to him on the frontlines. He, peace be upon him, led by example and knew the Almighty's reward for martyrdom is a short path to paradise.

VERSE 284

Lillaahi maa fissamaawaati wa maa fil ard; wa in tubdoo maa feee anfusikum aw tukhfoohu yuhaasibkum bihil laa; fayaghfiru li mai yashaaa'u wa yu'azzibu mai yashaaa'u;wallaahu 'alaa kulli shai in qadeer

To Allah belongs all that is in the heavens and the earth; and whether you reveal what is in your heart or conceal it, you will have to account for it to Allah who will pardon whom He please and punish whom He will, for Allah has the power over all things.

The verse starts with "To Allah belongs all that is in the heavens and the earth." But aren't many things in the skies and the earth owned by people? Don't countries own space satellites in orbit? Don't you and your relatives own pieces of land? We answer that Allah has allowed His creation to own land and property. However, this ownership is temporary and can be taken away at any time. Your property could be stolen or taken by force. You may die or decide to sell what you have.

So the phrase "To Allah belongs all" His creation indicates ultimate control because Allah is the true owner that no one can overcome. As for us humans, we may claim to own a piece of land today, but we cannot assure that we will own it tomorrow. In fact, none of us can guarantee him or herself to be alive an hour from now. Everything in existence belongs to Allah.

Since we are subject to change by circumstances outside our control, we must welcome the fact that Allah wants us to help one another. Allah informs us: to Me belongs whatever is in heavens and on earth, and I make matters of hardship and ease rotate among people. He says:

If you have suffered a blow, they too have suffered one like it. We deal out such days among people in turn, for Allah to find out who truly believes, for Him to choose martyrs from among you- Allah does not love evildoers- (3:140)

Thus, we say to those who have gained power, wealth, or status: beware when you feel that you have reached the top because humans are always subject to change. If you have all the wealth that you wanted, the children you desired, and a job you like, then watch out! You are a human being, and you are bound to change. A poet says:

When something is just right, it starts to decline

You see it vanishing the moment it is said: it is complete

Once a woman came to the caliph Haroon Alrasheed and said to him: 'May Allah complete His bounty upon you. May He make you rejoice with all that you have. Indeed you knew justice when you ruled.' The caliph asked, 'Where you are from?' She answered: 'I am from the tribe of Barmak' and left. The caliph knew that his army had defeated Barmak, killed most of its men, and ransacked its property. He asked those around him. Do you know what this woman has just said? They answered: 'She sang your praises; she loves you as all people love you.' The Caliph said to them: 'By Allah, you did not understand a word of what she said.' When she said: 'May Allah complete His bounty upon you,' she was referring to the poet who said:

When something is just right, it starts to decline

You see it vanishing the moment it is said: it is complete

When she supplicated: 'May Allah make you rejoice with all that you have,' she was referring to this verse: 'When they forgot what they had been reminded of, We opened up for them the doors to everything, until, when they rejoiced in the bounty they had been given, We suddenly seized them and at once they were in despair.' (6:44)

And when she said: 'Indeed you knew justice when you ruled,' she was referring to this verse in the Quran: 'as for the unjust - they are the fuel of hell.' (77:15)

This brings us back to the verse. Take note that the phrase "To Allah belongs all that is in the heavens and the earth" includes Allah owning each one of us. A poet said:

My soul which owns things is itself going to depart

Then why should I grieve over any possessions that depart me?

There is one thing, however, that will always belong to you, and never depart: Your deeds. Allah says: 'and whether you reveal what is in your heart or conceal it, you will have to account for it to Allah.' When your soul departs, you lose all your material possessions, and you are only left with your deeds. Allah will hold you accountable for what has been recorded in your register. He says:

'We have bound each human being's destiny to his neck. On the Day of Resurrection, We shall bring out a record for each of them, which they will find spread wide open. "Read your ledger; this day, you are sufficient to take your own account." (17: 13, 14)

Your account will have a balance of faith and good deeds for you on one side and a balance of ungratefulness and bad deeds against you on the other. This is further explained with the 'scale' in the following verse:

On that Day the weighing of deeds will be true and just: those whose good deeds are heavy on the scales will be the ones to prosper. And those whose scales are light, it is they who have made their souls suffer losses because they have been unjust with regard to Our Messages. (07:8-9)

Allah is just. Those whose scale of faith and good deeds is heavy will enter paradise, but those who disbelieved, sold themselves for worldly pleasures, and wronged others are destined to hellfire.

This leaves out one possibility. How about those whose good and bad deeds are in balance? We answer that such people will be the companions of Al-A'raf -a boundary between hell and heaven-. Allah says:

A barrier divides the two groups with men on its heights recognizing each group by their marks: they will call out to the people of the Garden, 'Peace be with you!'- They will not have entered, but they will be hoping, And when their eyes are turned towards the fellows of the Fire, they will say, `Our Lord! Place us not with these wrong-doing people.' (4:46, 47)

Scholars say that the people of A'raf will be pardoned by Allah because His forgiveness precedes His wrath.

Allah reassures you that whatever good you did will be multiplied in the balance pan. He also reassures you that He will compensate you for what you have suffered from evil and injustice. Good deeds are the currency of the Hereafter. Allah says:

And do not disgrace me on the Day when all people are resurrected: the Day when neither wealth nor children can help, except for him who comes to Allah with a pure heart. (26:87-89)

And in another chapter:

Those who disbelieve and die disbelievers will not be saved even if each offers enough gold to fill the entire earth. Agonizing torment is in store for them, and there will be no one to help them. (3:91)

Anyone who wronged a fellow human –regardless of their faith- will have to pay out of his or her good deeds to the one he or she wronged. In essence, if you wrong your neighbour, he or she will take from your scale and add to theirs. Thus, Allah guarantee comes from two angles: assurance that any good deed, regardless how small, will be accounted for, and assurance that any injustice, regardless of how insignificant, will also be accounted and compensated for. Allah says:

When the earth is shaken violently in its last quake; when the earth disgorges its burdens; when man cries, 'What is wrong with it?'; On that day it will relate its chronicles, for your Lord will have commanded it. On that Day, people will come forward in separate groups to be shown their deeds: whoever has done an atom's-weight of good will see it, and whoever has done an atom's-weight of evil will see that. (Chapter 99)

Verse 284

To Allah belongs all that is in the heavens and the earth; and whether you reveal what is in your heart or conceal it, you will have to account for it to Allah who will pardon whom He please and punish whom He will, for Allah has the power over all things.

To 'reveal what is in your heart,' means to turn your thoughts and feelings into action. How about when you 'conceal it'? Does it mean to keep your feelings to yourself and not to act on them? Not always. Not every feeling can be translated into practical action. For example, the feelings of love; you may love someone and not get a chance to declare your love. Thus, there are deeds which settle in the heart and remain there. Does Allah hold us accountable for such thoughts and feelings?

The answer to this very important question requires depth and reflection. We know that some of the Prophet's companions had struggled in this regard. When Abdullah bin Umar, heard this verse, he wept and said: 'if Allah punishes us for our thoughts, we will surely perish.' So did Ibn Abbas. Afterward, Allah revealed the following verse: "Allah does not burden any soul with more than it can bear: each gains whatever good it has done, and suffers its bad- '(from 2:286).

Let's get back to the question: Does Allah hold us accountable for our thoughts and feelings? We answer that, while there are countless thoughts and emotions, we can narrow things down into five different categories: First there are fleeting thoughts, second there are daydreams and fantasies, third are deep thoughts, fourth is intention, and lastly, determination. The first four categories often do not have any real-world outcomes, while the last one, determination, is when a person's plan becomes evident. Now, we will address each condition in detail.

A fleeting thought comes to the mind once and then disappears; it does not leave any lasting impression. While a daydream or fantasy is more developed and stays in the mind for a while. A deep thought is something you turn over in your mind and look at from different angles. It may resurface several times as you discuss the matter back and forth within yourself. As for intention, it is the first serious step towards considering action. You look at the means available to you to put your dreams and fantasies into action and fulfil your desires. Whereas, determination is the end of the thought process and the start of the implementation phase. The phrase "whether you reveal what is in your heart or conceal it, you will have to account for it to Allah," refers to determination.

Many scholars have questioned whether this verse has been nullified by the verse which followed it. In other words, the verse "Allah does not burden any soul with more than it can bear' may offer us relief from the burden of thought accountability. We answer that Allah only nullifies verses related to past religious rulings. He does not nullify matters of creed or verses narrating historical events. The verse under study, verse 284 does not fall into the category of a religious ruling. Thus, it cannot be nullified. The determination to do something is an act that Allah will take each one of us to account for.

The verse continues: 'you will have to account for it to Allah who will pardon whom He please.' Wouldn't you like to know the people who will be pardoned? Allah gives you the answer in the following verse:

Except those who repent, believe, and do good deeds: Allah will change the evil deeds of such people into good ones. He is most forgiving, most merciful. (25:70)

Perhaps the first thing that gets your attention in this verse is the phrase: 'Allah will change the evil deeds of such people into good ones.' How could this be? Does Allah really change the bad deeds of a sinner into good ones? The answer is simply, yes. But there are conditions. A person who has committed a sin, has to feel sincere regret and correct his or her action in order to be rewarded by Allah. Those who possess knowledge say: perhaps a sin which leads to feelings of regret and humbleness is better than obedience which leads to feelings of honour and arrogance.

Here is another example to clarify why Allah would 'change the evil deeds of such people into good ones.' Most Muslims have never drank alcohol in their lives. So it is very easy for any of them to pass by a bar or pub without noticing or feeling any desire to drink. However, a Muslim man who used to be an Alcoholic, then repented and gave up drinking for the sake of Allah would feel very differently. Each time he passes by a bar, he would feel the urge to drink. Each time he sees a beer advertisement on television, he would struggle to control his desire to drink. This daily struggle –done for the sake of Allah- earns this man Allah's reward. 'Allah will change the evil deeds of such people into good ones.'

You often find that the good in the world comes from people who have indulged into some type of sin which they later regretted and repented from. Take the example of a woman, who has a weakness for gossip and bad-mouthing people behind their backs. After many years, this woman repents from her sin and vows never to speak ill of anyone. Allah, the All-Merciful, forgives her. However, she may still be haunted by her sin and feel a constant need to do good deeds to make up for her past. For years, this long-forgiven sin may push the woman to be generous to her neighbours and volunteer to help the poor. Thus, much goodness around you may have come from those who have wronged themselves in the past. Be careful not to pass judgment on someone who has indulged in sin and repented.

On the other hand, a person who had never indulged in sin may not feel the urge to go the extra mile for others.

In explaining the phrase 'Allah will pardon whom He please and punish whom He will,' some scholars said that Allah left the matter of forgiveness to us. In other words, if you want the Almighty to forgive you, then be sincere and increase your good deeds. This is further evident in the following sacred narration: On the authority of Abu Hurairah who relayed that the Prophet, peace be upon him, said: "Allah, the All-Merciful says: 'I treat my servant as he hopes that I would treat him. I am with him whenever he remembers Me: if he remembers Me in his heart, I remember him in Mine; if he remembers Me in a gathering, I remember him in a gathering far better; if he draws near towards Me a hand-span, I draw near towards him an arm's length; if he draws near to Me an arm's length, I draw near to him a mile; and if he comes to Me walking, I go to him running.'"

Allah put the initiative in your hand. All you have to do is to be sincere in your strive to get closer to your Lord. Remember that Allah did not limit you to the five obligatory prayers. You can turn to Him in prayer at any time you wish, at any place you see fit, and speak to Him on whatever is troubling you because His door is wide open, for He Almighty never resigns until the servant does.

Contrast that to our worldly life. If you want to meet the president or the prime minister, you would have to request an appointment first. In the unlikely event that your request is approved, you would have to schedule a time that fits the president's schedule. You may have to submit a written outline for the reason of the meeting. Perhaps, ten minutes into the meeting, the president would stand and tell you that the meeting is over because he or she has other things to do. A poet said:

Being a servant of the Almighty is enough honour for me

I'm welcomed by the Lord without an appointment

He is on His holy throne, and I am at the time and place I like.

VERSE 285

Aamanar-Rasoolu bimaaa unzila ilaihi mir-Rabbihee walmu'minoon; kullun aamana billaahi wa Malaaa'ikathihee wa Kutubhihee wa Rusulihee laa nufarriqu baina ahadim-mir-Rusulih wa qaaloo sami'naa wa ata'naa ghufraanaka Rabbanaa wa ilaikal-maseer

The Messenger believes in what has been sent down to him from his Lord, and so do the believers; each one believes in Allah, and His angels, and His Books, and His Messengers: "We make no distinction between any of His Messengers." And they say: "We have heard the call to faith and obeyed. Our Lord, grant us Your forgiveness, and to You is the homecoming."

When you study this marvellous verse, you note that the first seed of faith in the One Allah started with our beloved Prophet Muhammad. Allah says: 'The Messenger believes in what has been sent down to him from his Lord.' After that, faith moved to those who the Prophet enlightened with his knowledge as the verse states: 'and so do the believers.' Then the faith of the Prophet and believers became one. Allah says referring to all: 'each one believes in Allah, and His angels, and His Books, and His Messengers.' So faith started with Prophet Muhammad who received it from his Lord, then he, peace be upon him, spread the message so he and all the believers would have one common creed.

Here is an interesting fact. It was not enough for our beloved Muhammad to be the first believer in Allah, he, peace be upon him, also had to believe that he is the messenger of Allah. There were many occasions where Muhammad would joyfully say: 'I bear testimony that I am the messenger of Allah.'? Here is an example:

The companion Jaber narrated: 'There was a Jewish merchant in Medina who used to lend me money when I was in need. We agreed to pay him back next season when I harvest dates from my palm trees. That particular year, my trees had very poor yield. And when the Jewish merchant came asking for his money, I explained my situation and asked if he can wait till next year's crop. He refused and became angry with me. I felt trapped. Prophet Muhammad heard about my situation from his companions. He asked them: "Take me to Jaber's land, maybe I can intervene and ask the merchant to give him another year." The merchant said to Muhammad: "O Abu Qasem, I cannot wait any longer for my money." The Prophet waited for a while and then asked the merchant again only to receive the same answer. The Prophet came to me and said: 'Jaber, show me which trees are yours?' I did. He, peace be upon him, continued: 'Can you get me a few of your dates and show me a good place to rest in your land.' So I did. The Prophet ate from my dates and took a nap between my trees. When he woke up, he went back to the Jewish merchant and asked again if he could wait till next year. The merchant refused. Prophet Muhammad looked at me and said: 'Jaber, go back to your land and harvest your trees.' I found my palm trees, that were bare earlier, overburdened with ripe dates. I collected the dates, paid the merchant and kept the rest for myself. I never had a better year. When Prophet Muhammad saw me coming back with bags of dates, he smiled and said: 'I bear witness that I am the Messenger of Allah.'

When you read the Quran, you find that Allah Almighty bears witness to His Lordship. He says:

Allah bears witness that there is no God but Him, as do the angels and those who have knowledge. He upholds justice. There is no God but Him, the Almighty, the All-Wise. (3:18)

So Allah bears witness to His Lordship, and the Prophet bears witness to Allah's Lordship and to his own Prophethood, and then he delivers the message to the believers completing the chain.

Allah tells us about the different elements of belief. He says: 'each one believes in Allah, and His angels, and His Books, and His Messengers: "We make no distinction between any of His Messengers." And they say: "We have heard the call to faith and obeyed. Our Lord, grant us Your forgiveness, and to You is the homecoming."' Why these elements, you may ask? We answer that faith –by definition- cannot be in something that is seen or even perceived. You cannot say I believe in my phone because you can see it and touch it.

Let's take a moment to study the different elements of faith Allah listed for us: Allah is unseen –you could not have known about Him had he not told you-. You may have concluded that a vast universe had to have a creator, but there is no way to know who the creator or creators are. Similarly, the angels are unseen. Had Allah not told us that He created angels, we would never have known. We know that Angels are magnificent obedient creatures who never disobey Allah.

Now we come to the faith in Prophets, messengers, and heavenly books. The first question that comes to mind: Well, Prophets and messengers were people, we could see them and touch them, the same goes for the Torah, Bible, and Quran, where is the faith in that? We answer: Have you –or even the companions- seen the Quran physically descend on the Prophet? Of course not. The matter of revelations is unseen.

The verse continues: "We make no distinction between any of His Messengers." Should we hold all the messengers as equal? We answer that all the heavenly messages since the time of Adam shared the same creed: 'There is no God but Allah.' Allah says in verse 13 of chapter 42:

In matters of faith, He has laid down for you the same commandment that He gave Noah, which We have revealed to you and which We enjoined on Abraham and Moses and Jesus

Heavenly religions differ in matters of social and economic teachings, but never in creed. Each message was sent to address certain societal ills to certain peoples at certain periods of time. Take the example of what Prophet Jesus said to his people -the children of Israel-:

I have come to confirm the truth of the Torah which preceded me, and to make some things lawful to you which used to be forbidden. I have come to you with a sign from your Lord. Be mindful of Allah, obey me (03:50)

Islam, the final message, holds within it the same exact creed as all the previous messages, but its social and economic teachings are for all people till the end of time.

The verse continues: 'And they say: "We have heard the call to faith and obeyed.' To hear the call means to have properly received the message of Islam, and 'to obey' means to follow Allah's teachings after hearing them.

Allah wants you to follow His teachings in all aspects of your life. Some people claim that religion is prayers and fasting, and that it is separate from daily living. We answer that Allah gave you commands related to this world and commands related to the hereafter. You should not take any of them lightly, nor pick and choose one over the other.

Look at the following verses: Allah says:

O you who believe, when the call to prayer is made on the day of congregation, hasten to remember Allah, putting aside your business. – –that is better for you if only you knew— then when the prayer is finished, disperse in the land and seek out Allah's bounty. Remember Allah often so that you may prosper. (62:9, 10)

Take note that Allah did not only order you to pray your Friday congregation prayers, but He also ordered you to go out and earn a living after the prayer is done. Both are acts of worship and obedience to Allah. Allah does not want you to be so involved in your business and worldly affairs that you come late or forget about your prayers. Likewise, He does not want you to spend all your time in the mosque and ignore your needs and those of your family. Allah brings balance to your life.

Both, the first command: 'When the call is made for the Prayer on Friday, then move promptly to the remembrance of Allah, and leave off your trading,' and the second command: 'when the prayer has ended, disperse in the land and seek out Allah's bounty' are from our Lord, and we should give them equal importance.

And just in case you forget about Allah's teachings and throw your life out of balance, Allah teaches you to say: 'Our Lord, grant us Your forgiveness, and to You is the homecoming.'

VERSE 286

Laa yukalliful-laahu nafsan illaa wus'ahaa; lahaa maa kasabat wa 'alaihaa maktasabat; Rabbanaa laa tu'aakhiznaaa in naseenaaa aw akhtaanaa; Rabbanaa wa laa tahmil-'alainaaa isran kamaa hamaltahoo 'alal-lazeena min qablinaa; Rabbanaa wa laa tuhammilnaa maa laa taaqata lanaa bih; wa'fu 'annaa waghfir lanaa warhamnaa; Anta mawlaanaa fansurnaa 'alal qawmil kaafireen

Allah does not burden any soul, except with something within its capacity: for it what it earned and against it what it had acquired. - 'Our Lord, do not take us to task if we have forgotten or erred. Lord, do not burden us as You burdened those before us. Lord, do not burden us with more than we have the strength to bear. Pardon us, forgive us, and have mercy on us. You are our guardian, so help us against the disbelievers.'
(Chapter 2: Verse 286)

When it comes to life's burdens, there are three conditions that you may face: The first is to encounter a task that is clearly overwhelming and outside your capacity. The second is to face a challenging task that pushes you to your limits. Lastly, there are tasks well within your capacity. Hence, the phrase: 'Allah does not burden any soul, except with something within its capacity,' means that Allah does not assign you any obligation unless it is clearly within your ability.

Every Muslim is obligated to pray five times a day, but don't you personally know people who offer ten prayers every day? Allah has obligated every Muslim to fast the entire month of Ramadan. Don't you personally know people who also fast Monday and Thursday of every week? Similar is the case of almsgiving –zakat-. Many people give far more than the obligated amount.

This means that all religious obligations are well within our capabilities. Once you complete your obligations, you are welcome to do more if you choose. Allah says in the 184th verse of Surah Baqarah: 'Should anyone do good of his own accord, that is better for him.'

It is narrated that when Allah heard His Messenger and the believers supplicate: "Lord, do not burden us as You burdened those before us." He replied: 'It is done.' And when He heard them supplicate: "Lord, do not burden us with more than we have the strength to bear." He replied: 'it is done.'

Allah did not obligate us with anything beyond our capacity, and that capacity is the average ability of all the believers. People who have greater abilities, or are more willing than others, can volunteer to do extra worship beyond the obligation.

As for those with less ability, Allah eased their burden according to their condition. For example, Islamic law recognizes the difficulty one may face during travel, so the traveller is encouraged not to fast Ramadan during trips, and to make up the days later. Those who are poor are not obligated to give the Zakat almsgiving or to make the Hajj pilgrimage. Here is another example from the Quran. Allah says:

But Allah has lightened your burden for now, knowing that there is a weakness in you—a steadfast hundreds of you will defeat two hundred, and a steadfast thousand of you will defeat two thousand, by Allah's permission: Allah is with the steadfast. (08:66)

Before the revelation of this verse, the proportion of fighters that obligated Muslims to stand up and fight their enemies was one against ten. Allah eased this requirement to one against two due to a weakness in the capacity of the believers.

Some people misinterpret verse 286 for their benefit. They think that it is up to them to decide what they can bear and what they are not able to do. When they are faced with a religious obligation that they like, they do it. When they are faced with a religious duty that is tough or inconvenient, such as fasting long summer days, they say we are not obligated to do it because 'Allah does not burden any soul, except with something within its capacity' In other words, they want to be the judge of which of Allah's commands applies to them.

The truth is exactly the opposite; Allah is the best judge, and He has absolute knowledge of what you and I can do. So, when Allah assigns a duty to you, then rest assured that it is well within your ability because ' Allah does not burden any soul, except with something within its capacity.' You do not define ability, and then measure the obligation against your opinion. If an obligation is assigned to you, then it is well within your ability.

The verse continues, 'for it what it earned and against it what it had acquired.' Here, we should pause and study Allah's words in the Arabic origin because they hold the key to understanding the verse. The word 'earned' is translated from the Arabic origin 'Kasaba.' The verb 'Kasaba' is often used to describe natural and lawful actions that do not require much effort. The phrase 'had acquired' is translated from the origin 'Iktasaba.' It is a longer verb that indicates an unnatural –often unlawful- action that requires deliberate effort and intention.

Take the example of a man looking at his beautiful wife; is he doing something unnatural or unlawful? Of course not. This man is relaxed enjoying his family. It is an action that falls under the 'kasaba' category. Contrast that to a man who wants to look at the wife of his friend. First, he would look around to make sure no one is paying attention; then he would take a quick glance at the woman, then he would turn around to make sure that no one caught him looking. This unlawful act requires a lot of deliberate effort and falls under the category of 'Iktasaba.'

When you read the Quran, you will come across the following verse:

Truly those who earn evil and are surrounded by their sins will be the inhabitants of the Fire, there to remain. (2:81)

It is interesting to note that, although the verse is talking about sin, Allah used the word 'earn' –Kasaba- rather than acquire –Iktasaba-.

Why, you may ask? We answer that this verse is talking about one of the calamities that can befall a society. It happens when people lose their sense of faith and decency and become accustomed to transgression. Note the description 'and are surrounded by their sins' indicating repetition and complete immersion in sin making it second nature to people.

Take the example of a person stealing for the very first time. He or she would plan for days and may hesitate whether to steal or not, and then, after the theft is committed, he or she would worry for days about every sound and every movement. You can say that this person 'Iktasaba' the stolen goods and money. However, as this person continues to steal for years, he or she becomes a professional thief, and stealing becomes second nature. There is less worry, and no hesitation to commit the crime over and over. At that point you can say that he or she 'kasaba' the stolen goods and money.

In another example, a man who cheats on his wife for the first time may feel guilty for months, however, if he continues down that path, self-blame would stop, and you may find him bragging to his friends about the affair. It is a real tragedy when a person, or a society, reaches a level where sin is widely acceptable.

So when you hear the phrase: 'for it what it earned and against it what it had acquired,' be smart and make sure that you pile on the good deeds and shift the balance in your favour.

Allah does not burden any soul, except with something within its capacity: for it what it earned and against it what it had acquired. - 'Our Lord, do not take us to task if we have forgotten or erred. Lord, do not burden us as You burdened those before us. Lord, do not burden us with more than we have the strength to bear. Pardon us, forgive us, and have mercy on us. You are our guardian, so help us against the disbelievers.' (Chapter 2: Verse 286)

Allah narrates the supplication of the believers: 'Our Lord, do not take us to task if we have forgotten or erred.' Prophet Muhammad, peace be upon him, said: "Allah has absolved my followers from matters of error, forgetfulness, and what they were coerced into doing."

Here you may ask, why does the Quran talk about something that has already been forgiven? There are two possible answers. The first answer is that matters of error, forgetfulness, and coercion may not have been forgiven from the very beginning; perhaps forgiveness only took place after the Prophet and the early believers supplicated their Lord and asked for ease. The second possibility is that if matters of error, forgetfulness, and coercion were forgiven from the very beginning, then the supplication is indicative of the utmost purity of faith. In other words, it is an acknowledgment from the believers that Allah should not be disobeyed except by inadvertent error or forgetfulness. Allah should never be disobeyed intentionally. A true believer values the close connection with Allah so much, that he or she would never disobey Him except out of forgetfulness or error. Allah says:

We also commanded Adam before you, but he forgot and We found him lacking in resolve. (20:115)

Allah referred to Adam's forgetfulness as a sin, but later, He honored the nation of Muhammad and absolved them from sins that came out of forgetfulness.

Here we should pause and compare our forgetfulness to that of Adam. First, Adam, peace be upon him, was created by the hand of Allah, while we were created by the laws of reproduction. Allah says:

He said, 'satan, what prevented you prostrating to what I created with My own Hands? Were you overcome by arrogance or are you one of the exalted?' (38:75)

Second, Adam received teachings from Allah directly and not through a messenger. Lastly, Adam was tasked with a single obligation: 'do not to go near a particular tree in paradise.' So how could he forget? Adams forgetfulness was surely a sin. It was not appropriate for him to forget this single mandate that was instructed directly by Allah. Perhaps Adam was made to forget for wisdom only known by Allah. It may have been so that he can reside on earth as Allah's successor, or to teach humanity how to repent from mistakes.

We supplicate: 'Our Lord, do not take us to task if we have forgotten or erred.' What exactly is an error? Error is translated from the Arabic origin 'Akhtana.' In the Arabic language, there are two words that denote making a mistake. The first is Akhta –to err-, and the second is Khate'a –to make a mistake-. A person who errs –Akhta- is a person who does not know the rule, or is not fully aware that what he or she is doing is wrong. Thus, a person who errs –Akhta- needs education and correction for his or her actions. On the other hand, a person who makes a mistake -khate'a- is a person who is fully aware of the rules, and deliberately breaks them. This is sin in its truest sense.

For example, during a physics class, a student learns that speed is calculated by dividing distance over time. This rule is taught again and again in the classroom with multiple examples and problems to solve so it sticks in the student's mind. During this time, the teacher corrects errors and gives advice. But would the teacher correct any mistakes as the student is sitting for the final exam? Of course not, the student is now penalized for mistakes by getting a lower grade.

In the verse under study, the verb Akhta أخطا is used. It means that as a believer, I may make mistakes only unintentionally out of ignorance. This might be because a specific ruling was not taught to me, or I may have been taught once and forgot; just as a physics student may make mistakes as he or she is learning the subject. But once the student sits down and studies, he or she develops a strong grip on the subject and stops making errors.

Take the example of a young girl learning to type on a keyboard. Initially, she would find it very difficult to look at the screen and strike the correct letters with her fingers. She knows the rules of typing but makes several errors. The process of learning may take weeks or months, and may even require scolding a few times from the typing instructor. But once she learns and practices, typing becomes automatic. Her speed and accuracy go up. Now, the young girl can hold a conversation, or watch a video, while typing flawlessly without as much as a glance at the keyboard or the screen. She has acquired an ingrained skill.

The same happens for students of Islamic jurisprudence. If you ask a first-year student at Al-Azhar University a question, he or she would have to take the time to look through the sources and find the correct ruling. But if you ask the same question to a trained scholar, he or she would know the answer and can tell you the exact references for the rule.

The supplication continues: 'Lord, do not burden us as You burdened those before us. Lord, do not burden us with more than we have the strength to bear.' A burden is something that is heavy to carry around. For example, after the children of Israel had wronged themselves by worshiping a golden calf, Allah ordered those who wanted to repent to kill themselves or give away one-fourth of their wealth in almsgiving. As for the followers of our beloved Muhammad, he, peace be upon him, told us that after the supplication of 'Lord, do not burden us as You burdened those before us,' Allah replied: 'yes, it is done.' Our Lord blessed Islam with ease and removed difficulty from its teachings.

Verse 286

a continuation

Allah does not burden any soul, except with something within its capacity: for it what it earned and against it what it had acquired. - 'Our Lord, do not take us to task if we have forgotten or erred. Lord, do not burden us as You burdened those before us. Lord, do not burden us with more than we have the strength to bear. Pardon us, forgive us, and have mercy on us. You are our guardian, so help us against the disbelievers.' (Chapter 2: Verse 286)

We continue with the supplication of the believers: 'Pardon us, forgive us, and have mercy on us.' We turn to you, Lord, raise our hands and ask: Our Lord, you know that no matter how much awareness we have; No matter how Allah-fearing we are, we will never be able to properly fulfill your right, so we turn to you and supplicate for pardon.

What is the meaning of 'pardon us,' you may ask? 'Pardon' is translated from the Arabic 'Afu.' It has its roots in the desert environment where footprints left by travelers in the sand are erased by the wind. Similarly, if you do something wrong, your sins leave a trace. When Allah pardons your sin, He erases its traces -as if it never happened-.

How about 'forgive us, and have mercy on us'? How is it different from 'Pardon us'? "forgive us" is translated from the Arabic origin 'Eghfir Lana.' Say for example, that your neighbour wronged you and threw trash by your door. Now you have a choice; you can treat the neighbour the same way he treated you and throw trash at his door. You can suppress your anger and do nothing —although you still feel livid.- Or you can choose to forgive and forget.

But how about your Creator? If you sin, Allah may not punish you for your sin, but He may still be angry with you. And who among us can bear Allah's anger? Therefore, we ask for forgiveness and supplicate: "forgive us."

Lastly, we ask our Lord for mercy which is the best of all things. To receive mercy is to be spared from sin from the very beginning. Allah says:

We send down the Quran as healing and mercy to those who believe; as for those who disbelieve, it only increases their loss. (17:82)

Take note that healing means to be cured of a disease that you are already afflicted with. Mercy, on the other hand, means that you are spared the affliction entirely.

The verse continues: "You are our guardian, so help us against the disbelievers.' This is an acknowledgment that Allah is our Creator, the Executors of our affairs, and our Supporter. He supports us against the disbelieving people. Hence, the last verse of 'The Cow' is in harmony with the first few verses:

Alif, Lam, Meem. This is the Book in which there is no doubt, containing guidance for those who are mindful of Allah. Those who believe in the unseen, establish prayer and spend out of what We have provided for them. Those who believe in the revelation sent down to you, and in what was sent before you, and those who have firm faith in the Hereafter. Those are upon guidance from their Lord, and those are the successful. As for Those who willfully persist in unbelief: it is alike to them whether you warn them or do not warn them; they will not believe. Allah has set a seal on their hearts, and on their ears and over their eyes there is a dark covering, and for them is great torment. (2:1-7)

At the beginning of the chapter, Allah gave us the examples of the believers and their counterparts -the disbelievers and the hypocrites-. Here, Allah ends the chapter with the supplication of the believers: "You are our guardian, so help us against the disbelievers' indicating an ongoing conflict between faith and disbelief.

A true believer always upholds the commandment of Allah whenever and wherever disbelief and corruption are found. He or she has complete trust and confidence that Allah is the Savoir and Protector. The moment Islam is challenged, the believer stands up for his or her faith. This implies that the believer must always remain attentive to the conspiracies of disbelief. Why? We answer that the ultimate goal of those with no faith is to replace Allah's rules with their own. They aim to tilt the balance of life in their favour. They want to exploit the weak, impoverish others by drowning them in interest-bearing and predatory loans, and raid natural resources even if that lays the environment to waste. Allah's teachings are the one major obstacle in the way of corruption. Thus, it is critical for the believers to defend faith and work diligently to guard Allah's teachings. In this struggle, the believers ask Allah for support: 'You are our guardian, so help us against the disbelievers'

This supplication also suggests that your personal belief in Allah is not enough. You should work tirelessly to help others and let your faith shine to all creations around you. The conflict between those on the straight path and the corrupt will cause life to be miserable and exhausting, especially for the believers. Why, you may ask? We answer that if a person is honest and upright, his good character mostly benefits others, and would not necessarily benefit him.

Similarly, if a person is corrupt, his corruption hurts others, and may not necessarily hurt him. An excellent surgeon benefits all patients, but if the surgeon needs surgery, he or she will have to go to a lesser doctor. Think about your hands: if you are right-handed, your right-hand does a great job on everything else except itself. When you trim your nails, you do a great job using your right hand to trim the left hand's nails. But when it comes to trimming the nails of your right hand, you use your left hand which is far less skilled. Thus, make sure that all those around you are righteous so you can reap the benefits of their faith.

Allah honored humanity by entrusting us as His successors on earth and making us superior over other creations. The entire universe is at our service. If we apply Allah's teachings, tranquillity and peace would prevail, and humanity will be in perfect harmony with all creation. Allah says:

We create man in the finest state, then reduce him to the lowest of the low, except those who believe and do righteous deeds. There awaits them a never-ending reward. What, then, can make you deny the Divine System of life! (95:4-7)

Faith in Allah does not mean to isolate yourself from the rest of the world. To the contrary, it means engaging people and living life to the fullest. But there will always be those who benefit from corruption because it serves their interests, and thus a struggle arises; a battle in which everyone wants to be victorious. Allah teaches you to ask for His aid and victory over the disbelievers. We supplicate: 'Lord, do not burden us as You burdened those before us. Lord, do not burden us with more than we have the strength to bear. Pardon us, forgive us, and have mercy on us. You are our guardian, so help us against the disbelievers.'

Allah's help, however, is not without conditions. A believer must face conflicts with untainted faith, pure motives, and adequate preparation. If the believers are defeated, they should re-examine which part of their faith they did not uphold. Allah says: 'and the ones who support Our cause will be the victors' (37:173)

You should use all the means Allah put at your disposal first, then supplicate: 'You are our guardian, so help us against the disbelievers.' Allah says:

Prepare against them whatever arms and cavalry you can muster, that you may strike terror in the hearts of the enemies of Allah and yours, and others besides them not known to you, but known to Allah. Whatever you spend in the way of Allah will be paid back to you in full, and no wrong will be done to you. (08:60)

Allah asks you to work hard, utilize the materials He deposited for you in the earth, and exercise your thoughtful mind. Once you have exhausted all the means at your disposal, you would truly be eligible for Allah's support and victory.

www.ingramcontent.com/pod-product-compliance
Lightning Source LLC
Chambersburg PA
CBHW030539080526
44585CB00012B/205